Cheeky Brat

Mitsubachi Miyuki

2

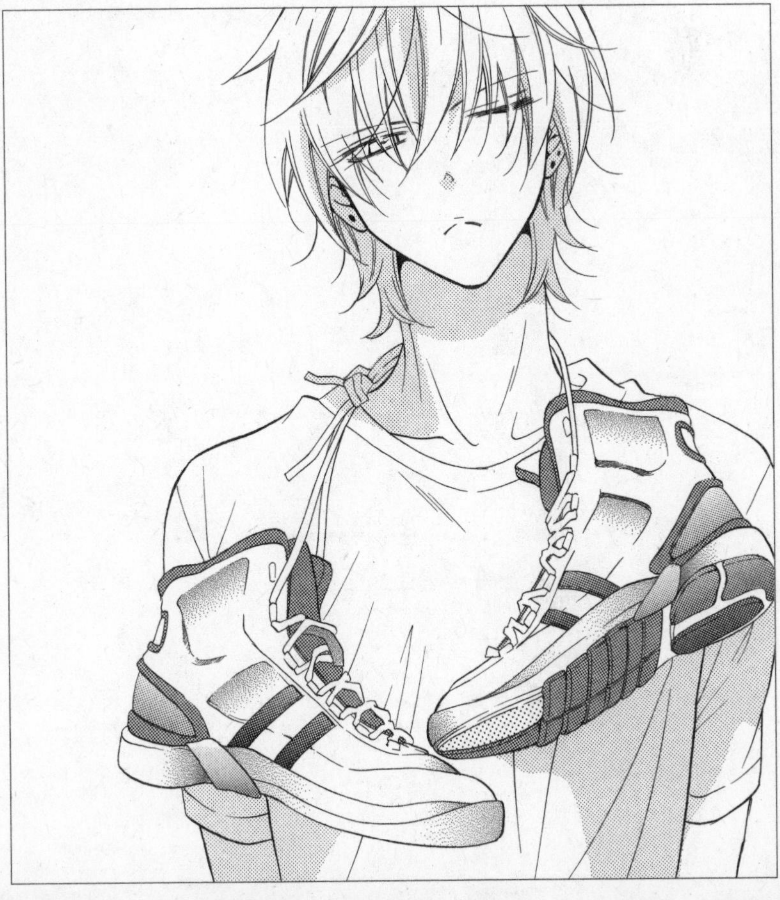

Cheeky Brat

Contents

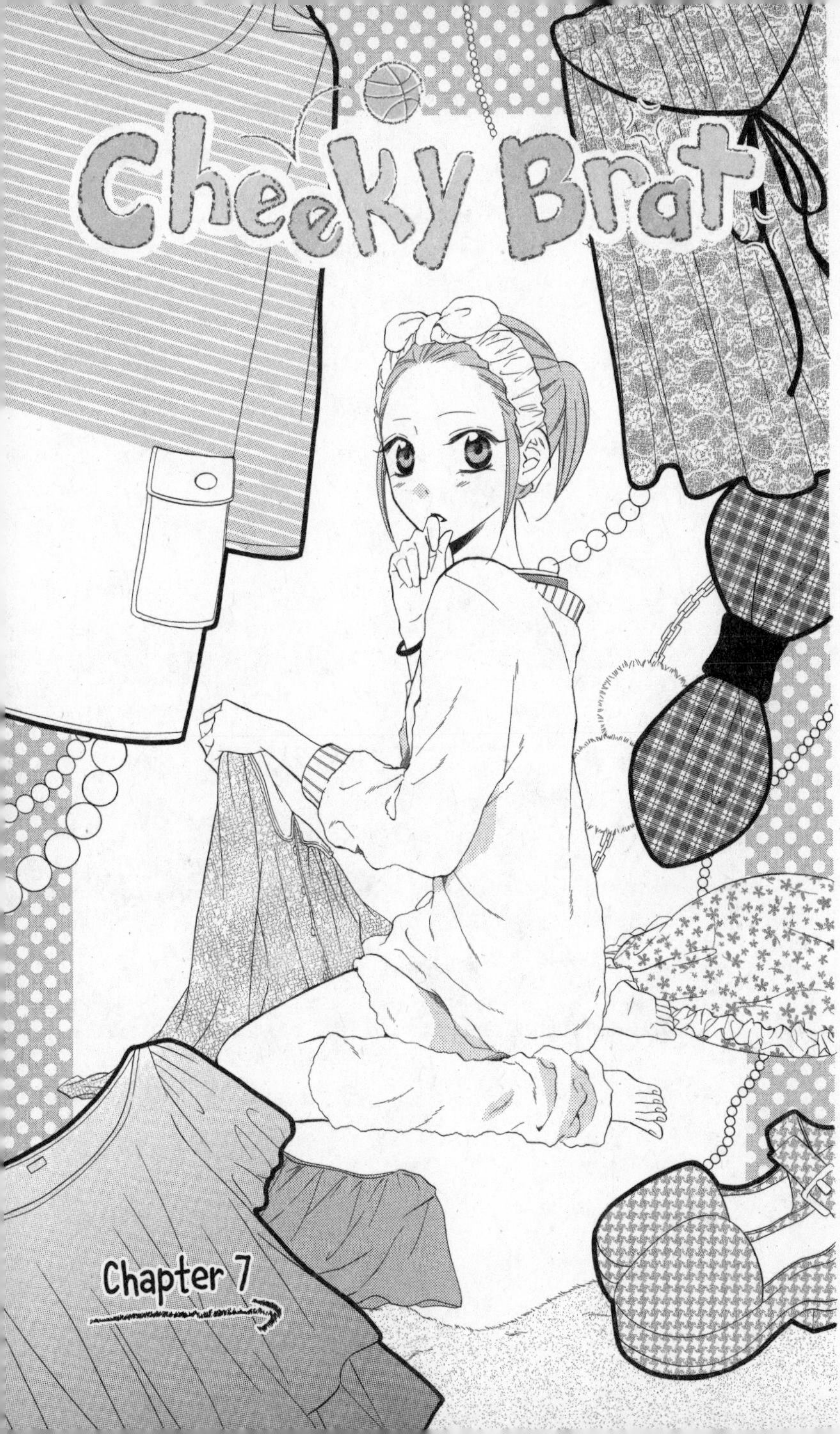
Cheeky Brat
Chapter 7

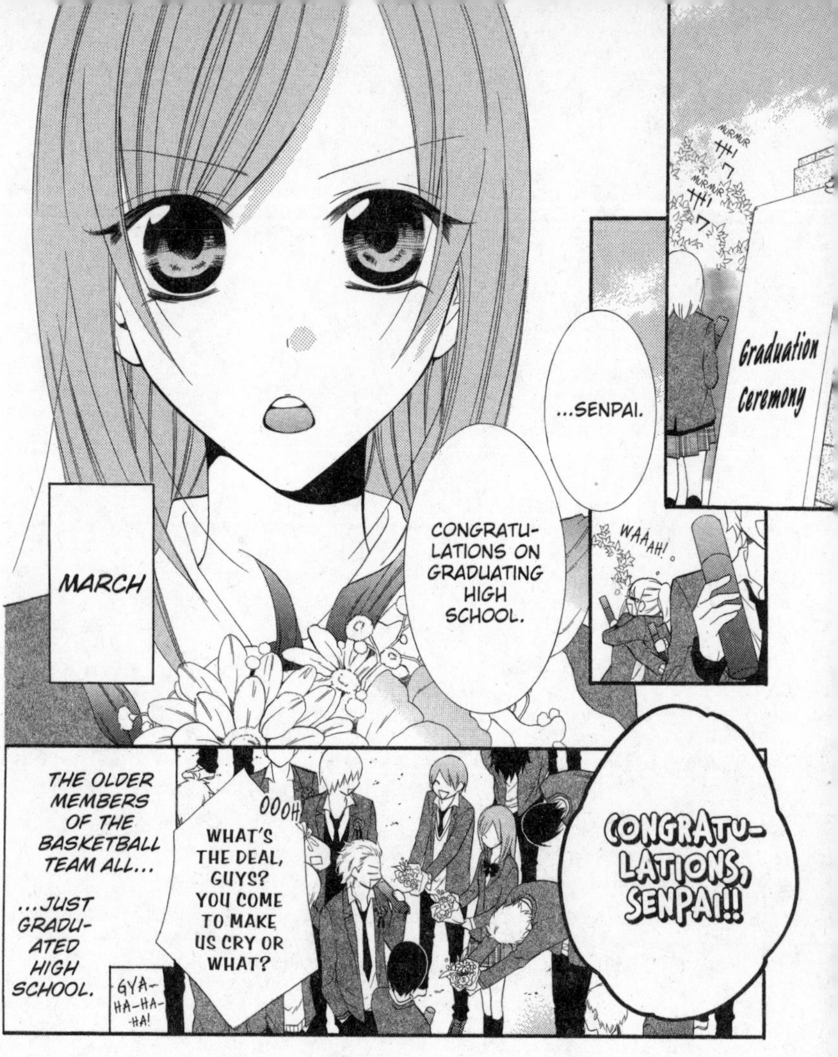
MURMUR
MURMUR
Graduation Ceremony
...SENPAI.
WAAAH!
MARCH
CONGRATU-LATIONS ON GRADUATING HIGH SCHOOL.
CONGRATU-LATIONS, SENPAI!!
OOOH
WHAT'S THE DEAL, GUYS? YOU COME TO MAKE US CRY OR WHAT?
THE OLDER MEMBERS OF THE BASKETBALL TEAM ALL...
...JUST GRADU-ATED HIGH SCHOOL.
GYA-HA-HA-HA!

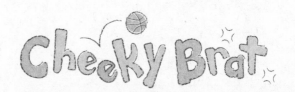

Cheeky Brat

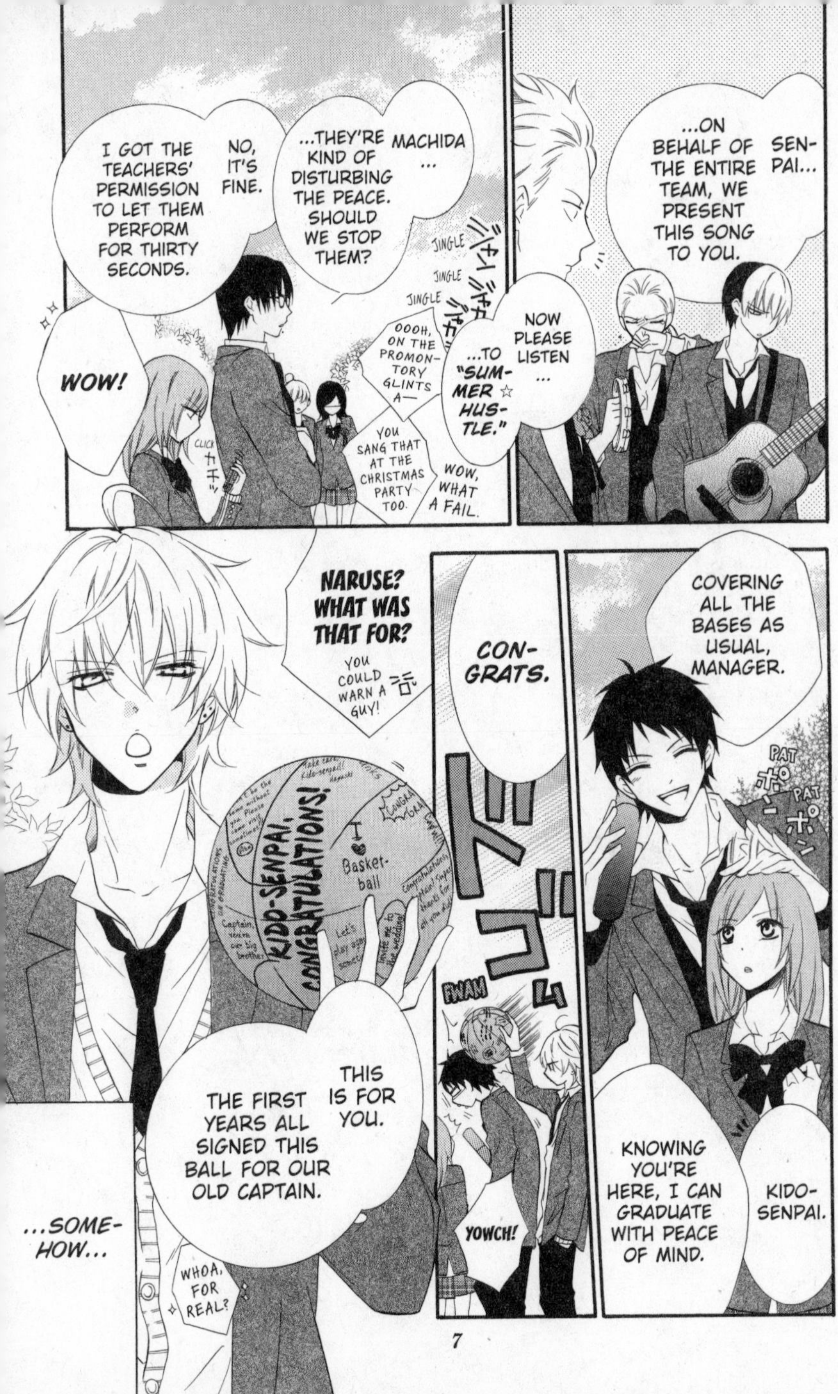
SEN-PAI...
...ON BEHALF OF THE ENTIRE TEAM, WE PRESENT THIS SONG TO YOU.
NOW PLEASE LISTEN...
...TO "SUMMER☆HUSTLE."
JINGLE JINGLE JINGLE
MACHIDA...
...THEY'RE KIND OF DISTURBING THE PEACE. SHOULD WE STOP THEM?
NO, IT'S FINE.
I GOT THE TEACHERS' PERMISSION TO LET THEM PERFORM FOR THIRTY SECONDS.
OOOH, ON THE PROMONTORY GLINTS A—
YOU SANG THAT AT THE CHRISTMAS PARTY TOO.
WOW, WHAT A FAIL.
WOW!
CLICK
COVERING ALL THE BASES AS USUAL, MANAGER.
PAT PAT
KIDO-SENPAI.
KNOWING YOU'RE HERE, I CAN GRADUATE WITH PEACE OF MIND.
CON-GRATS.
FWAM
YOWCH!
NARUSE? WHAT WAS THAT FOR?
YOU COULD WARN A GUY!
KIDO-SENPAI, CONGRATULATIONS!
I ♥ Basket-ball
THIS IS FOR YOU.
THE FIRST YEARS ALL SIGNED THIS BALL FOR OUR OLD CAPTAIN.
WHOA, FOR REAL?
...SOME-HOW...

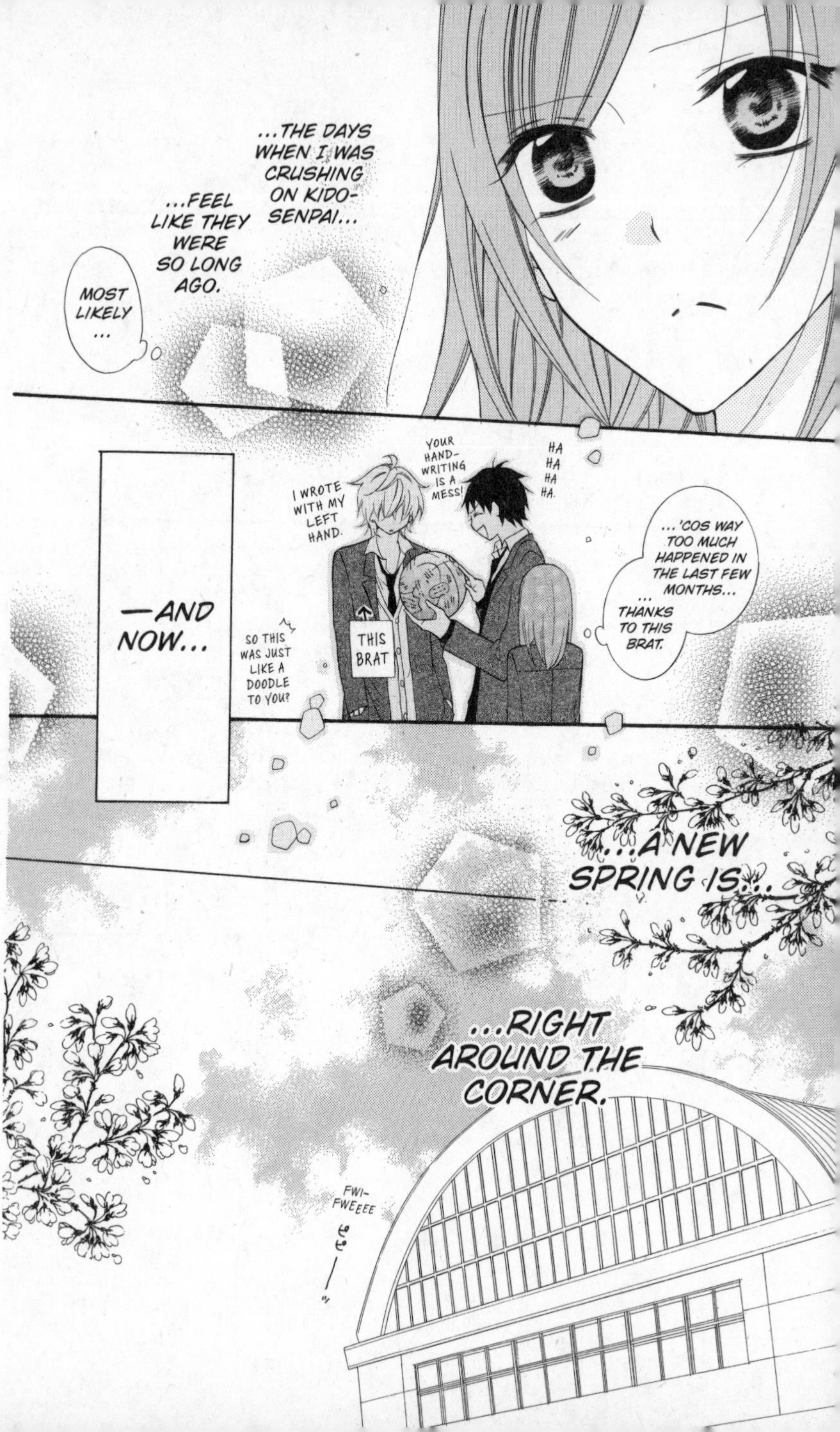
...THE DAYS WHEN I WAS CRUSHING ON KIDO-SENPAI...
...FEEL LIKE THEY WERE SO LONG AGO.
MOST LIKELY...
...'COS WAY TOO MUCH HAPPENED IN THE LAST FEW MONTHS... THANKS TO THIS BRAT.
HA HA HA HA.
YOUR HAND-WRITING IS A MESS!
I WROTE WITH MY LEFT HAND.
THIS BRAT
SO THIS WAS JUST LIKE A DOODLE TO YOU?
—AND NOW...
...A NEW SPRING IS...
...RIGHT AROUND THE CORNER.
FWI-FWEEEE

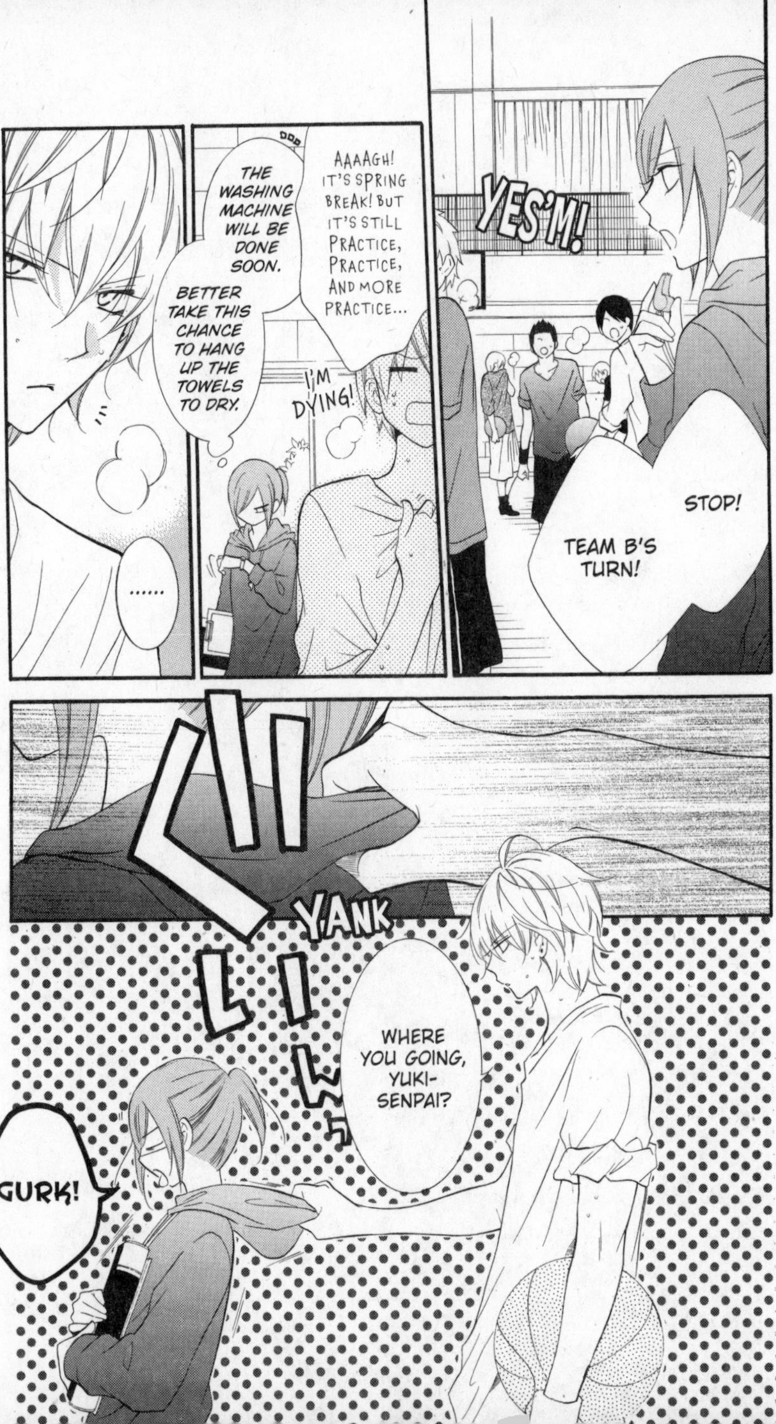
STOP!
TEAM B'S TURN!
YES'M!
AAAAGH! IT'S SPRING BREAK! BUT IT'S STILL PRACTICE, PRACTICE, AND MORE PRACTICE...
I'M DYING!
THE WASHING MACHINE WILL BE DONE SOON.
BETTER TAKE THIS CHANCE TO HANG UP THE TOWELS TO DRY.
......
YANK
WHERE YOU GOING, YUKI-SENPAI?
GURK!

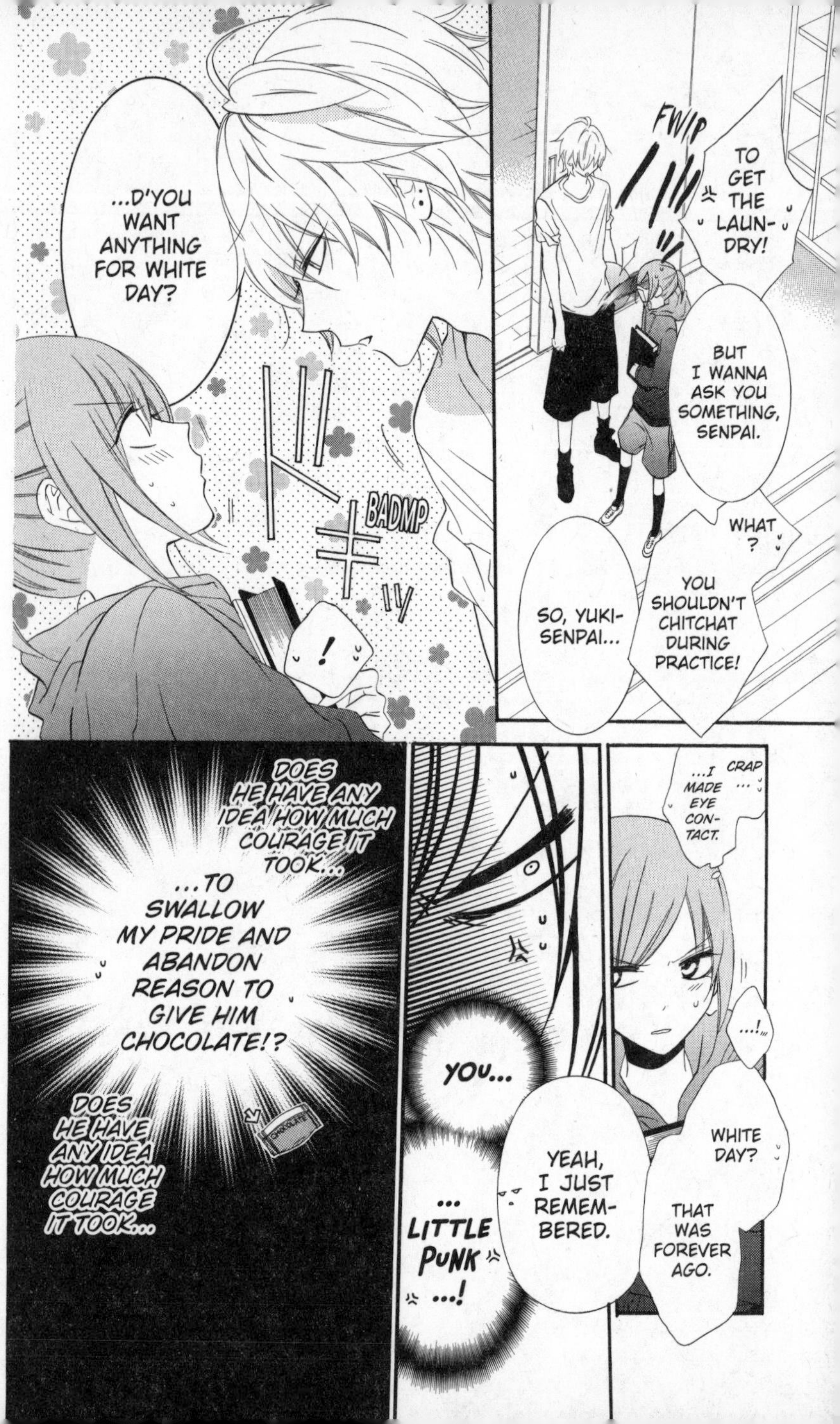
FWIP
TO GET THE LAUNDRY!
BUT I WANNA ASK YOU SOMETHING, SENPAI.
WHAT?
YOU SHOULDN'T CHITCHAT DURING PRACTICE!
SO, YUKI-SENPAI...
...D'YOU WANT ANYTHING FOR WHITE DAY?
BADMP
!
CRAP...
...I MADE EYE CONTACT.
...!
WHITE DAY?
THAT WAS FOREVER AGO.
YEAH, I JUST REMEMBERED.
YOU...
...LITTLE PUNK...!
DOES HE HAVE ANY IDEA HOW MUCH COURAGE IT TOOK...
...TO SWALLOW MY PRIDE AND ABANDON REASON TO GIVE HIM CHOCOLATE!?
CHOCOLATE
DOES HE HAVE ANY IDEA HOW MUCH COURAGE IT TOOK...

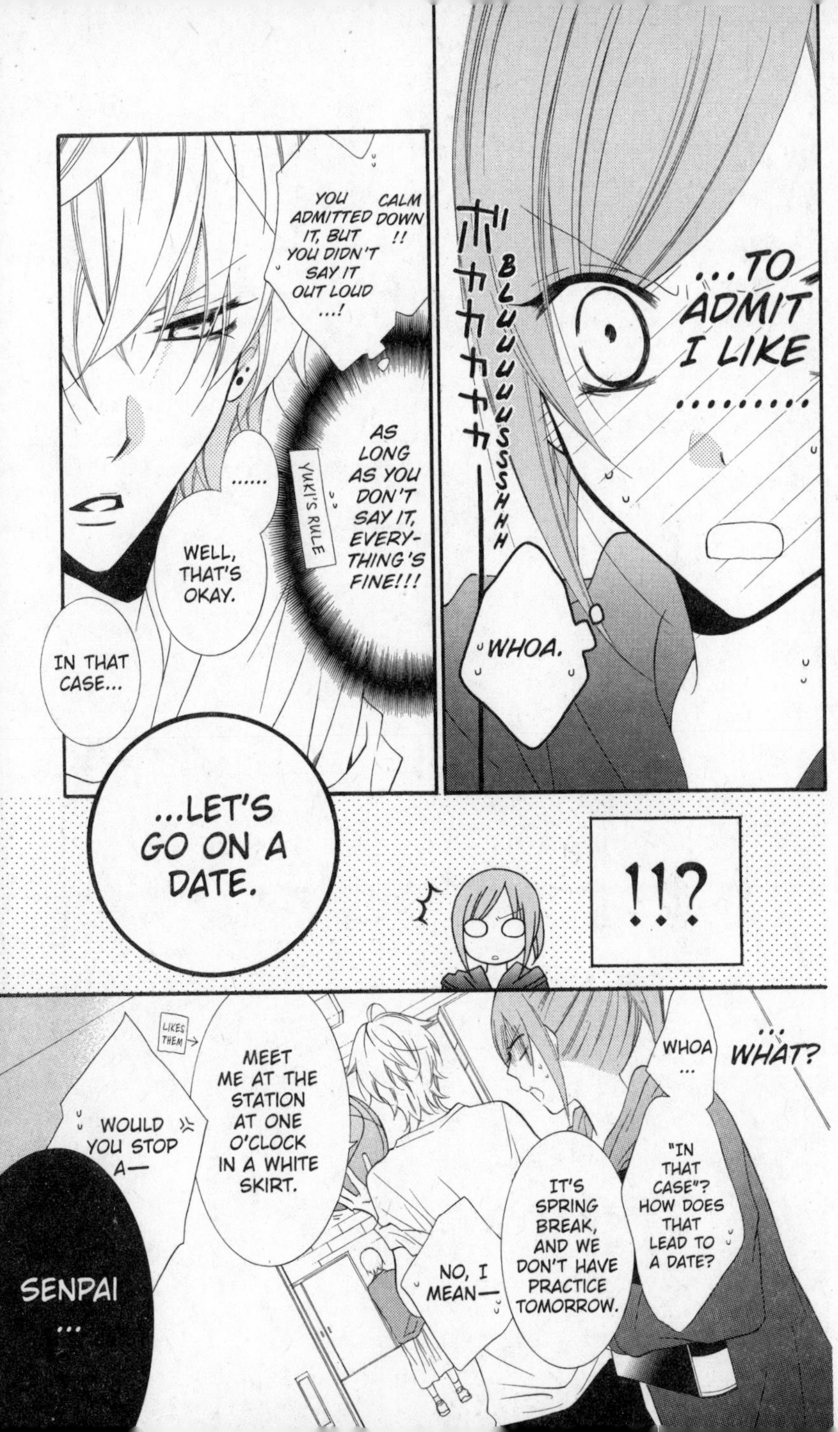
...TO ADMIT I LIKE ....
BLUUUUUUSSSHHH
WHOA.
CALM DOWN !!
YOU ADMITTED IT, BUT YOU DIDN'T SAY IT OUT LOUD ...!
AS LONG AS YOU DON'T SAY IT, EVERY-THING'S FINE!!!
YUKI'S RULE
......
WELL, THAT'S OKAY.
IN THAT CASE...
!!?
...LET'S GO ON A DATE.
...WHAT?
WHOA ...
"IN THAT CASE"? HOW DOES THAT LEAD TO A DATE?
IT'S SPRING BREAK, AND WE DON'T HAVE PRACTICE TOMORROW.
NO, I MEAN—
MEET ME AT THE STATION AT ONE O'CLOCK IN A WHITE SKIRT.
LIKES THEM
WOULD YOU STOP A—
SENPAI ...

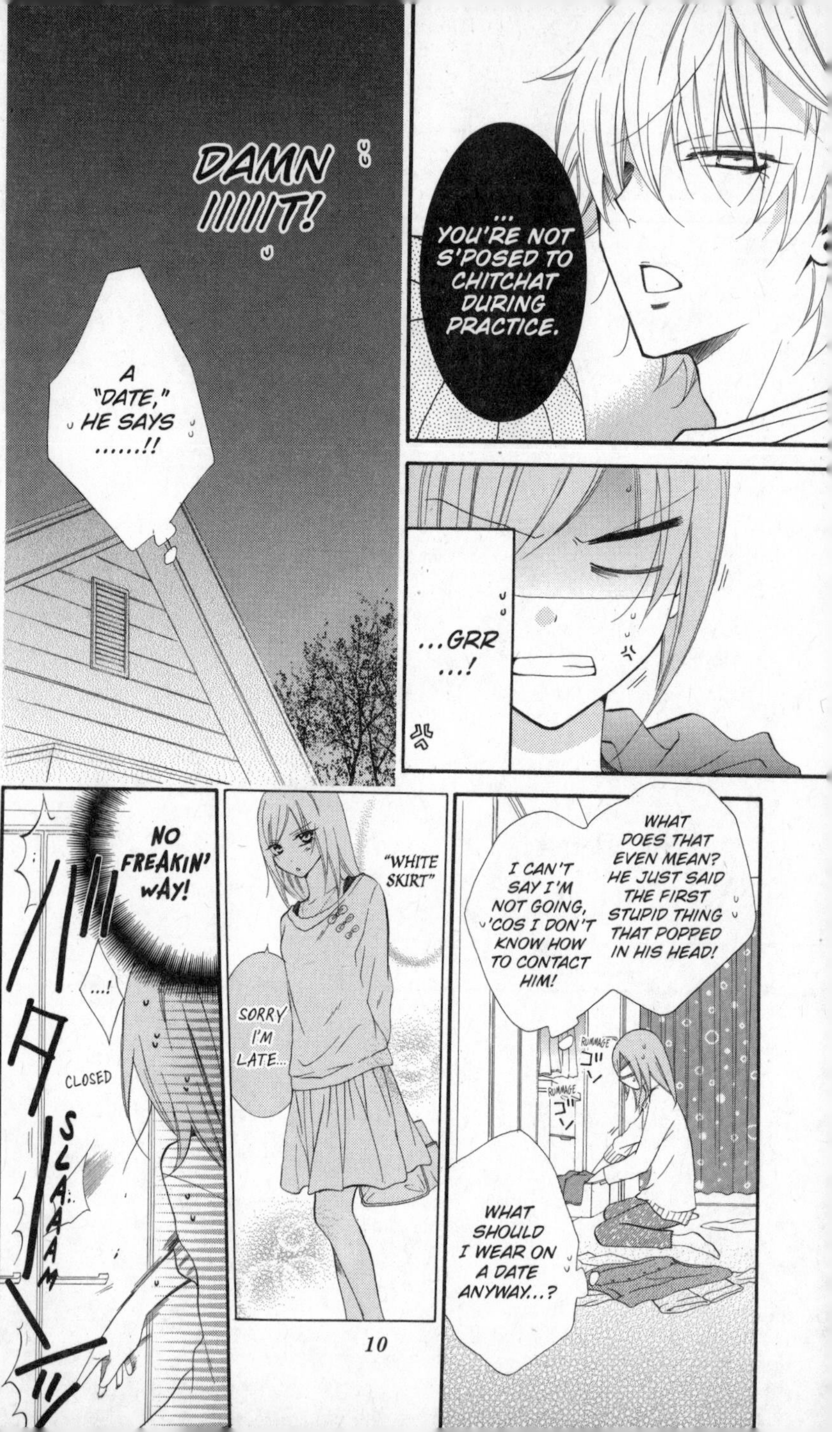
... YOU'RE NOT S'POSED TO CHITCHAT DURING PRACTICE.
...GRR ...!
DAMN IIIIIT!
A "DATE," HE SAYS ......!!
WHAT DOES THAT EVEN MEAN? HE JUST SAID THE FIRST STUPID THING THAT POPPED IN HIS HEAD!
I CAN'T SAY I'M NOT GOING, 'COS I DON'T KNOW HOW TO CONTACT HIM!
RUMMAGE
RUMMAGE
WHAT SHOULD I WEAR ON A DATE ANYWAY...?
"WHITE SKIRT"
SORRY I'M LATE...
NO FREAKIN' WAY!
...!
CLOSED
SLAAAAM

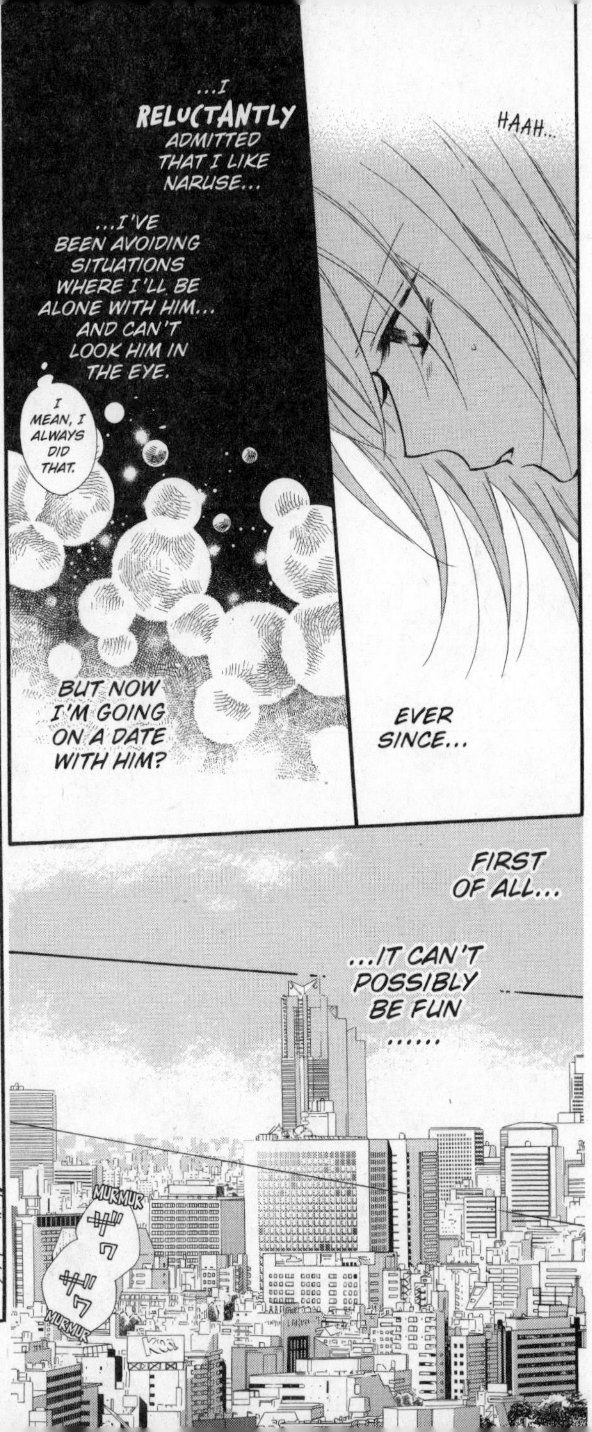
HAAH...
EVER SINCE...
...I RELUCTANTLY ADMITTED THAT I LIKE NARUSE...
...I'VE BEEN AVOIDING SITUATIONS WHERE I'LL BE ALONE WITH HIM... AND CAN'T LOOK HIM IN THE EYE.
I MEAN, I ALWAYS DID THAT.
BUT NOW I'M GOING ON A DATE WITH HIM?
FIRST OF ALL...
...IT CAN'T POSSIBLY BE FUN ......
MURMUR
ザワ
ザワ
MURMUR

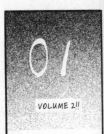

01

VOLUME 2!!

Nice to meet you, or hello again! I'm Mitsubachi Miyuki!!!

This is *Cheeky Brat*. Volume 2. To those of you who own volume 1, and to those of you who are like, "But I don't, though!", thank you for picking up volume 2.

It's volume 2!! I myself really like this series and have a lot of fun drawing it, so producing a volume 1 that continues on to a volume 2 makes me so happy that I start bouncing off the walls. I'll line the two books up and take pictures.

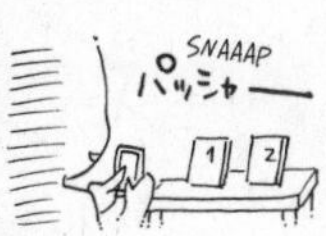
SNAAAP
パッシャー
1
2

Let's go, *Cheeky Brat* 2!!!

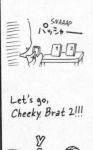

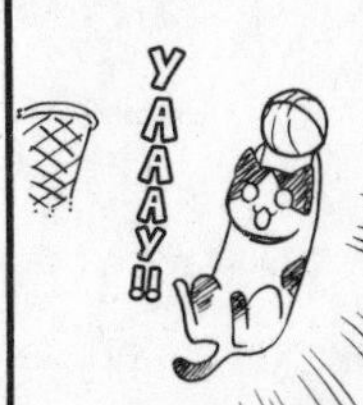
YAAAAY!!

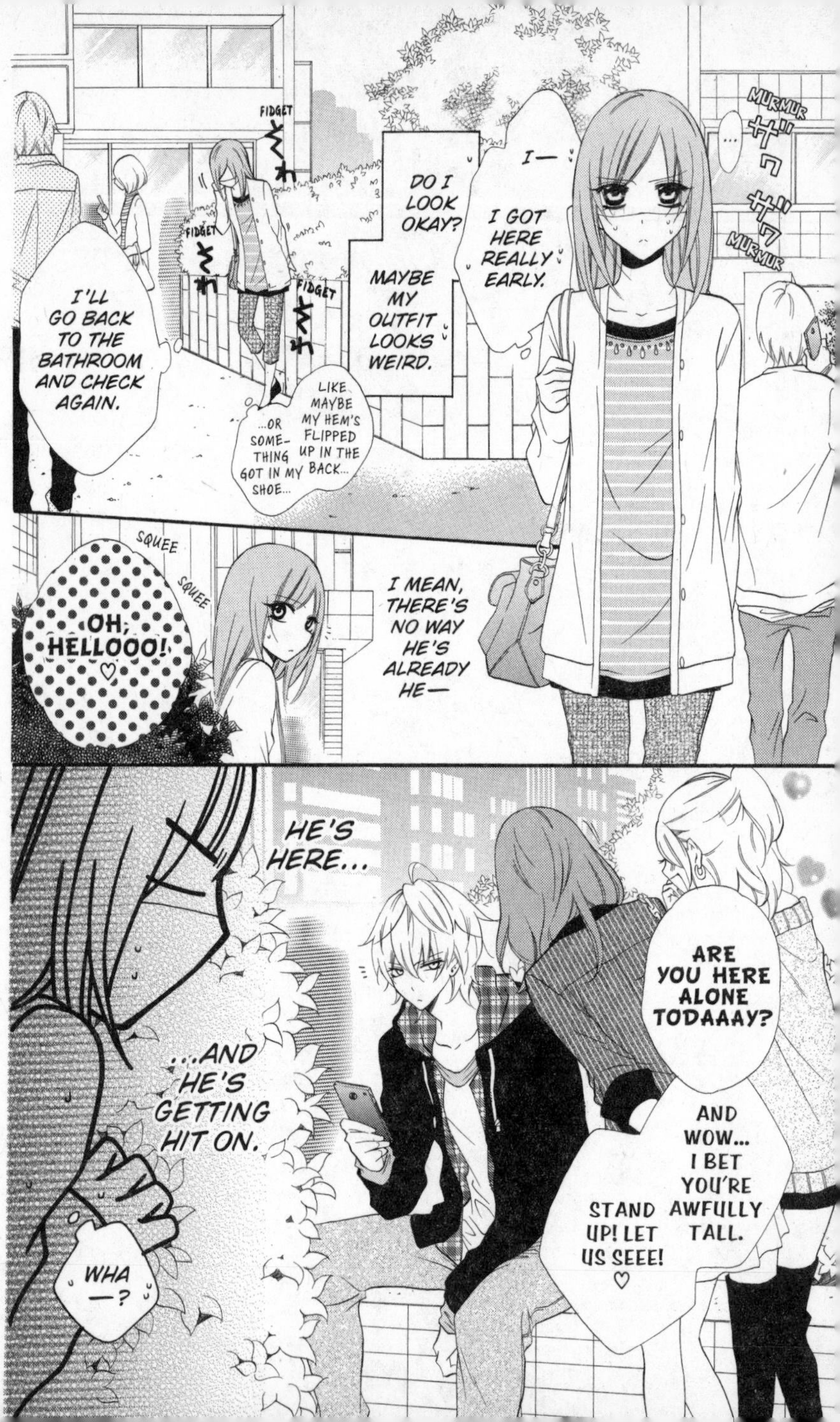
MURMUR
MURMUR
…
I—
I GOT HERE REALLY EARLY.
DO I LOOK OKAY?
MAYBE MY OUTFIT LOOKS WEIRD.
FIDGET
FIDGET
FIDGET
LIKE MAYBE MY HEM'S FLIPPED UP IN THE BACK…
…OR SOMETHING GOT IN MY SHOE…
I'LL GO BACK TO THE BATHROOM AND CHECK AGAIN.
I MEAN, THERE'S NO WAY HE'S ALREADY HE—
SQUEE
SQUEE
OH, HELLOOO! ♡
ARE YOU HERE ALONE TODAAAY?
AND WOW… I BET YOU'RE AWFULLY TALL.
STAND UP! LET US SEEE! ♡
HE'S HERE…
…AND HE'S GETTING HIT ON.
WHA—?

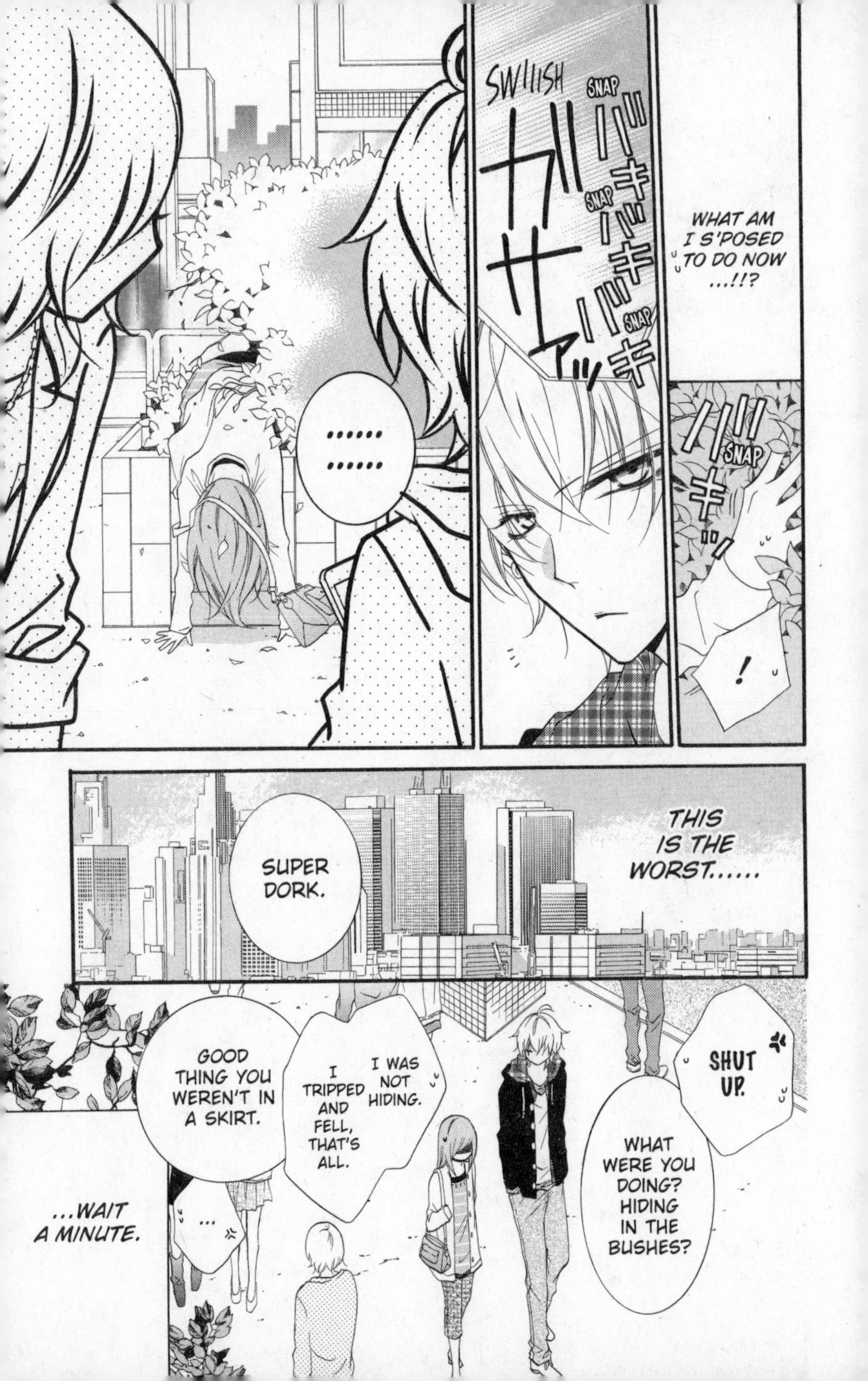
WHAT AM I S'POSED TO DO NOW ...!!?
SNAP
バキッ
!
SWIISH
ガサァッ
SNAP
SNAP
SNAP
バキバキバキ
......
......
THIS IS THE WORST......
SUPER DORK.
SHUT UP.
WHAT WERE YOU DOING? HIDING IN THE BUSHES?
I WAS NOT HIDING.
I TRIPPED AND FELL, THAT'S ALL.
GOOD THING YOU WEREN'T IN A SKIRT.
...
...WAIT A MINUTE.

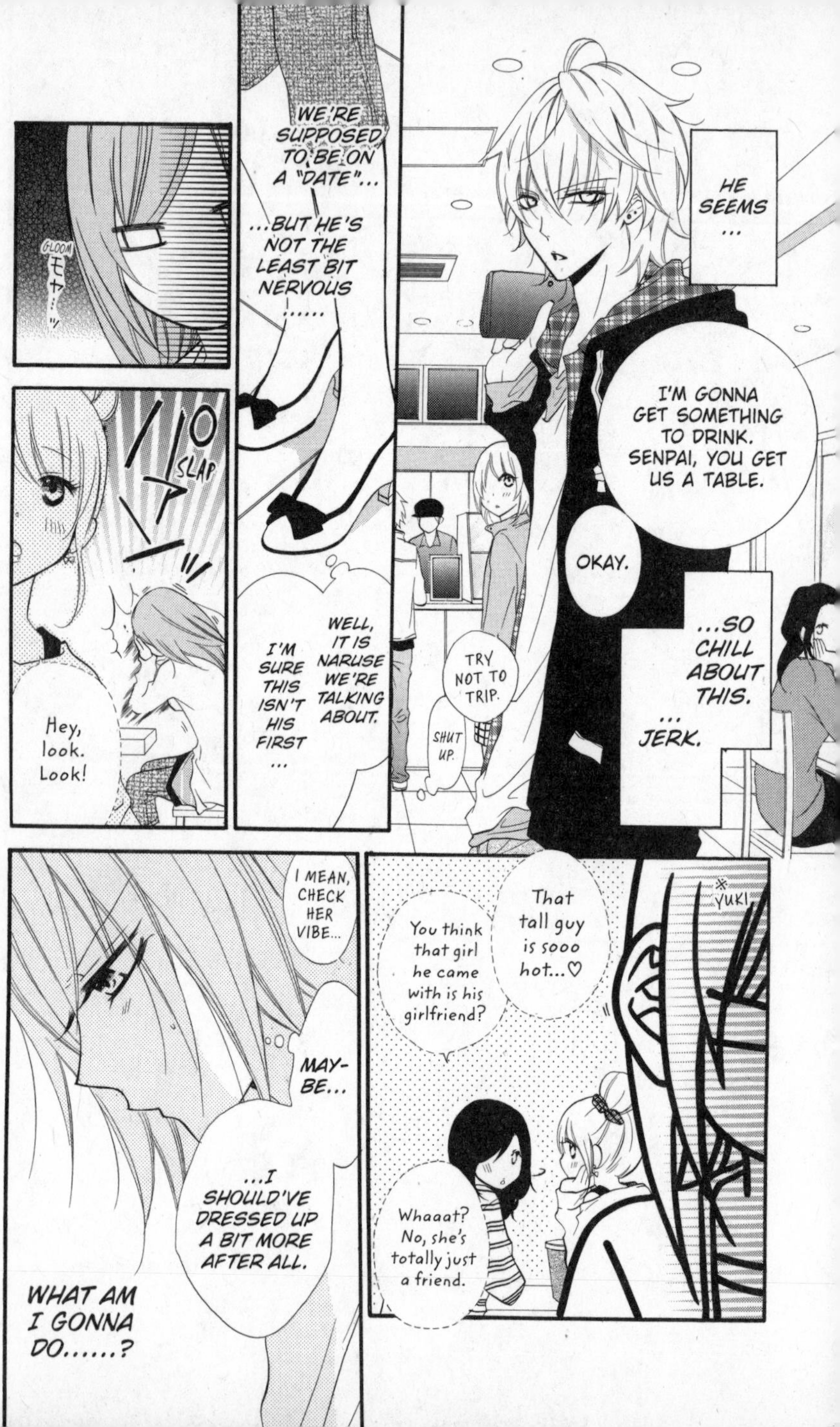

HE SEEMS...
I'M GONNA GET SOMETHING TO DRINK. SENPAI, YOU GET US A TABLE.
OKAY.
...SO CHILL ABOUT THIS.
...JERK.
TRY NOT TO TRIP.
SHUT UP.
WE'RE SUPPOSED TO BE ON A "DATE"...
...BUT HE'S NOT THE LEAST BIT NERVOUS......
WELL, IT IS NARUSE WE'RE TALKING ABOUT.
I'M SURE THIS ISN'T HIS FIRST...
GLOOM
モヤ…ッ
SLAP
Hey, look. Look!
*YUKI
That tall guy is sooo hot...♡
You think that girl he came with is his girlfriend?
Whaaat? No, she's totally just a friend.
I MEAN, CHECK HER VIBE...
MAY-BE...
...I SHOULD'VE DRESSED UP A BIT MORE AFTER ALL.
WHAT AM I GONNA DO......?

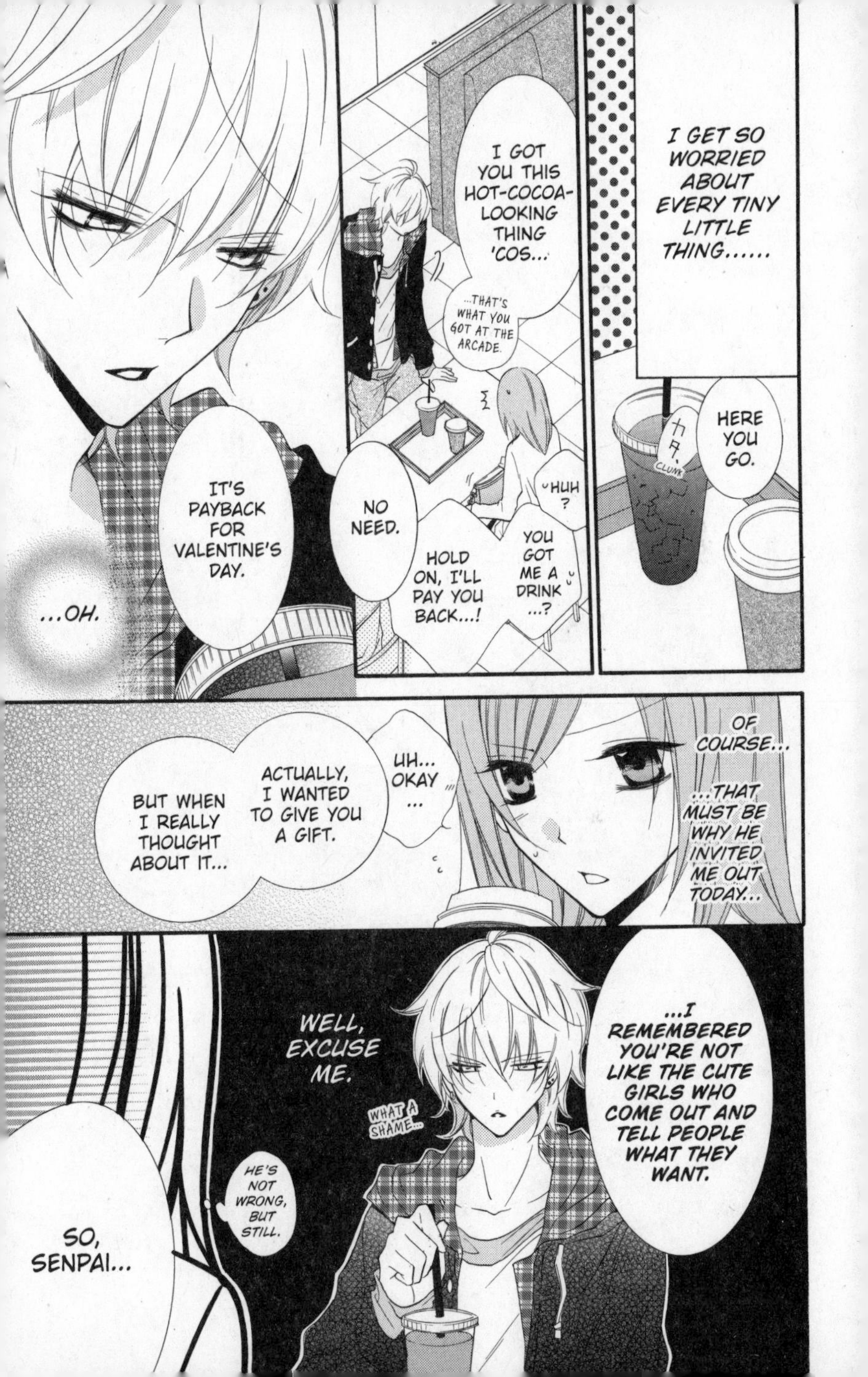
I GET SO WORRIED ABOUT EVERY TINY LITTLE THING......
HERE YOU GO.
カタ
CLUNK
I GOT YOU THIS HOT-COCOA-LOOKING THING 'COS...
...THAT'S WHAT YOU GOT AT THE ARCADE.
HUH?
YOU GOT ME A DRINK...?
HOLD ON, I'LL PAY YOU BACK...!
NO NEED.
IT'S PAYBACK FOR VALENTINE'S DAY.
...OH.
OF COURSE...
...THAT MUST BE WHY HE INVITED ME OUT TODAY...
UH... OKAY...
ACTUALLY, I WANTED TO GIVE YOU A GIFT.
BUT WHEN I REALLY THOUGHT ABOUT IT...
...I REMEMBERED YOU'RE NOT LIKE THE CUTE GIRLS WHO COME OUT AND TELL PEOPLE WHAT THEY WANT.
WELL, EXCUSE ME.
WHAT A SHAME...
HE'S NOT WRONG, BUT STILL.
SO, SENPAI...

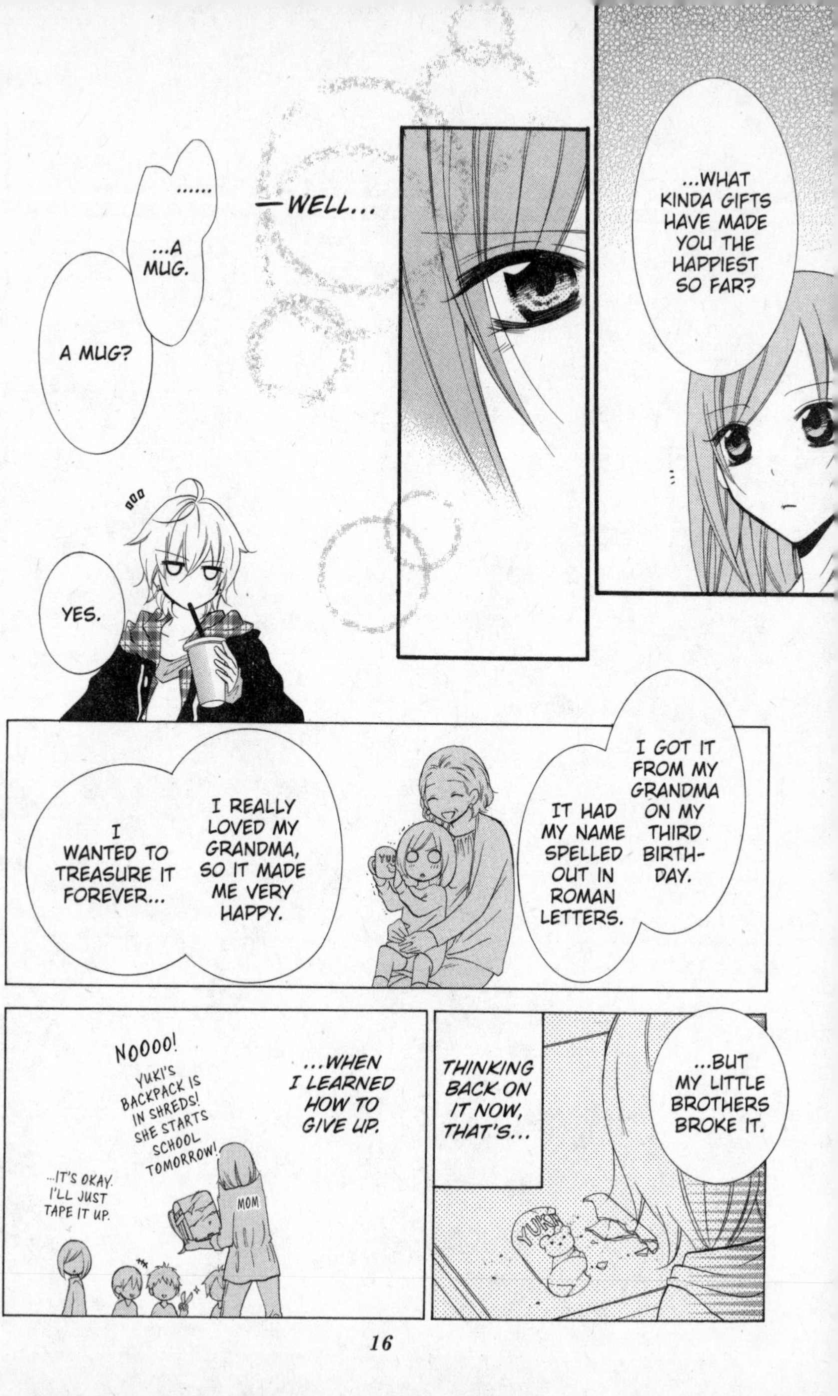
...WHAT KINDA GIFTS HAVE MADE YOU THE HAPPIEST SO FAR?
—WELL...
......
...A MUG.
A MUG?
YES.
I GOT IT FROM MY GRANDMA ON MY THIRD BIRTH-DAY.
IT HAD MY NAME SPELLED OUT IN ROMAN LETTERS.
I REALLY LOVED MY GRANDMA, SO IT MADE ME VERY HAPPY.
I WANTED TO TREASURE IT FOREVER...
...BUT MY LITTLE BROTHERS BROKE IT.
YUKI
THINKING BACK ON IT NOW, THAT'S...
...WHEN I LEARNED HOW TO GIVE UP.
NOOOO!
YUKI'S BACKPACK IS IN SHREDS! SHE STARTS SCHOOL TOMORROW!
MOM
...IT'S OKAY. I'LL JUST TAPE IT UP.

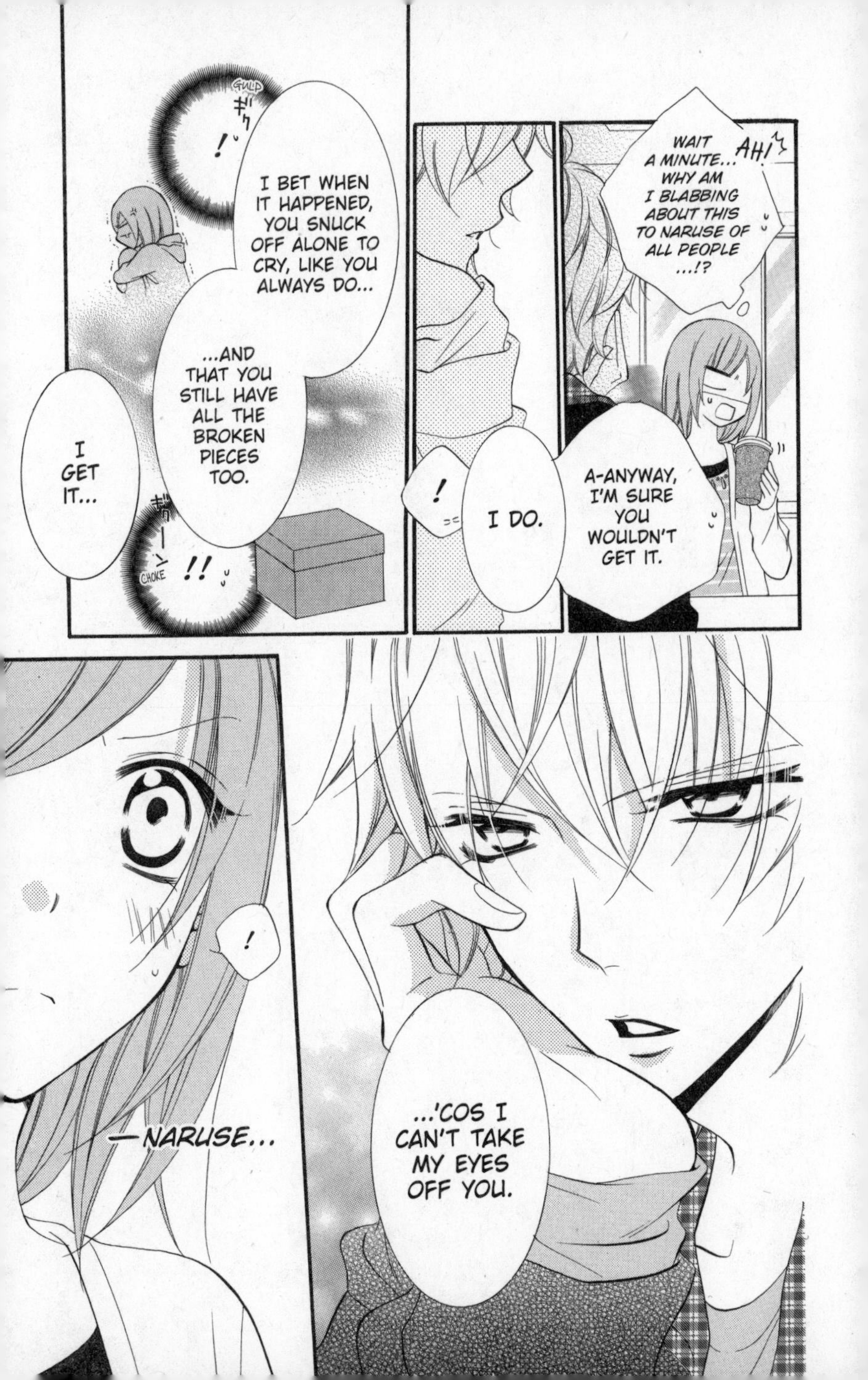
AH!
WAIT A MINUTE... WHY AM I BLABBING ABOUT THIS TO NARUSE OF ALL PEOPLE ...!?
A-ANYWAY, I'M SURE YOU WOULDN'T GET IT.
!
I DO.
GULP
!
I BET WHEN IT HAPPENED, YOU SNUCK OFF ALONE TO CRY, LIKE YOU ALWAYS DO...
...AND THAT YOU STILL HAVE ALL THE BROKEN PIECES TOO.
I GET IT...
CHOKE
!!
...'COS I CAN'T TAKE MY EYES OFF YOU.
!
—NARUSE...

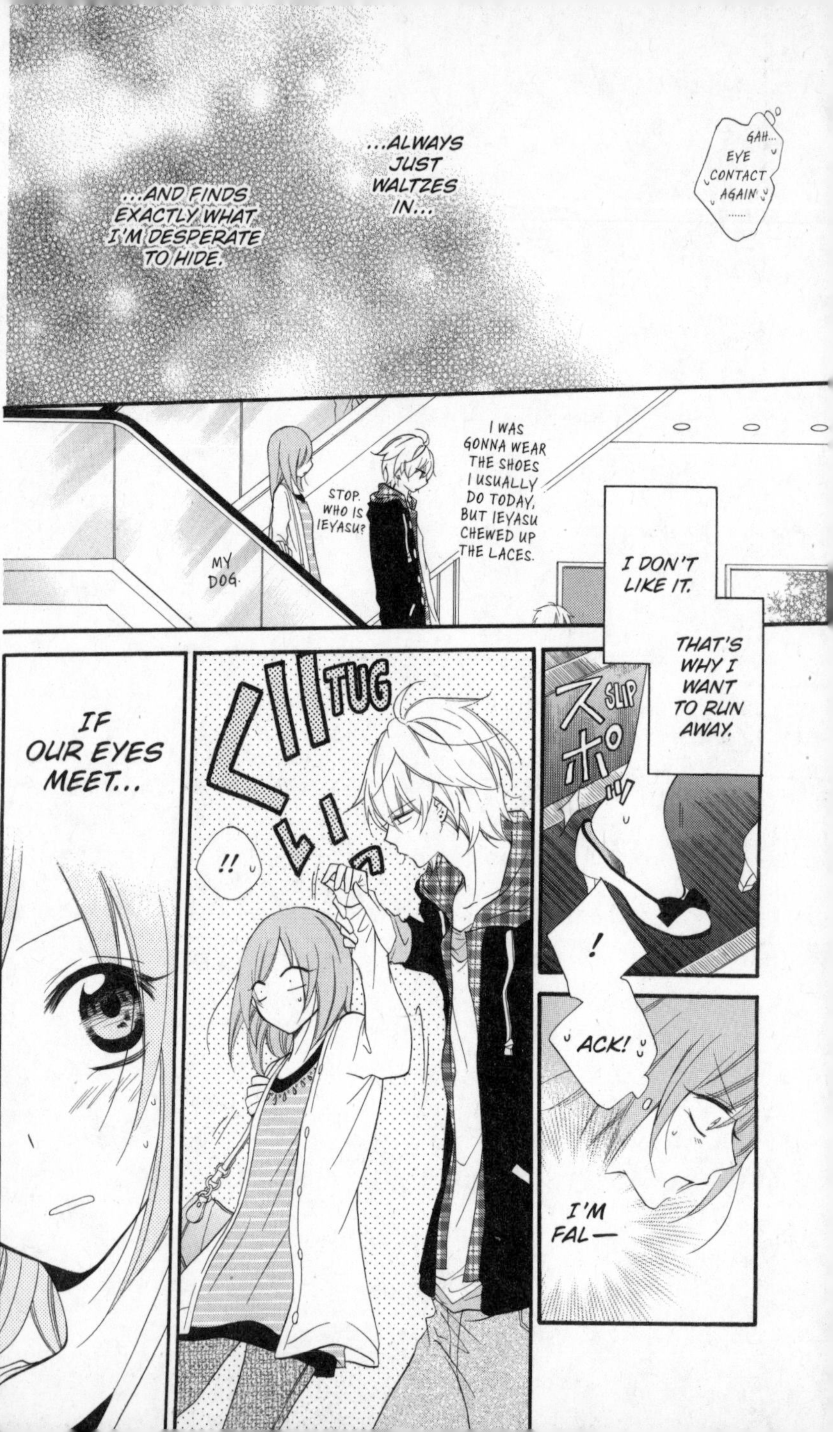
GAH... EYE CONTACT AGAIN ......
...ALWAYS JUST WALTZES IN...
...AND FINDS EXACTLY WHAT I'M DESPERATE TO HIDE.
I WAS GONNA WEAR THE SHOES I USUALLY DO TODAY, BUT IEYASU CHEWED UP THE LACES.
STOP. WHO IS IEYASU?
MY DOG.
I DON'T LIKE IT.
THAT'S WHY I WANT TO RUN AWAY.
SLIP
!
ACK!
I'M FAL—
TUG
!!
IF OUR EYES MEET...

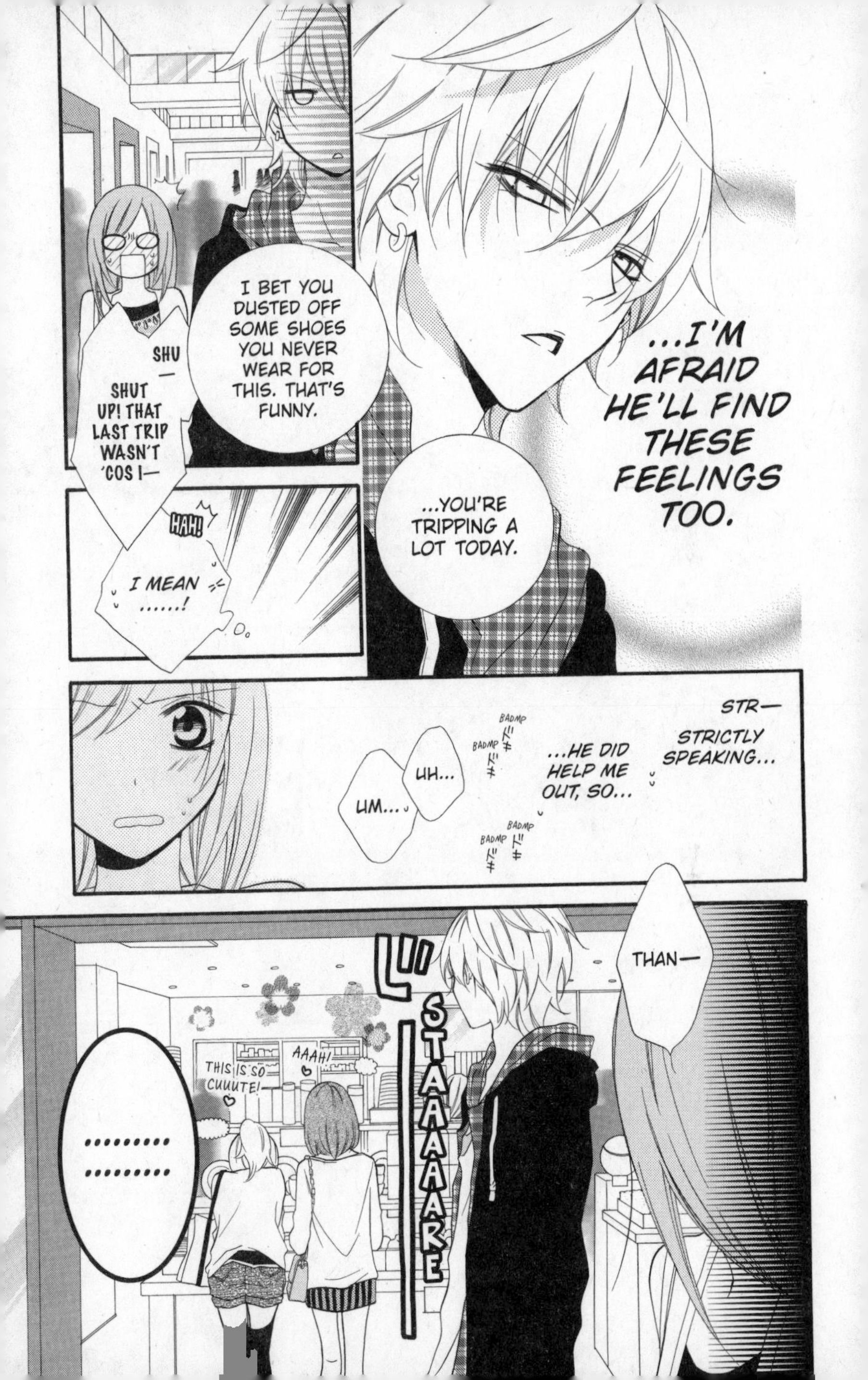
...I'M AFRAID HE'LL FIND THESE FEELINGS TOO.
...YOU'RE TRIPPING A LOT TODAY.
I BET YOU DUSTED OFF SOME SHOES YOU NEVER WEAR FOR THIS. THAT'S FUNNY.
SHU—
SHUT UP! THAT LAST TRIP WASN'T 'COS I—
HAH!
I MEAN ......!
STR—
STRICTLY SPEAKING...
...HE DID HELP ME OUT, SO...
BADMP
BADMP
BADMP
BADMP
UH...
UM...
THAN—
STAAAAARE
AAAH!
THIS IS SO CUUUTE!
....
....

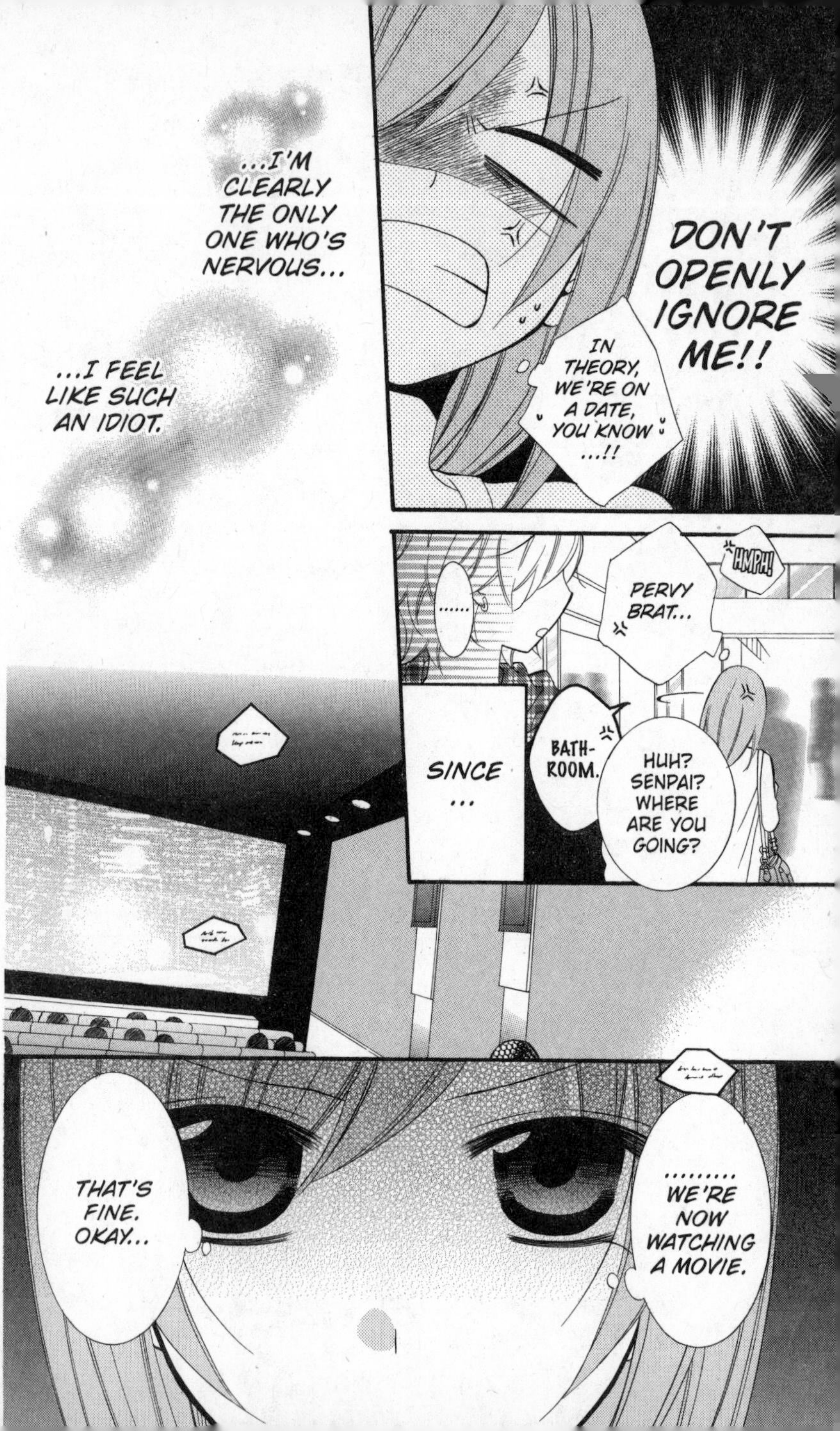
DON'T OPENLY IGNORE ME!!
IN THEORY, WE'RE ON A DATE, YOU KNOW ...!!
...I'M CLEARLY THE ONLY ONE WHO'S NERVOUS...
...I FEEL LIKE SUCH AN IDIOT.
HMPH!
PERVY BRAT...
......
HUH? SENPAI? WHERE ARE YOU GOING?
BATH-ROOM.
SINCE ...
....
WE'RE NOW WATCHING A MOVIE.
THAT'S FINE. OKAY...

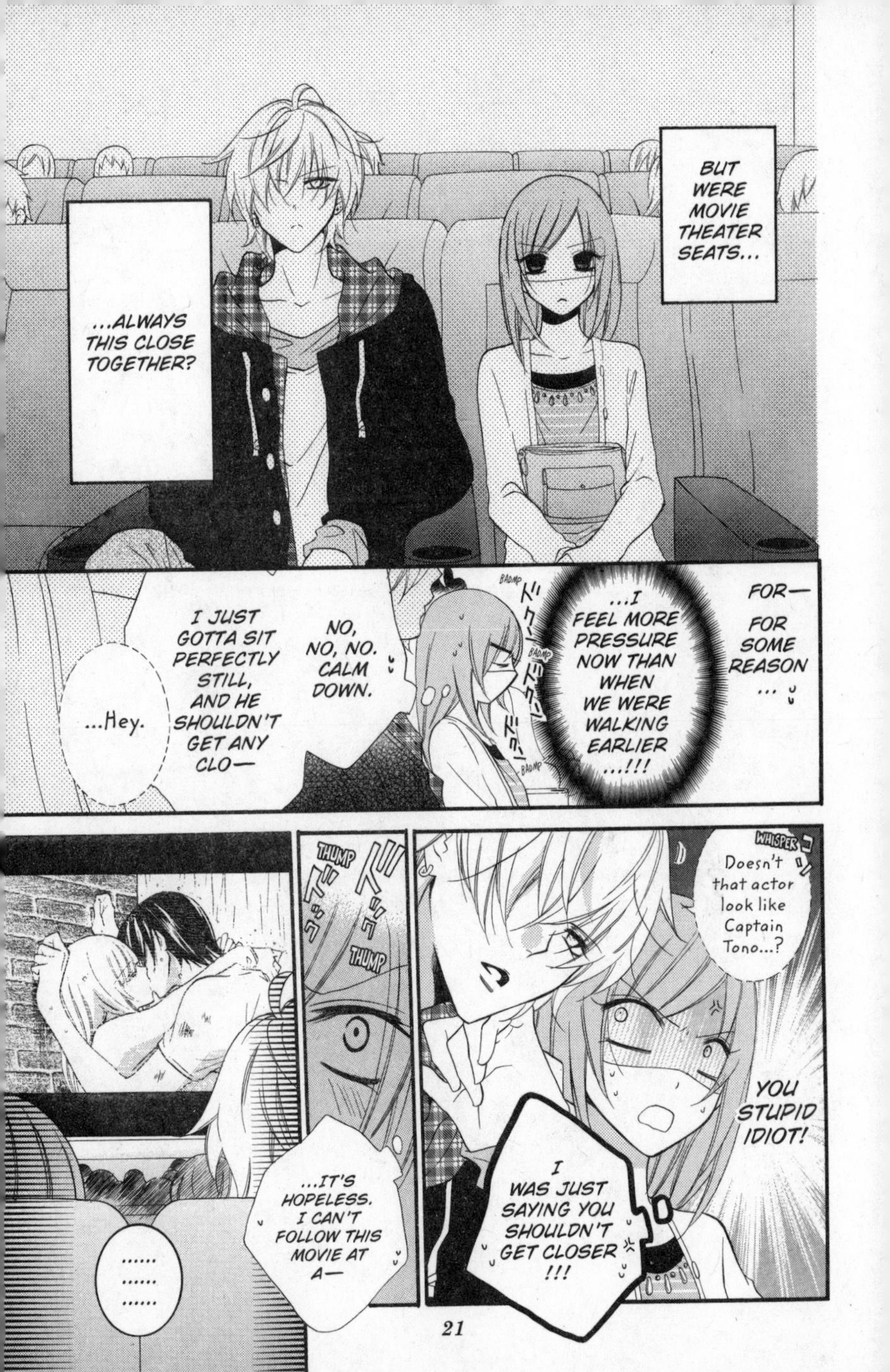
BUT WERE MOVIE THEATER SEATS...
...ALWAYS THIS CLOSE TOGETHER?
FOR— FOR SOME REASON...
...I FEEL MORE PRESSURE NOW THAN WHEN WE WERE WALKING EARLIER...!!!
BADMP
BADMP
BADMP
NO, NO, NO. CALM DOWN.
I JUST GOTTA SIT PERFECTLY STILL, AND HE SHOULDN'T GET ANY CLO—
...Hey.
WHISPER
Doesn't that actor look like Captain Tono...?
YOU STUPID IDIOT!
I WAS JUST SAYING YOU SHOULDN'T GET CLOSER!!!
THUMP
THUMP
...IT'S HOPELESS. I CAN'T FOLLOW THIS MOVIE AT A—
....

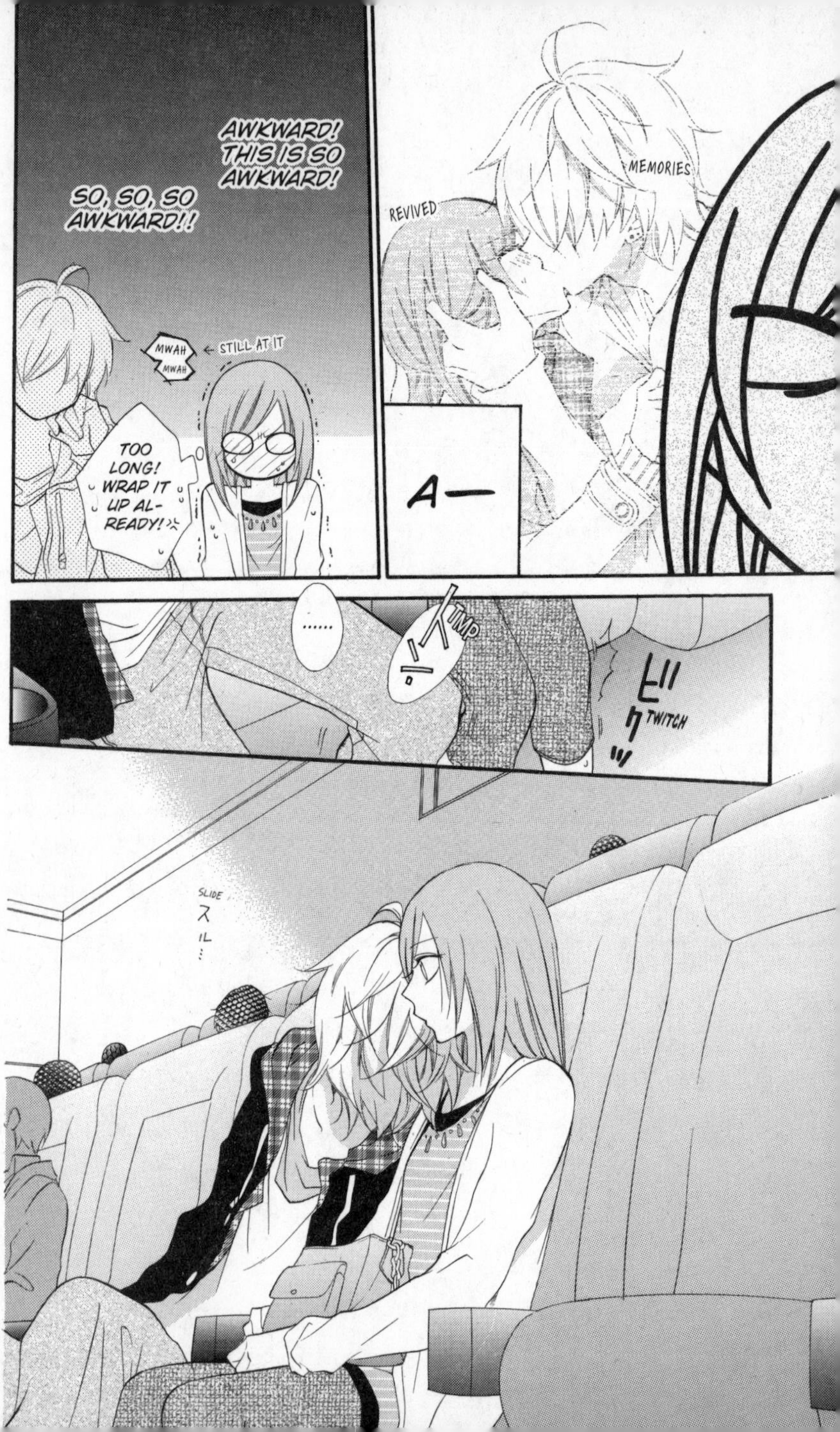
MEMORIES
REVIVED
A—
AWKWARD! THIS IS SO AWKWARD!
SO, SO, SO AWKWARD!!
MWAH MWAH
← STILL AT IT
TOO LONG! WRAP IT UP AL-READY!
TWITCH
TMP
......
SLIDE

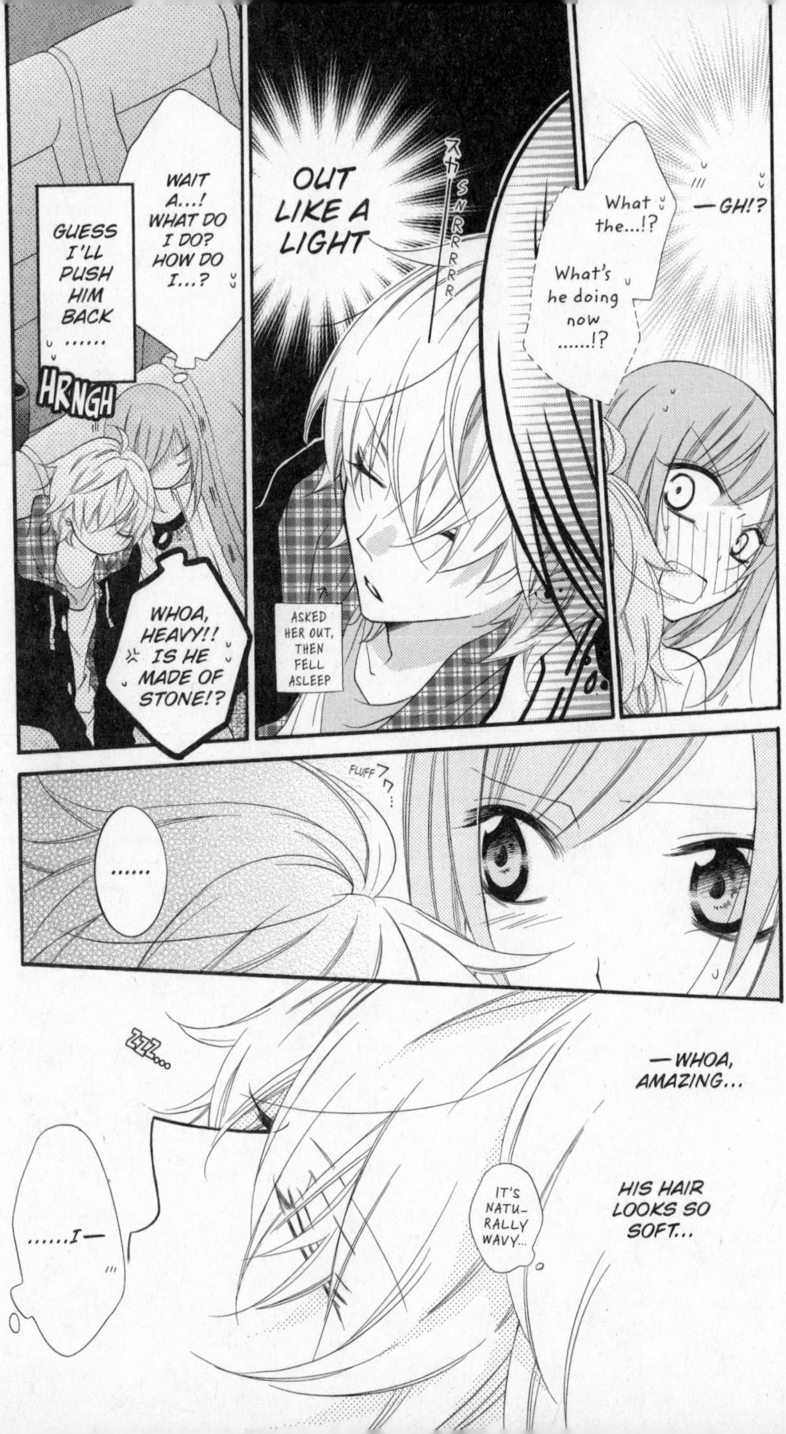
—GH!?
What the...!?
What's he doing now......!?
OUT LIKE A LIGHT
SNRRRRR
ASKED HER OUT, THEN FELL ASLEEP
WAIT A...! WHAT DO I DO? HOW DO I...?
GUESS I'LL PUSH HIM BACK......
HRNGH
WHOA, HEAVY!! IS HE MADE OF STONE!?
FLUFF
......
—WHOA, AMAZING...
HIS HAIR LOOKS SO SOFT...
IT'S NATU-RALLY WAVY...
ZZZ...
......I—

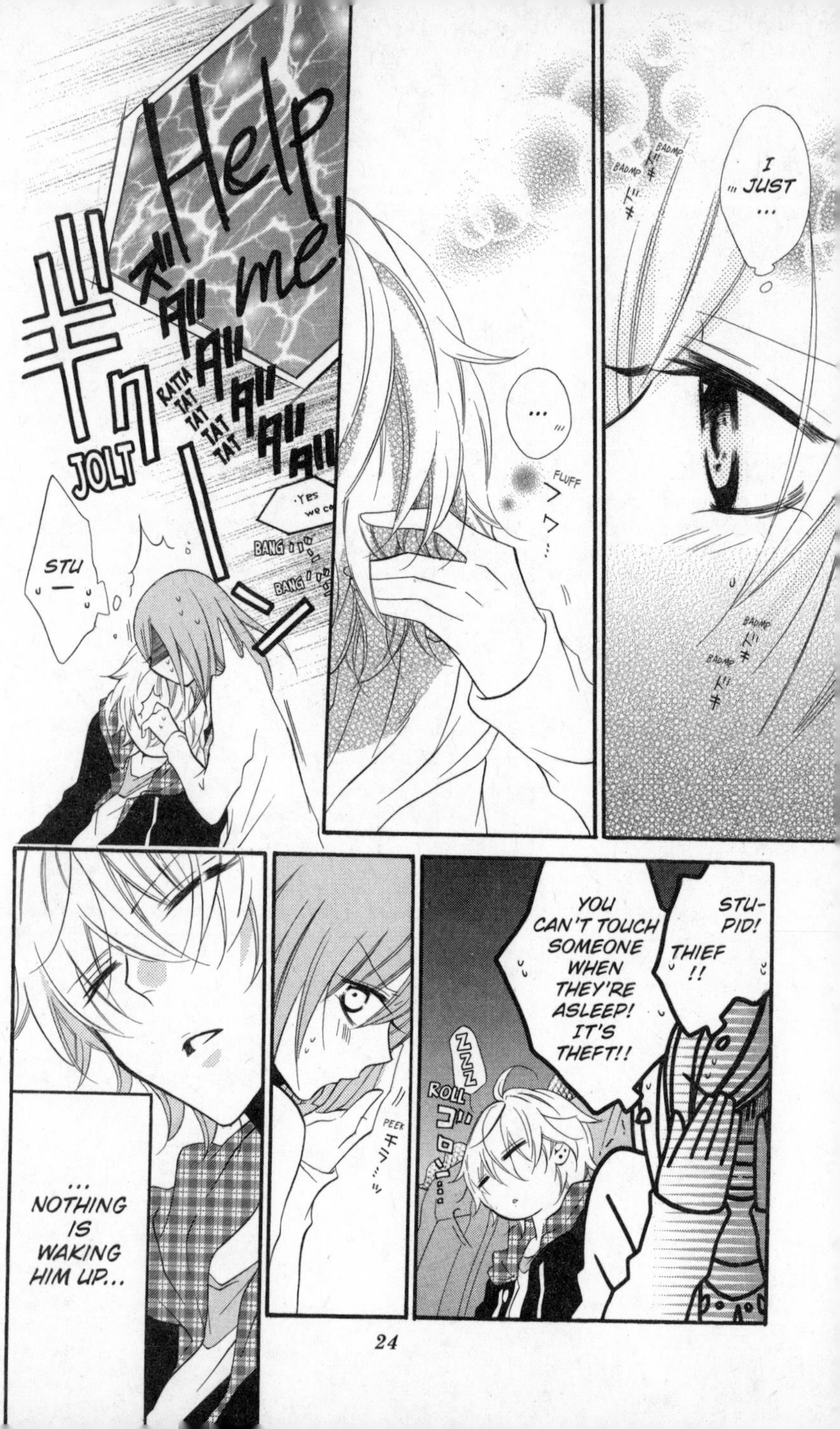

BADMP
BADMP
I JUST ...
BADMP
BADMP
...
FLUFF
Help me!
RATTA TAT TAT TAT TAT
JOLT
·Yes we ca
BANG
BANG
STU—
STU-PID!
THIEF!!
YOU CAN'T TOUCH SOMEONE WHEN THEY'RE ASLEEP! IT'S THEFT!!
ZZZ
ROLL
PEEK
... NOTHING IS WAKING HIM UP...

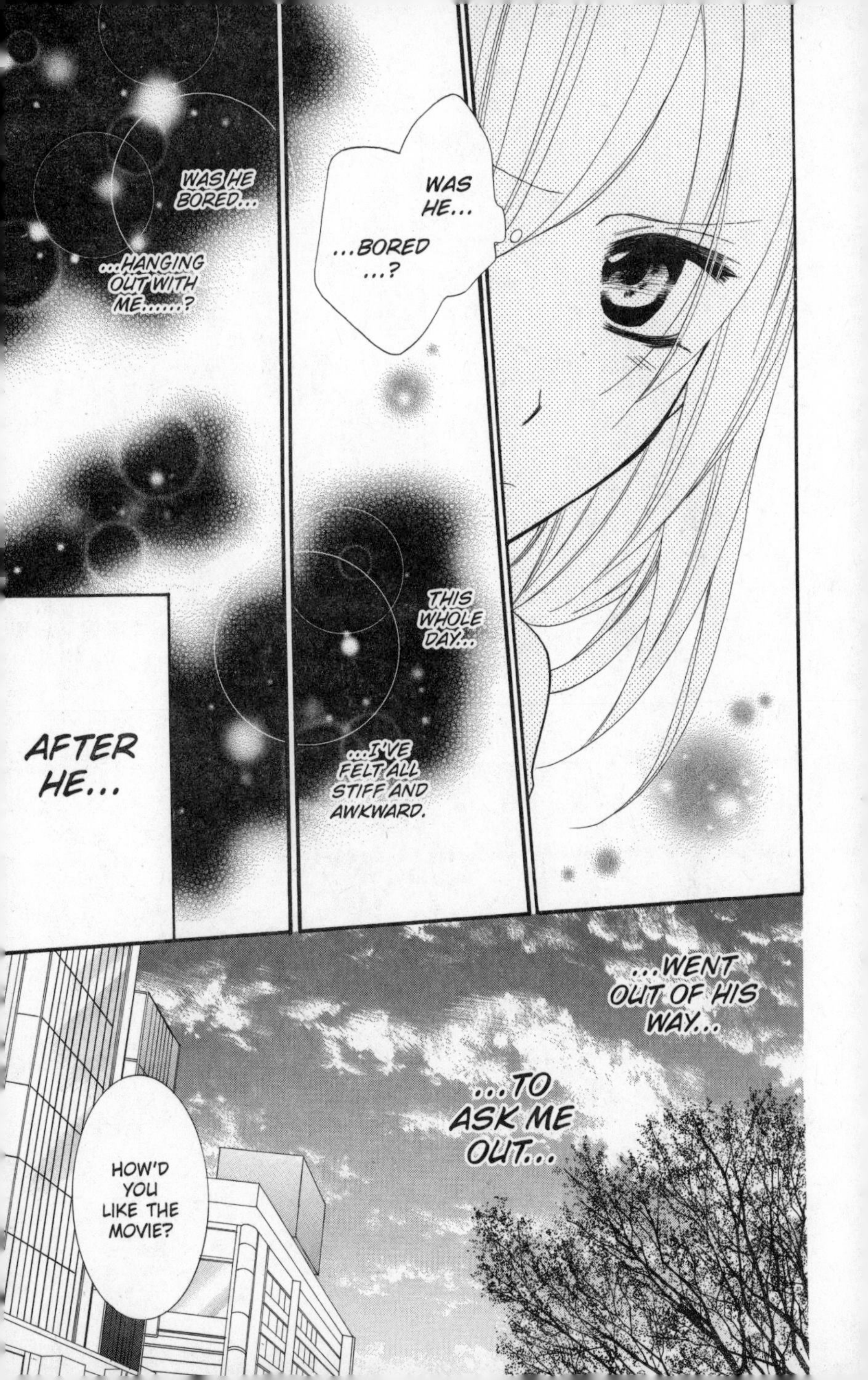
WAS HE... ...BORED ...?
THIS WHOLE DAY...
...I'VE FELT ALL STIFF AND AWKWARD.
WAS HE BORED...
...HANGING OUT WITH ME......?
AFTER HE...
...WENT OUT OF HIS WAY...
...TO ASK ME OUT...
HOW'D YOU LIKE THE MOVIE?

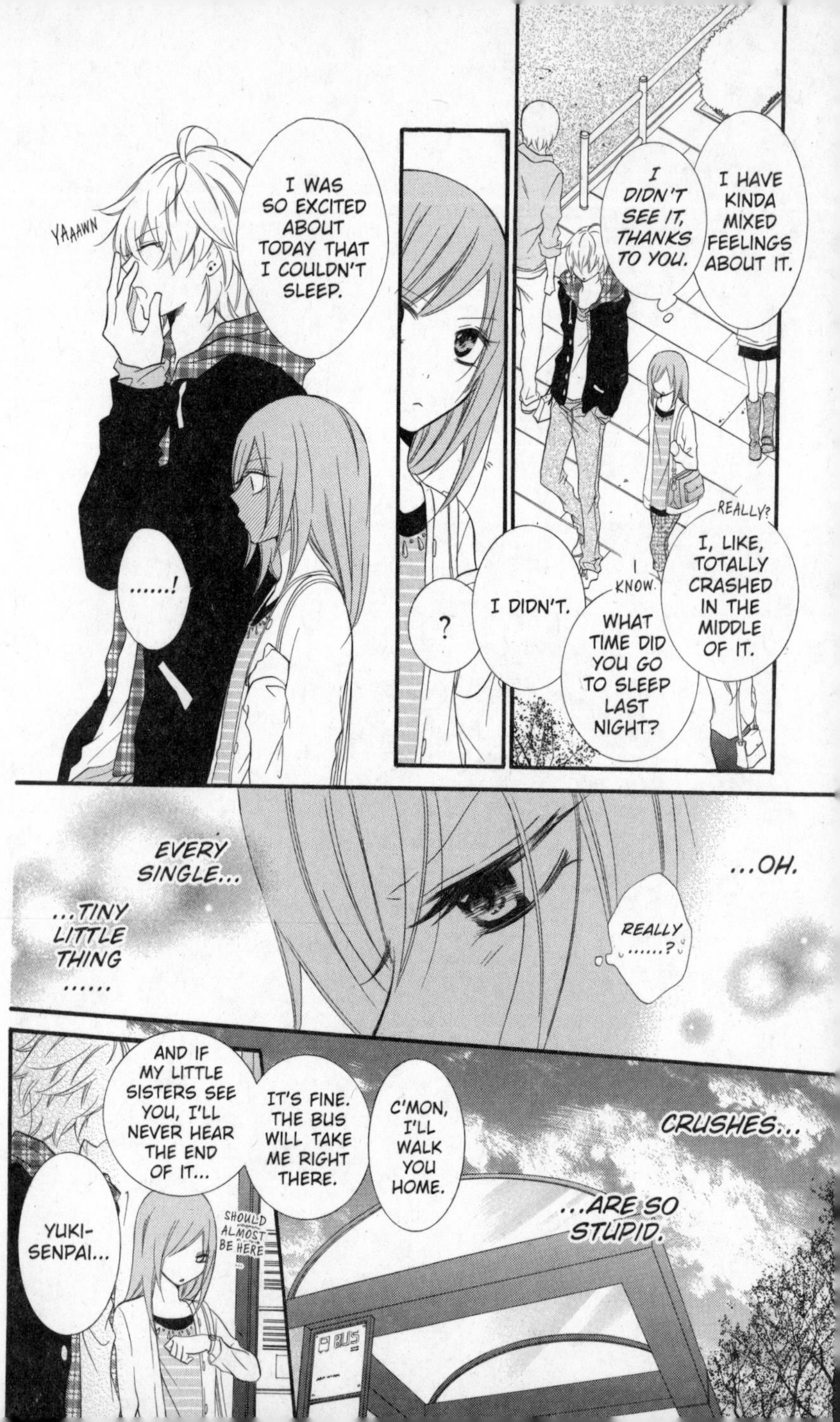
I HAVE KINDA MIXED FEELINGS ABOUT IT.
I DIDN'T SEE IT, THANKS TO YOU.
REALLY?
I, LIKE, TOTALLY CRASHED IN THE MIDDLE OF IT.
I KNOW.
WHAT TIME DID YOU GO TO SLEEP LAST NIGHT?
I DIDN'T.
?
I WAS SO EXCITED ABOUT TODAY THAT I COULDN'T SLEEP.
YAAAWN
......!
...OH.
REALLY ......?
EVERY SINGLE...
...TINY LITTLE THING ......
CRUSHES...
...ARE SO STUPID.
C'MON, I'LL WALK YOU HOME.
IT'S FINE. THE BUS WILL TAKE ME RIGHT THERE.
AND IF MY LITTLE SISTERS SEE YOU, I'LL NEVER HEAR THE END OF IT...
SHOULD ALMOST BE HERE ...
YUKI-SENPAI...

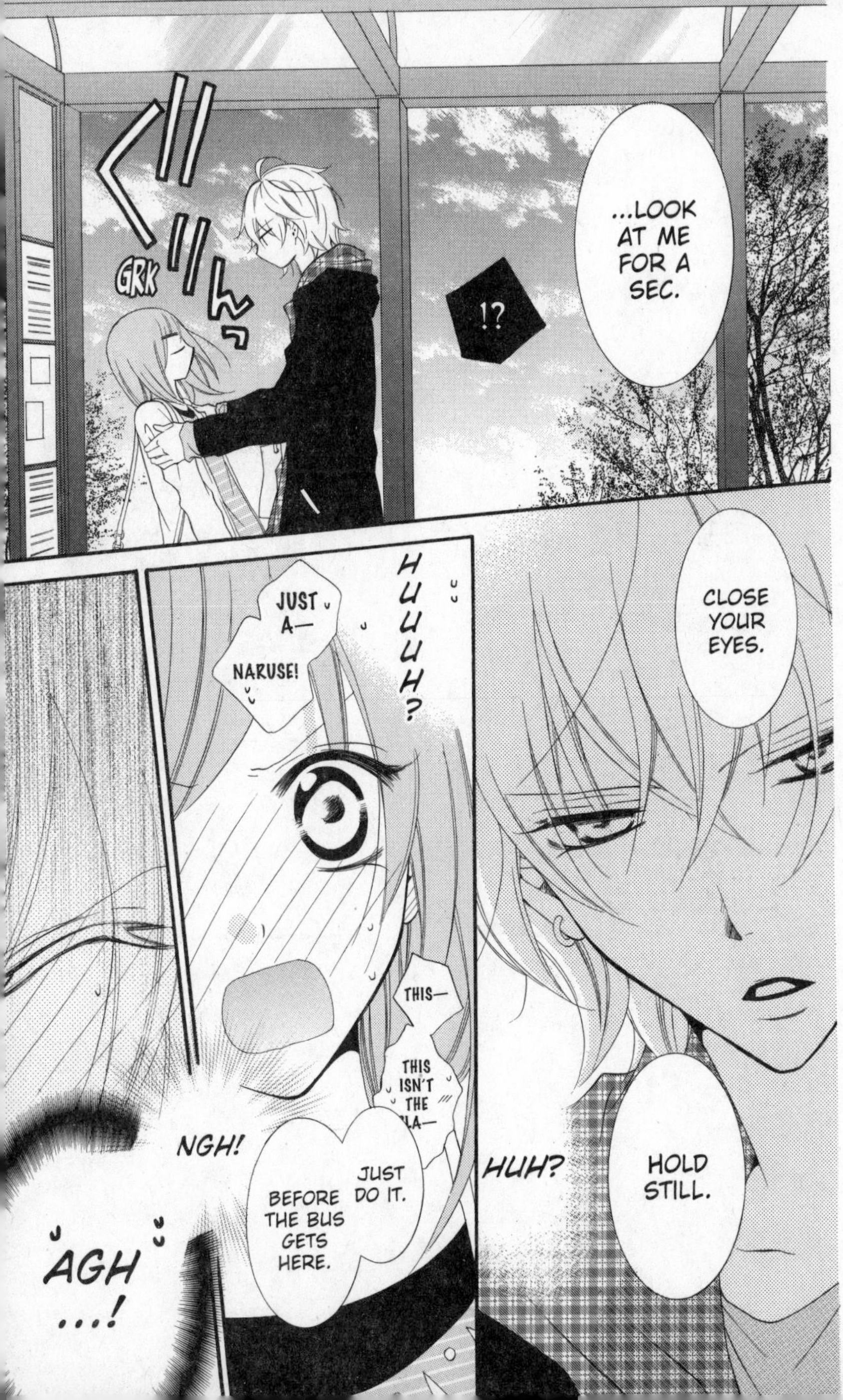

...LOOK AT ME FOR A SEC.
!?
GRK
CLOSE YOUR EYES.
HOLD STILL.
HUH?
HUUUH?
JUST A—
NARUSE!
THIS—
THIS ISN'T THE LA—
JUST DO IT.
BEFORE THE BUS GETS HERE.
NGH!
AGH ...!

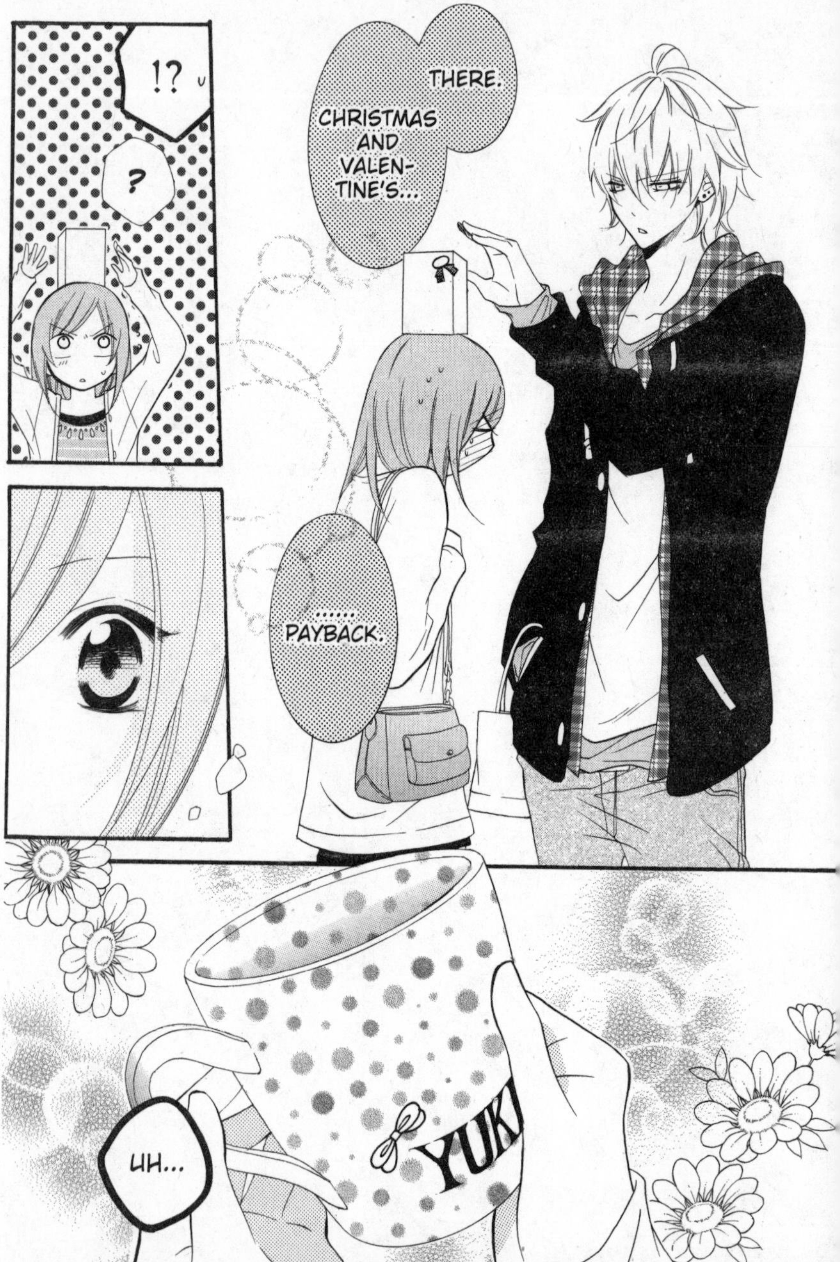
THERE.
CHRISTMAS AND VALEN-TINE'S...
......PAYBACK.
!?
?
UH...

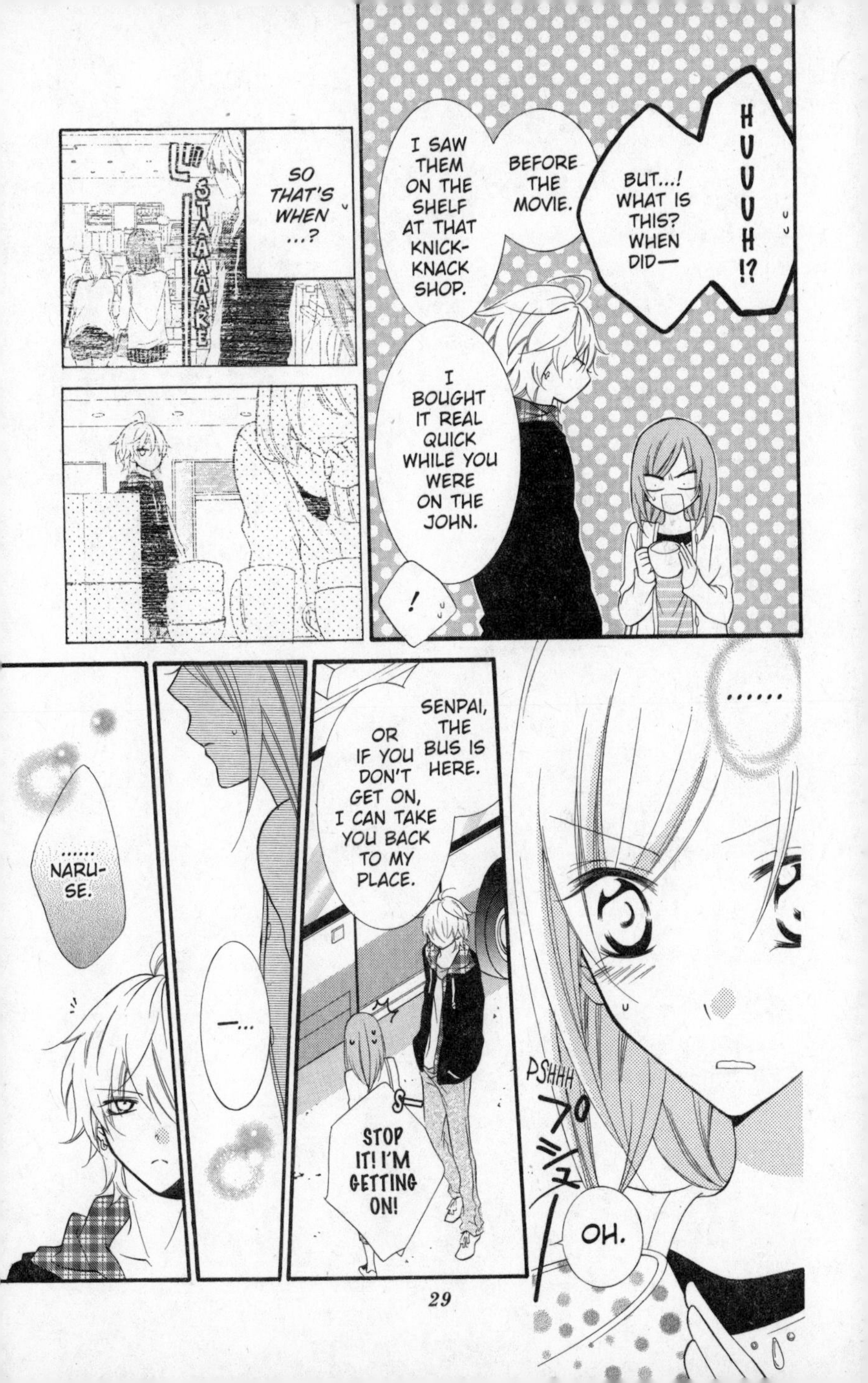
HUUUUH!?
BUT...! WHAT IS THIS? WHEN DID—
BEFORE THE MOVIE.
I SAW THEM ON THE SHELF AT THAT KNICK-KNACK SHOP.
I BOUGHT IT REAL QUICK WHILE YOU WERE ON THE JOHN.
!
SO THAT'S WHEN ...?
STAAAAAKE
......
PSHHH
OH.
SENPAI, THE BUS IS HERE.
OR IF YOU DON'T GET ON, I CAN TAKE YOU BACK TO MY PLACE.
STOP IT! I'M GETTING ON!
—...
......NARU-SE.

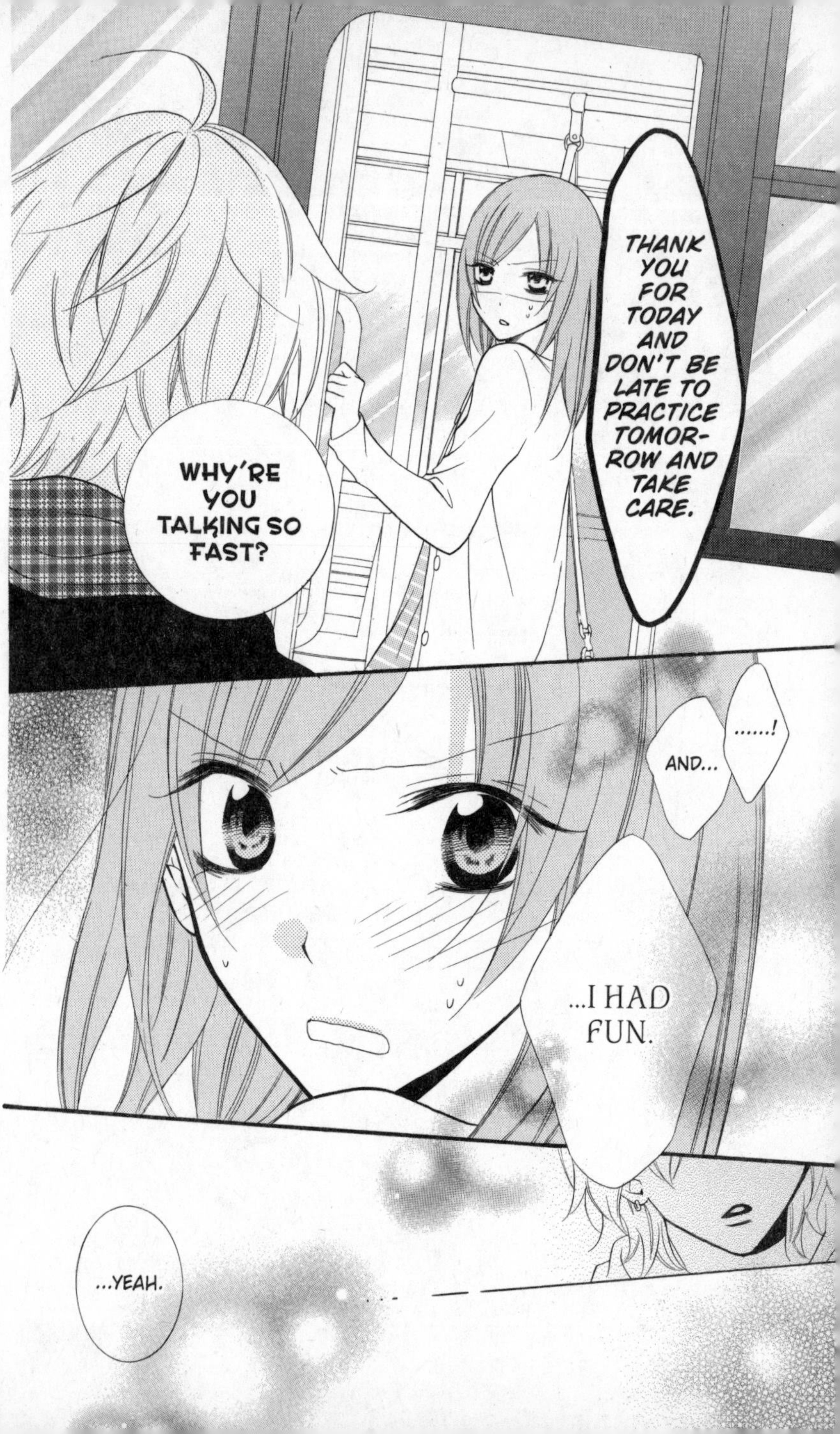
THANK YOU FOR TODAY AND DON'T BE LATE TO PRACTICE TOMOR-ROW AND TAKE CARE.
WHY'RE YOU TALKING SO FAST?
......!
AND...
...I HAD FUN.
...YEAH.

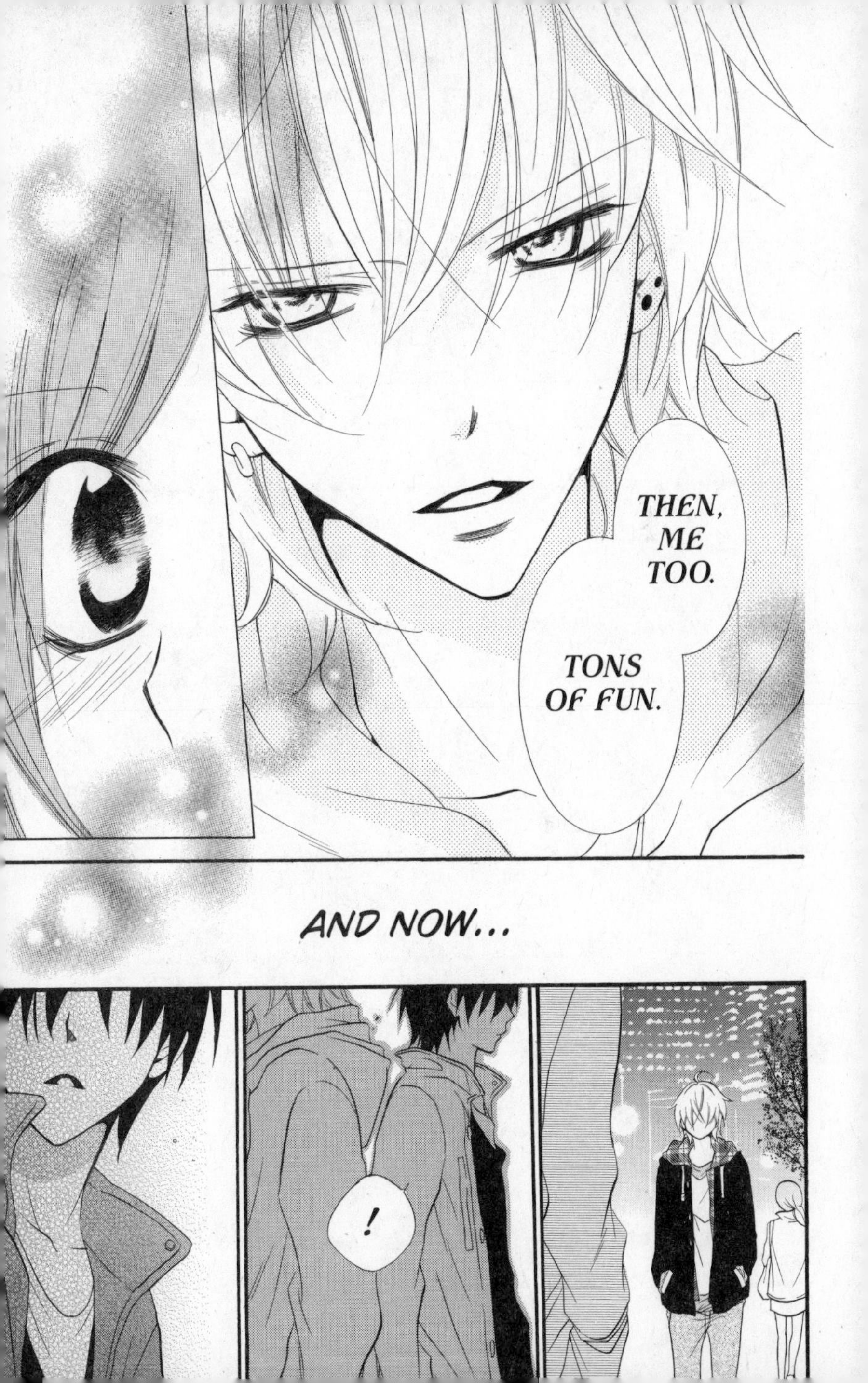
THEN, ME TOO.
TONS OF FUN.
AND NOW...
!

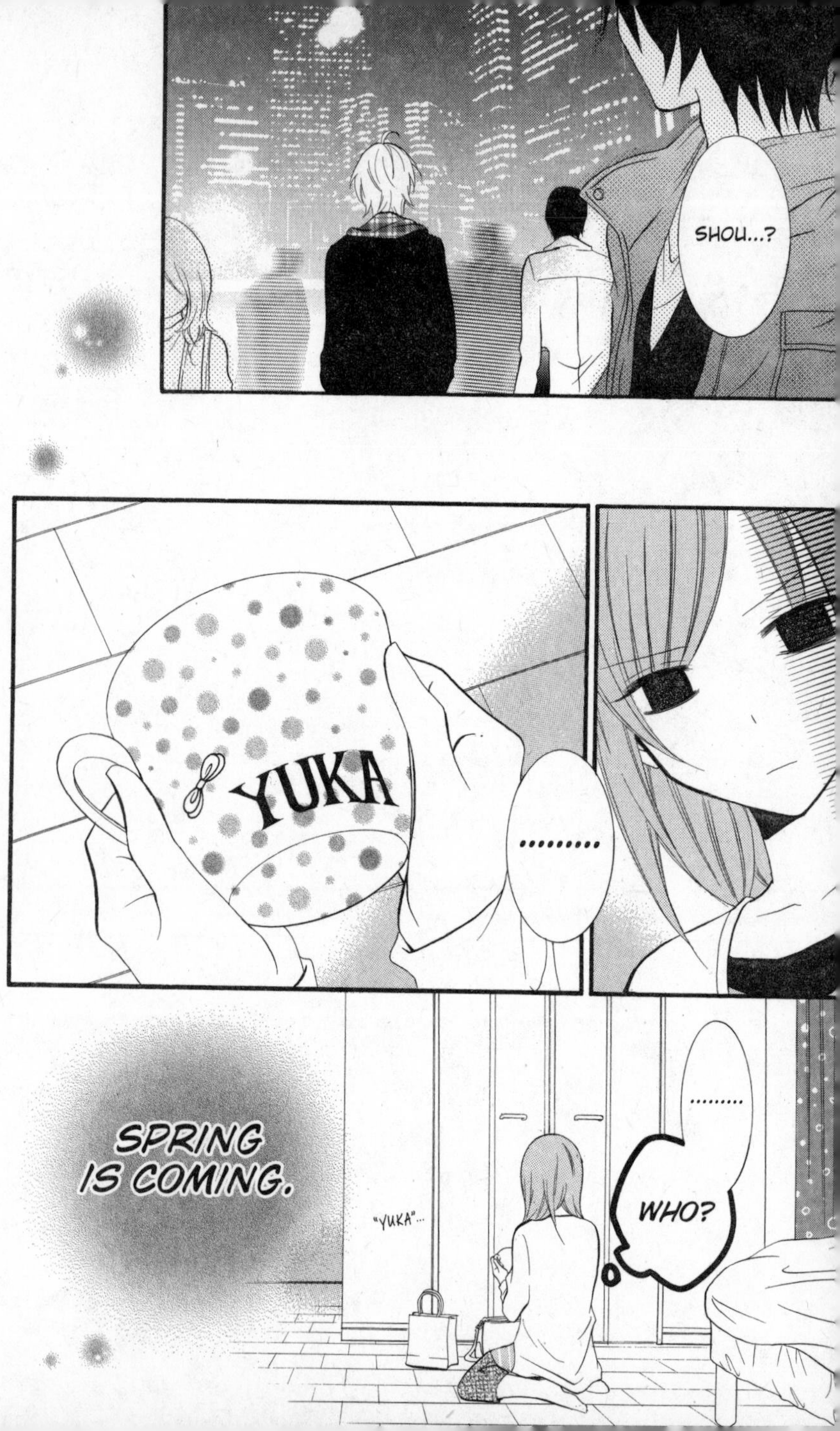
SHOU...?
....
YUKA
....
WHO?
"YUKA"...
SPRING
IS COMING.

Chapter 8

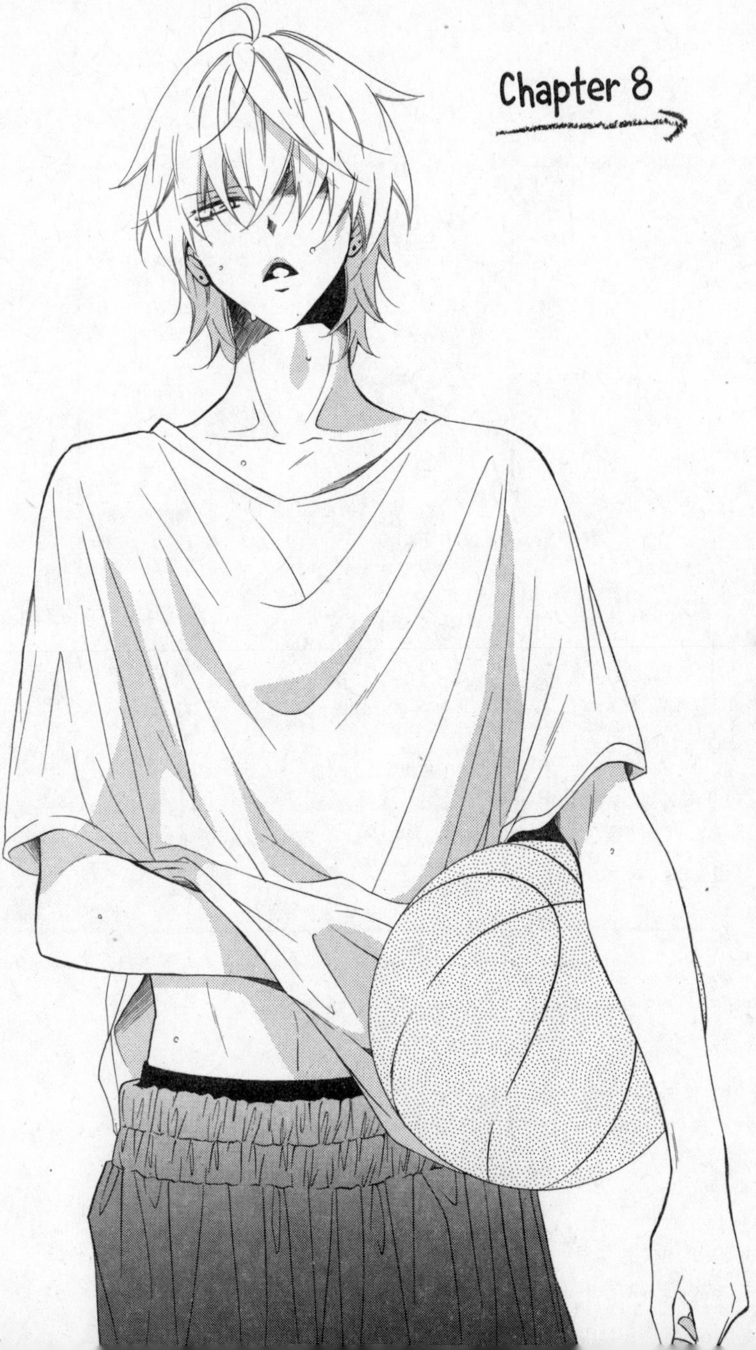

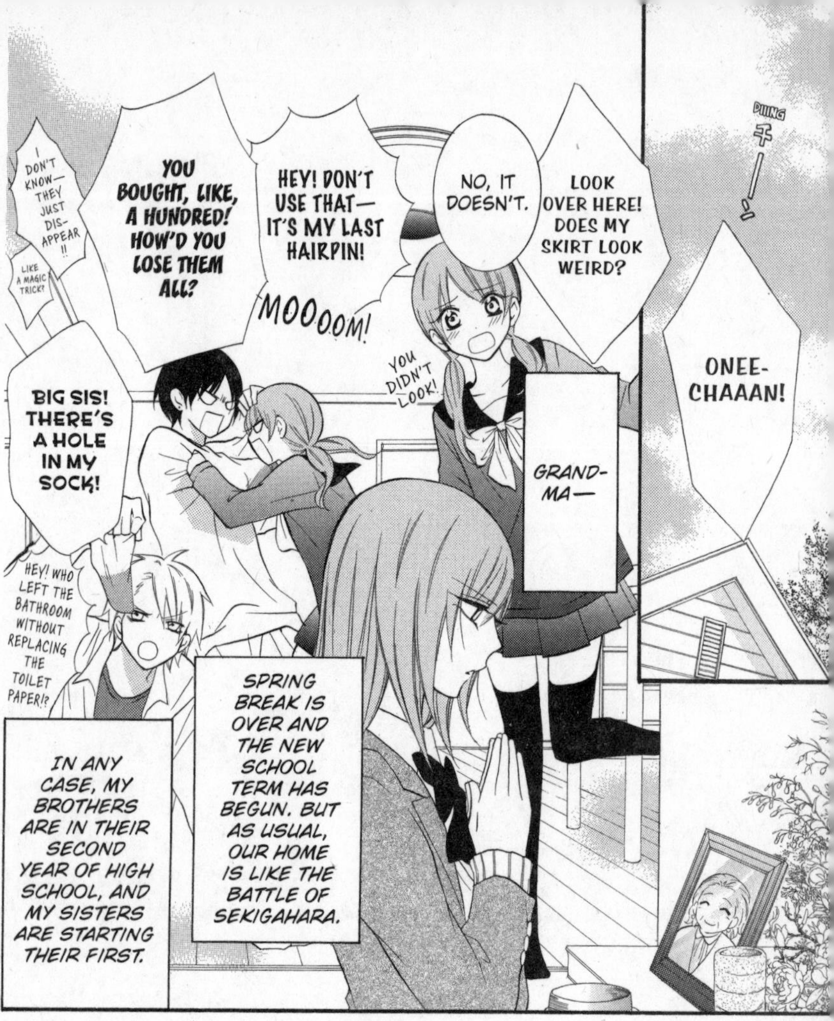
DIIING
チーン
ONEE-CHAAAN!
LOOK OVER HERE! DOES MY SKIRT LOOK WEIRD?
NO, IT DOESN'T.
HEY! DON'T USE THAT— IT'S MY LAST HAIRPIN!
MOOOOM!
YOU DIDN'T LOOK!
YOU BOUGHT, LIKE, A HUNDRED! HOW'D YOU LOSE THEM ALL?
I DON'T KNOW— THEY JUST DIS-APPEAR!!
LIKE A MAGIC TRICK?
BIG SIS! THERE'S A HOLE IN MY SOCK!
GRAND-MA—
HEY! WHO LEFT THE BATHROOM WITHOUT REPLACING THE TOILET PAPER!?
SPRING BREAK IS OVER AND THE NEW SCHOOL TERM HAS BEGUN. BUT AS USUAL, OUR HOME IS LIKE THE BATTLE OF SEKIGAHARA.
IN ANY CASE, MY BROTHERS ARE IN THEIR SECOND YEAR OF HIGH SCHOOL, AND MY SISTERS ARE STARTING THEIR FIRST.

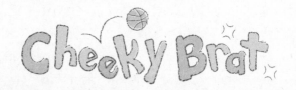

Cheeky Brat

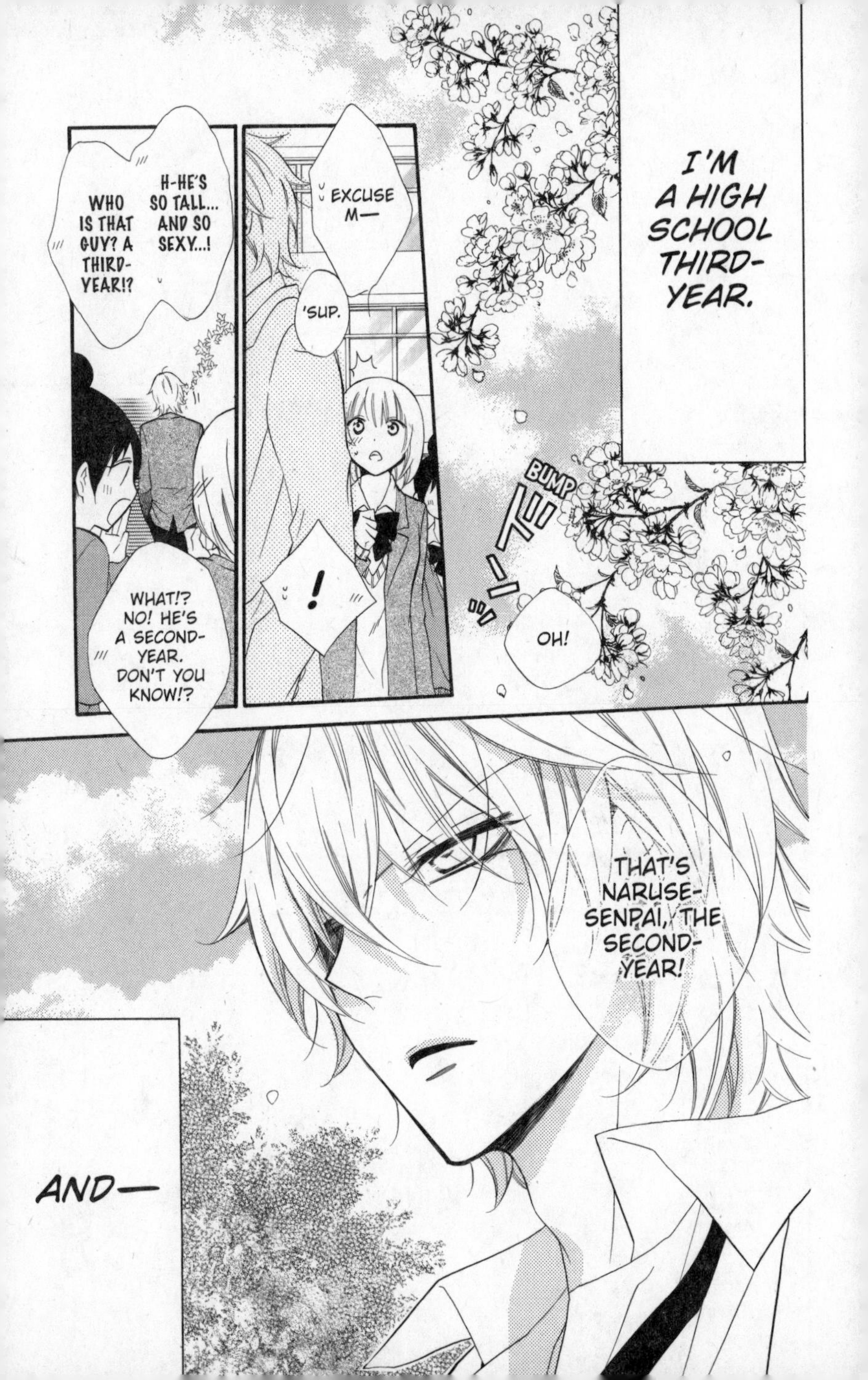
I'M A HIGH SCHOOL THIRD-YEAR.
BUMP
OH!
EXCUSE M—
'SUP.
!
H-HE'S SO TALL... AND SO SEXY...!
WHO IS THAT GUY? A THIRD-YEAR!?
WHAT!? NO! HE'S A SECOND-YEAR. DON'T YOU KNOW!?
THAT'S NARUSE-SENPAI, THE SECOND-YEAR!
AND—

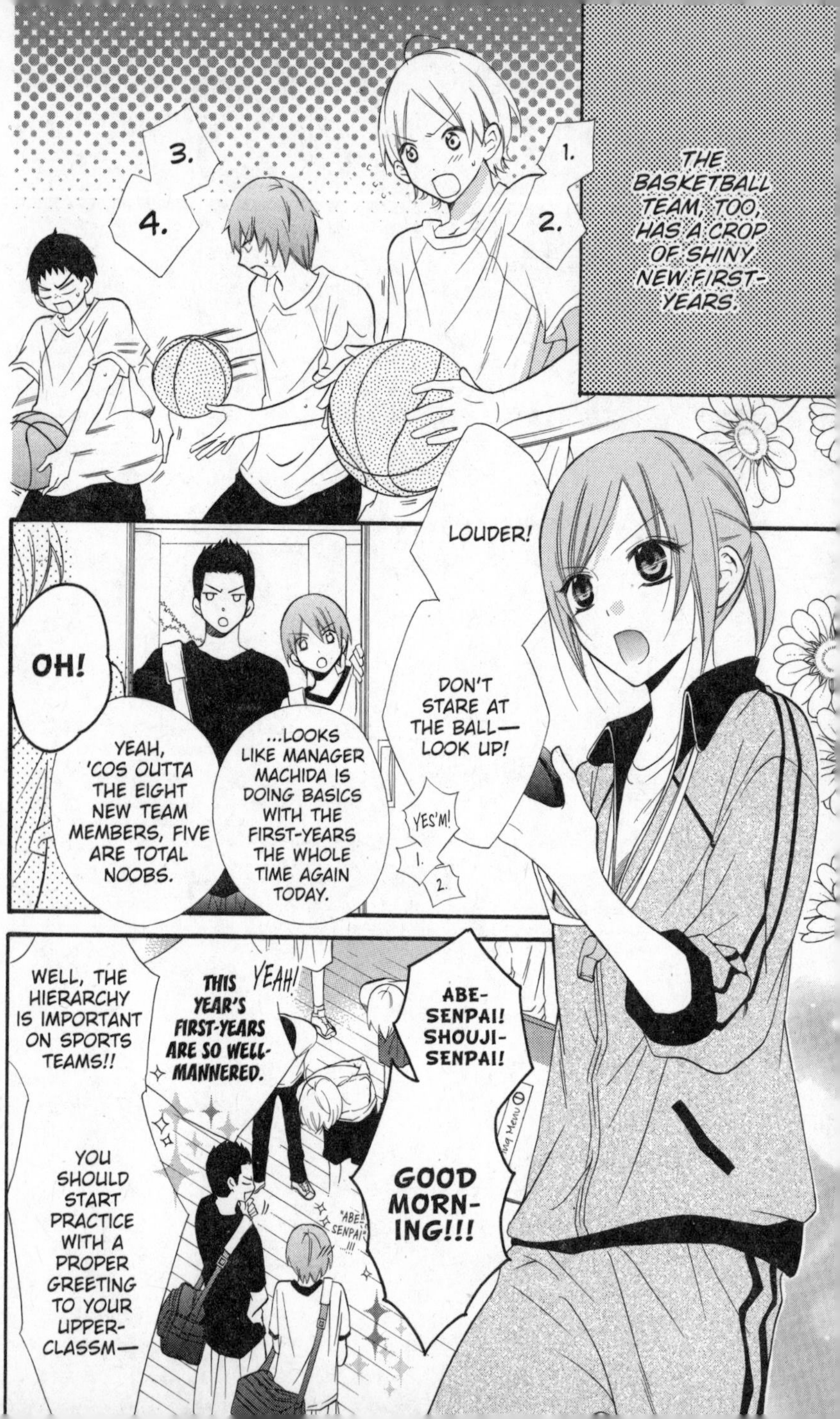
THE BASKETBALL TEAM, TOO, HAS A CROP OF SHINY NEW FIRST-YEARS.
1.
2.
3.
4.
LOUDER!
DON'T STARE AT THE BALL—LOOK UP!
YES'M!
1.
2.
...LOOKS LIKE MANAGER MACHIDA IS DOING BASICS WITH THE FIRST-YEARS THE WHOLE TIME AGAIN TODAY.
YEAH, 'COS OUTTA THE EIGHT NEW TEAM MEMBERS, FIVE ARE TOTAL NOOBS.
OH!
ABE-SENPAI! SHOUJI-SENPAI!
GOOD MORNING!!!
YEAH!
THIS YEAR'S FIRST-YEARS ARE SO WELL-MANNERED.
WELL, THE HIERARCHY IS IMPORTANT ON SPORTS TEAMS!!
YOU SHOULD START PRACTICE WITH A PROPER GREETING TO YOUR UPPER-CLASSM—

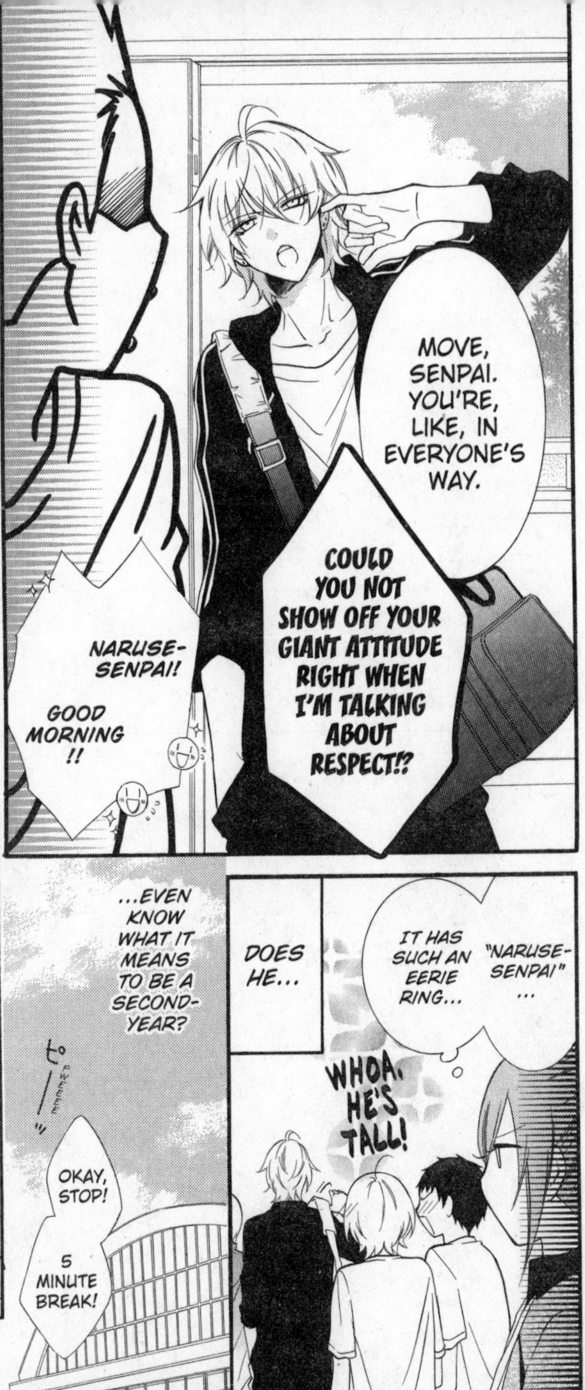
MOVE, SENPAI. YOU'RE, LIKE, IN EVERYONE'S WAY.
COULD YOU NOT SHOW OFF YOUR GIANT ATTITUDE RIGHT WHEN I'M TALKING ABOUT RESPECT!?
NARUSE-SENPAI!
GOOD MORNING!!
"NARUSE-SENPAI"...
IT HAS SUCH AN EERIE RING...
DOES HE...
WHOA, HE'S TALL!
...EVEN KNOW WHAT IT MEANS TO BE A SECOND-YEAR?
PWEEEE
OKAY, STOP!
5 MINUTE BREAK!

02

1ST AUTOGRAPH SIGNING

To commemorate the sale of the previous volume of *Cheeky Brat*, or actually, because *Hana to Yume* is celebrating its 40th anniversary✧ Wow! this year, to my inner delight, I was able to ride the coattails of the celebration and do an autograph signing...!!

1st Autograph signing.
In Yokohama.
So fancy.

The bookstore that hosted the event even went so far as to create a sort of Mitsubachi Miyuki corner featuring all my published works, which really only exacerbated the nerves I had been suffering from since the previous day. I took pictures while I was freaking out.

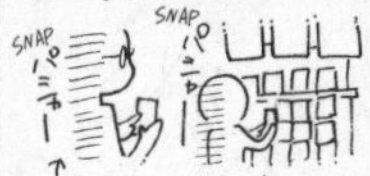
SNAP
SNAP

My editor took pictures of me freaking out.

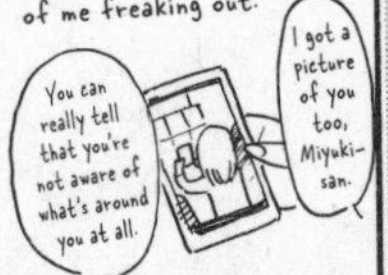
You can really tell that you're not aware of what's around you at all.
I got a picture of you too, Miyuki-san.

I felt like I was going to vomit from my nerves while I practiced signing my autograph.

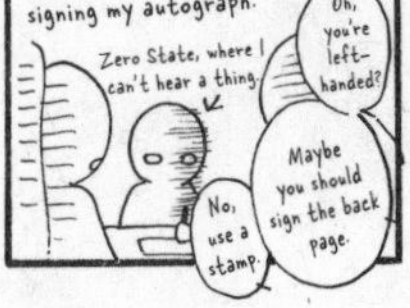
Zero State, where I can't hear a thing.
Oh, you're left-handed?
Maybe you should sign the back page.
No, use a stamp.

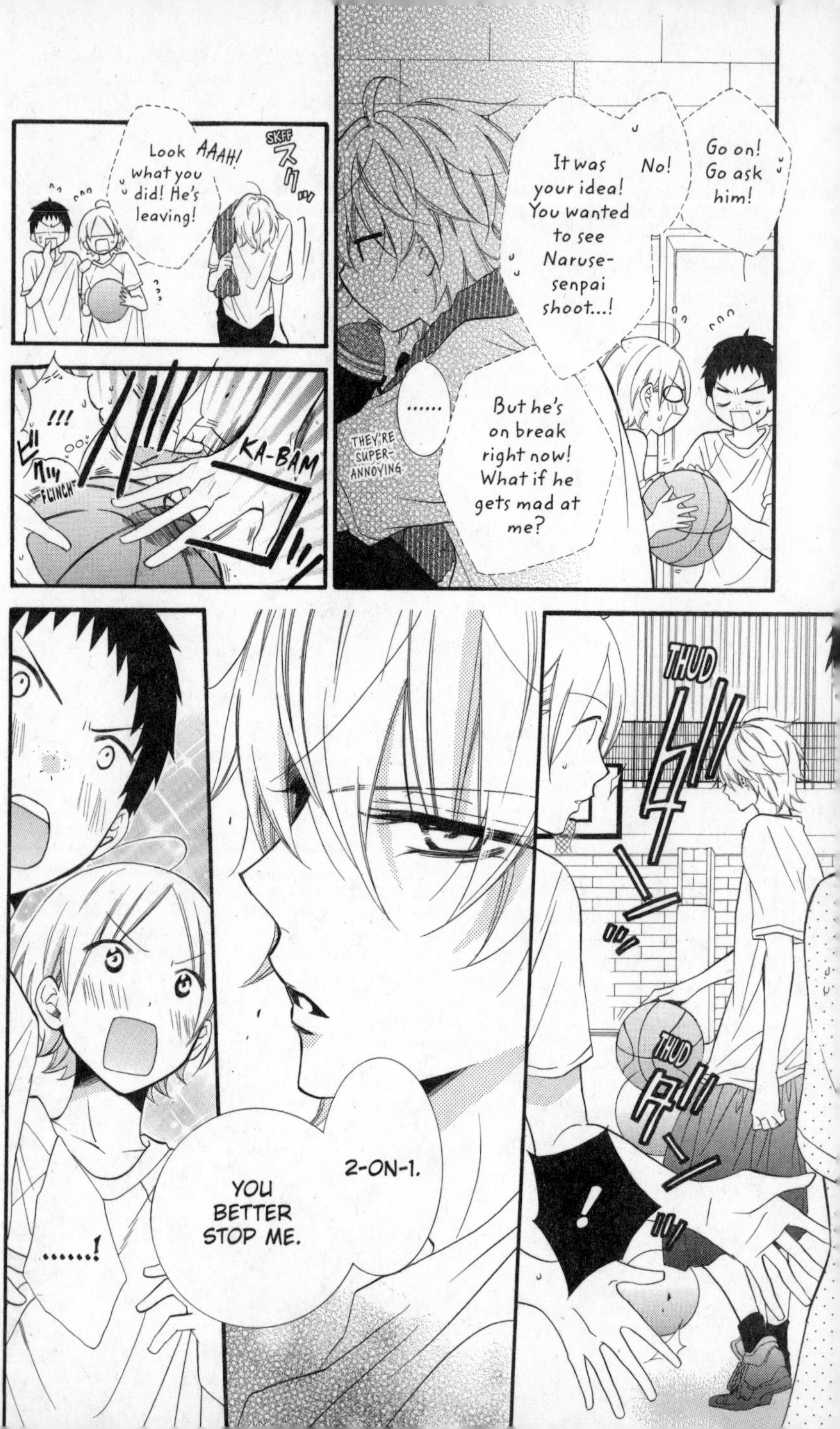
Go on! Go ask him!
No!
It was your idea! You wanted to see Naruse-senpai shoot...!
But he's on break right now! What if he gets mad at me?
......
THEY'RE SUPER-ANNOYING.
SKFF
AAAH!
Look what you did! He's leaving!
KA-BAM
!!!
FLINCH
THUD
THUD
!
2-ON-1.
YOU BETTER STOP ME.
......!

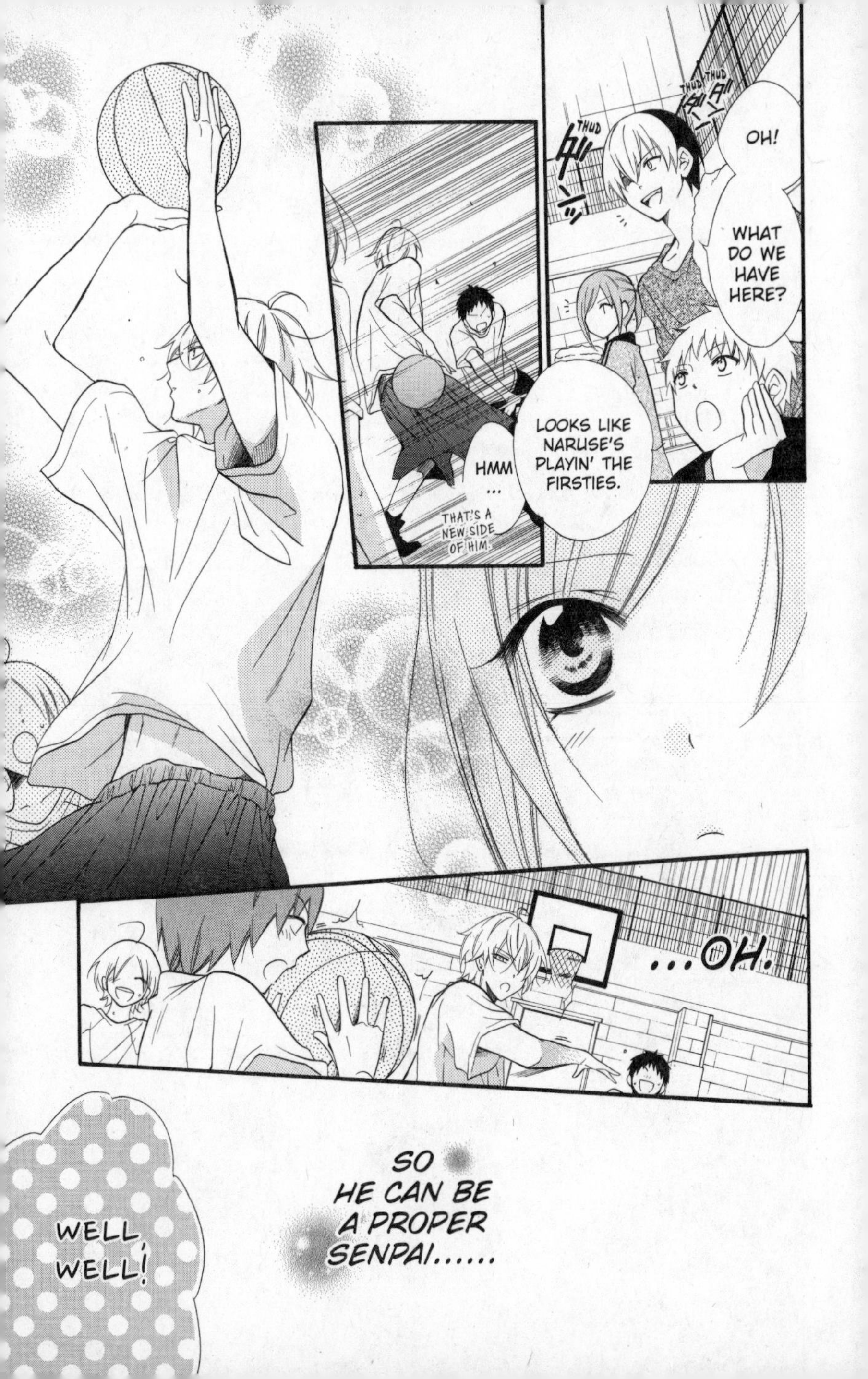
THUD THUD
THUD
OH!
WHAT DO WE HAVE HERE?
LOOKS LIKE NARUSE'S PLAYIN' THE FIRSTIES.
HMM ...
THAT'S A NEW SIDE OF HIM.
...OH.
SO HE CAN BE A PROPER SENPAI......
WELL WELL!

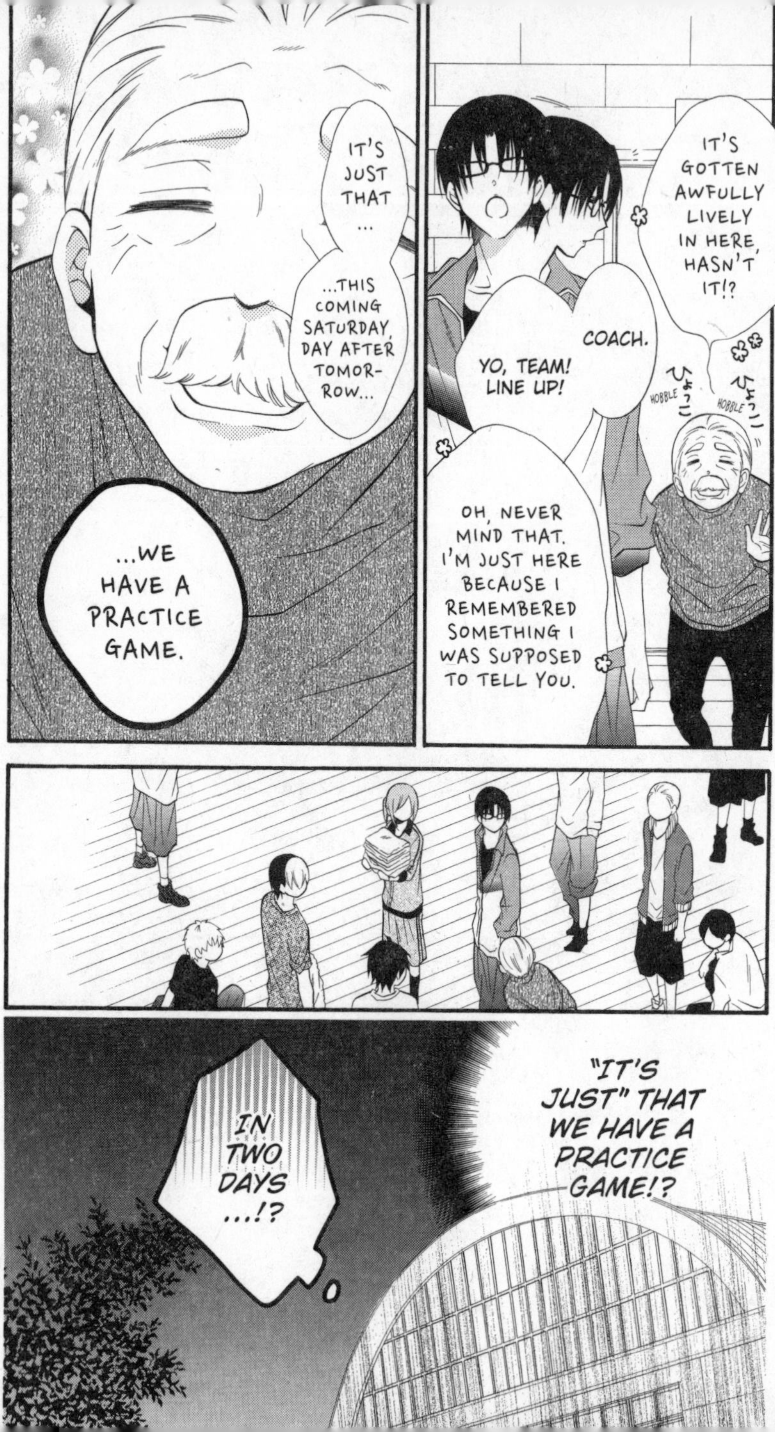
IT'S GOTTEN AWFULLY LIVELY IN HERE, HASN'T IT!?
ひょっこ
HOBBLE
ひょっこ
HOBBLE
COACH.
YO, TEAM! LINE UP!
OH, NEVER MIND THAT. I'M JUST HERE BECAUSE I REMEMBERED SOMETHING I WAS SUPPOSED TO TELL YOU.
IT'S JUST THAT ...
...THIS COMING SATURDAY, DAY AFTER TOMOR-ROW...
...WE HAVE A PRACTICE GAME.
"IT'S JUST" THAT WE HAVE A PRACTICE GAME!?
IN TWO DAYS ...!?

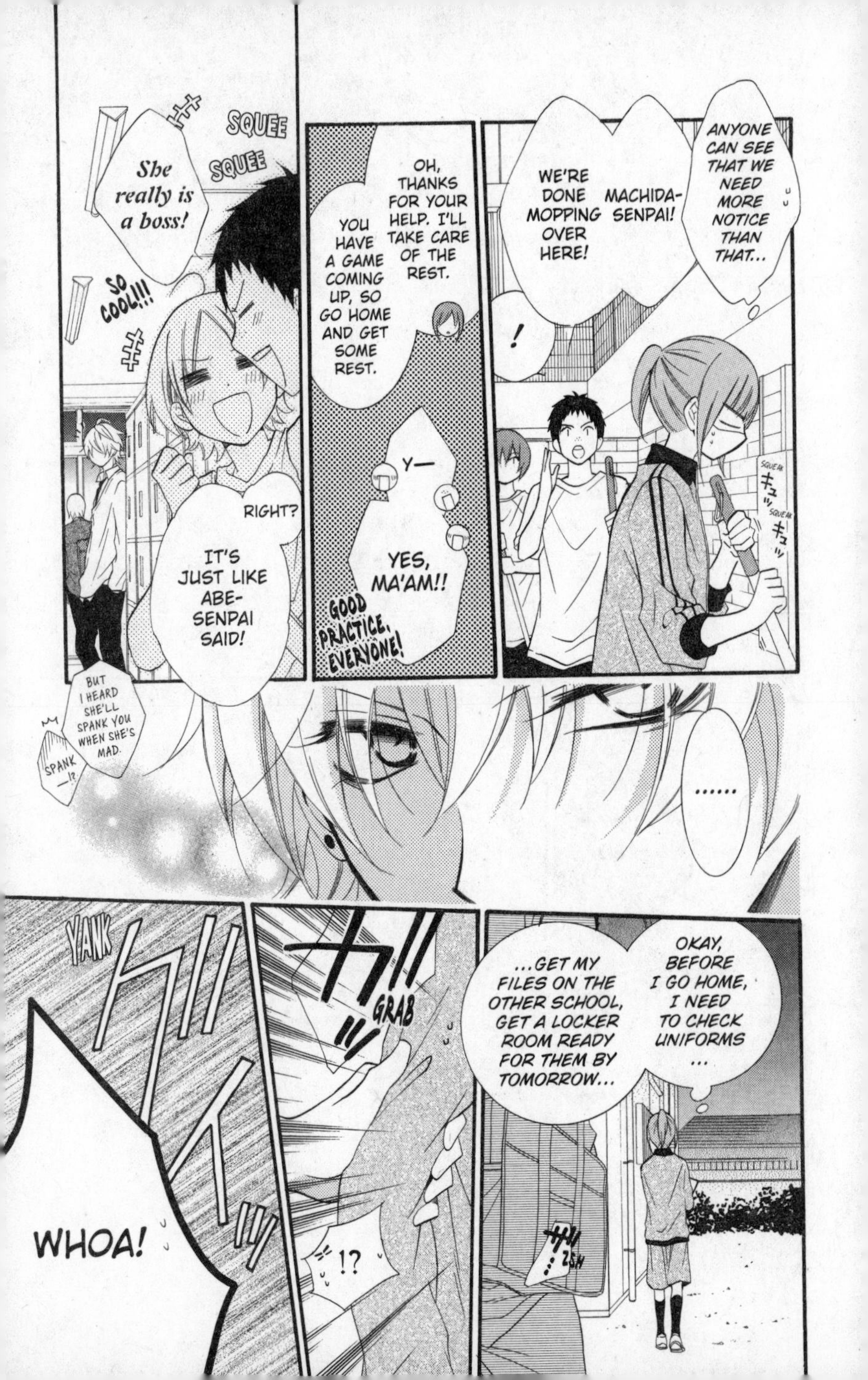
ANYONE CAN SEE THAT WE NEED MORE NOTICE THAN THAT...
MACHIDA-SENPAI!
WE'RE DONE MOPPING OVER HERE!
!
SQUEAK
SQUEAK
OH, THANKS FOR YOUR HELP. I'LL TAKE CARE OF THE REST.
YOU HAVE A GAME COMING UP, SO GO HOME AND GET SOME REST.
Y—
YES, MA'AM!!
GOOD PRACTICE, EVERYONE!
SQUEE
SQUEE
She really is a boss!
SO COOL!!!
RIGHT?
IT'S JUST LIKE ABE-SENPAI SAID!
BUT I HEARD SHE'LL SPANK YOU WHEN SHE'S MAD.
SPANK—!?
......
OKAY, BEFORE I GO HOME, I NEED TO CHECK UNIFORMS...
...GET MY FILES ON THE OTHER SCHOOL, GET A LOCKER ROOM READY FOR THEM BY TOMORROW...
ZSH
GRAB
!?
YANK
WHOA!

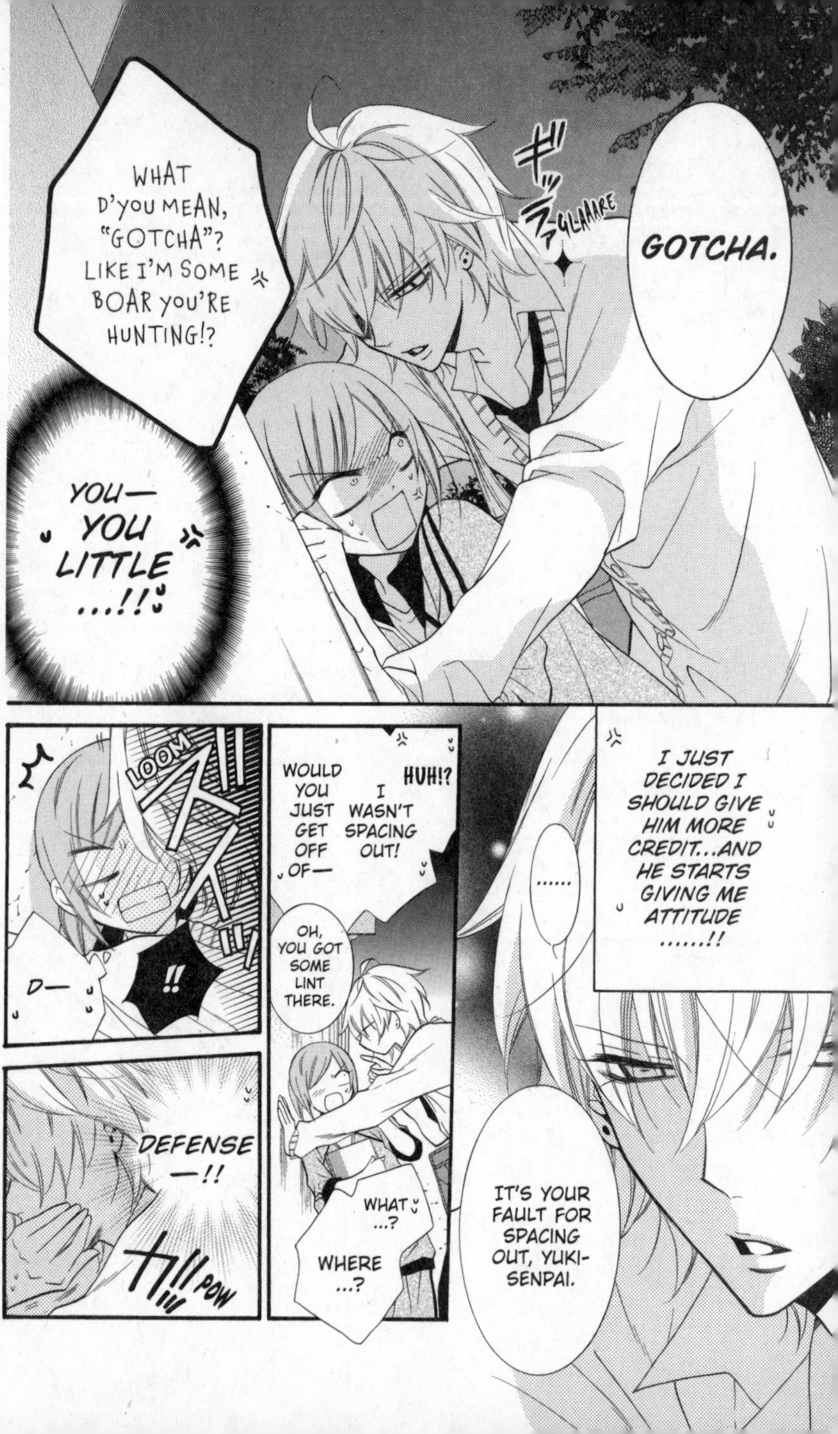
GOTCHA.
GL-AAARE
WHAT D'YOU MEAN, "GOTCHA"? LIKE I'M SOME BOAR YOU'RE HUNTING!?
YOU— YOU LITTLE...!!
I JUST DECIDED I SHOULD GIVE HIM MORE CREDIT...AND HE STARTS GIVING ME ATTITUDE ......!!
......
IT'S YOUR FAULT FOR SPACING OUT, YUKI-SENPAI.
HUH!? I WASN'T SPACING OUT!
WOULD YOU JUST GET OFF OF—
OH, YOU GOT SOME LINT THERE.
WHAT ...?
WHERE ...?
LOOM
!!
D—
DEFENSE—!!
POW

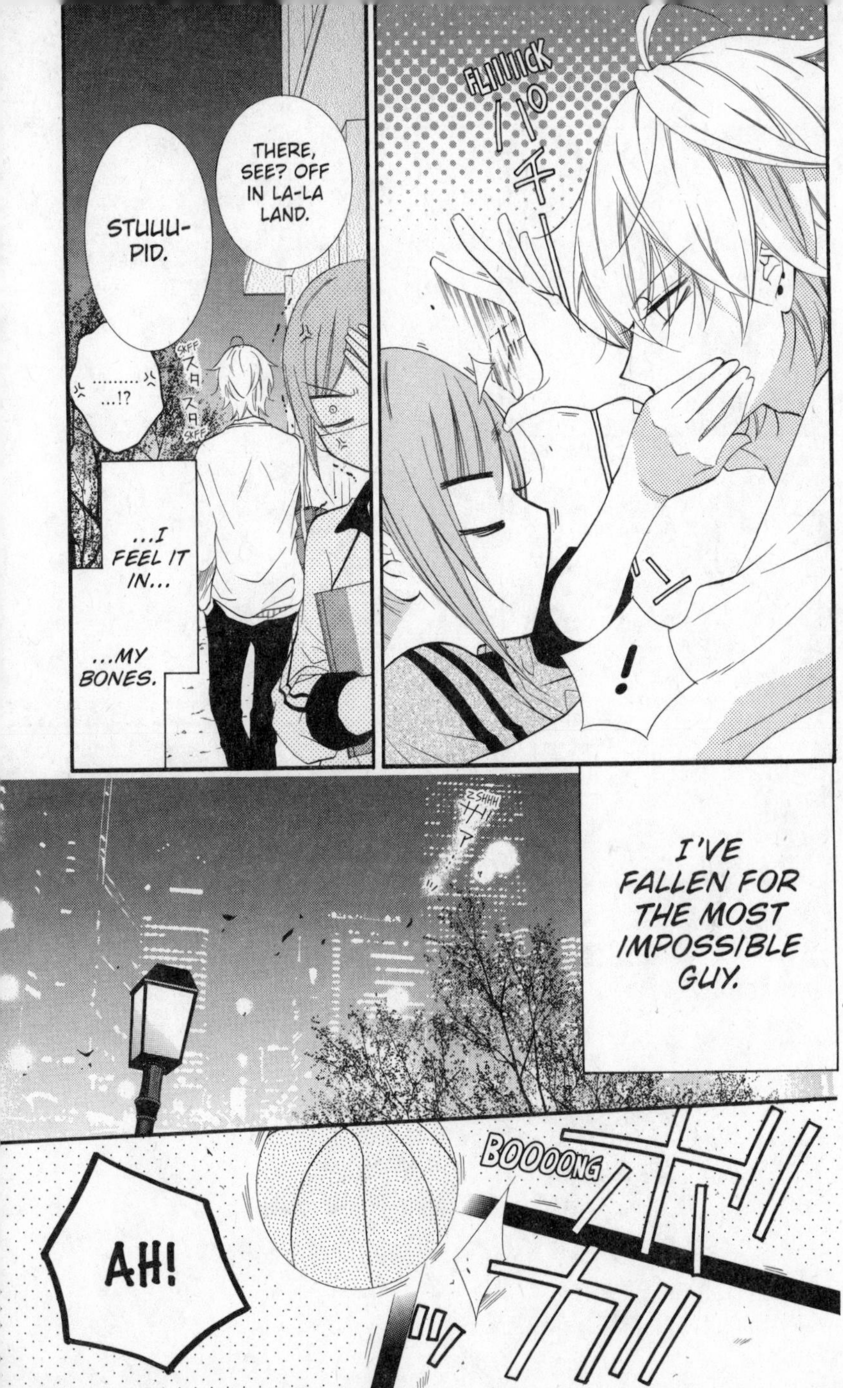
FLIIIIICK
!
THERE, SEE? OFF IN LA-LA LAND.
STUUU-PID.
SKFF
SKFF
.........!?
...I FEEL IT IN...
...MY BONES.
I'VE FALLEN FOR THE MOST IMPOSSIBLE GUY.
ZSHHH
BOOOoONG
AH!

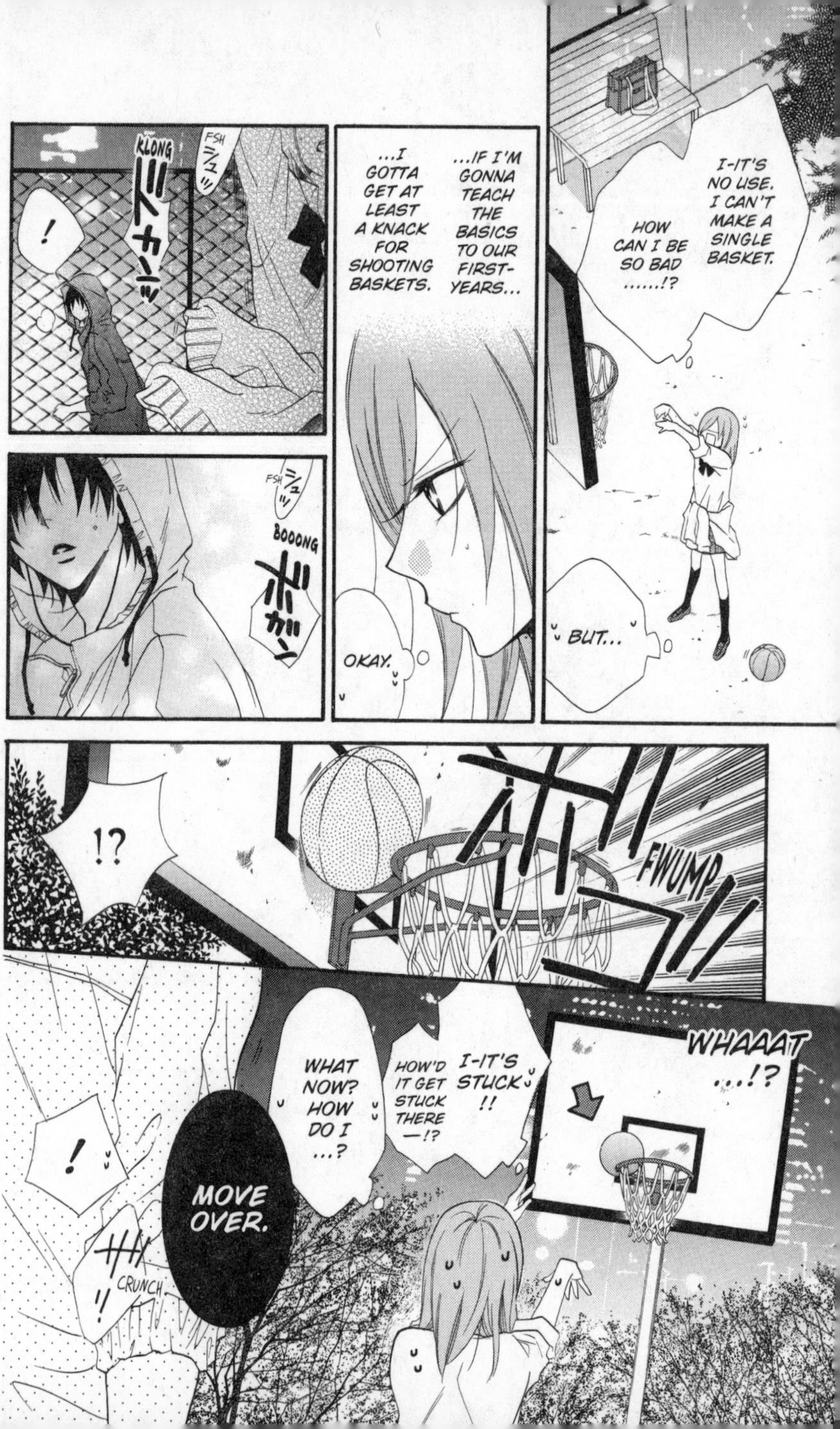
I-IT'S NO USE. I CAN'T MAKE A SINGLE BASKET.
HOW CAN I BE SO BAD ......!?
BUT...
...IF I'M GONNA TEACH THE BASICS TO OUR FIRST-YEARS...
...I GOTTA GET AT LEAST A KNACK FOR SHOOTING BASKETS.
OKAY.
FSH
KLONG
!
FSH
BOOONG
FWUMP
!?
WHAAAT ...!?
I-IT'S STUCK !!
HOW'D IT GET STUCK THERE—!?
WHAT NOW? HOW DO I ...?
MOVE OVER.
!
CRUNCH

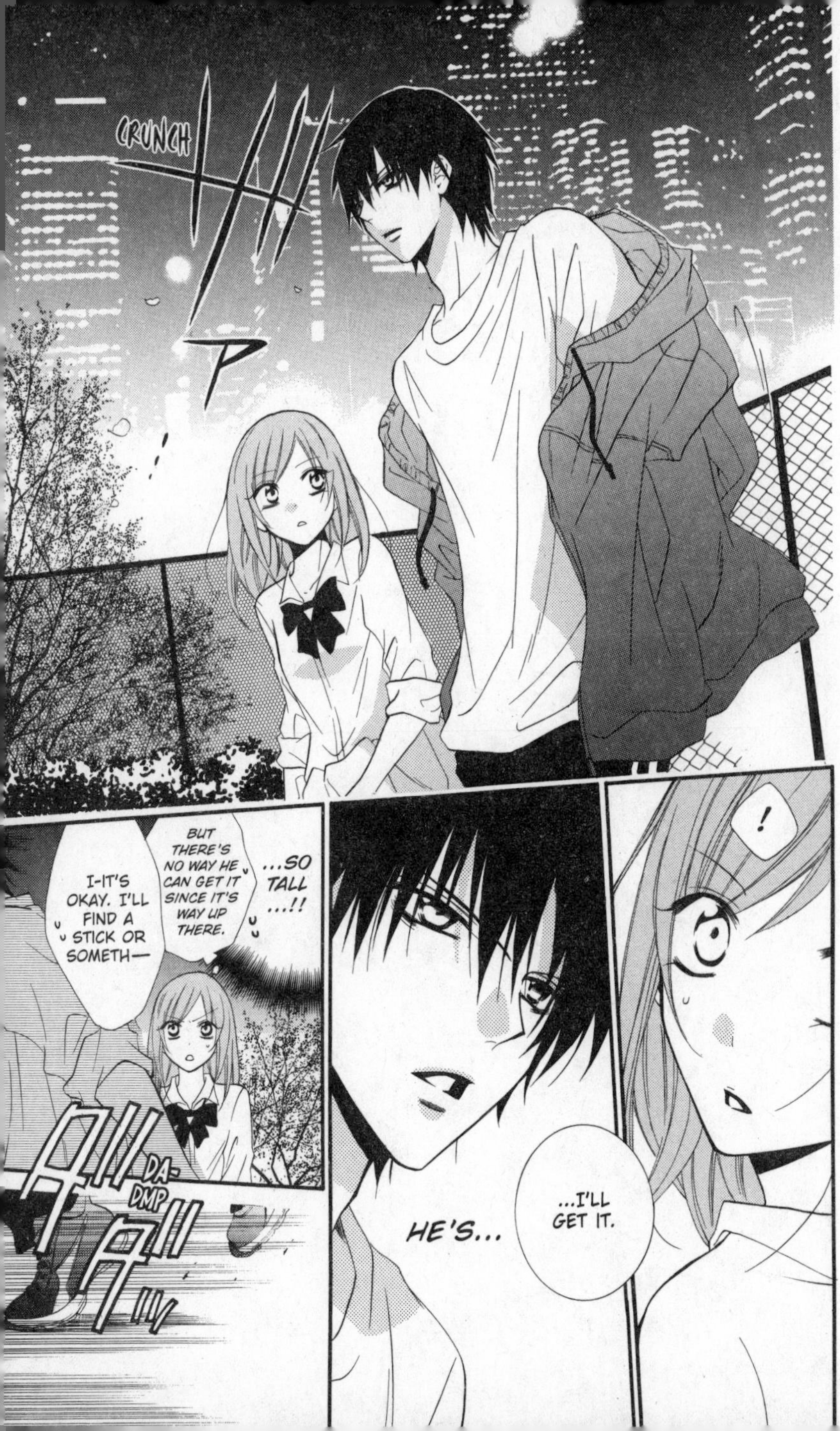
CRUNCH
P
!
!
...I'LL GET IT.
HE'S...
...SO TALL ...!!
BUT THERE'S NO WAY HE CAN GET IT SINCE IT'S WAY UP THERE.
I-IT'S OKAY. I'LL FIND A STICK OR SOMETH—
DA-DMP

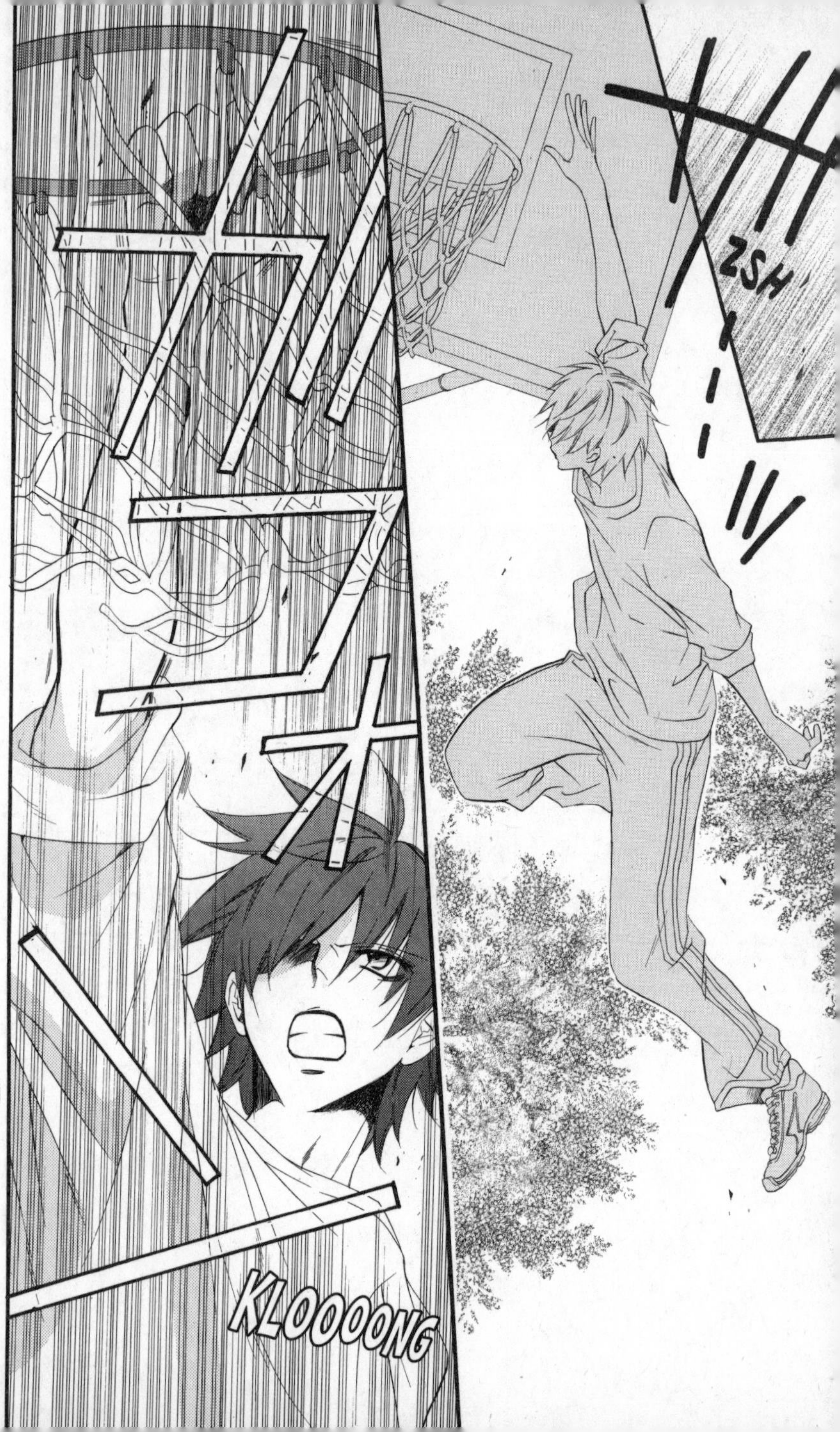
ZSH
KLOOOONG

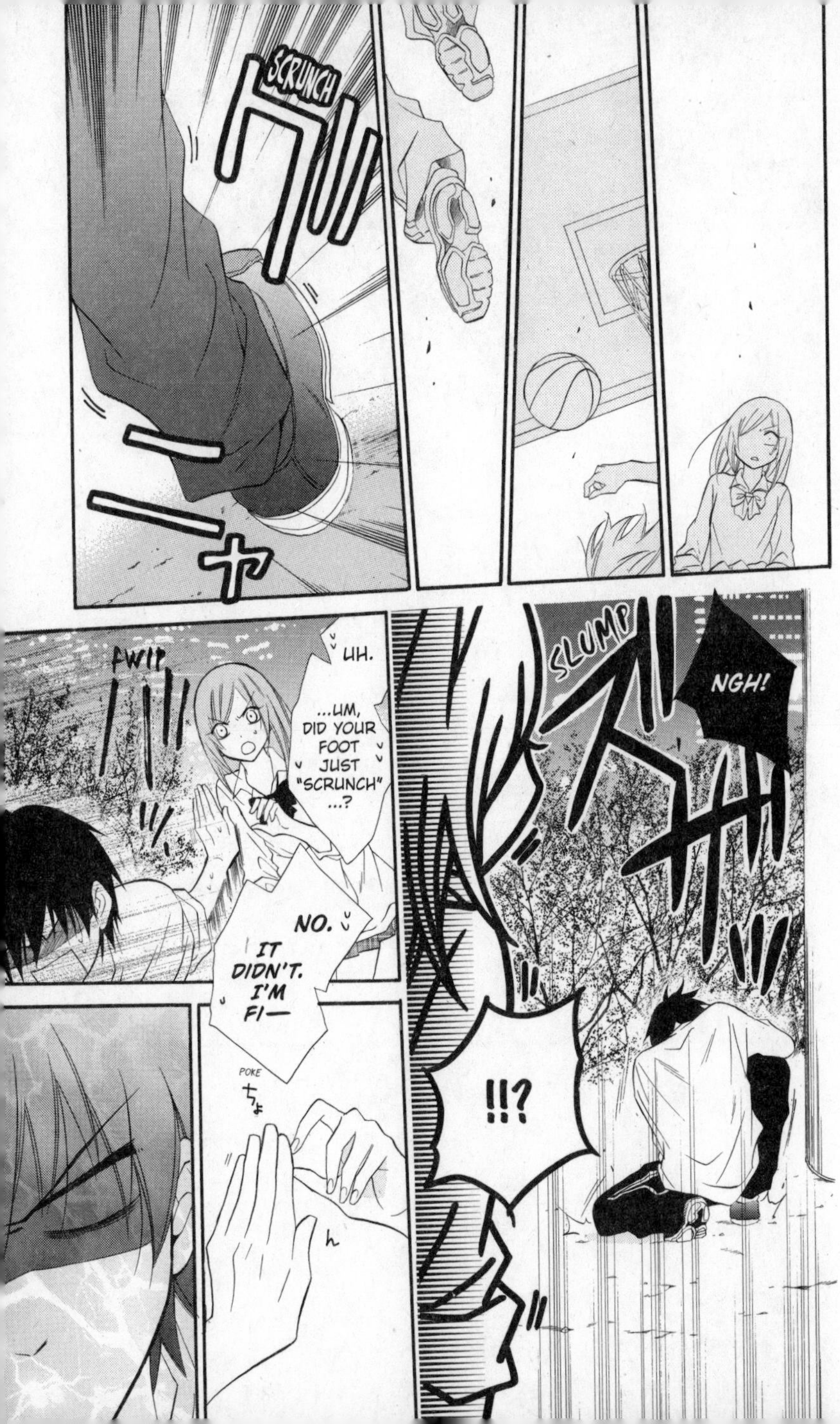
SCRUNCH
SLUMP
NGH!
!!?
UH.
...UM, DID YOUR FOOT JUST "SCRUNCH" ...?
FWIP
NO. IT DIDN'T. I'M FI—
POKE

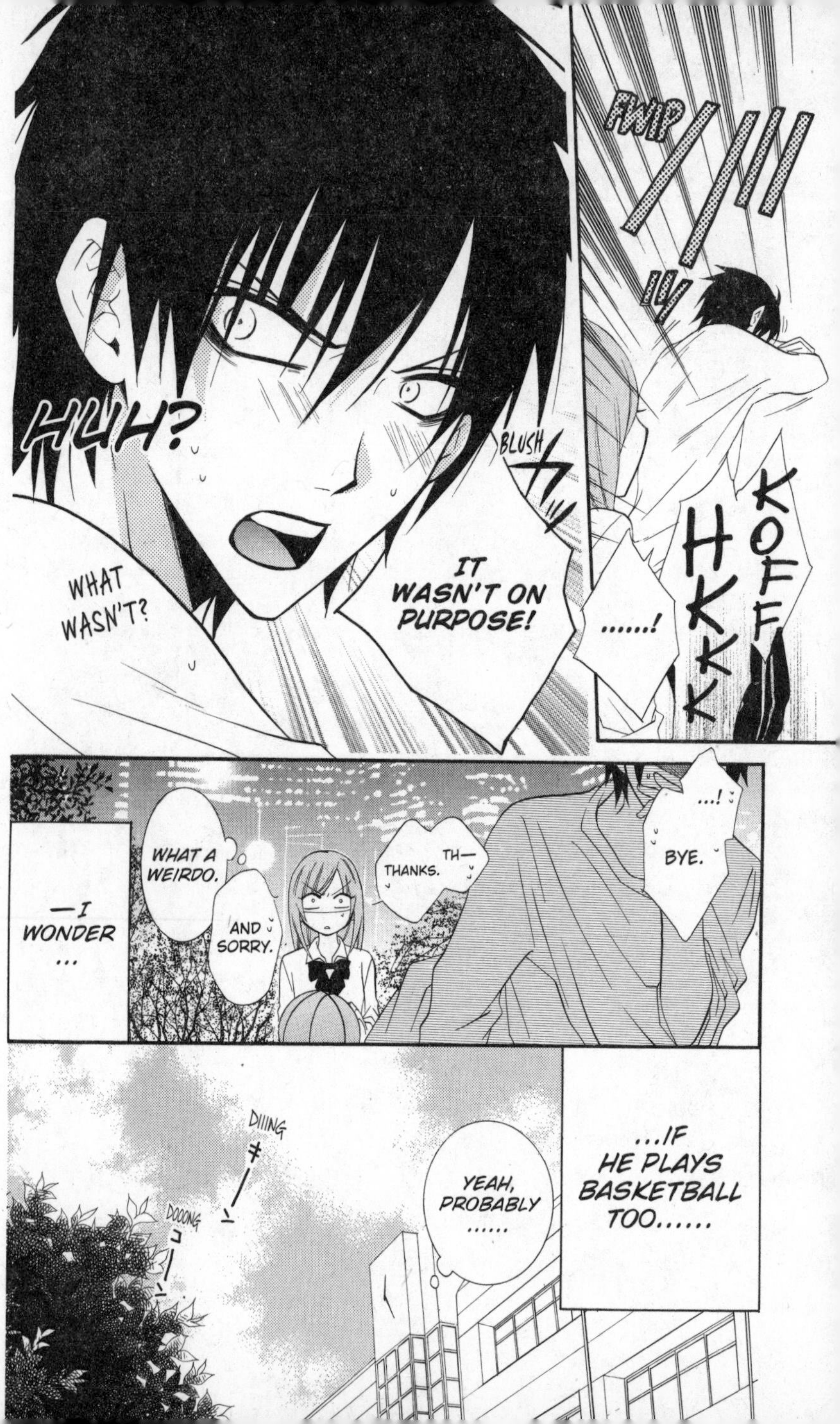
FWIP
HKKK
KOFF
......!
HUH?
BLUSH
IT WASN'T ON PURPOSE!
WHAT WASN'T?
...!
BYE.
TH— THANKS.
AND SORRY.
WHAT A WEIRDO.
—I WONDER ...
...IF HE PLAYS BASKETBALL TOO......
YEAH, PROBABLY ......
DIIING
キーン
DOOONG
コーン

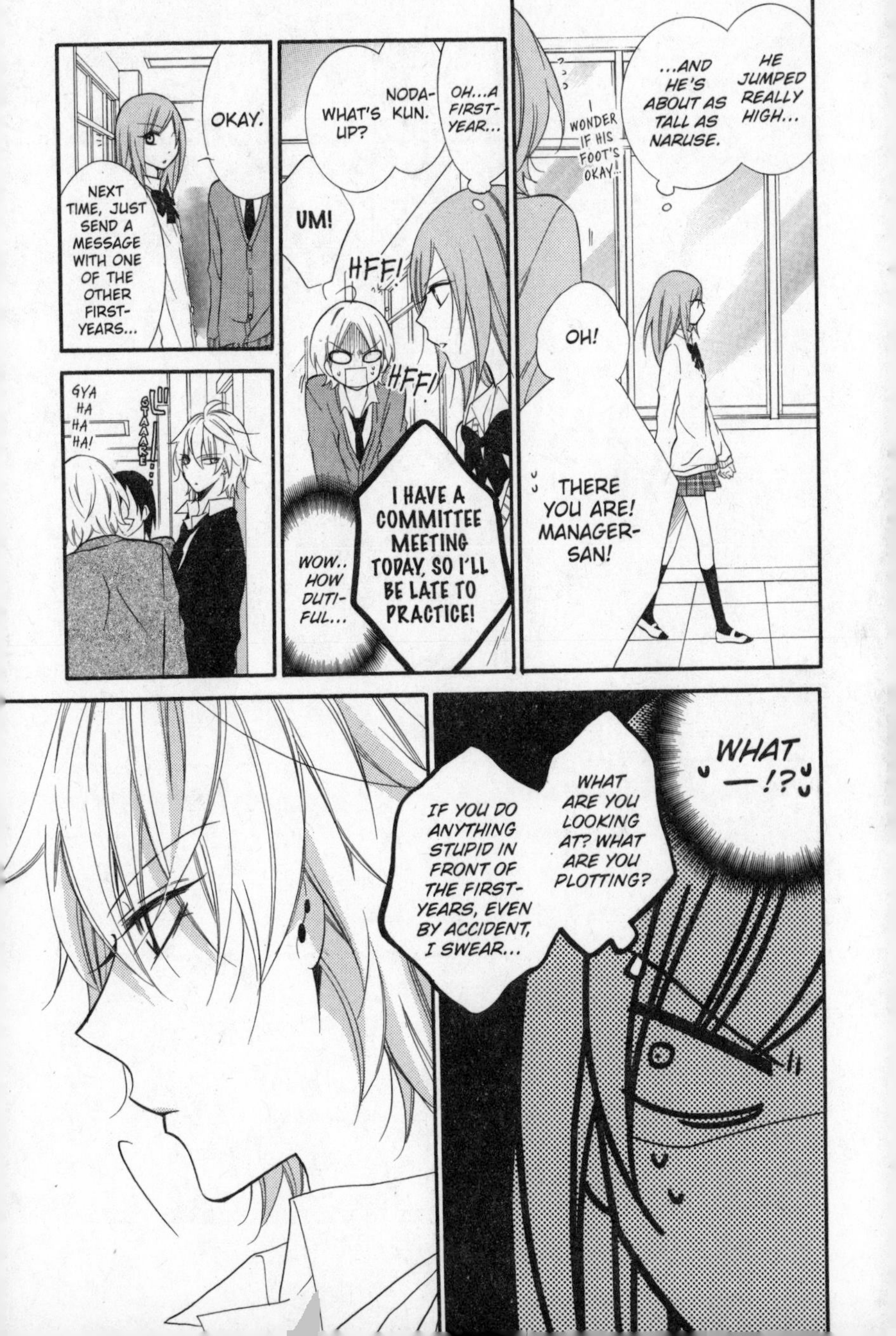
HE JUMPED REALLY HIGH...
...AND HE'S ABOUT AS TALL AS NARUSE.
I WONDER IF HIS FOOT'S OKAY...
OH!
THERE YOU ARE! MANAGER-SAN!
OH...A FIRST-YEAR...
NODA-KUN. WHAT'S UP?
UM!
HFF!
HFF!
I HAVE A COMMITTEE MEETING TODAY, SO I'LL BE LATE TO PRACTICE!
WOW.. HOW DUTIFUL...
OKAY.
NEXT TIME, JUST SEND A MESSAGE WITH ONE OF THE OTHER FIRST-YEARS...
GYA HA HA HA!
STAAARE...
WHAT—!?
WHAT ARE YOU LOOKING AT? WHAT ARE YOU PLOTTING?
IF YOU DO ANYTHING STUPID IN FRONT OF THE FIRST-YEARS, EVEN BY ACCIDENT, I SWEAR...

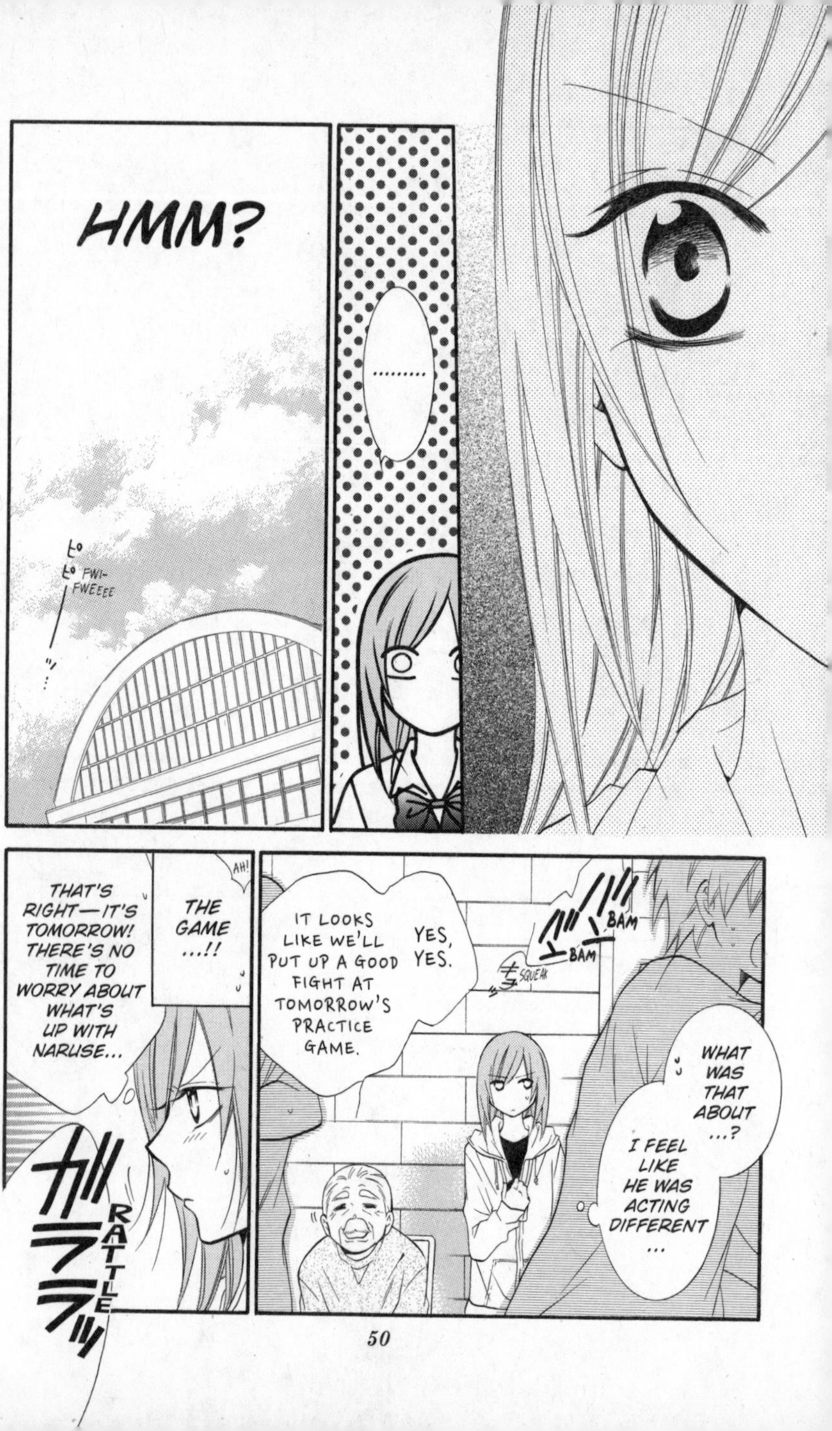
....
HMM?
FWI-FWEEEE
BAM
BAM
SQUEAK
WHAT WAS THAT ABOUT...?
I FEEL LIKE HE WAS ACTING DIFFERENT...
YES, YES.
IT LOOKS LIKE WE'LL PUT UP A GOOD FIGHT AT TOMORROW'S PRACTICE GAME.
AH!
THE GAME...!!
THAT'S RIGHT—IT'S TOMORROW! THERE'S NO TIME TO WORRY ABOUT WHAT'S UP WITH NARUSE...
RATTLE

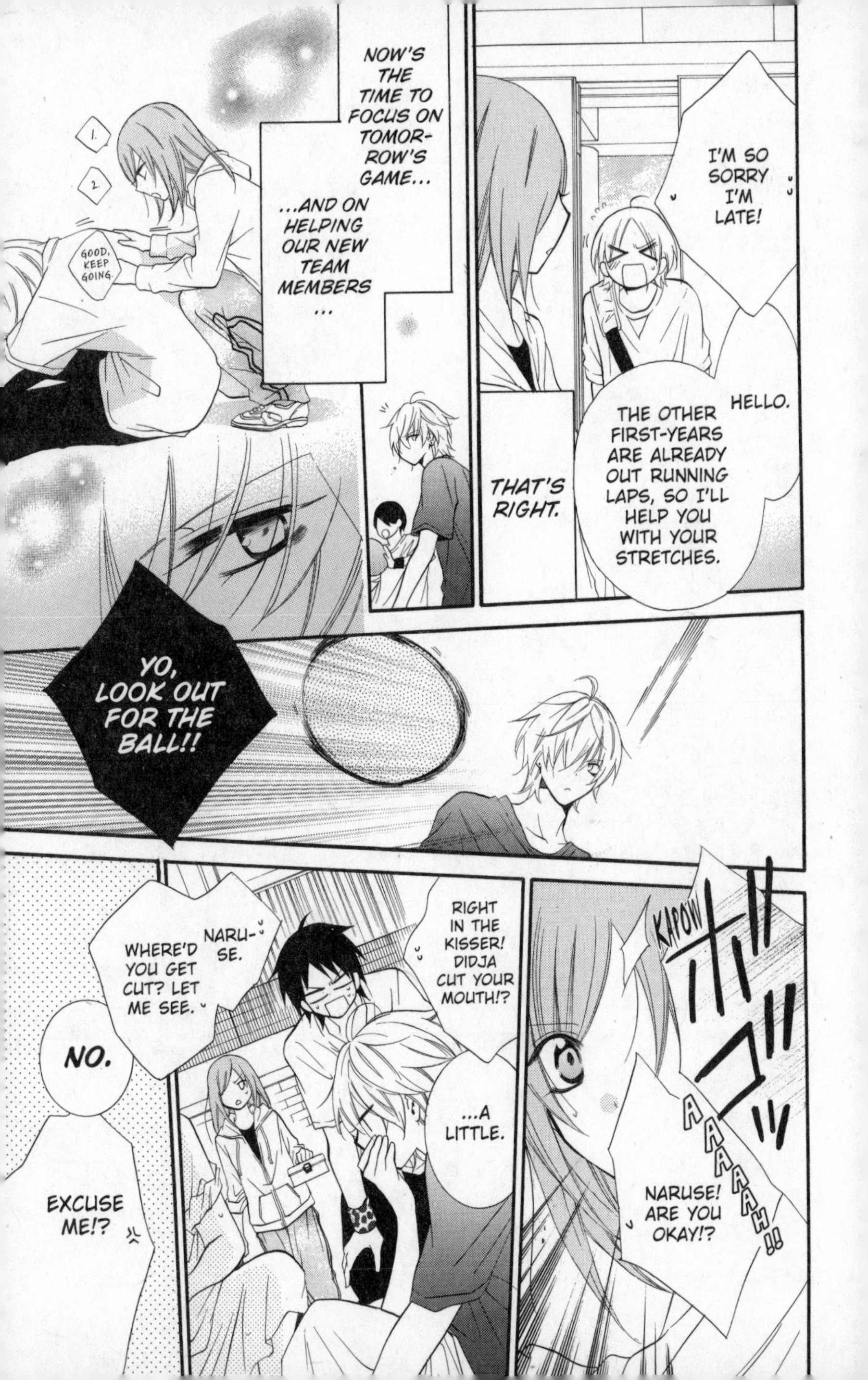
I'M SO SORRY I'M LATE!
HELLO.
THE OTHER FIRST-YEARS ARE ALREADY OUT RUNNING LAPS, SO I'LL HELP YOU WITH YOUR STRETCHES.
THAT'S RIGHT.
1.
2.
GOOD, KEEP GOING.
NOW'S THE TIME TO FOCUS ON TOMOR-ROW'S GAME...
...AND ON HELPING OUR NEW TEAM MEMBERS...
YO, LOOK OUT FOR THE BALL!!
KAPOW
AAAAAAH!!
NARUSE! ARE YOU OKAY!?
RIGHT IN THE KISSER! DIDJA CUT YOUR MOUTH!?
...A LITTLE.
NARU-SE.
WHERE'D YOU GET CUT? LET ME SEE.
NO.
EXCUSE ME!?

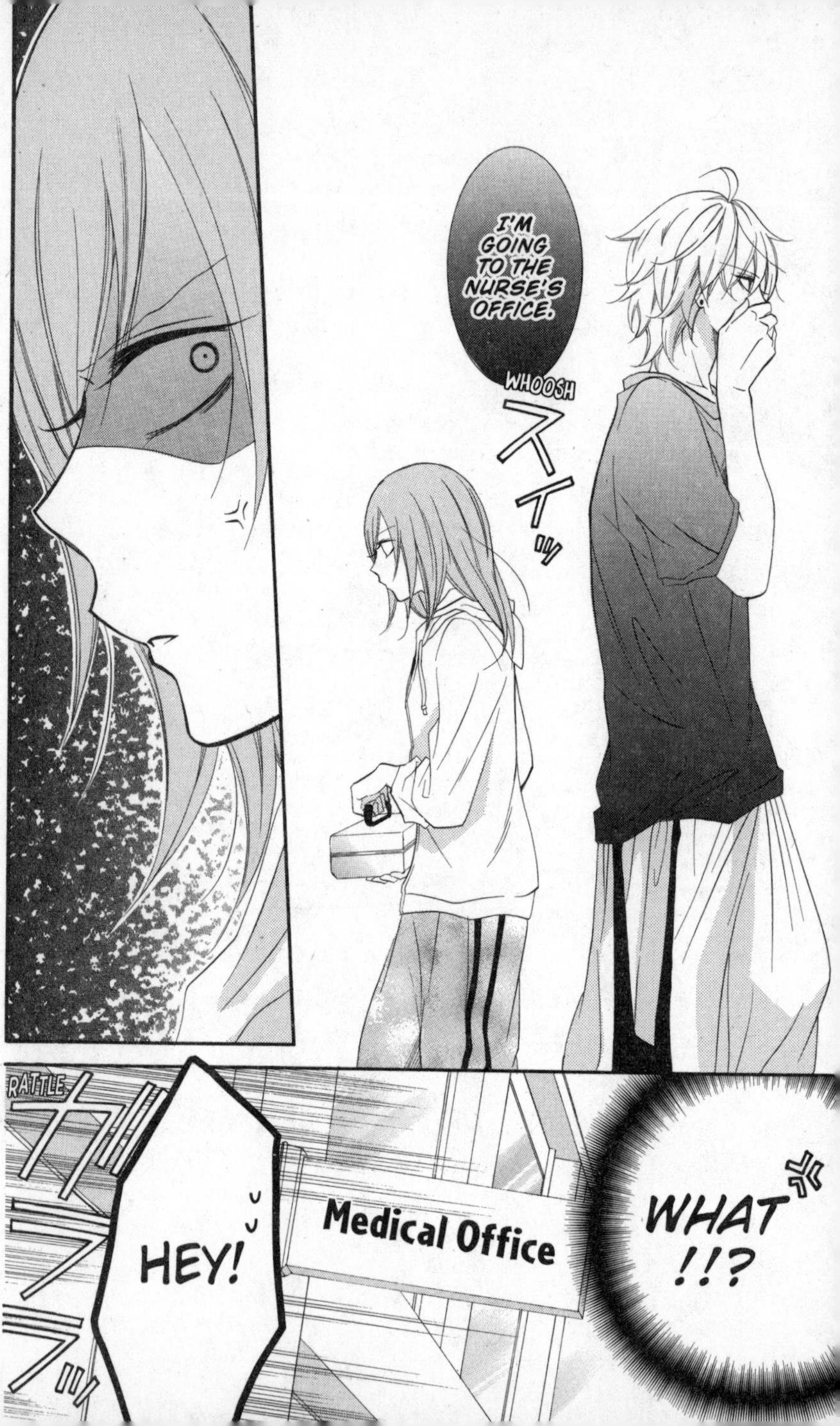
I'M GOING TO THE NURSE'S OFFICE.
WHOOSH
スイッ
WHAT!!?
Medical Office
HEY!
RATTLE
ガララッ

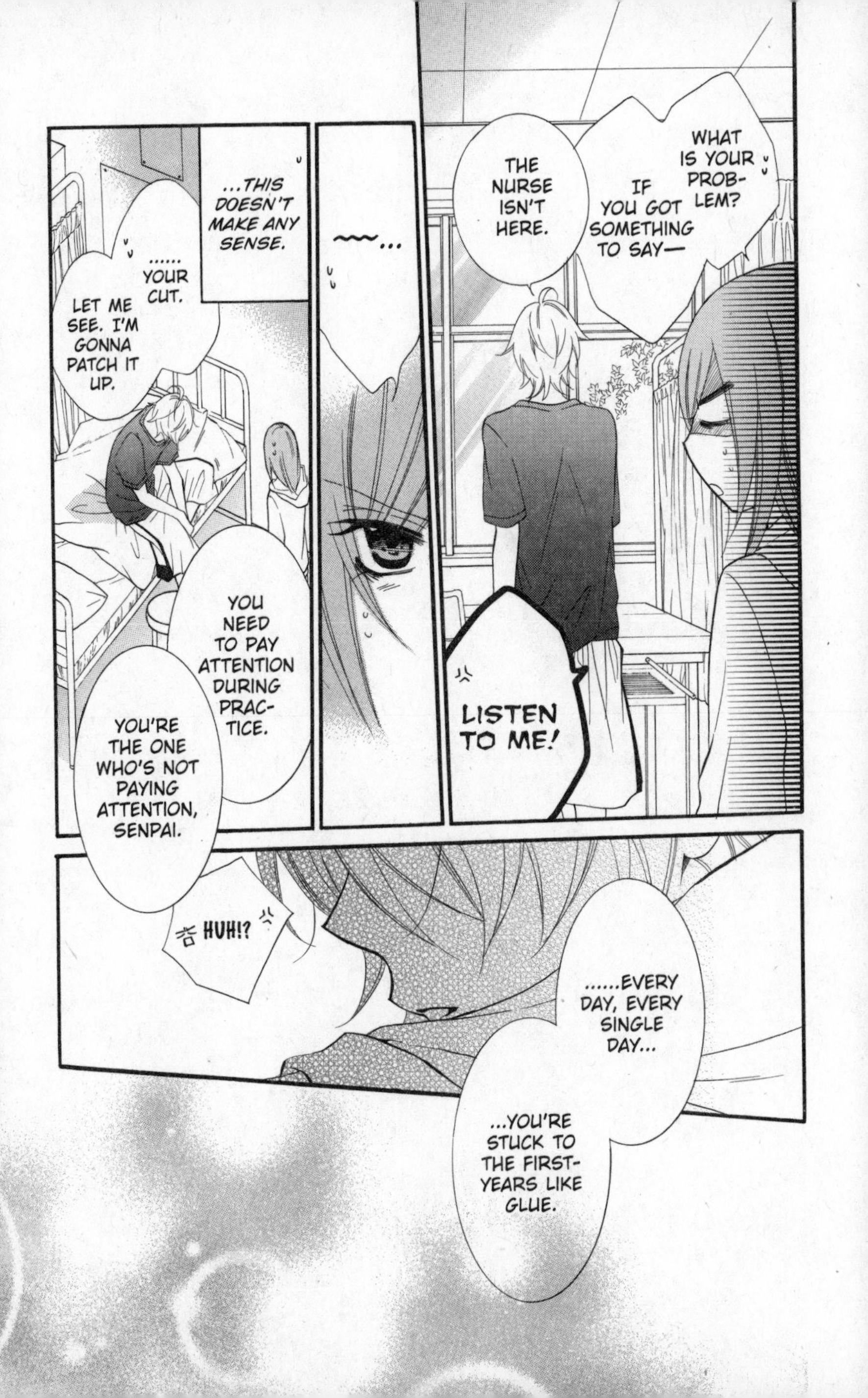
WHAT IS YOUR PROB-LEM?
IF YOU GOT SOMETHING TO SAY—
THE NURSE ISN'T HERE.
LISTEN TO ME!
~~~...
...THIS DOESN'T MAKE ANY SENSE.
......YOUR CUT.
LET ME SEE. I'M GONNA PATCH IT UP.
YOU NEED TO PAY ATTENTION DURING PRAC-TICE.
YOU'RE THE ONE WHO'S NOT PAYING ATTENTION, SENPAI.
HUH!?
......EVERY DAY, EVERY SINGLE DAY...
...YOU'RE STUCK TO THE FIRST-YEARS LIKE GLUE.
~~~

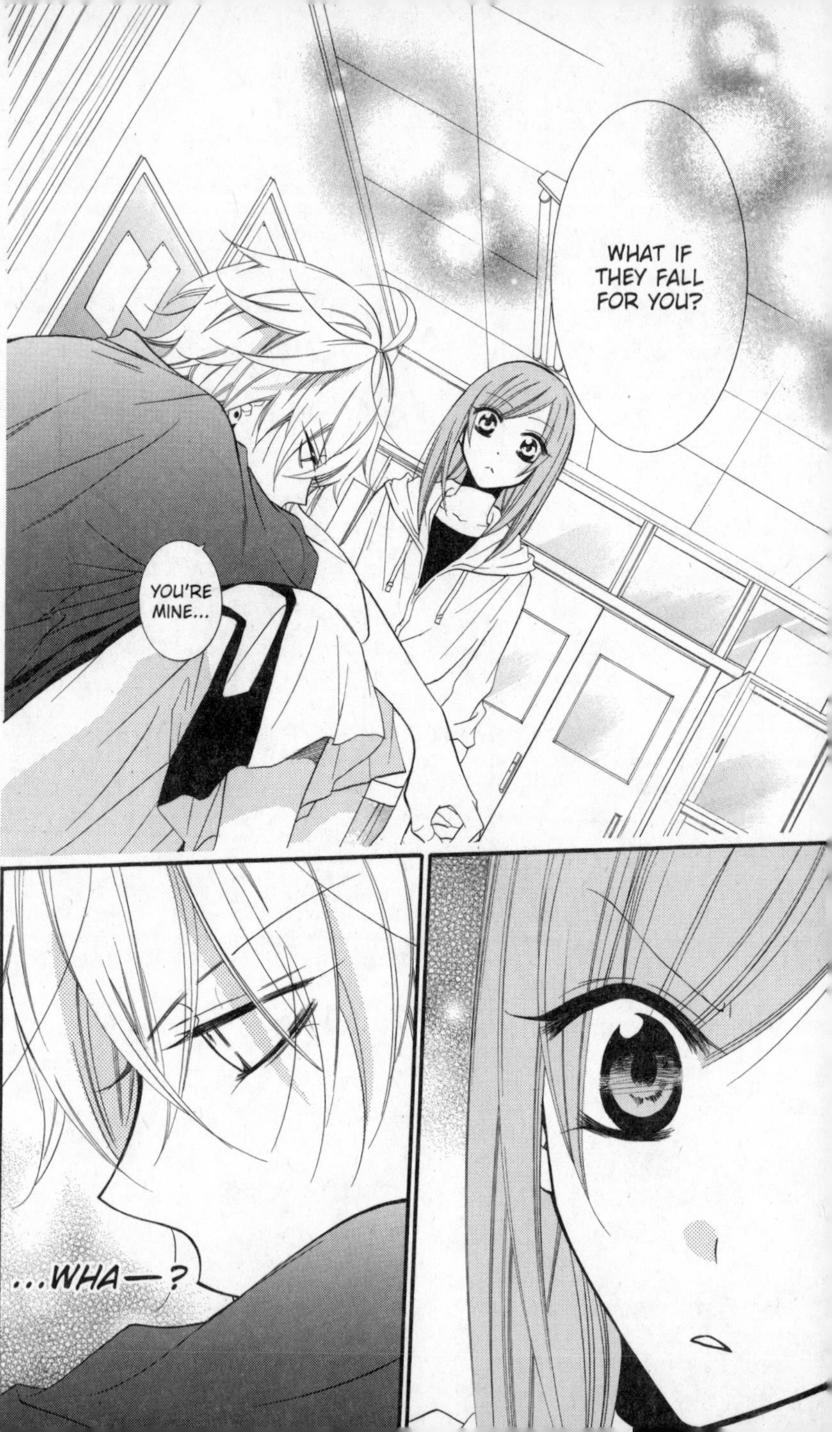
WHAT IF THEY FALL FOR YOU?
YOU'RE MINE...
...WHA—?

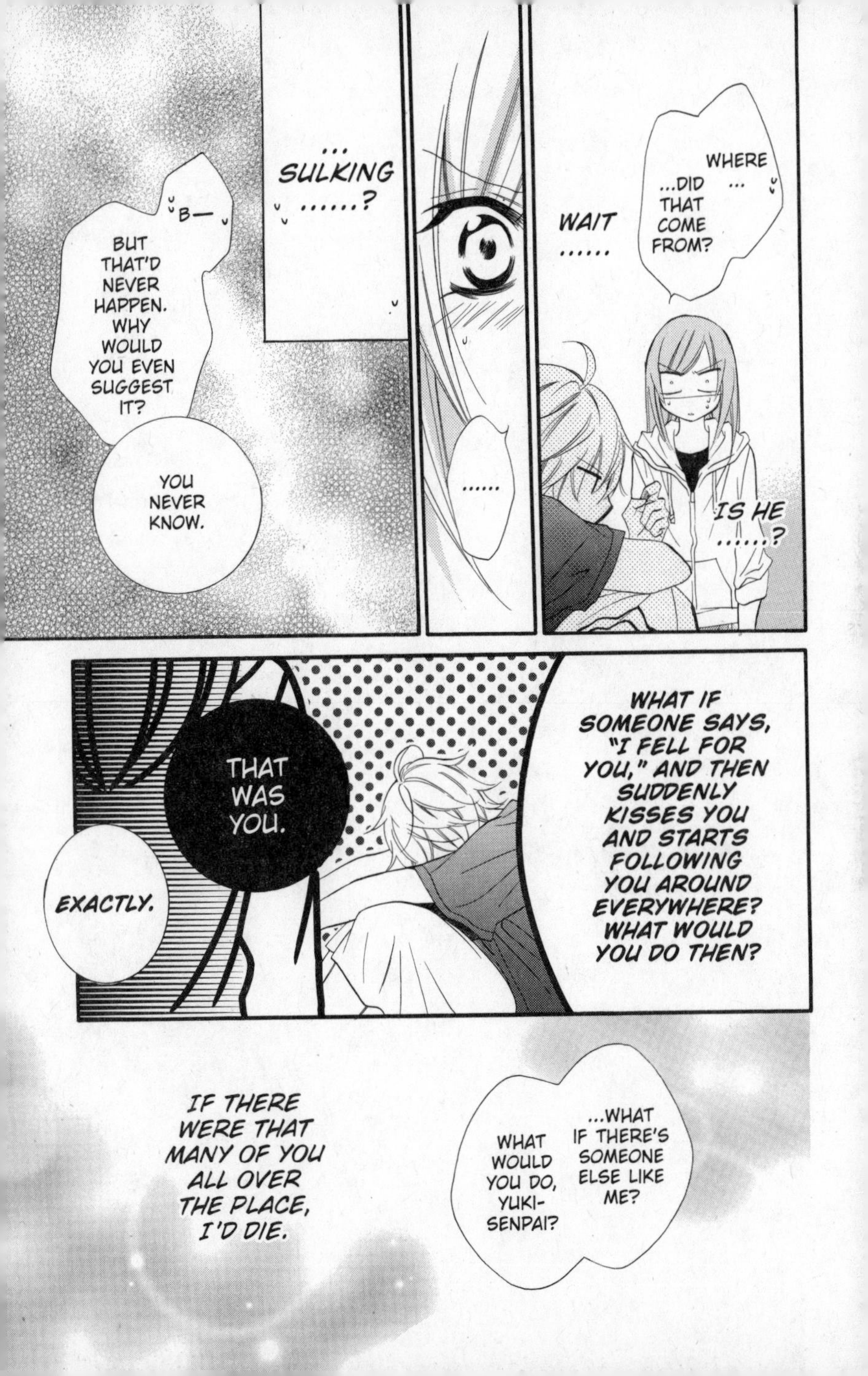
WHERE ... ...DID THAT COME FROM?
WAIT ......
IS HE ......?
......
...SULKING ......?
B— BUT THAT'D NEVER HAPPEN. WHY WOULD YOU EVEN SUGGEST IT?
YOU NEVER KNOW.
WHAT IF SOMEONE SAYS, "I FELL FOR YOU," AND THEN SUDDENLY KISSES YOU AND STARTS FOLLOWING YOU AROUND EVERYWHERE? WHAT WOULD YOU DO THEN?
THAT WAS YOU.
EXACTLY.
...WHAT IF THERE'S SOMEONE ELSE LIKE ME?
WHAT WOULD YOU DO, YUKI-SENPAI?
IF THERE WERE THAT MANY OF YOU ALL OVER THE PLACE, I'D DIE.

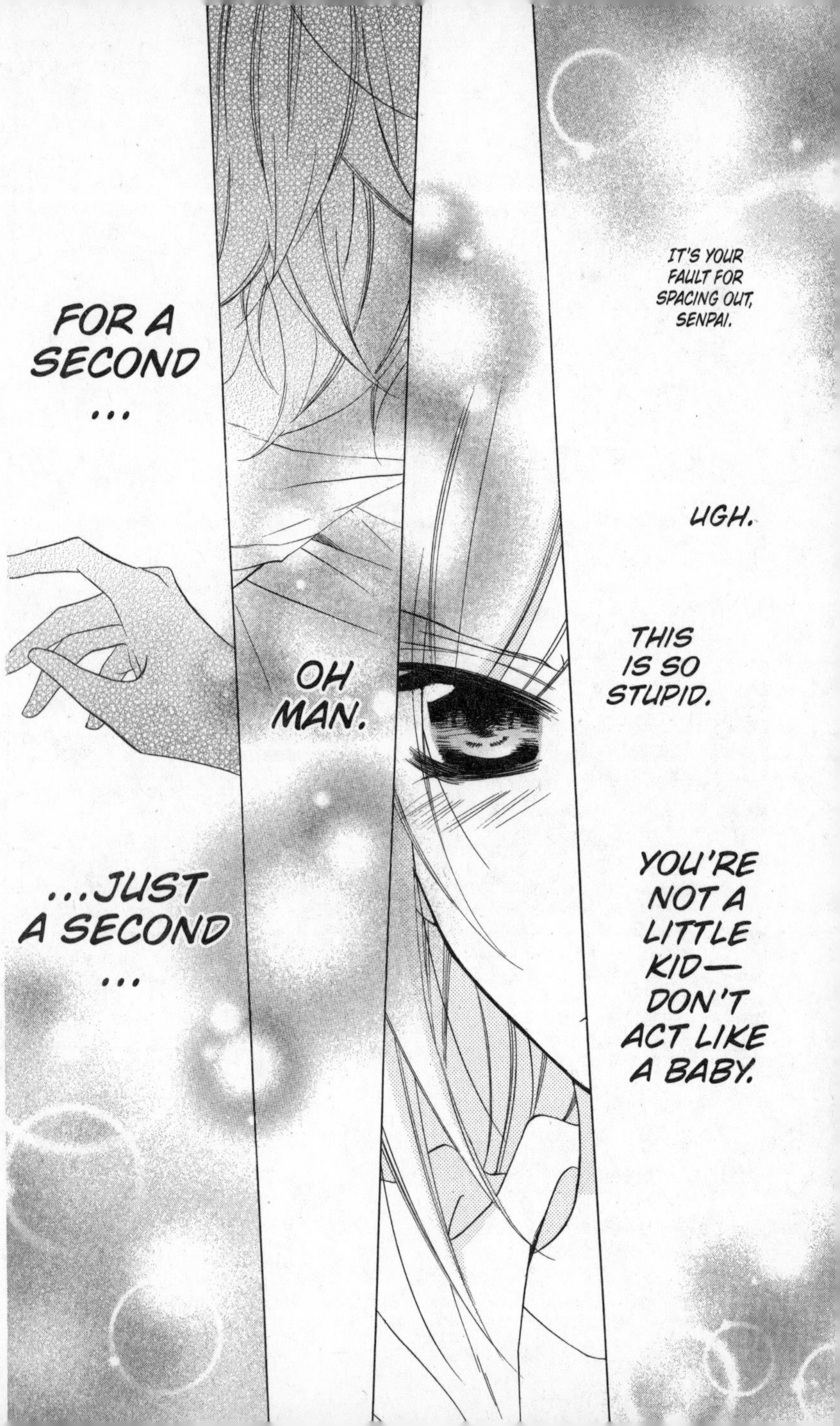
IT'S YOUR FAULT FOR SPACING OUT, SENPAI.
UGH.
THIS IS SO STUPID.
YOU'RE NOT A LITTLE KID—DON'T ACT LIKE A BABY.
OH MAN.
FOR A SECOND ...
...JUST A SECOND ...

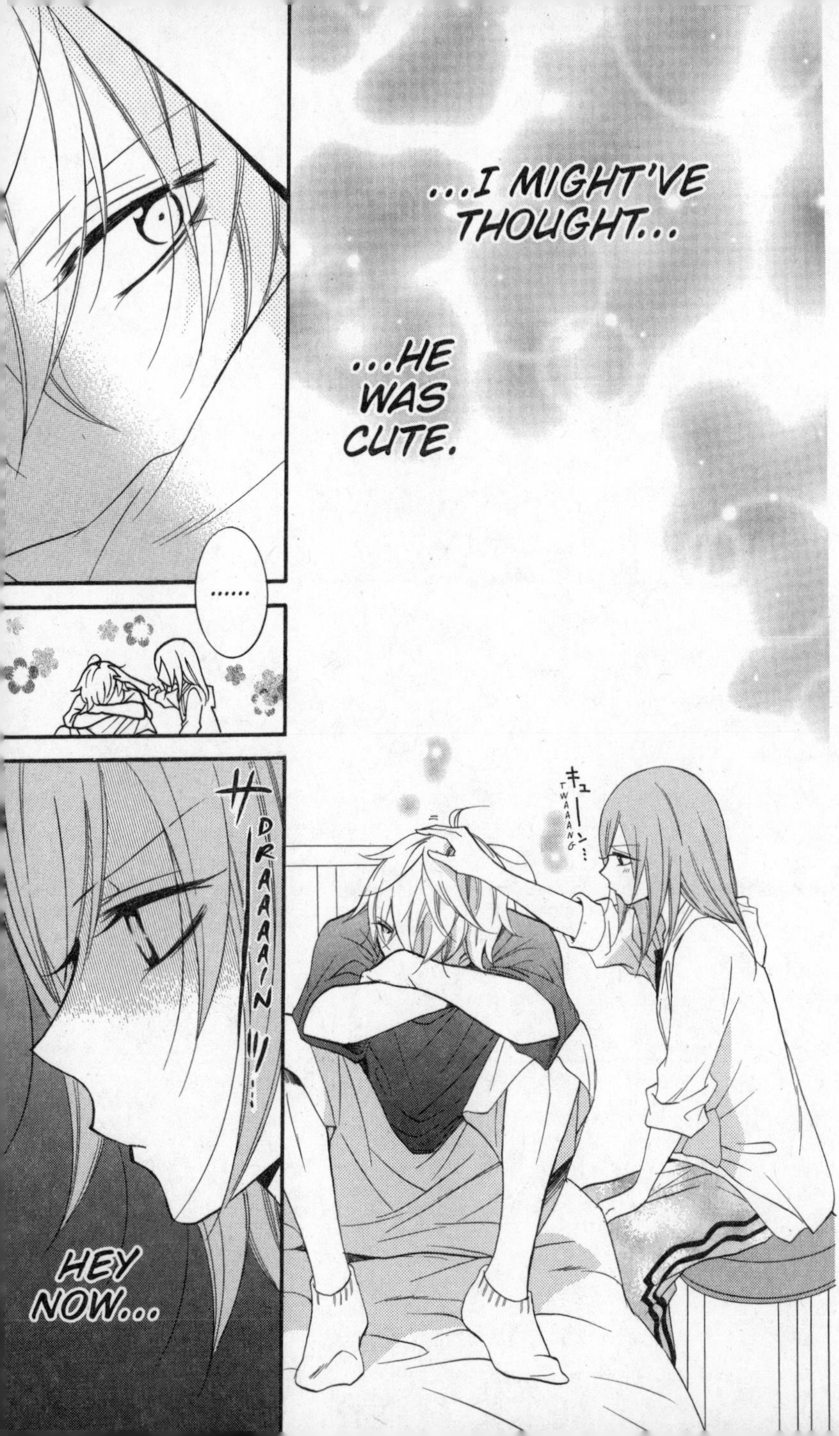

...I MIGHT'VE THOUGHT...
...HE WAS CUTE.
キュ一ン…
TWAAANG
......
DRAAAAIN
HEY NOW...

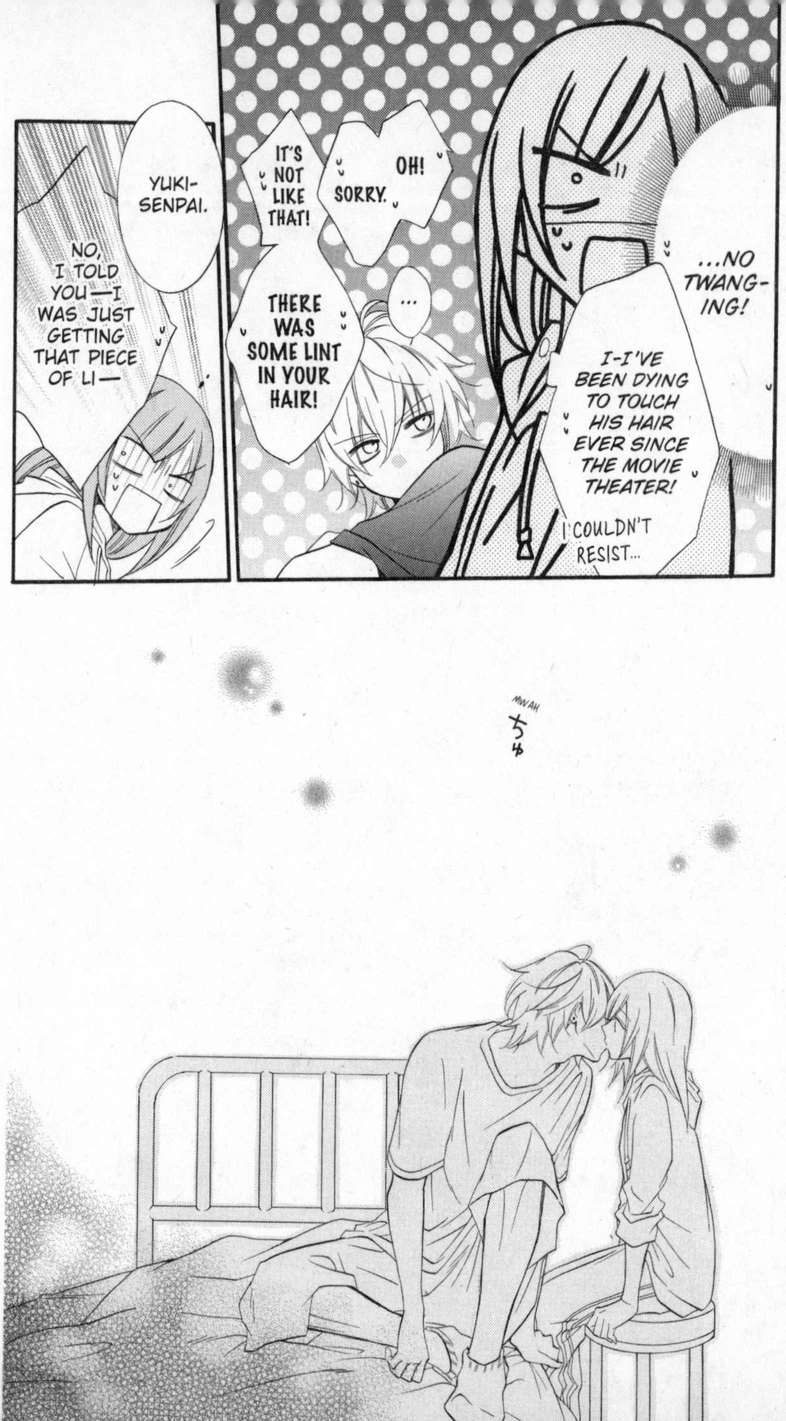
...NO TWANG-ING!
I-I'VE BEEN DYING TO TOUCH HIS HAIR EVER SINCE THE MOVIE THEATER!
I COULDN'T RESIST...
OH! SORRY.
IT'S NOT LIKE THAT!
...
THERE WAS SOME LINT IN YOUR HAIR!
YUKI-SENPAI.
NO, I TOLD YOU—I WAS JUST GETTING THAT PIECE OF LI—
MWAH
ちゅ

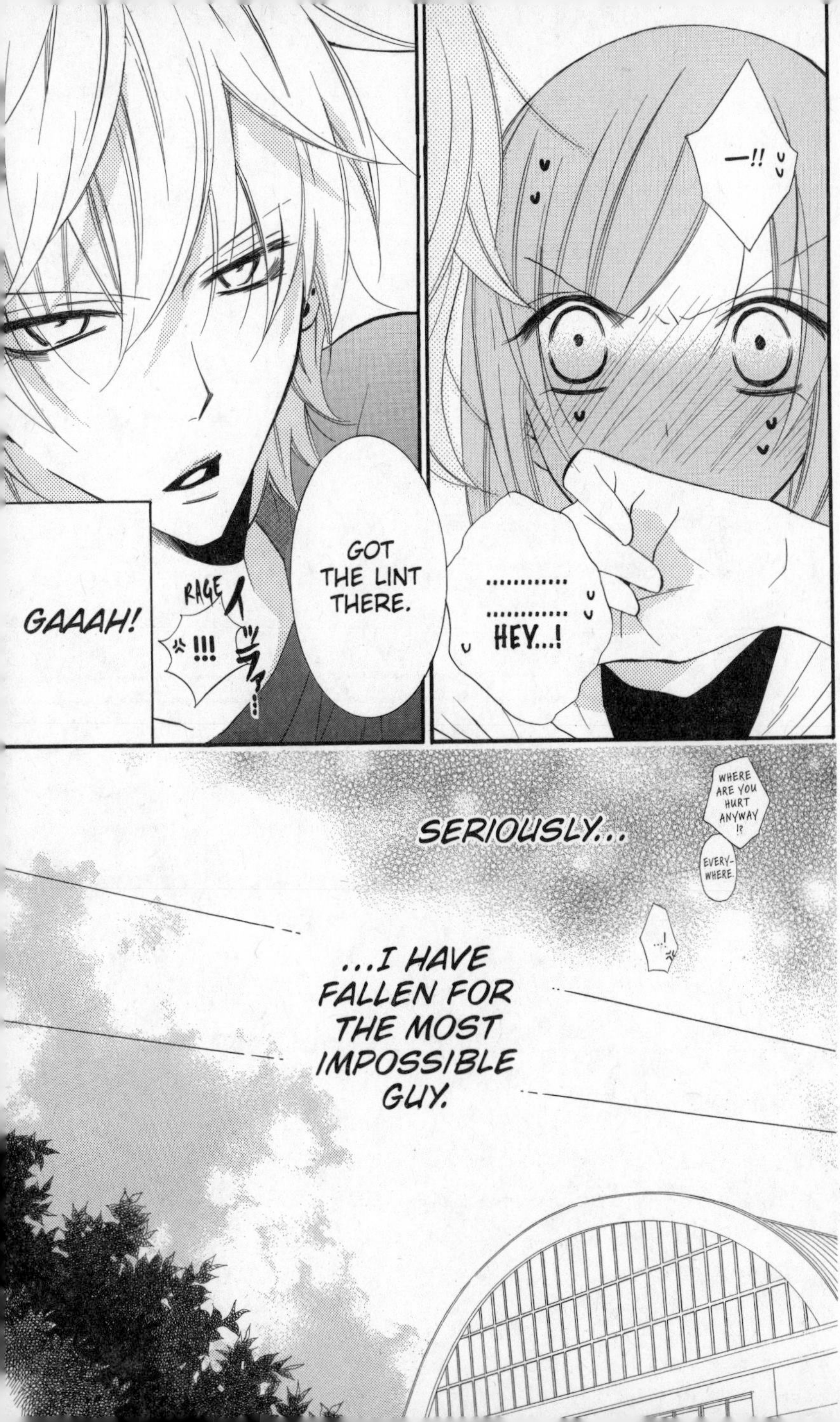
—!!
.... HEY...!
GOT THE LINT THERE.
RAGE !!!
GAAAH!
WHERE ARE YOU HURT ANYWAY!?
EVERY-WHERE.
...!
SERIOUSLY...
...I HAVE FALLEN FOR THE MOST IMPOSSIBLE GUY.

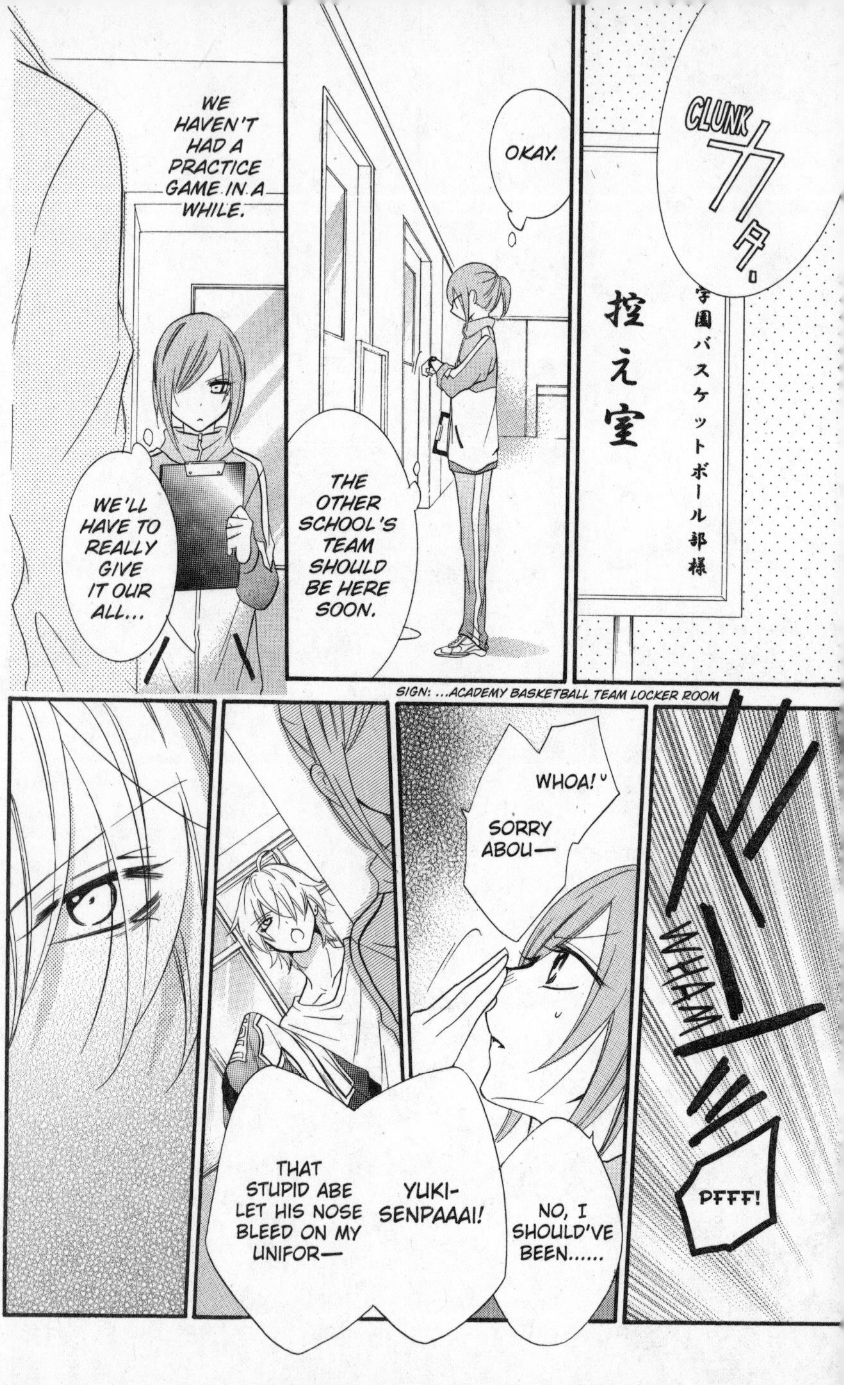
CLUNK
カタ。
学園バスケットボール部様
控え室
SIGN: ...ACADEMY BASKETBALL TEAM LOCKER ROOM
OKAY.
THE OTHER SCHOOL'S TEAM SHOULD BE HERE SOON.
WE HAVEN'T HAD A PRACTICE GAME IN A WHILE.
WE'LL HAVE TO REALLY GIVE IT OUR ALL...
WHAM
PFFF!
WHOA!
SORRY ABOU—
NO, I SHOULD'VE BEEN......
YUKI-SENPAAAI!
THAT STUPID ABE LET HIS NOSE BLEED ON MY UNIFOR—

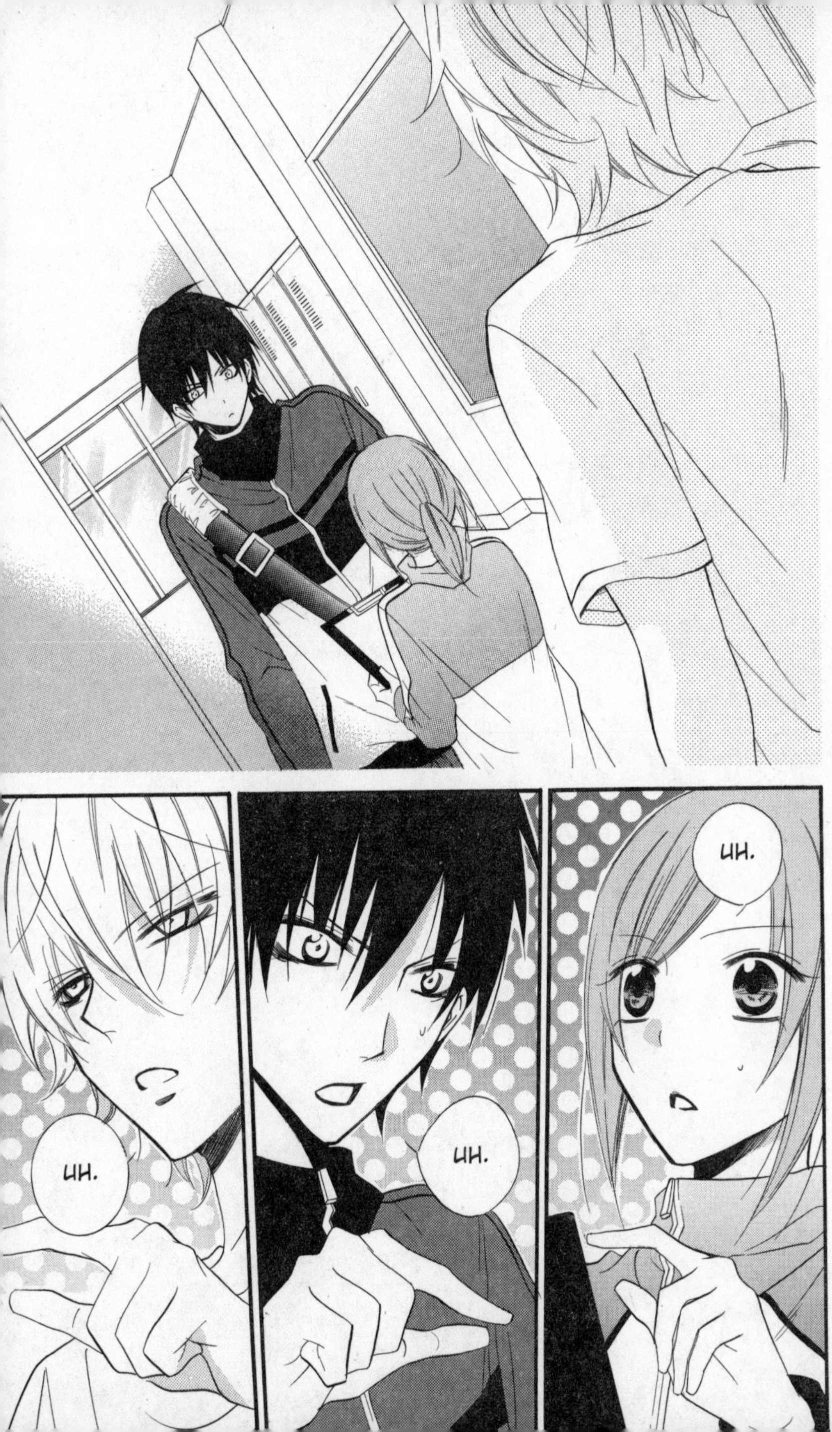
UH.
UH.
UH.

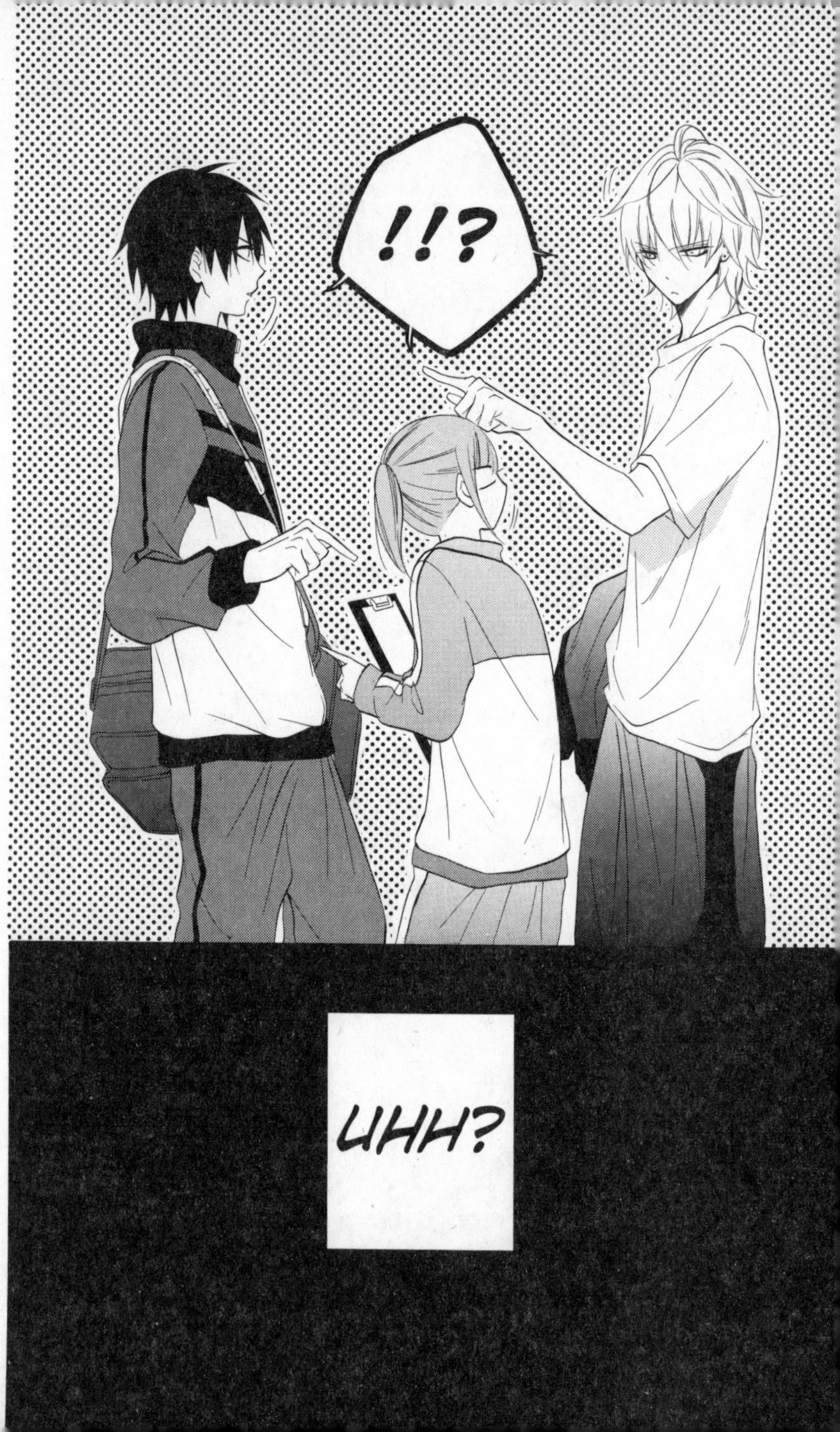
!!?
UHH?

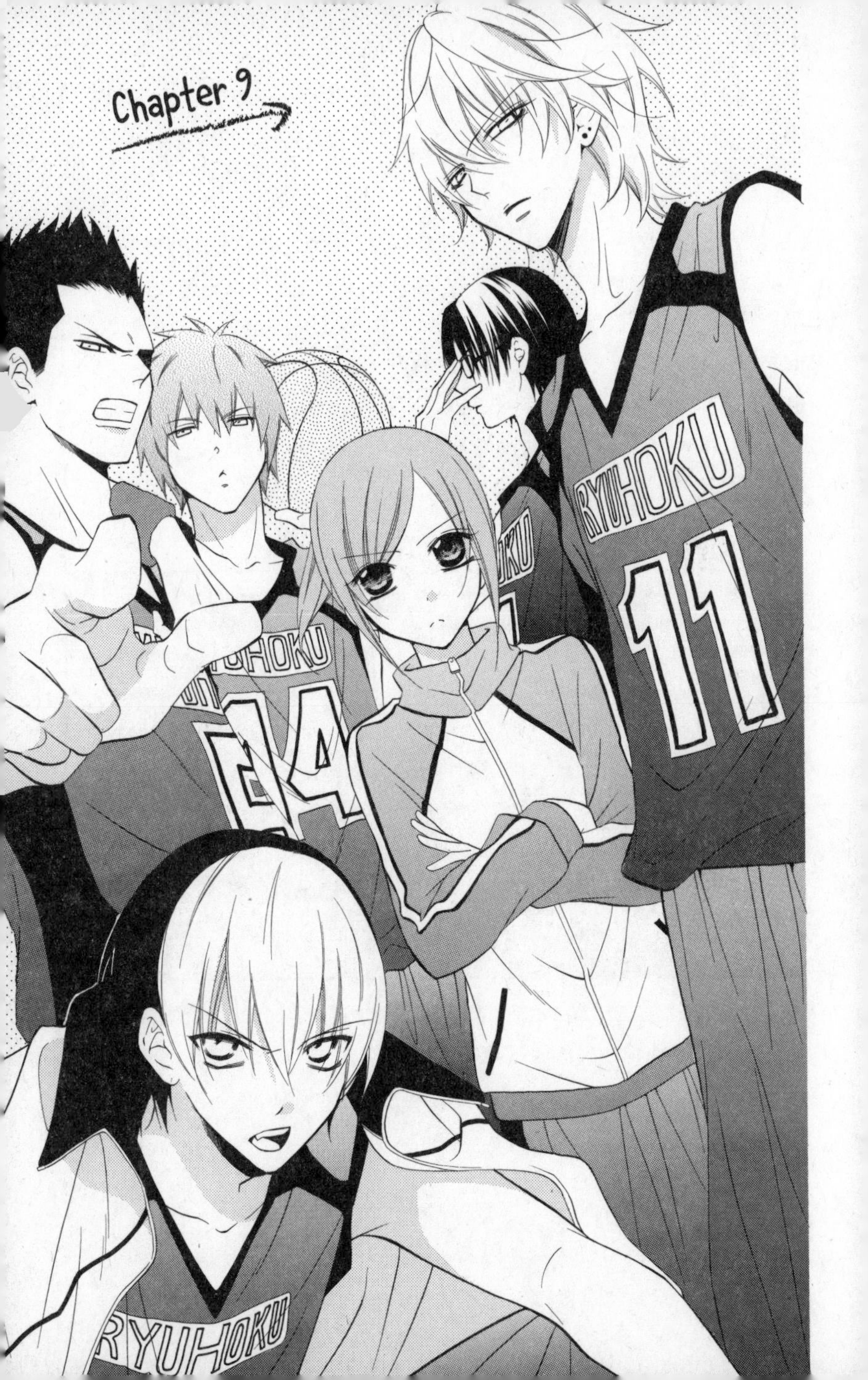
Chapter 9
RYUHOKU
11
RYUHOKU

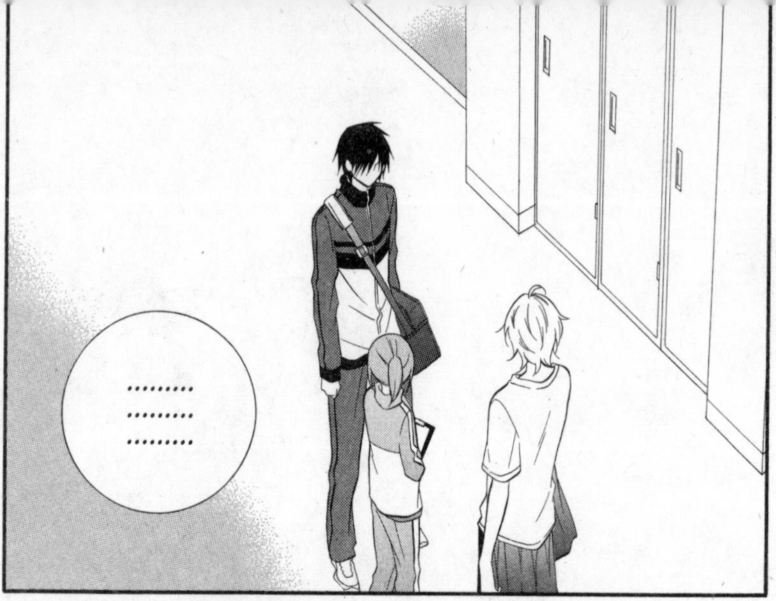
....
....
....

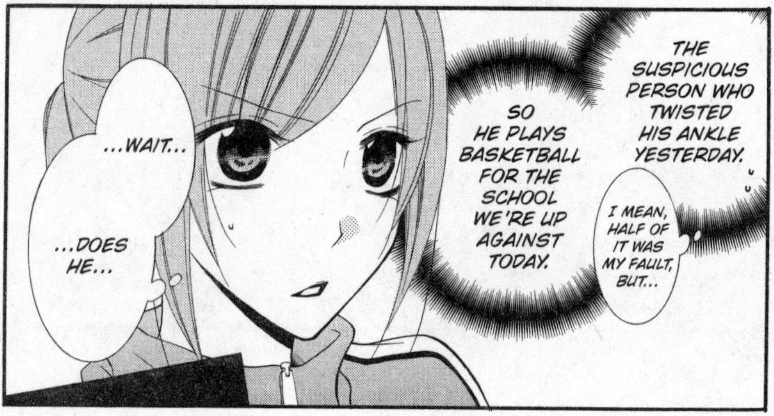
THE SUSPICIOUS PERSON WHO TWISTED HIS ANKLE YESTERDAY.
I MEAN, HALF OF IT WAS MY FAULT, BUT...
SO HE PLAYS BASKETBALL FOR THE SCHOOL WE'RE UP AGAINST TODAY.
...WAIT...
...DOES HE...

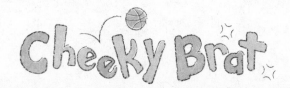

Cheeky Brat

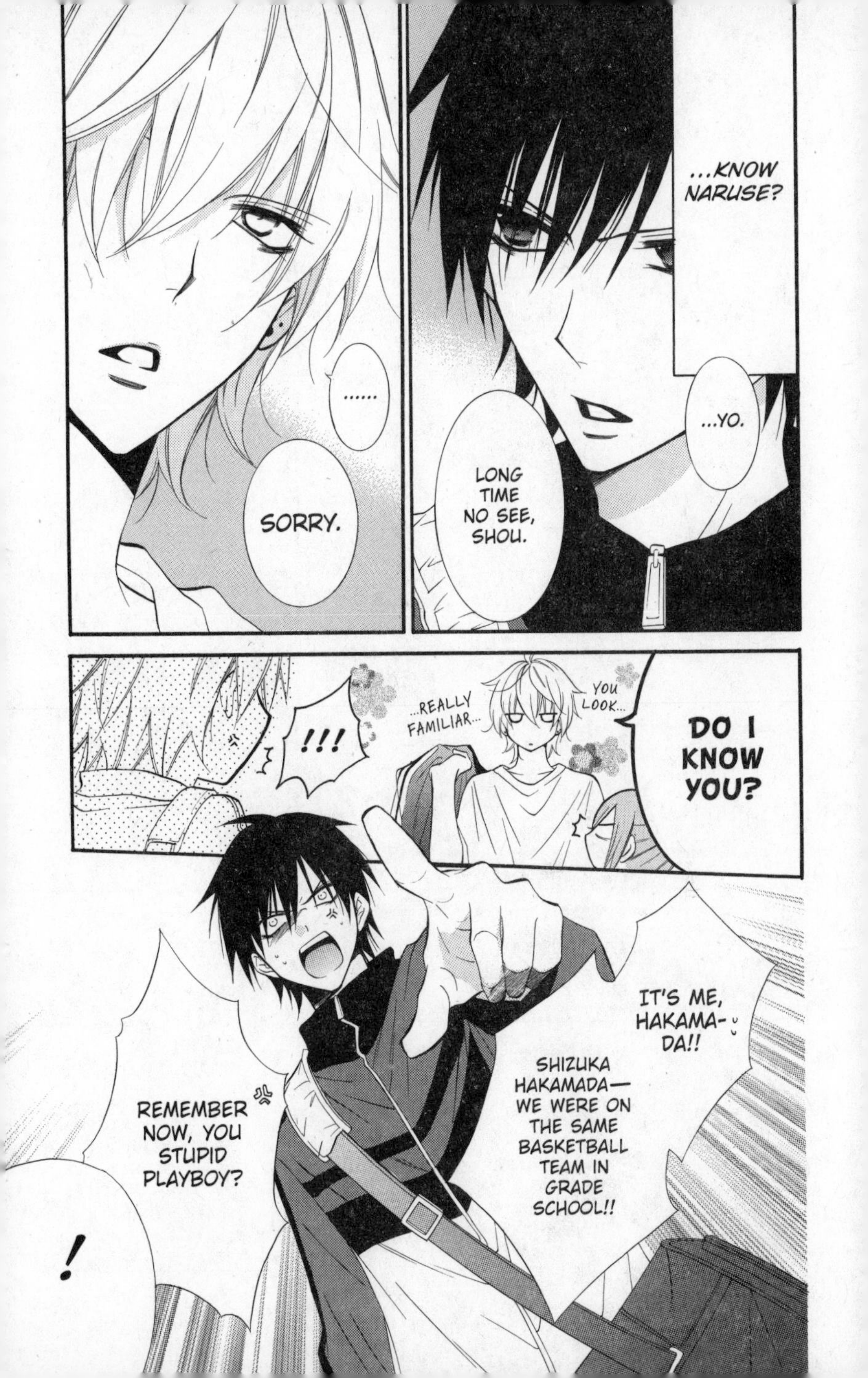
...KNOW NARUSE?
...YO.
LONG TIME NO SEE, SHOU.
......
SORRY.
DO I KNOW YOU?
YOU LOOK...
...REALLY FAMILIAR...
!!!
IT'S ME, HAKAMA-DA!!
SHIZUKA HAKAMADA—WE WERE ON THE SAME BASKETBALL TEAM IN GRADE SCHOOL!!
REMEMBER NOW, YOU STUPID PLAYBOY?
!

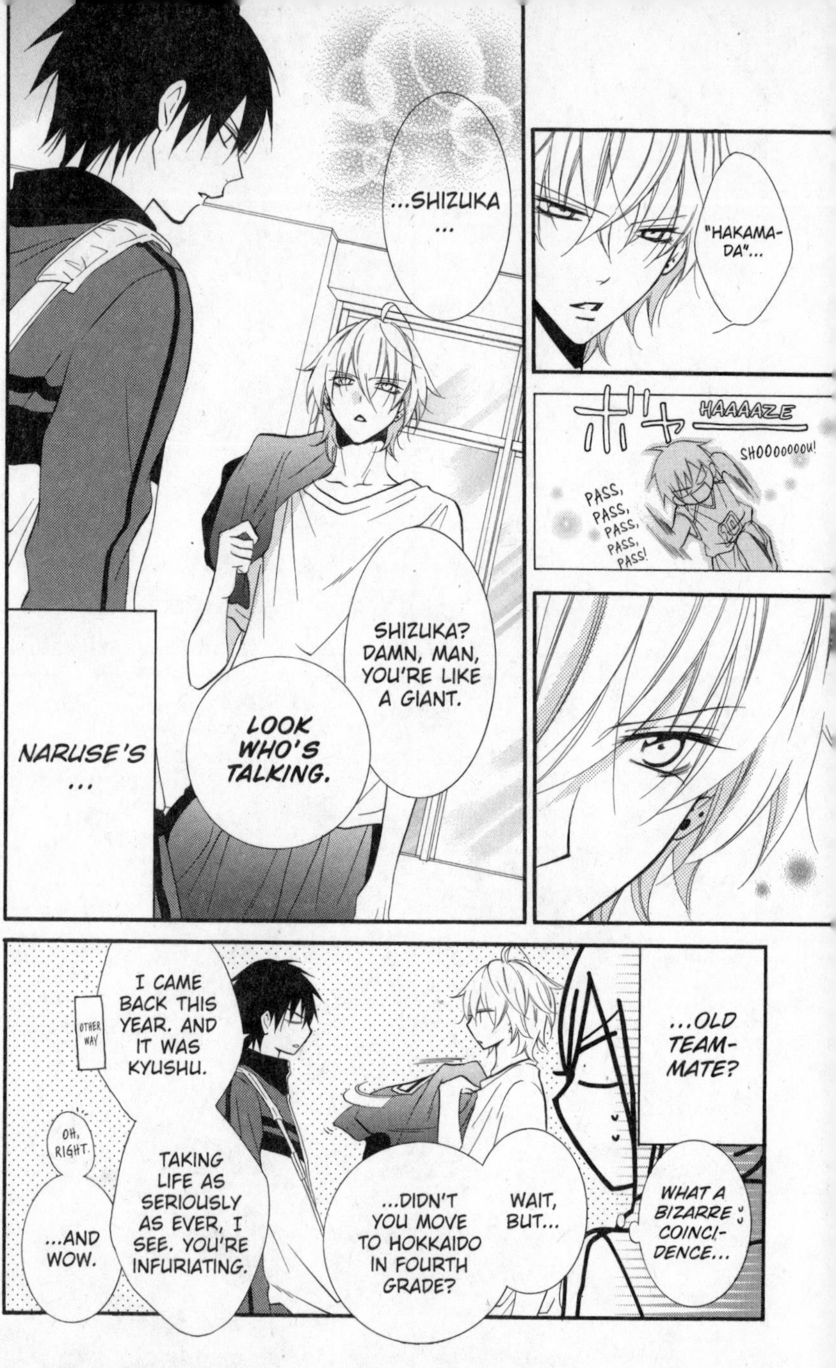
"HAKAMA-DA"...
HAAAAZE
SHOOOOOOOU!
PASS, PASS, PASS, PASS, PASS!
...SHIZUKA...
SHIZUKA? DAMN, MAN, YOU'RE LIKE A GIANT.
LOOK WHO'S TALKING.
NARUSE'S...
...OLD TEAM-MATE?
WHAT A BIZARRE COINCI-DENCE...
WAIT, BUT...
...DIDN'T YOU MOVE TO HOKKAIDO IN FOURTH GRADE?
TAKING LIFE AS SERIOUSLY AS EVER, I SEE. YOU'RE INFURIATING.
I CAME BACK THIS YEAR. AND IT WAS KYUSHU.
OTHER WAY
OH, RIGHT.
...AND WOW.

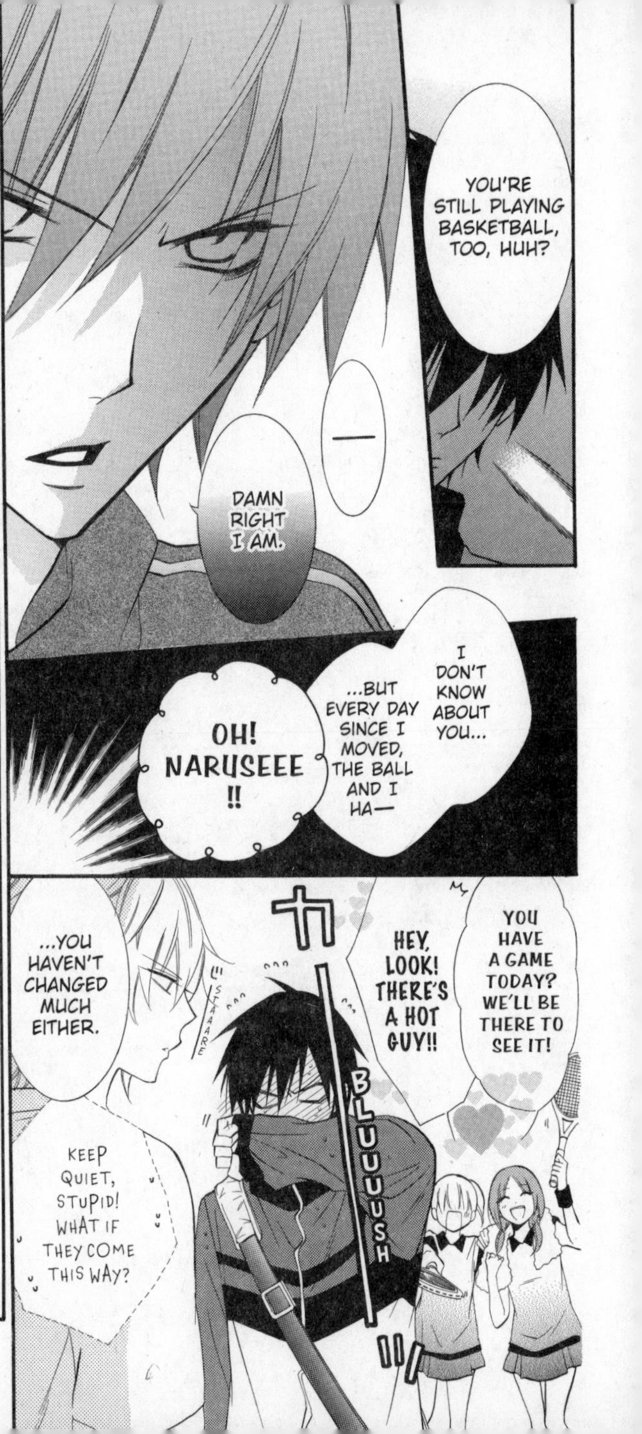
YOU'RE STILL PLAYING BASKETBALL, TOO, HUH?
—
DAMN RIGHT I AM.
I DON'T KNOW ABOUT YOU...
...BUT EVERY DAY SINCE I MOVED, THE BALL AND I HA—
OH! NARUSEEE!!
YOU HAVE A GAME TODAY? WE'LL BE THERE TO SEE IT!
HEY, LOOK! THERE'S A HOT GUY!!
BLUUUUSH
STAAARE
...YOU HAVEN'T CHANGED MUCH EITHER.
KEEP QUIET, STUPID! WHAT IF THEY COME THIS WAY?

03

CONTINUATION

And when the autograph session finally started, no amount of deep breathing helped me get air.

But my kind readers approached my cowardly self with smiles on their faces.

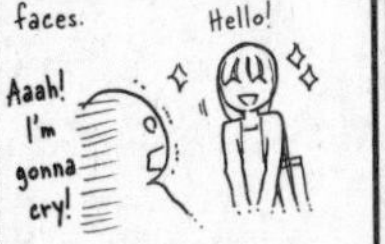
Hello!
Aaah! I'm gonna cry!

Some people told me they were from Yokohama, and others came all the way from Osaka...I was so touched, I was shaking...... Then a storm of failures unfolded.

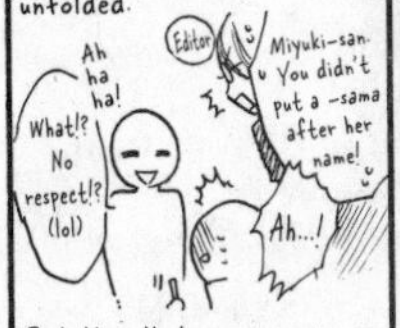
Ah ha ha!
What!? No respect!? (lol)
Editor
Miyuki-san. You didn't put a -sama after her name!
Ah...!

But the all-too-magnanimous reader laughed it off and forgave me...how divine...

I haven't had the chance to say this yet, but really, thank you so much. It felt like I was living in a dream, surrounded by all of your love...!!! I really appreciated the drawings, letters, flowers, and all the other gifts!!! To the employees at the bookstore, the editorial team, and the sales department, thank you for all you've done for me. m(_ _)m

Thank you very much!!!

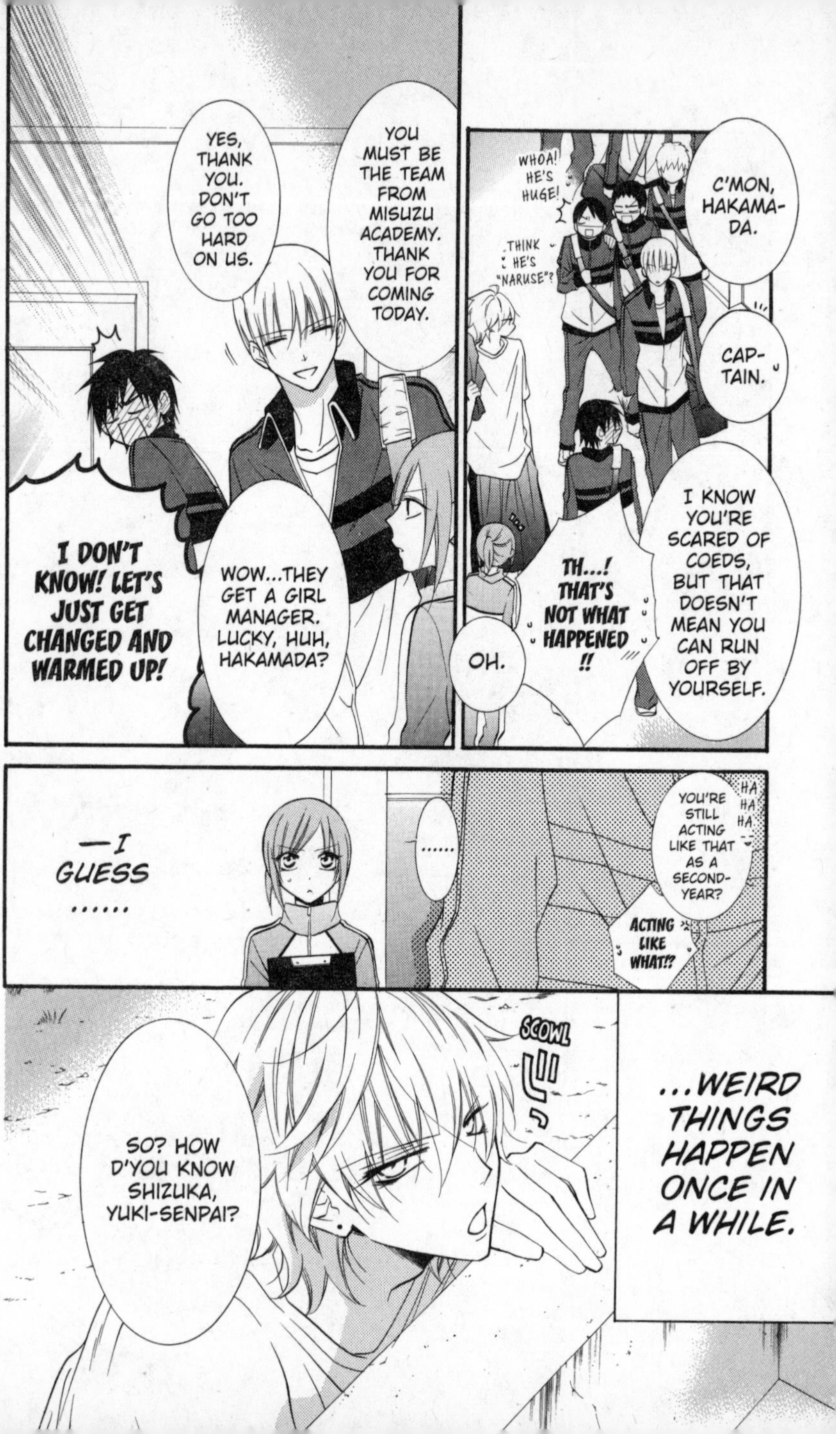

C'MON, HAKAMADA.
WHOA! HE'S HUGE!
THINK HE'S "NARUSE"?
CAPTAIN.
I KNOW YOU'RE SCARED OF COEDS, BUT THAT DOESN'T MEAN YOU CAN RUN OFF BY YOURSELF.
TH...! THAT'S NOT WHAT HAPPENED!!
OH.
YOU MUST BE THE TEAM FROM MISUZU ACADEMY. THANK YOU FOR COMING TODAY.
YES, THANK YOU. DON'T GO TOO HARD ON US.
WOW...THEY GET A GIRL MANAGER. LUCKY, HUH, HAKAMADA?
I DON'T KNOW! LET'S JUST GET CHANGED AND WARMED UP!
YOU'RE STILL ACTING LIKE THAT AS A SECOND-YEAR?
HA HA HA
ACTING LIKE WHAT!?
......
—I GUESS ......
...WEIRD THINGS HAPPEN ONCE IN A WHILE.
SCOWL
SO? HOW D'YOU KNOW SHIZUKA, YUKI-SENPAI?

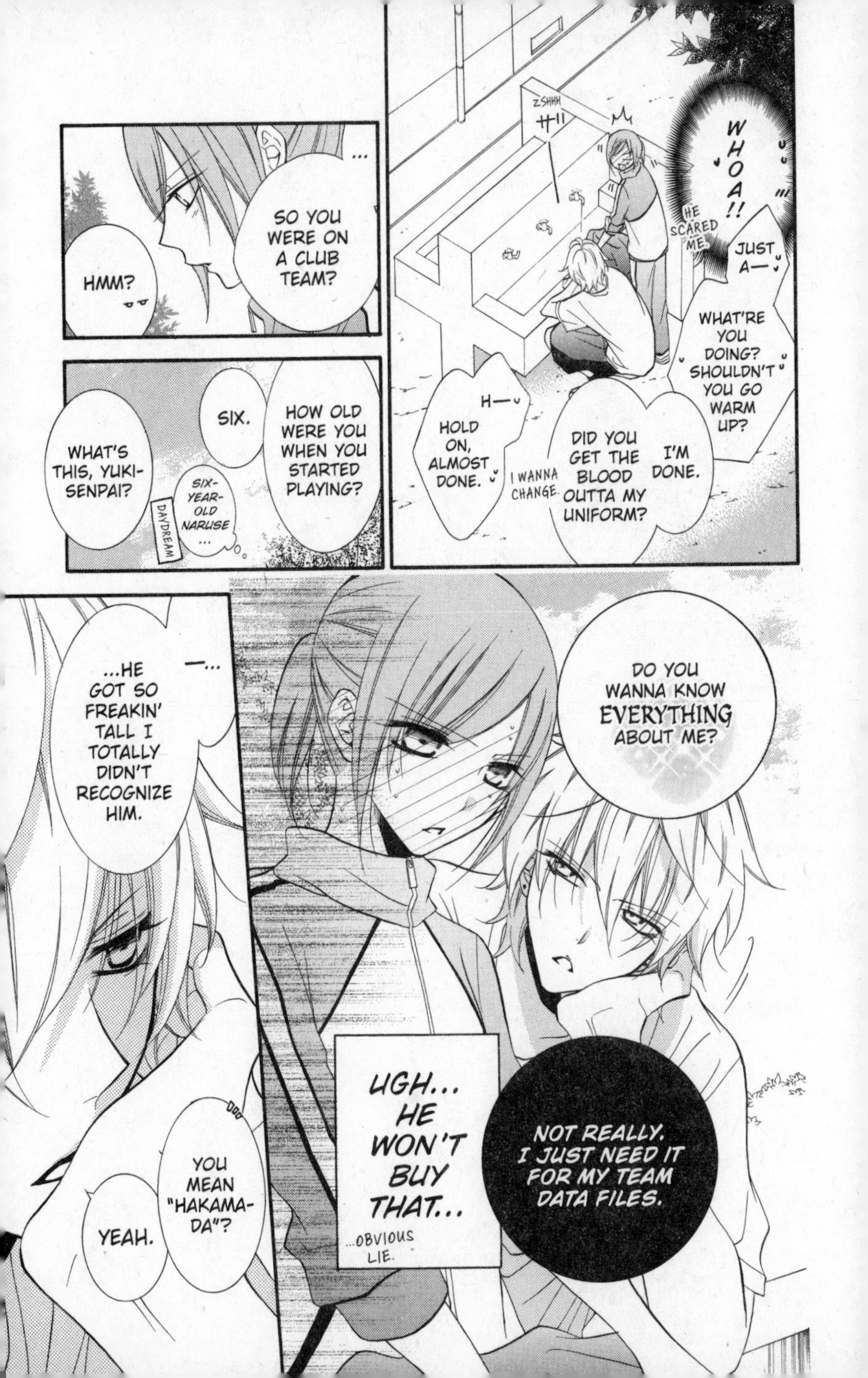
ZSHHH
WHOA!!
HE SCARED ME.
JUST A—
WHAT'RE YOU DOING? SHOULDN'T YOU GO WARM UP?
I'M DONE.
DID YOU GET THE BLOOD OUTTA MY UNIFORM?
H—
HOLD ON, ALMOST DONE.
I WANNA CHANGE.
...
SO YOU WERE ON A CLUB TEAM?
HMM?
HOW OLD WERE YOU WHEN YOU STARTED PLAYING?
SIX.
SIX-YEAR-OLD NARUSE...
DAYDREAM
WHAT'S THIS, YUKI-SENPAI?
DO YOU WANNA KNOW EVERYTHING ABOUT ME?
NOT REALLY. I JUST NEED IT FOR MY TEAM DATA FILES.
UGH... HE WON'T BUY THAT...
...OBVIOUS LIE.
—...
...HE GOT SO FREAKIN' TALL I TOTALLY DIDN'T RECOGNIZE HIM.
YOU MEAN "HAKAMA-DA"?
YEAH.

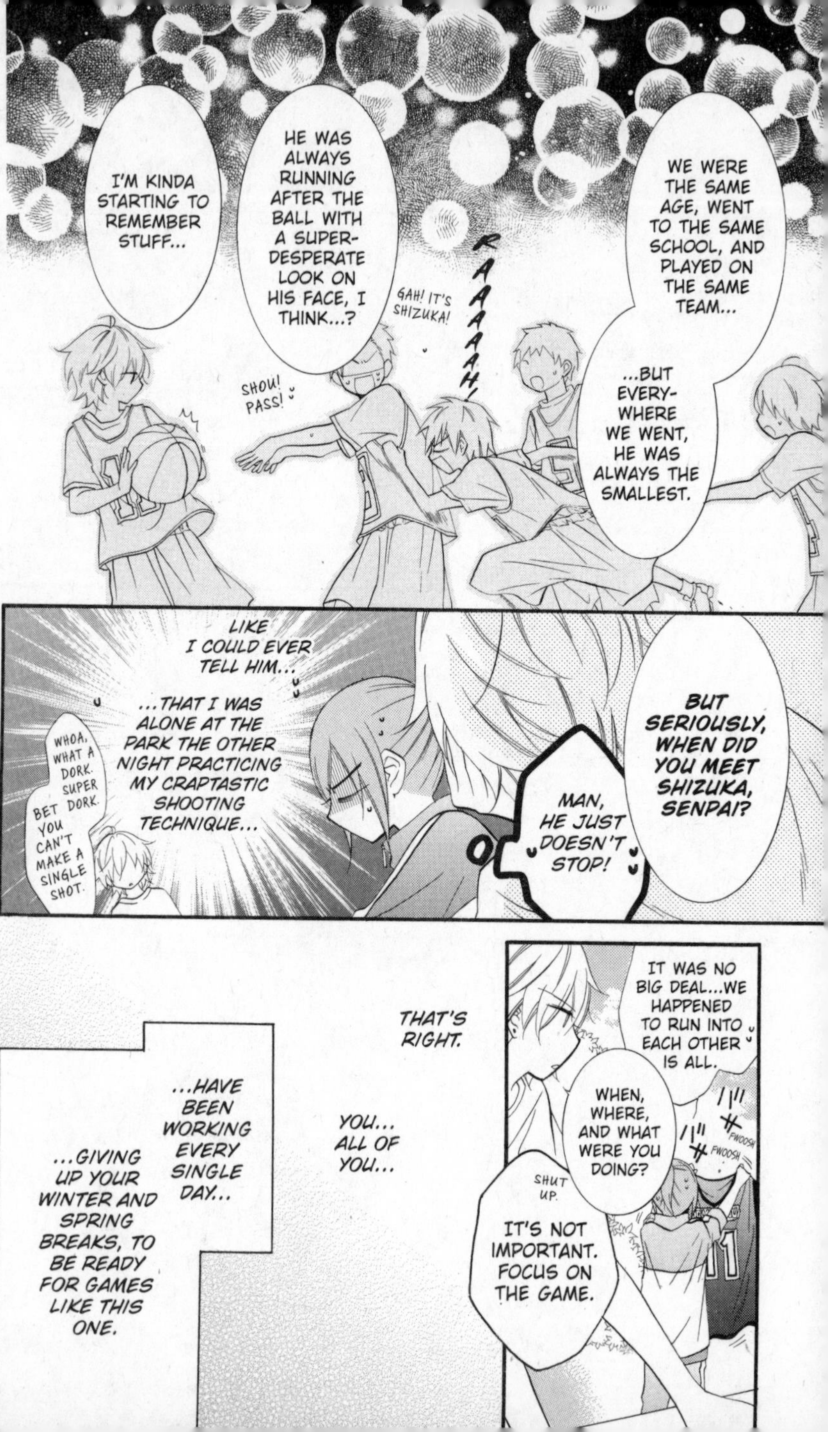
WE WERE THE SAME AGE, WENT TO THE SAME SCHOOL, AND PLAYED ON THE SAME TEAM...
...BUT EVERYWHERE WE WENT, HE WAS ALWAYS THE SMALLEST.
RAAAAAAH!
GAH! IT'S SHIZUKA!
HE WAS ALWAYS RUNNING AFTER THE BALL WITH A SUPER-DESPERATE LOOK ON HIS FACE, I THINK...?
SHOU! PASS!
I'M KINDA STARTING TO REMEMBER STUFF...
BUT SERIOUSLY, WHEN DID YOU MEET SHIZUKA, SENPAI?
MAN, HE JUST DOESN'T STOP!
LIKE I COULD EVER TELL HIM...
...THAT I WAS ALONE AT THE PARK THE OTHER NIGHT PRACTICING MY CRAPTASTIC SHOOTING TECHNIQUE...
WHOA, WHAT A DORK. SUPER DORK.
BET YOU CAN'T MAKE A SINGLE SHOT.
IT WAS NO BIG DEAL...WE HAPPENED TO RUN INTO EACH OTHER IS ALL.
WHEN, WHERE, AND WHAT WERE YOU DOING?
FWOOSH
FWOOSH
SHUT UP.
IT'S NOT IMPORTANT. FOCUS ON THE GAME.
THAT'S RIGHT.
YOU... ALL OF YOU...
...HAVE BEEN WORKING EVERY SINGLE DAY...
...GIVING UP YOUR WINTER AND SPRING BREAKS, TO BE READY FOR GAMES LIKE THIS ONE.

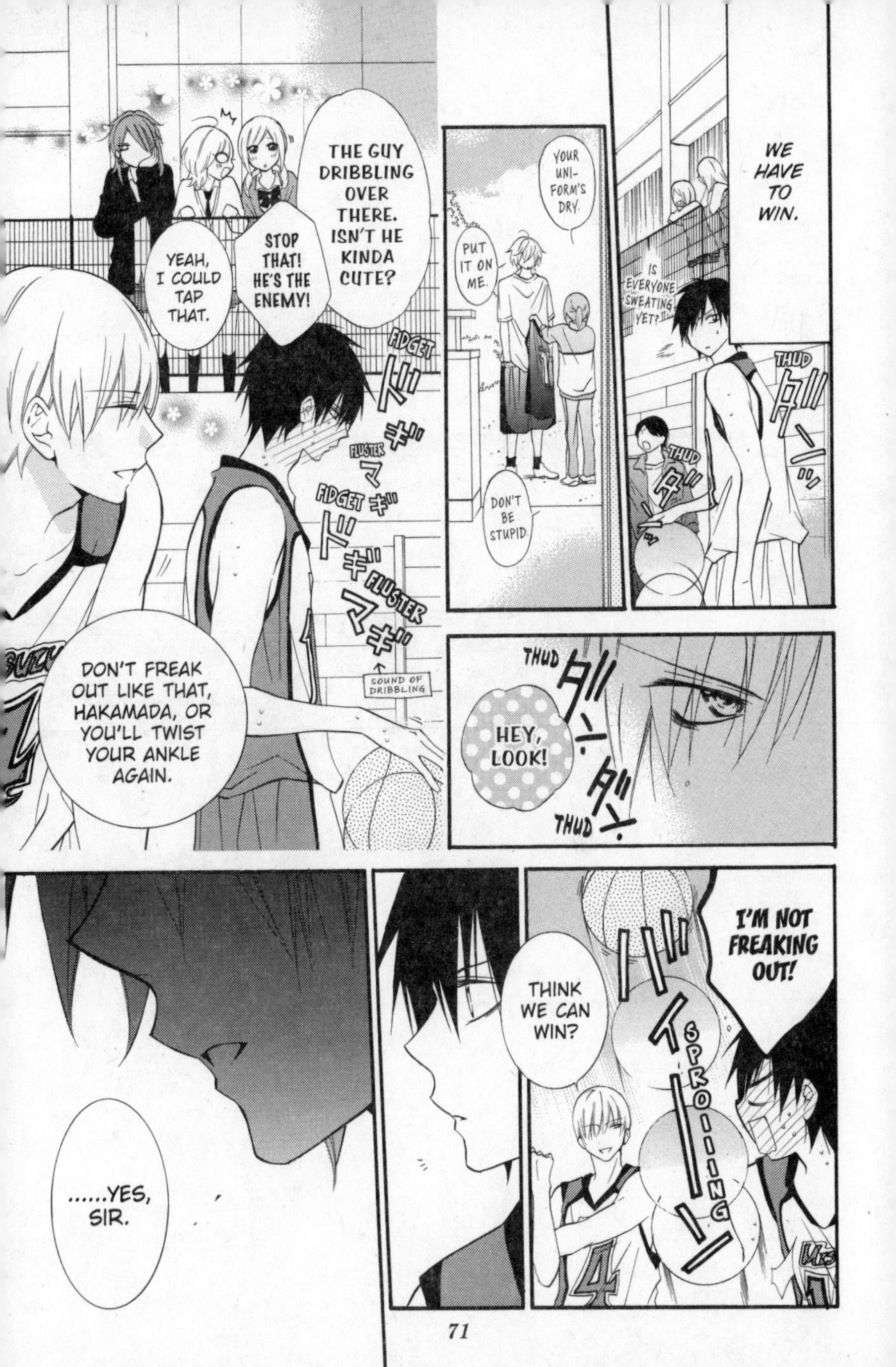
WE HAVE TO WIN.
IS EVERYONE SWEATING YET?
THUD
THUD
YOUR UNI-FORM'S DRY.
PUT IT ON ME.
DON'T BE STUPID.
THUD
HEY, LOOK!
THUD
THE GUY DRIBBLING OVER THERE. ISN'T HE KINDA CUTE?
STOP THAT! HE'S THE ENEMY!
YEAH, I COULD TAP THAT.
FIDGET
FLUSTER
FIDGET
FLUSTER
SOUND OF DRIBBLING
DON'T FREAK OUT LIKE THAT, HAKAMADA, OR YOU'LL TWIST YOUR ANKLE AGAIN.
I'M NOT FREAKING OUT!
SPROIIING
THINK WE CAN WIN?
......YES, SIR.

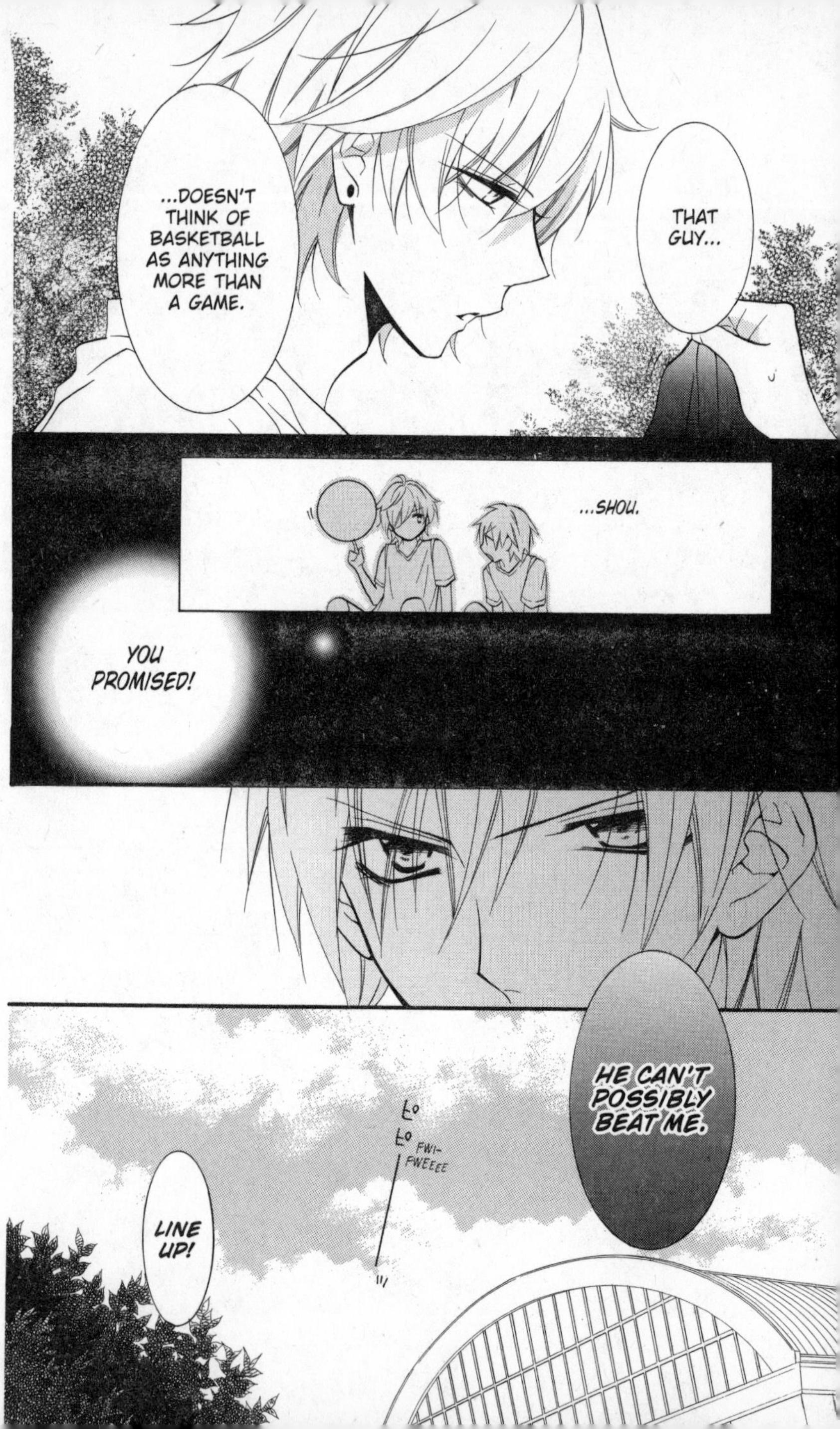
THAT GUY...
...DOESN'T THINK OF BASKETBALL AS ANYTHING MORE THAN A GAME.
...SHOU.
YOU PROMISED!
HE CAN'T POSSIBLY BEAT ME.
FWI-FWEEEE
LINE UP!

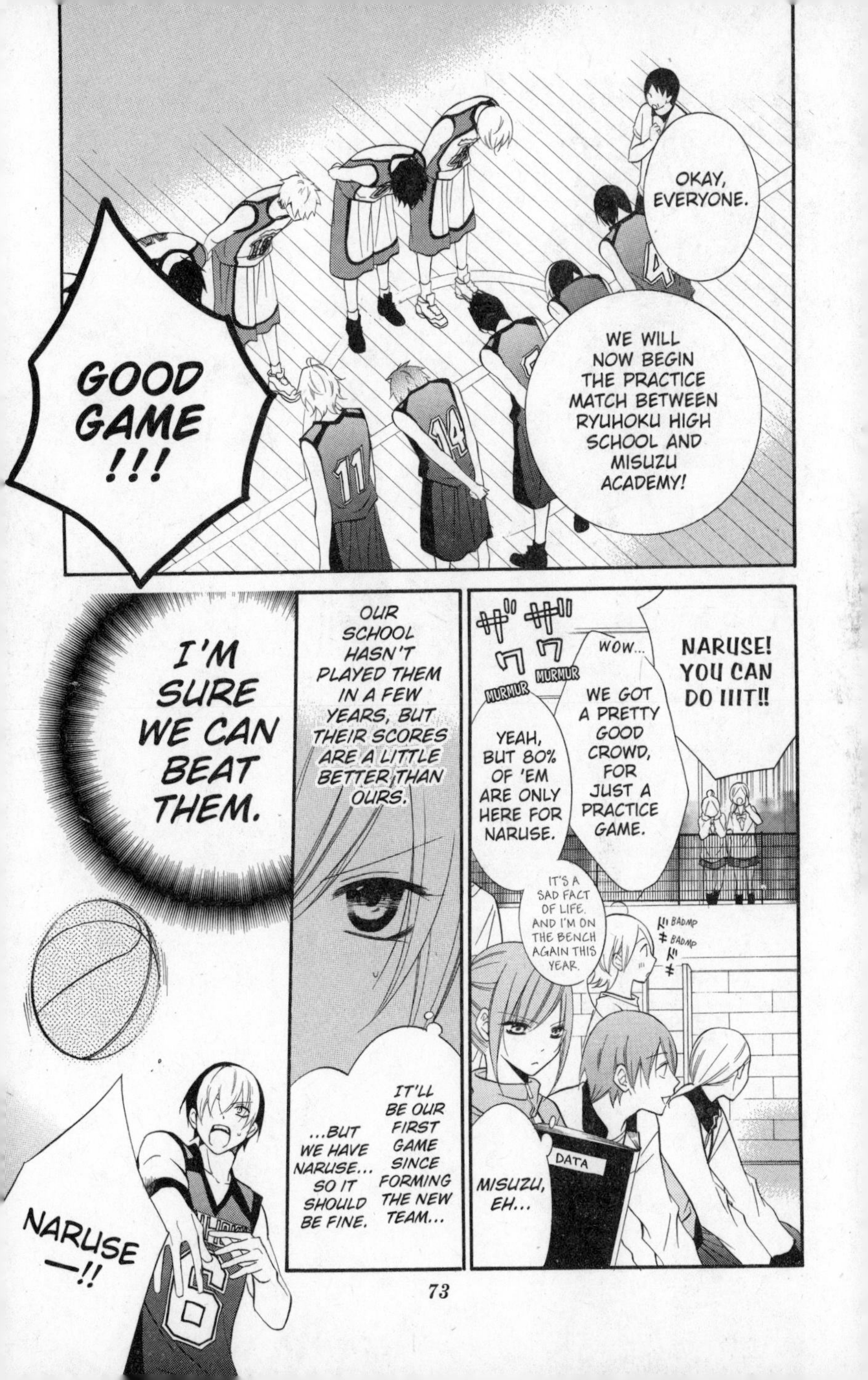
OKAY, EVERYONE.
WE WILL NOW BEGIN THE PRACTICE MATCH BETWEEN RYUHOKU HIGH SCHOOL AND MISUZU ACADEMY!
GOOD GAME!!!
ザワザワ
MURMUR
MURMUR
NARUSE! YOU CAN DO IIIT!!
WOW...
WE GOT A PRETTY GOOD CROWD, FOR JUST A PRACTICE GAME.
YEAH, BUT 80% OF 'EM ARE ONLY HERE FOR NARUSE.
IT'S A SAD FACT OF LIFE. AND I'M ON THE BENCH AGAIN THIS YEAR.
BADMP
BADMP
DATA
MISUZU, EH...
OUR SCHOOL HASN'T PLAYED THEM IN A FEW YEARS, BUT THEIR SCORES ARE A LITTLE BETTER THAN OURS.
IT'LL BE OUR FIRST GAME SINCE FORMING THE NEW TEAM...
...BUT WE HAVE NARUSE... SO IT SHOULD BE FINE.
I'M SURE WE CAN BEAT THEM.
NARUSE—!!

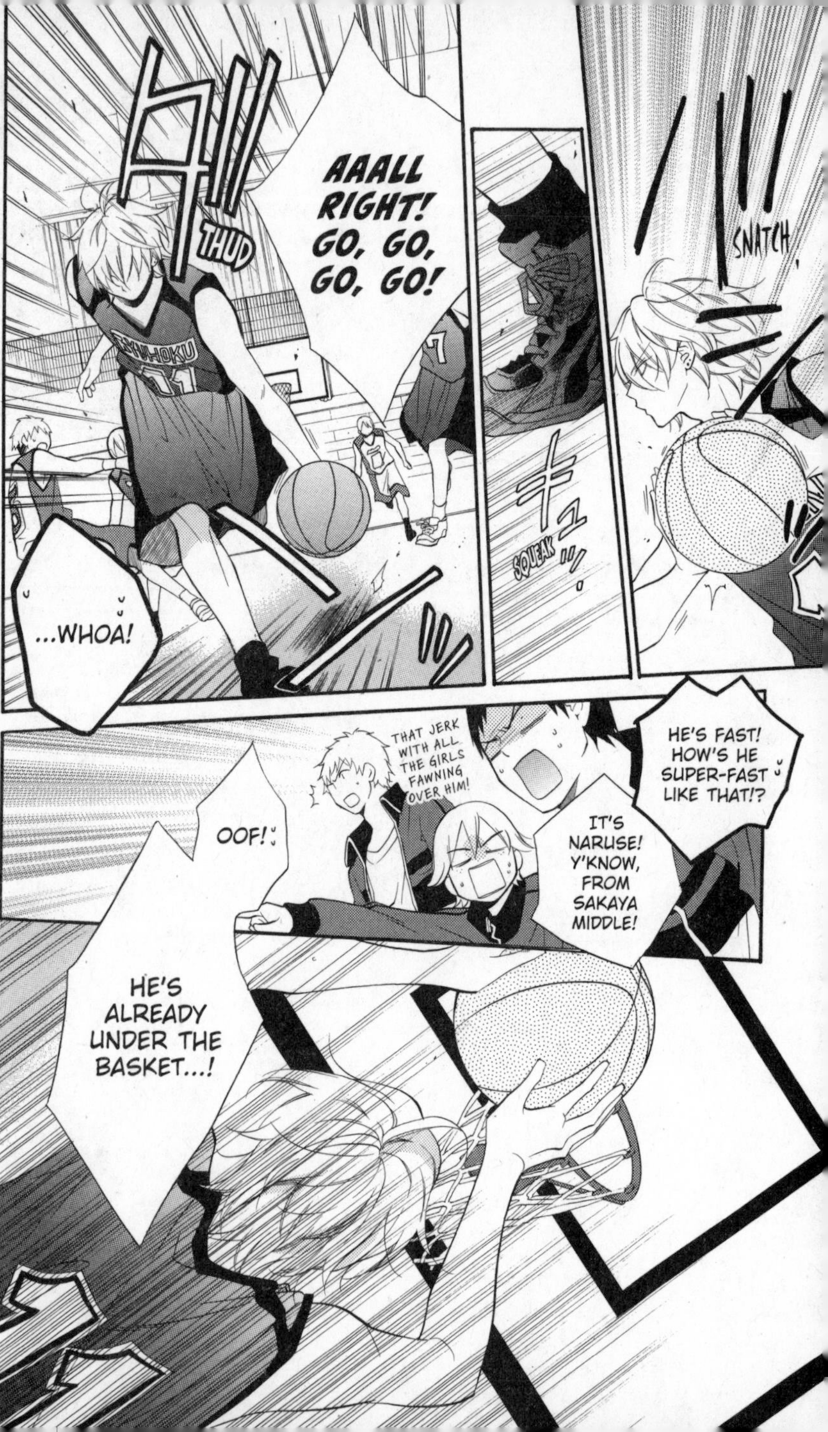
SNATCH
SQUEAK
THUD
AAALL RIGHT! GO, GO, GO, GO!
...WHOA!
HE'S FAST! HOW'S HE SUPER-FAST LIKE THAT!?
IT'S NARUSE! Y'KNOW, FROM SAKAYA MIDDLE!
THAT JERK WITH ALL THE GIRLS FAWNING OVER HIM!
OOF!
HE'S ALREADY UNDER THE BASKET...!

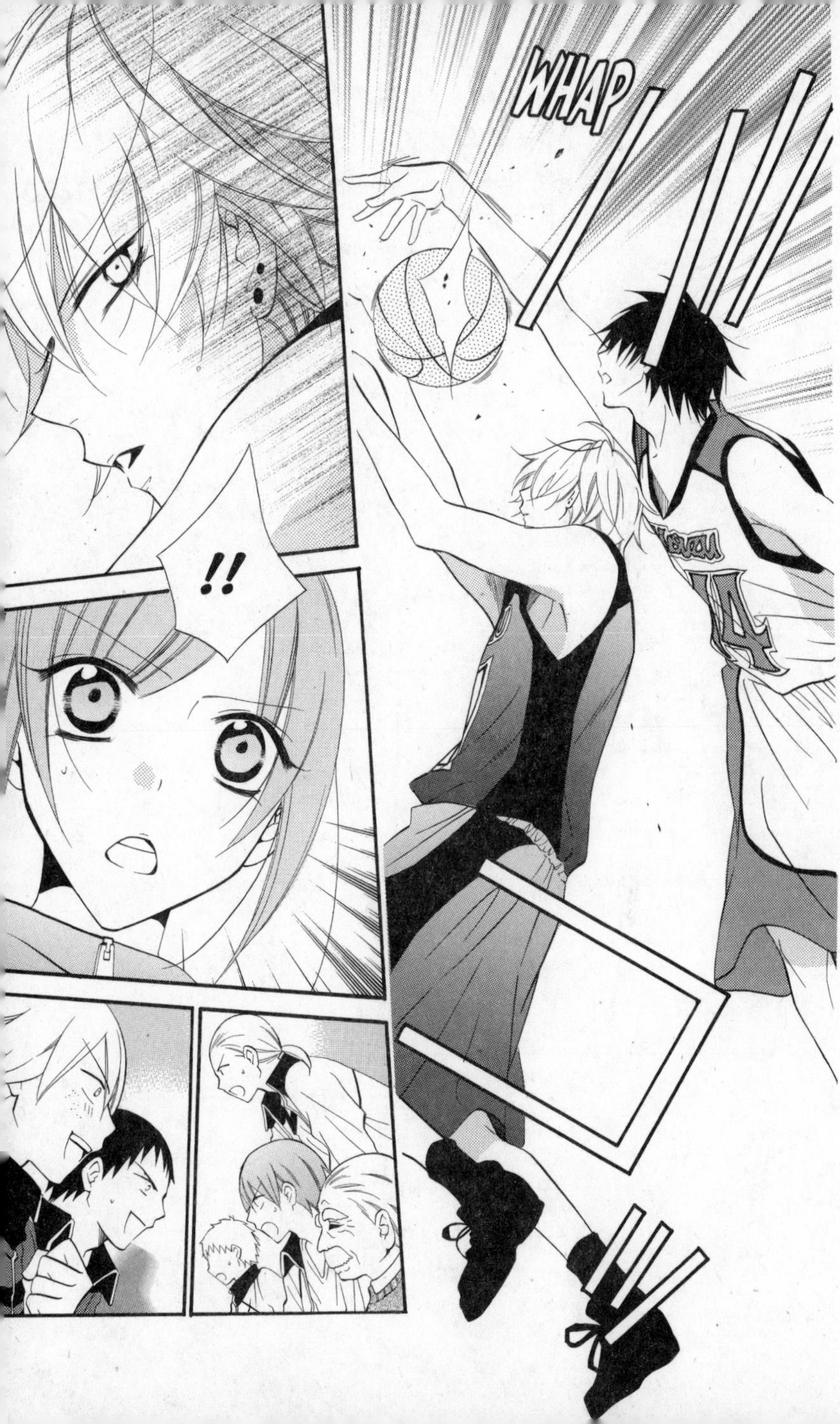
WHAP
!!

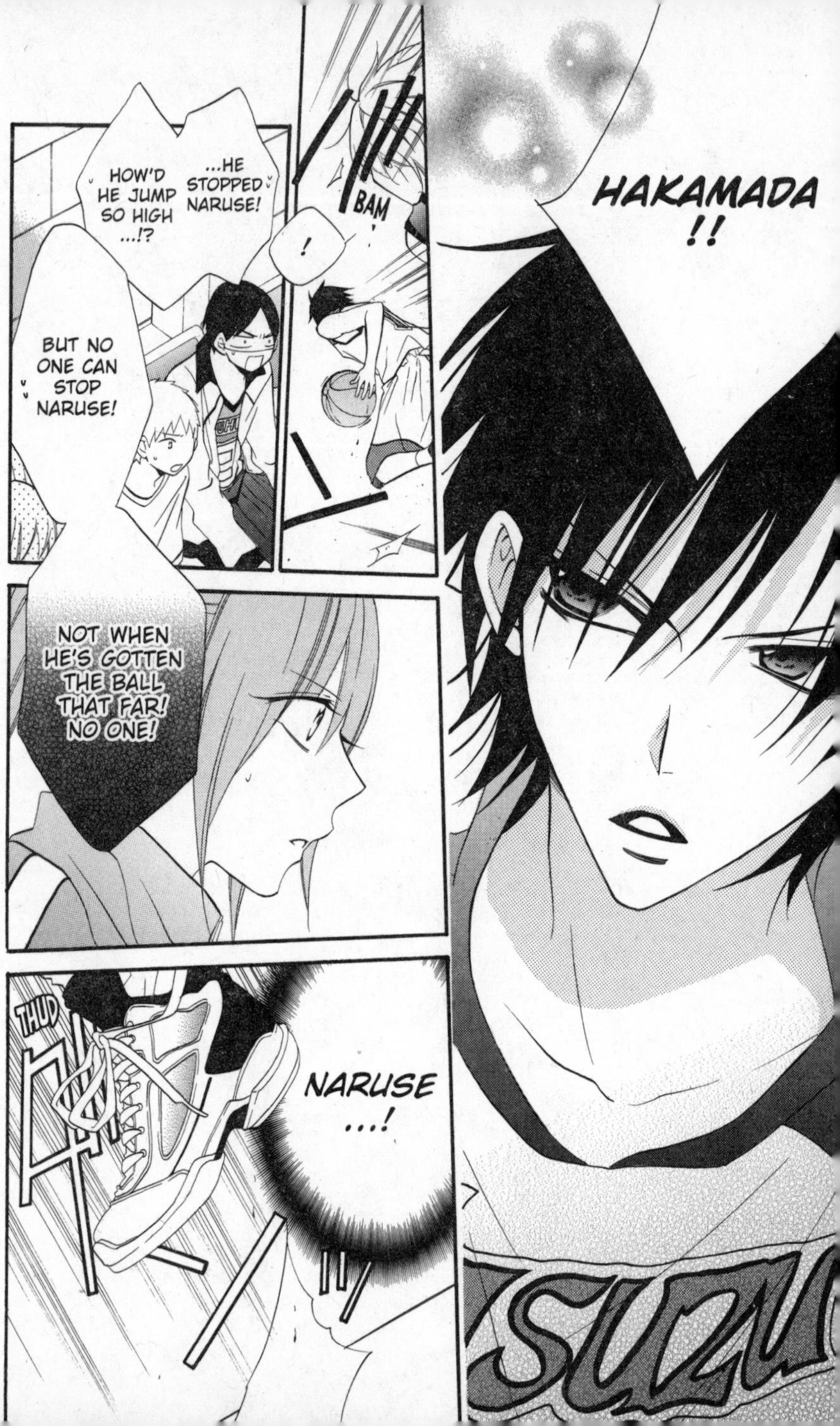
HAKAMADA !!
BAM
!
...HE STOPPED NARUSE!
HOW'D HE JUMP SO HIGH ...!?
BUT NO ONE CAN STOP NARUSE!
NOT WHEN HE'S GOTTEN THE BALL THAT FAR! NO ONE!
THUD
NARUSE ...!

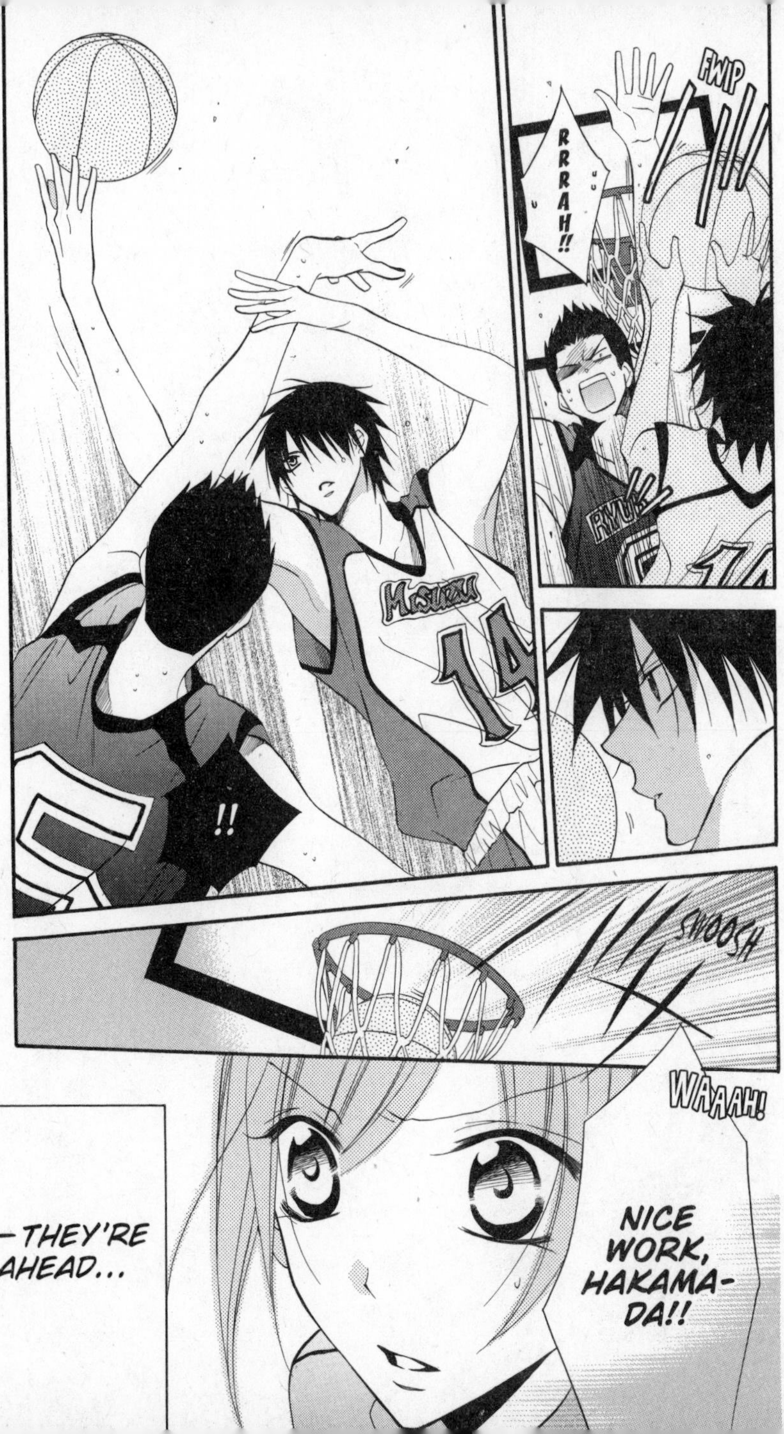
FWIP
RRRAH!!
!!
SWOOSH
WAAAH!
NICE WORK, HAKAMA-DA!!
—THEY'RE AHEAD...

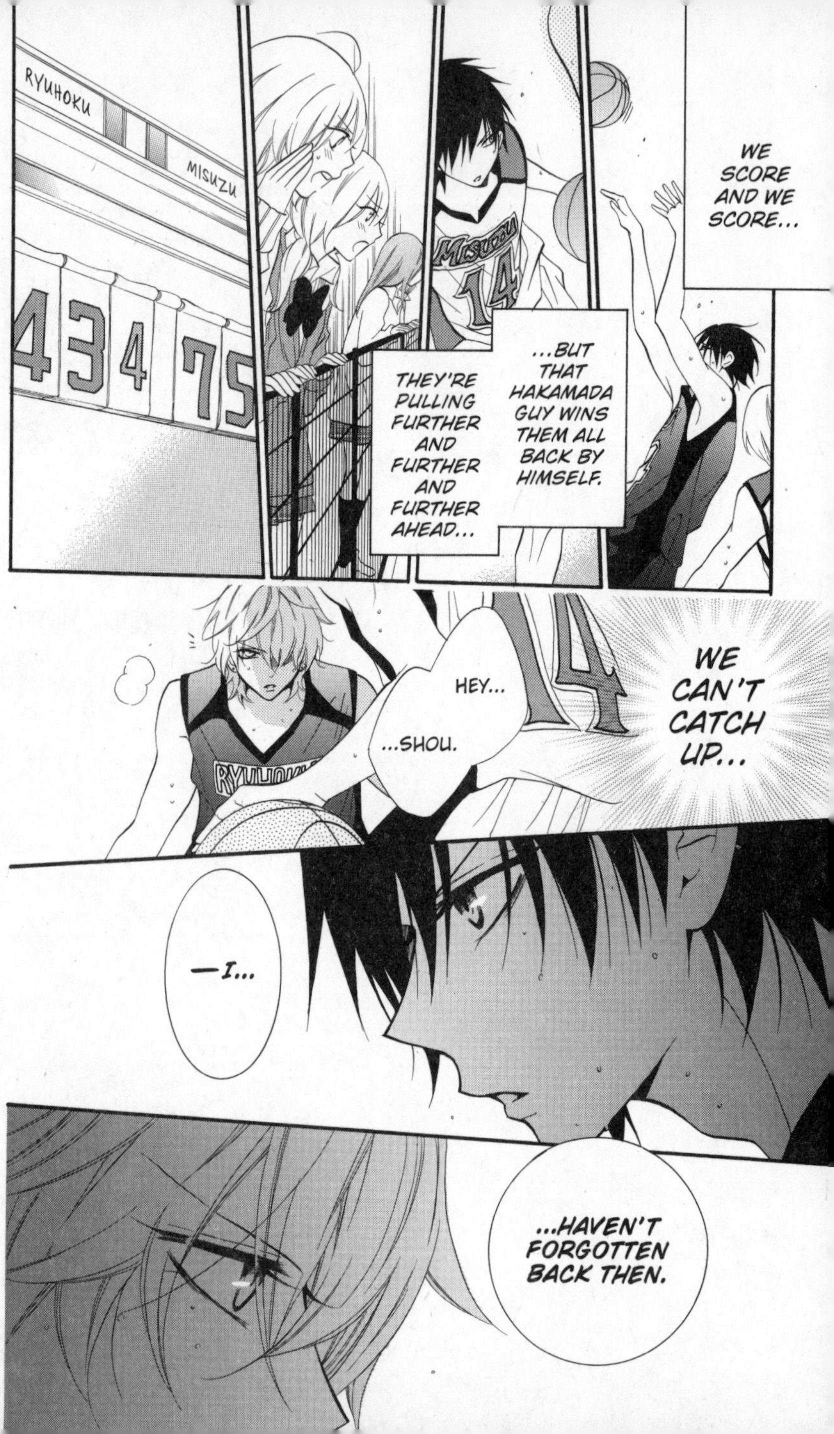
WE SCORE AND WE SCORE...
...BUT THAT HAKAMADA GUY WINS THEM ALL BACK BY HIMSELF.
THEY'RE PULLING FURTHER AND FURTHER AND FURTHER AHEAD...
MISUZU 14
RYUHOKU
MISUZU
434 75
WE CAN'T CATCH UP...
HEY...
...SHOU.
RYUHOKU
—I...
...HAVEN'T FORGOTTEN BACK THEN.

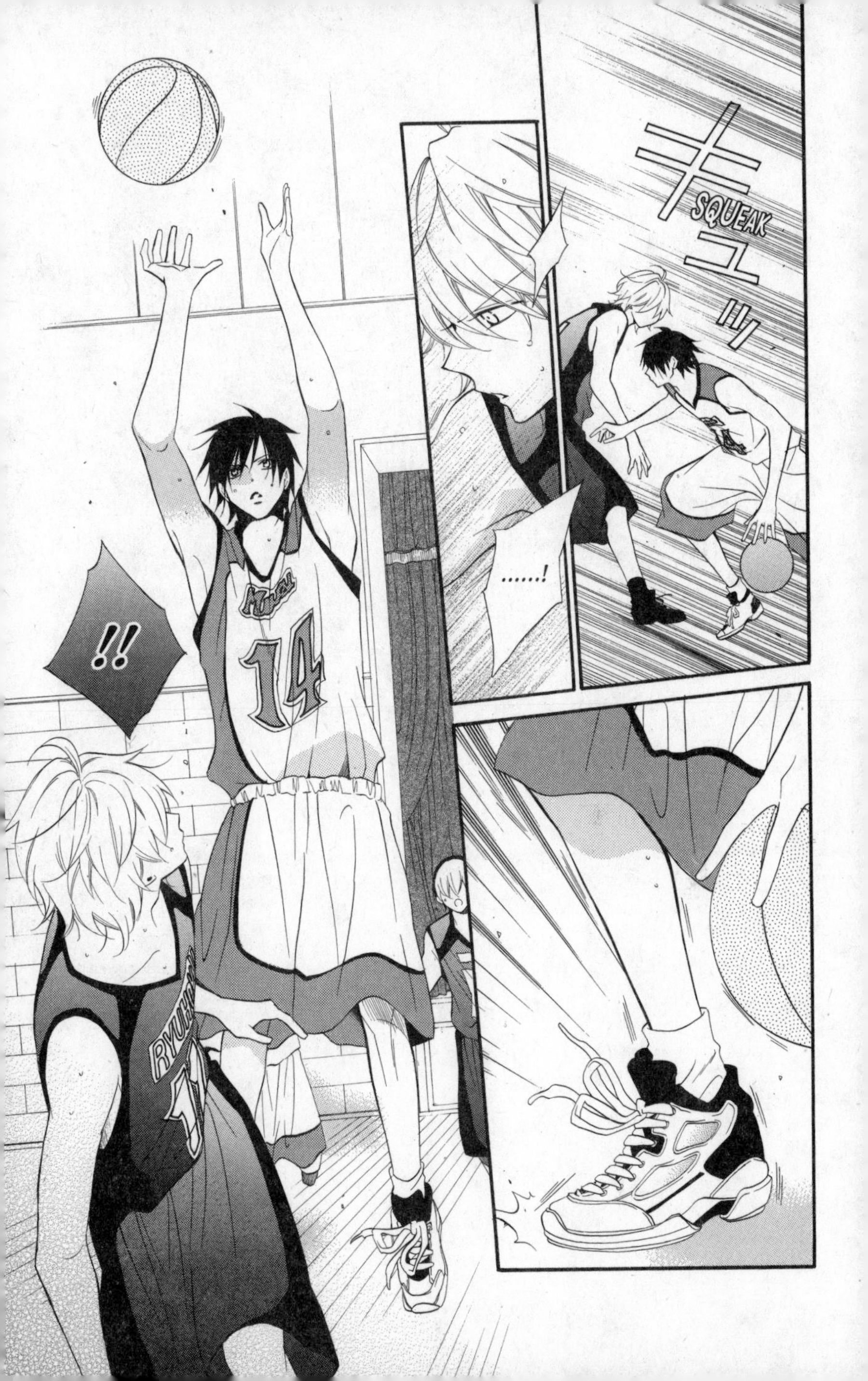
キュッ
SQUEAK
......!
!!

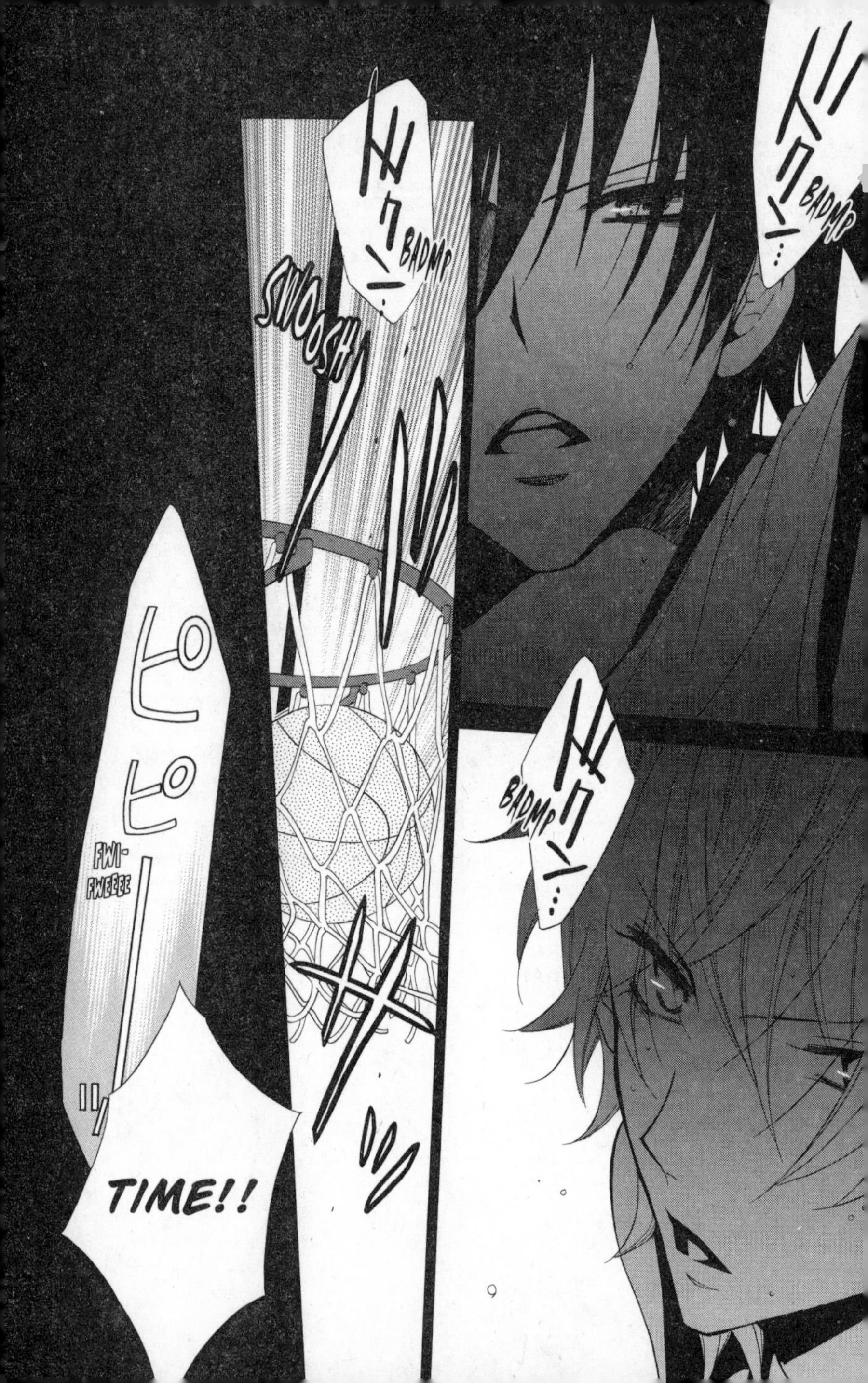

BADMP
BADMP
BADMP
SWOOSH
FWI-FWEEEE
TIME!!

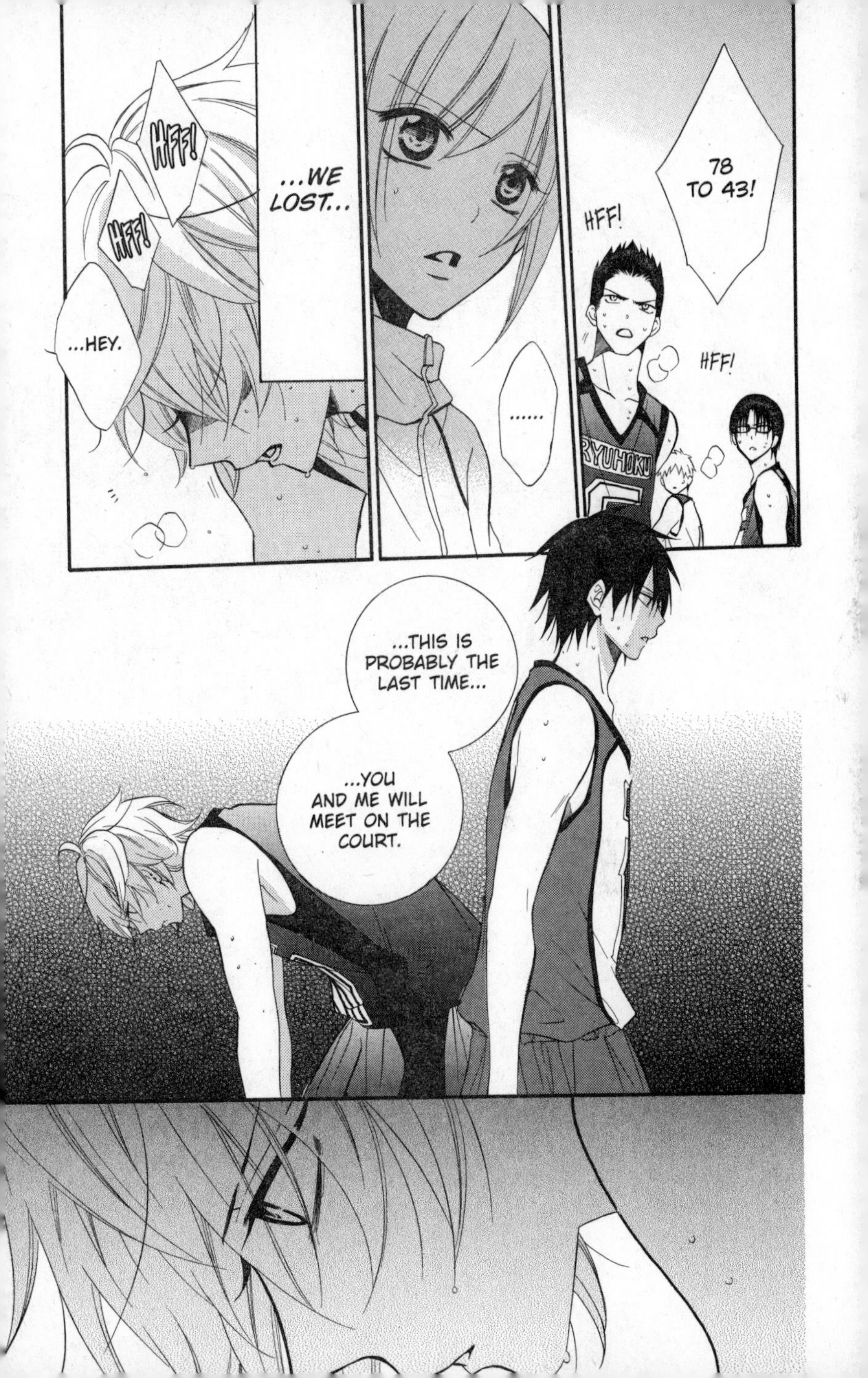
78 TO 43!
HFF!
HFF!
......
...WE LOST...
HFF!
HFF!
...HEY.
...THIS IS PROBABLY THE LAST TIME...
...YOU AND ME WILL MEET ON THE COURT.

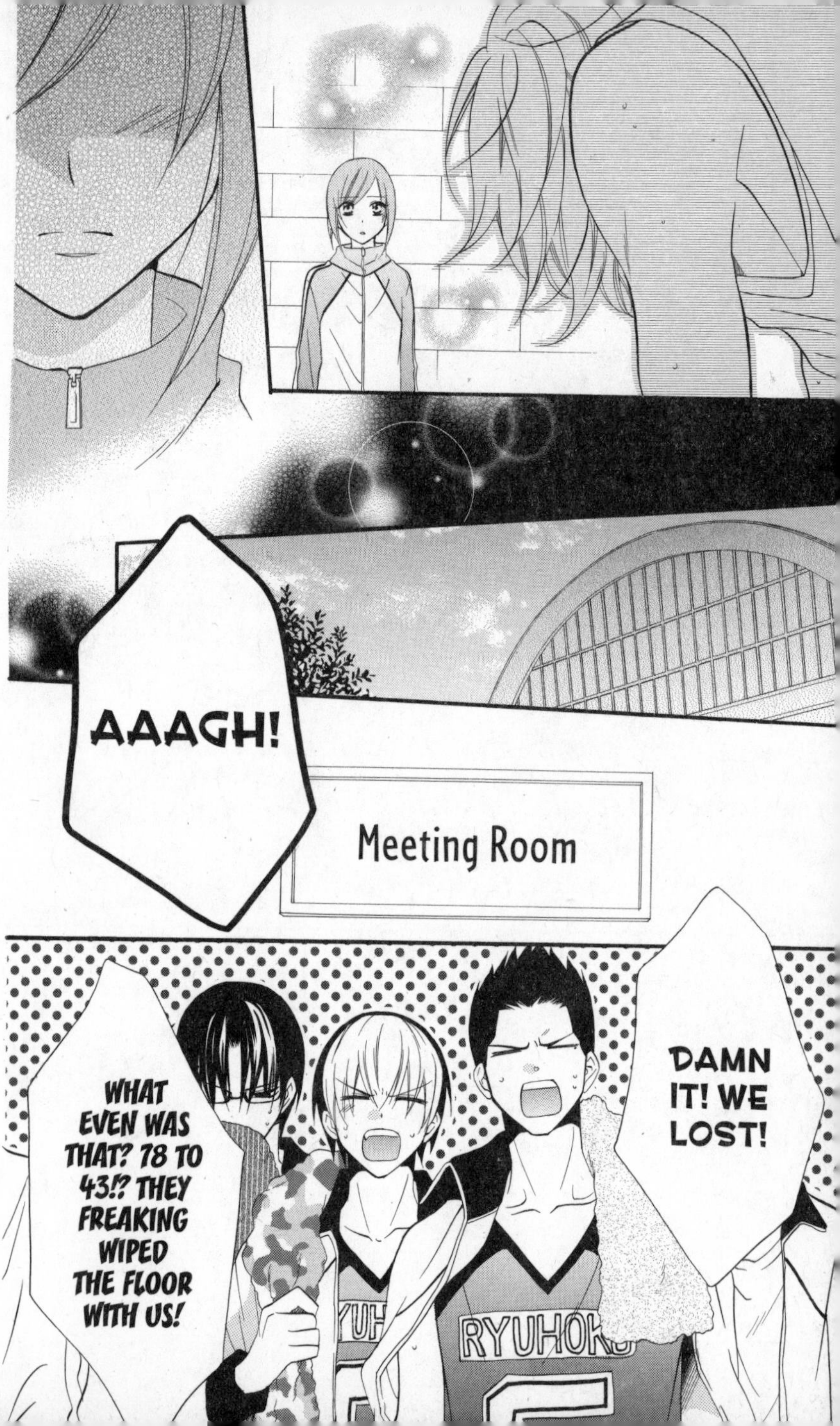
AAAGH!
Meeting Room
DAMN IT! WE LOST!
WHAT EVEN WAS THAT? 78 TO 43!? THEY FREAKING WIPED THE FLOOR WITH US!
RYUHOKU

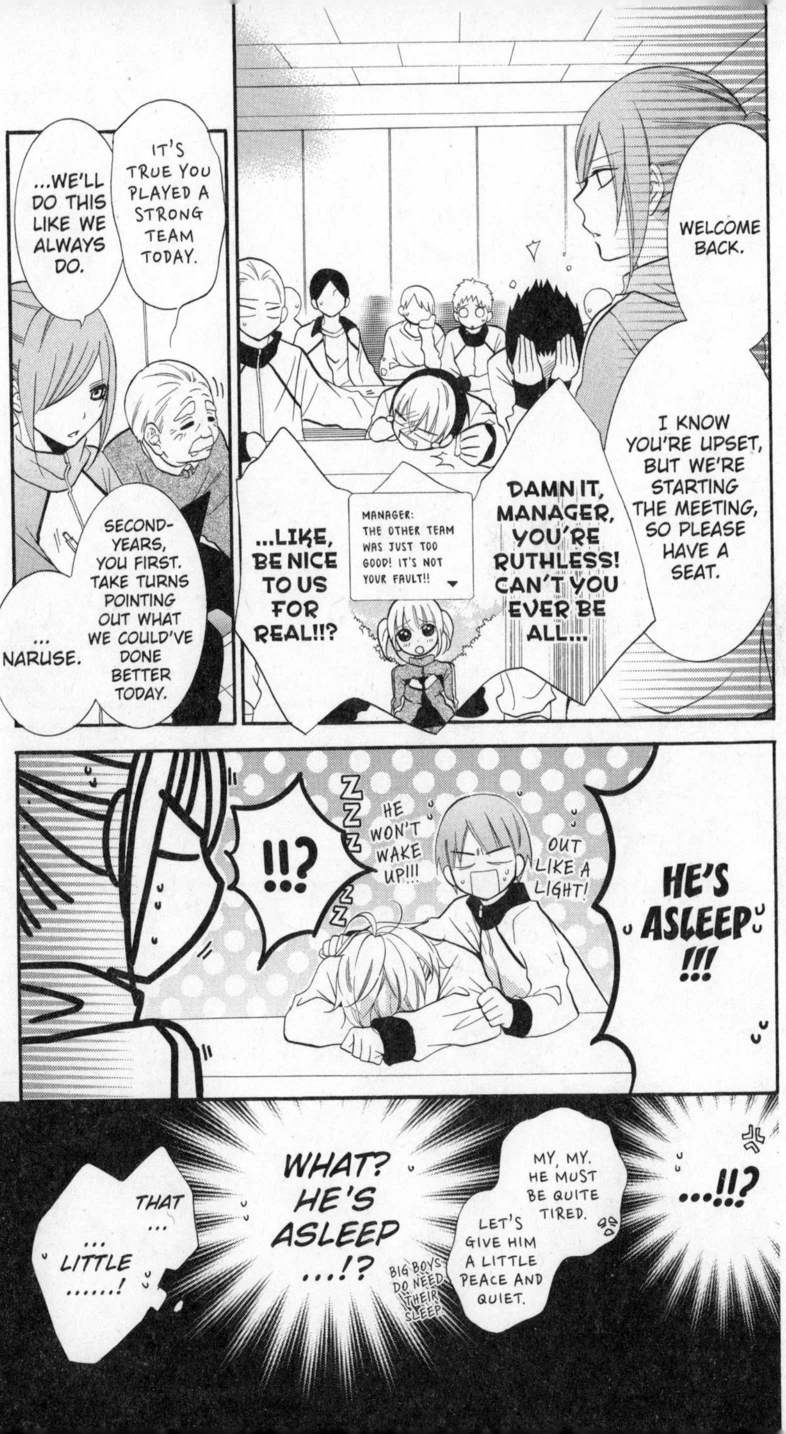

WELCOME BACK.
I KNOW YOU'RE UPSET, BUT WE'RE STARTING THE MEETING, SO PLEASE HAVE A SEAT.
DAMN IT, MANAGER, YOU'RE RUTHLESS! CAN'T YOU EVER BE ALL...
MANAGER: THE OTHER TEAM WAS JUST TOO GOOD! IT'S NOT YOUR FAULT!!
...LIKE, BE NICE TO US FOR REAL!!?
IT'S TRUE YOU PLAYED A STRONG TEAM TODAY.
...WE'LL DO THIS LIKE WE ALWAYS DO.
SECOND-YEARS, YOU FIRST. TAKE TURNS POINTING OUT WHAT WE COULD'VE DONE BETTER TODAY.
... NARUSE.
HE'S ASLEEP!!!
OUT LIKE A LIGHT!
HE WON'T WAKE UP!!!
ZZZ
ZZ
!!?
...!!?
MY, MY. HE MUST BE QUITE TIRED.
LET'S GIVE HIM A LITTLE PEACE AND QUIET.
BIG BOYS DO NEED THEIR SLEEP.
WHAT? HE'S ASLEEP ...!?
THAT ... ... LITTLE ......!

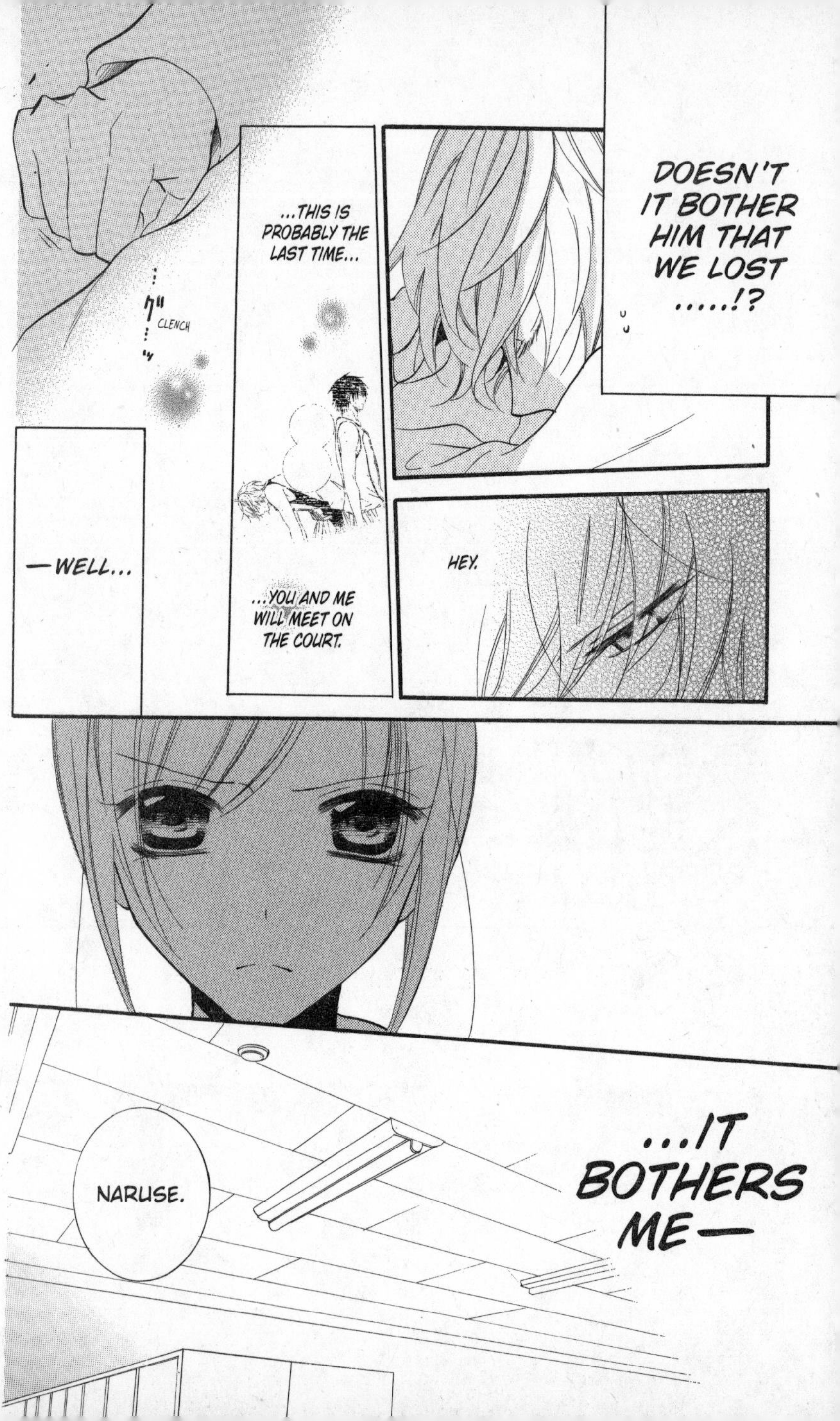
DOESN'T IT BOTHER HIM THAT WE LOST .....!?
HEY.
...THIS IS PROBABLY THE LAST TIME...
...YOU AND ME WILL MEET ON THE COURT.
CLENCH
—WELL...
...IT BOTHERS ME—
NARUSE.

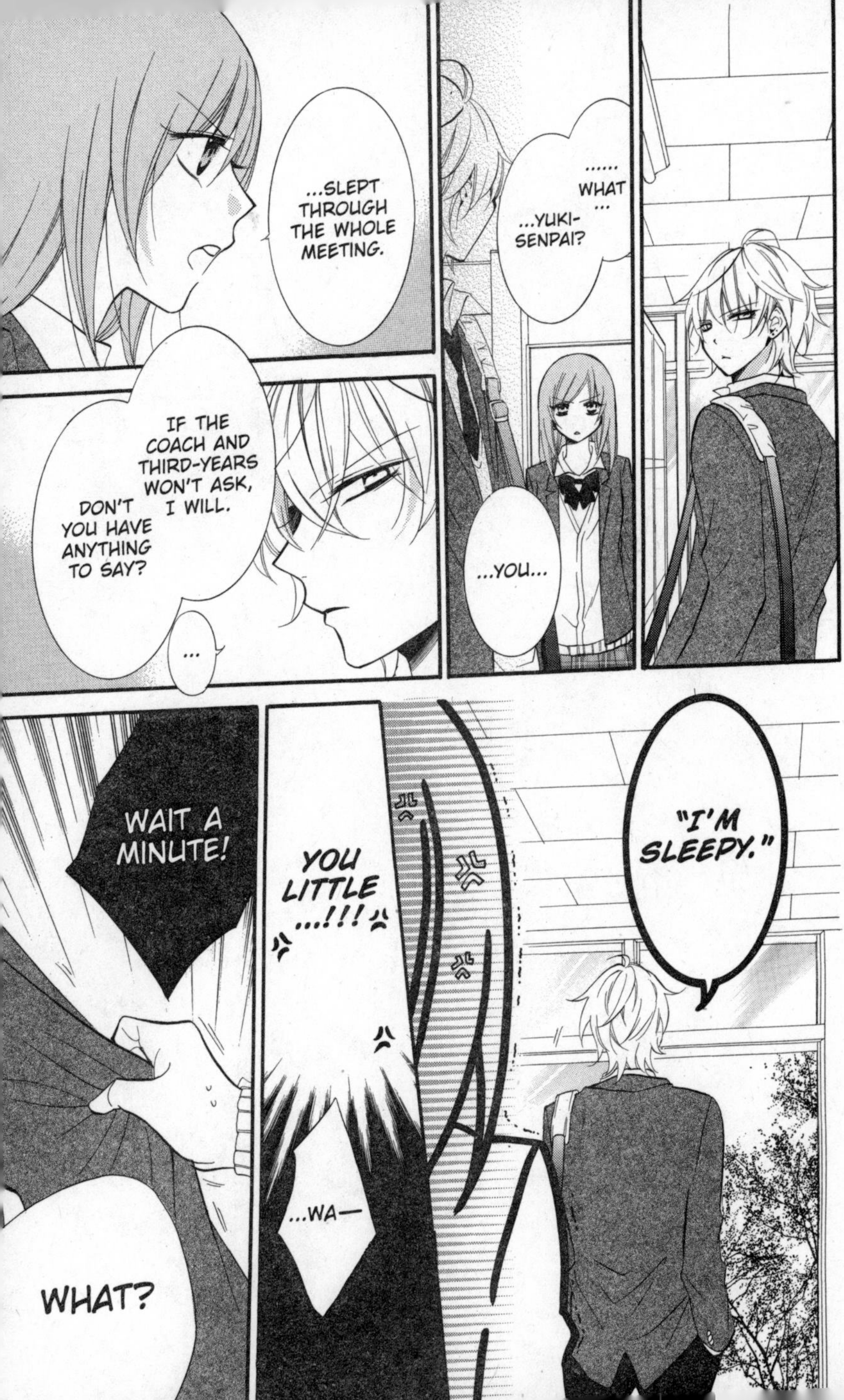
......WHAT... ...YUKI-SENPAI?
...YOU...
...SLEPT THROUGH THE WHOLE MEETING.
IF THE COACH AND THIRD-YEARS WON'T ASK, I WILL.
DON'T YOU HAVE ANYTHING TO SAY?
...
"I'M SLEEPY."
YOU LITTLE ...!!!
...WA—
WAIT A MINUTE!
WHAT?

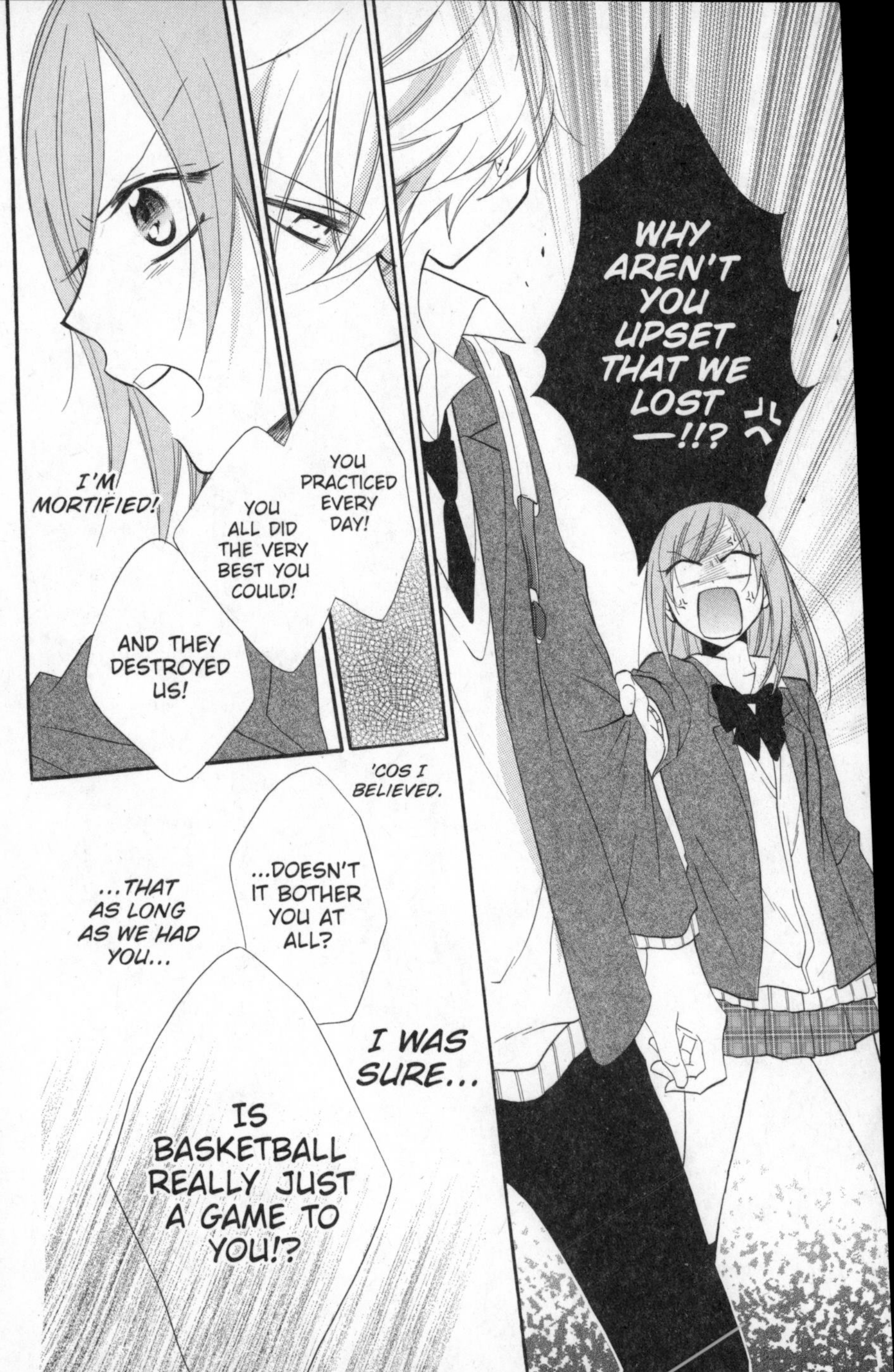
WHY AREN'T YOU UPSET THAT WE LOST—!!?
YOU PRACTICED EVERY DAY!
YOU ALL DID THE VERY BEST YOU COULD!
I'M MORTIFIED!
AND THEY DESTROYED US!
'COS I BELIEVED.
...DOESN'T IT BOTHER YOU AT ALL?
...THAT AS LONG AS WE HAD YOU...
I WAS SURE...
IS BASKETBALL REALLY JUST A GAME TO YOU!?

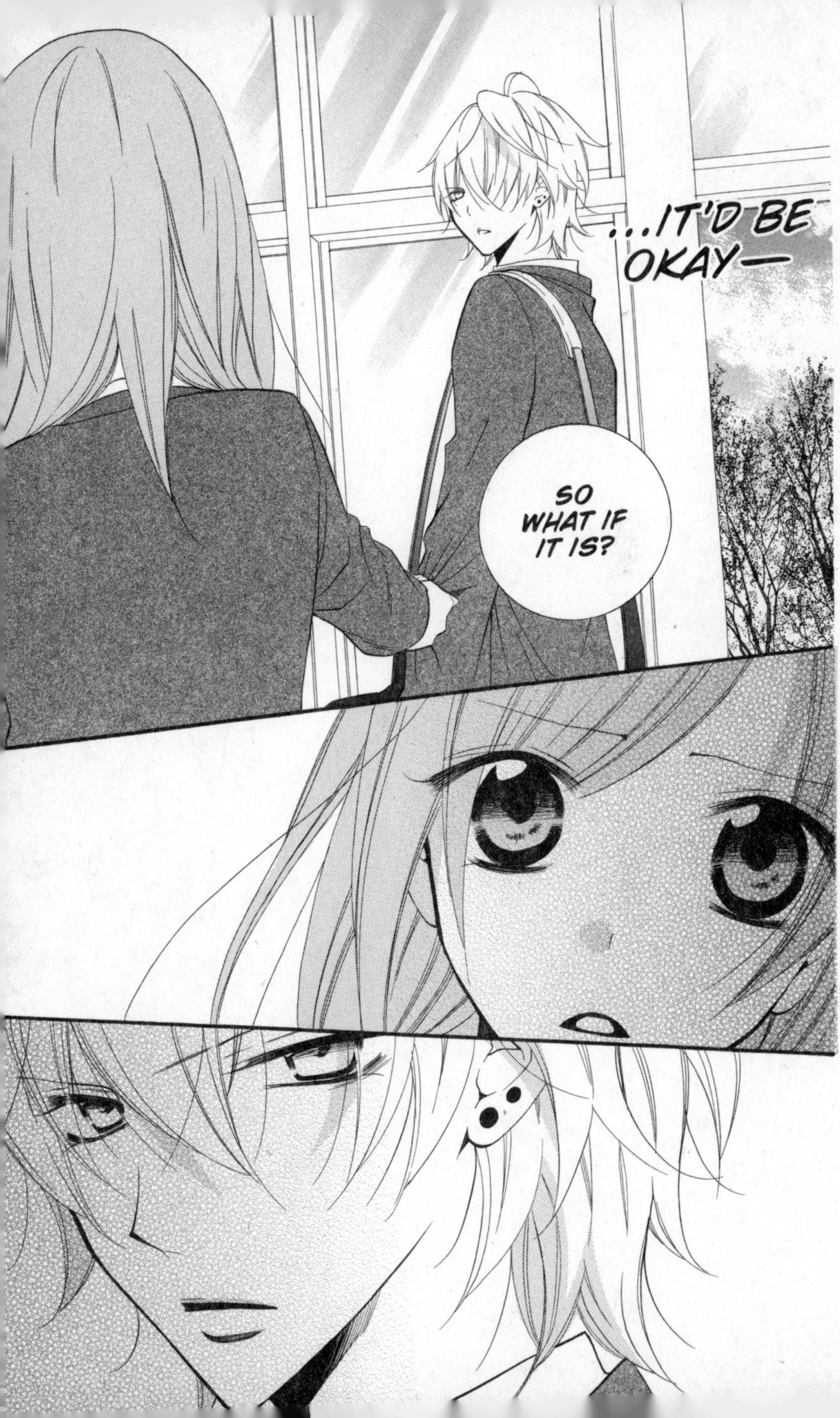
...IT'D BE OKAY—
SO WHAT IF IT IS?

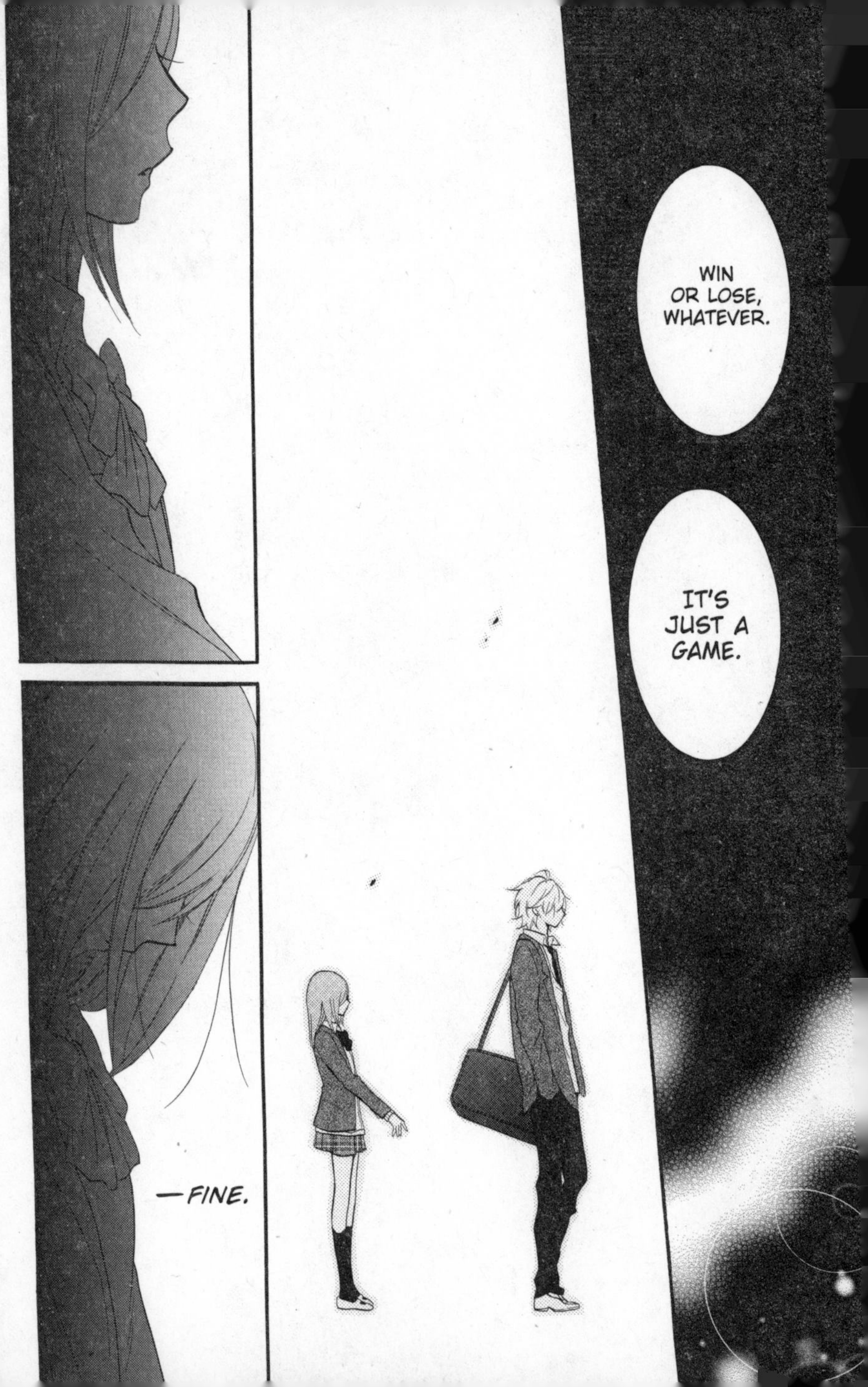
WIN OR LOSE, WHATEVER.
IT'S JUST A GAME.
—FINE.

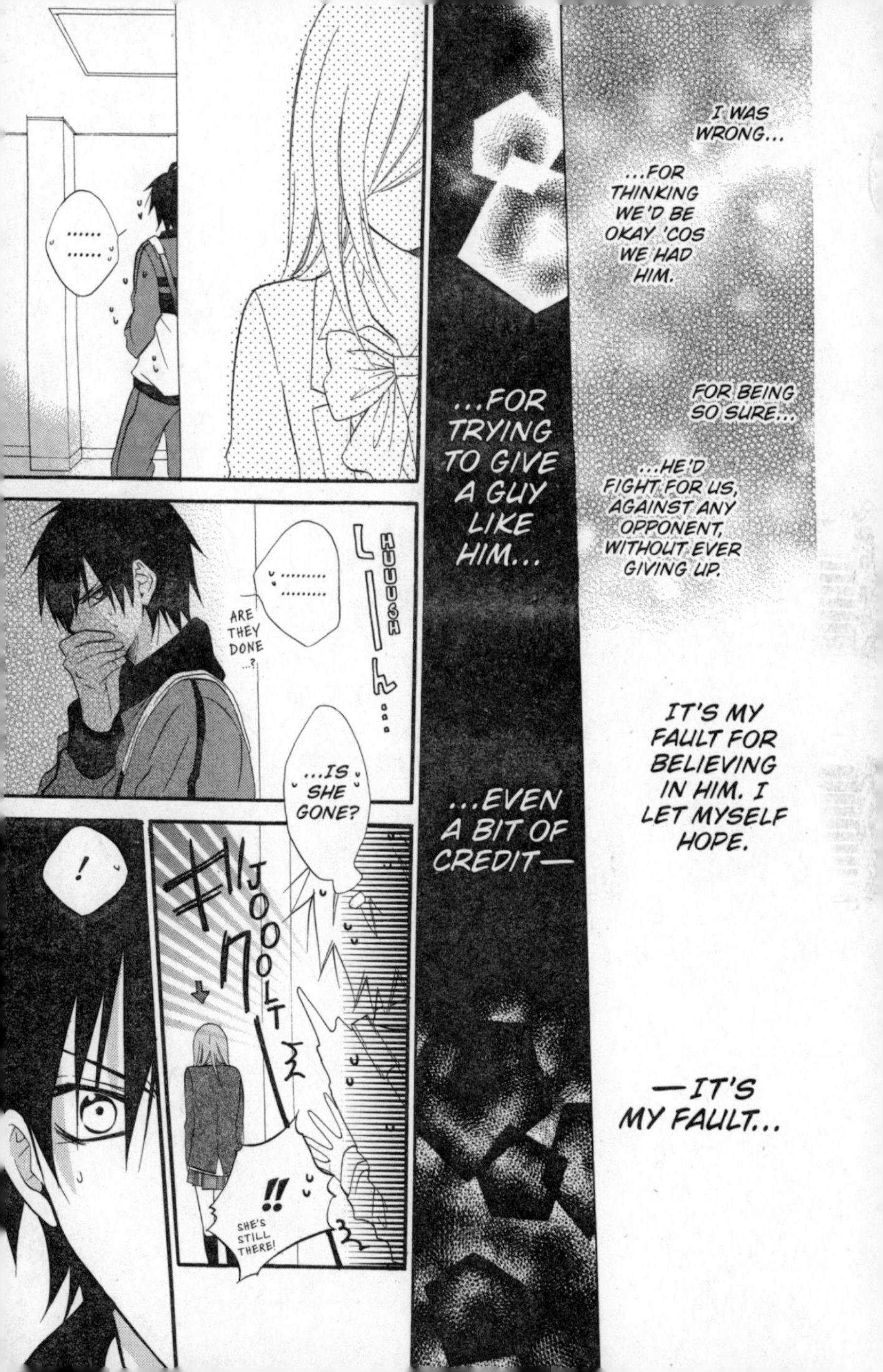
I WAS WRONG...
...FOR THINKING WE'D BE OKAY 'COS WE HAD HIM.
FOR BEING SO SURE...
...FOR TRYING TO GIVE A GUY LIKE HIM...
...HE'D FIGHT FOR US, AGAINST ANY OPPONENT, WITHOUT EVER GIVING UP.
IT'S MY FAULT FOR BELIEVING IN HIM. I LET MYSELF HOPE.
...EVEN A BIT OF CREDIT—
—IT'S MY FAULT...
......
......
HUUUSH
......
......
ARE THEY DONE ...?
...IS SHE GONE?
JOOOLT
!!
SHE'S STILL THERE!
!

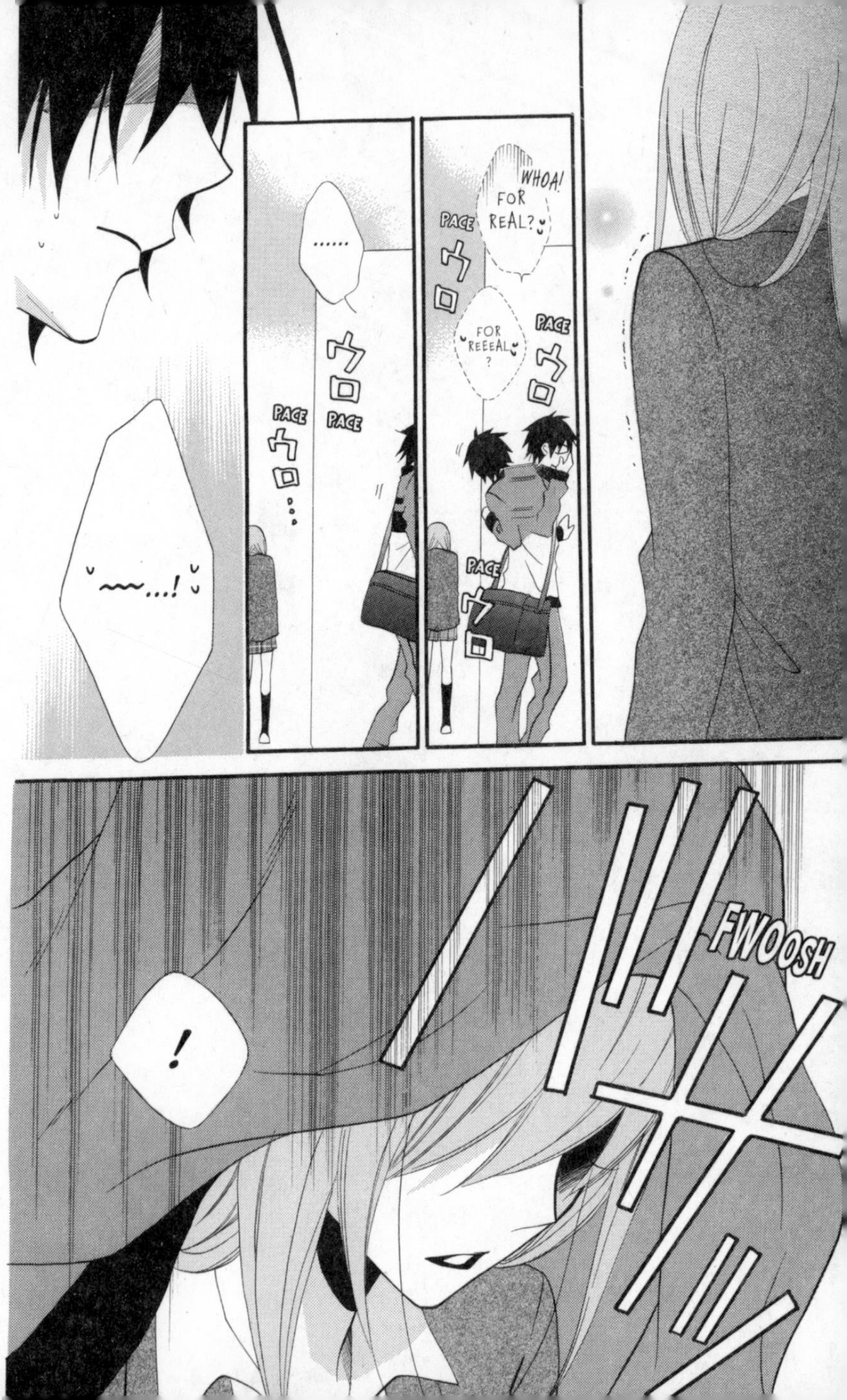
WHOA! FOR REAL?
PACE ウロ
PACE ウロ
FOR REEEAL?
PACE ウロ
......
ウロ PACE
PACE ウロ...
~~...!
FWOOSH
!

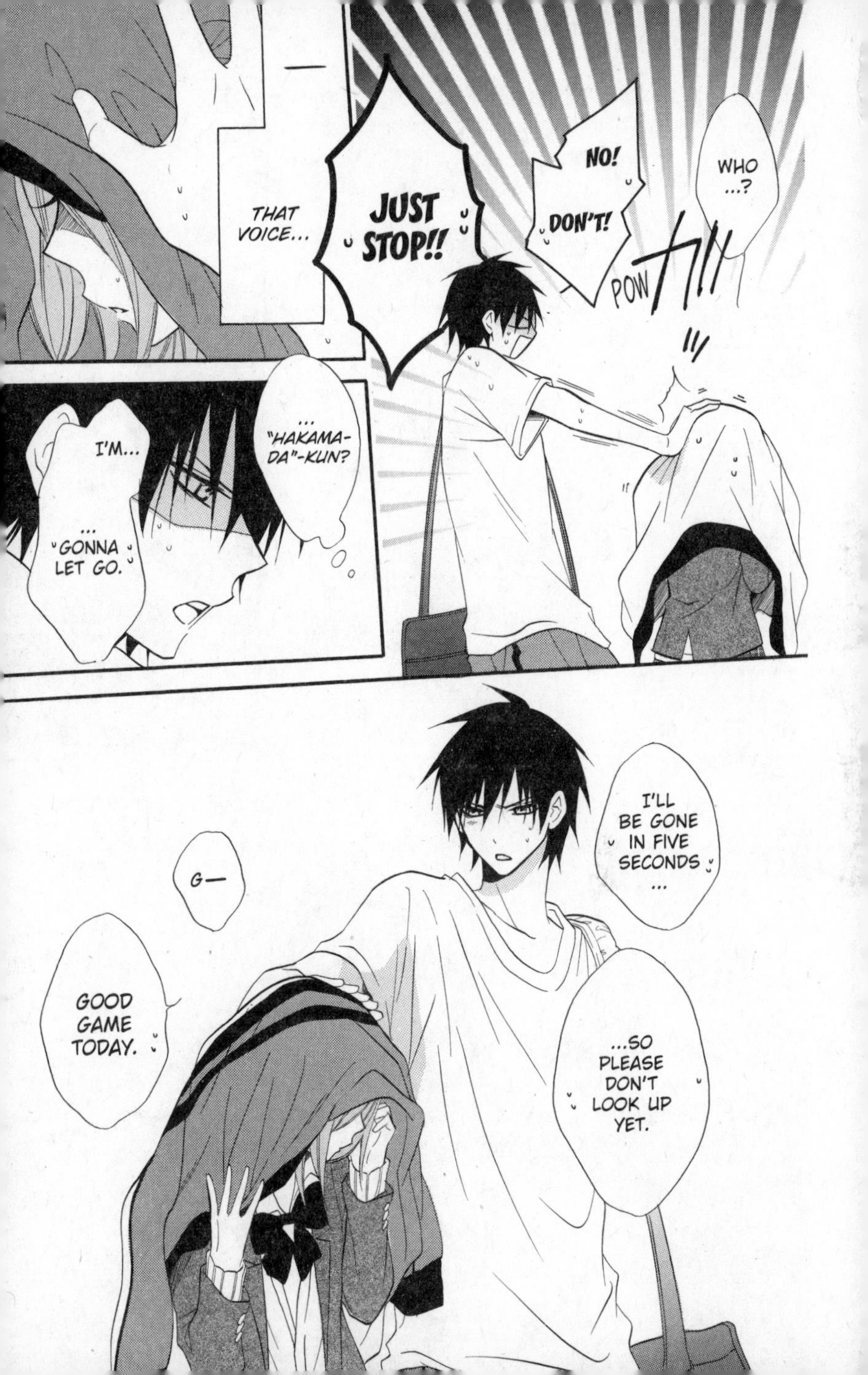
WHO ...?
NO! DON'T!
JUST STOP!!
POW
THAT VOICE...
—
... "HAKAMADA"-KUN?
I'M... ...GONNA LET GO.
I'LL BE GONE IN FIVE SECONDS ...
G—
...SO PLEASE DON'T LOOK UP YET.
GOOD GAME TODAY.

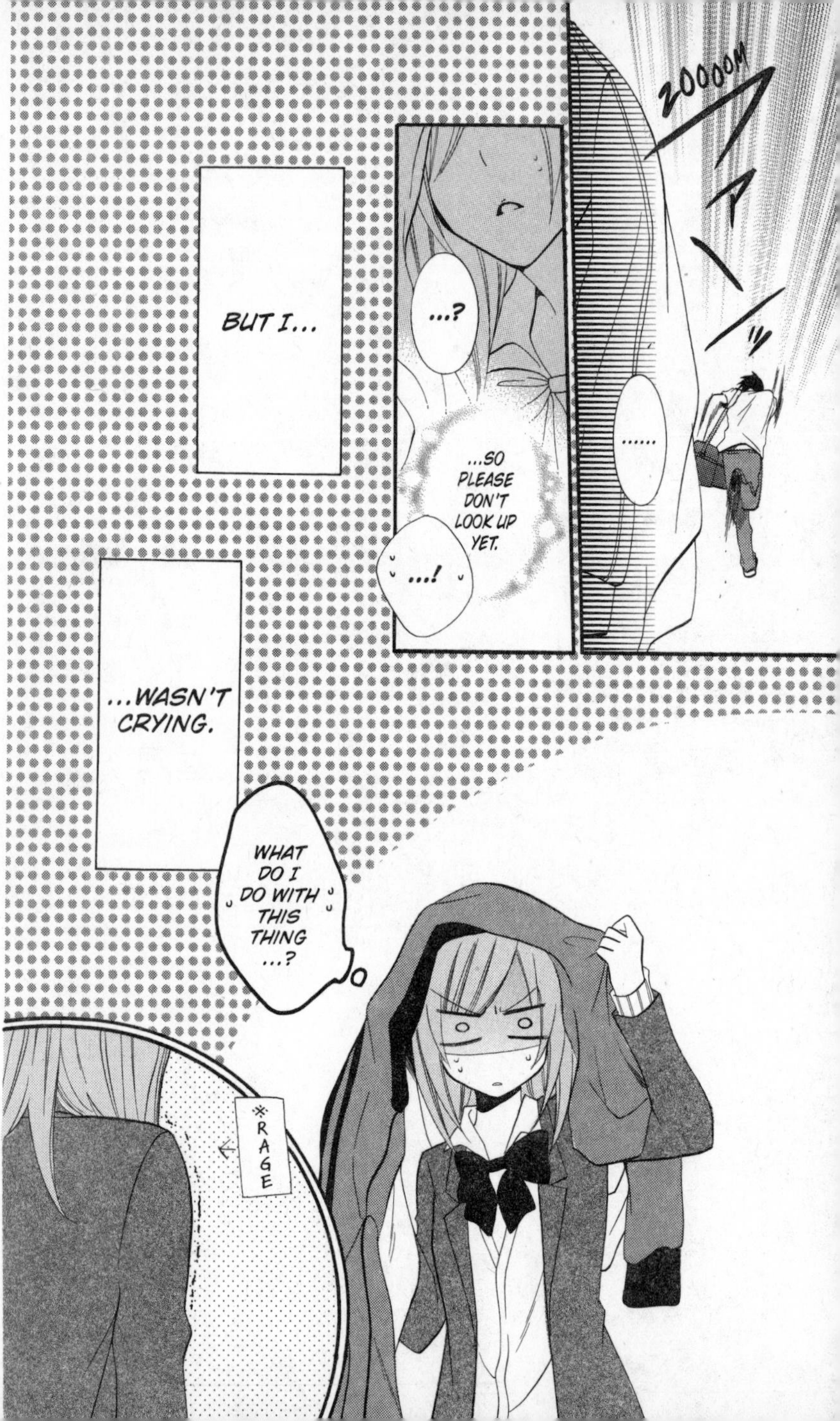
ZOOOOM
......
...?
...SO PLEASE DON'T LOOK UP YET.
...!
BUT I...
...WASN'T CRYING.
WHAT DO I DO WITH THIS THING ...?
※RAGE

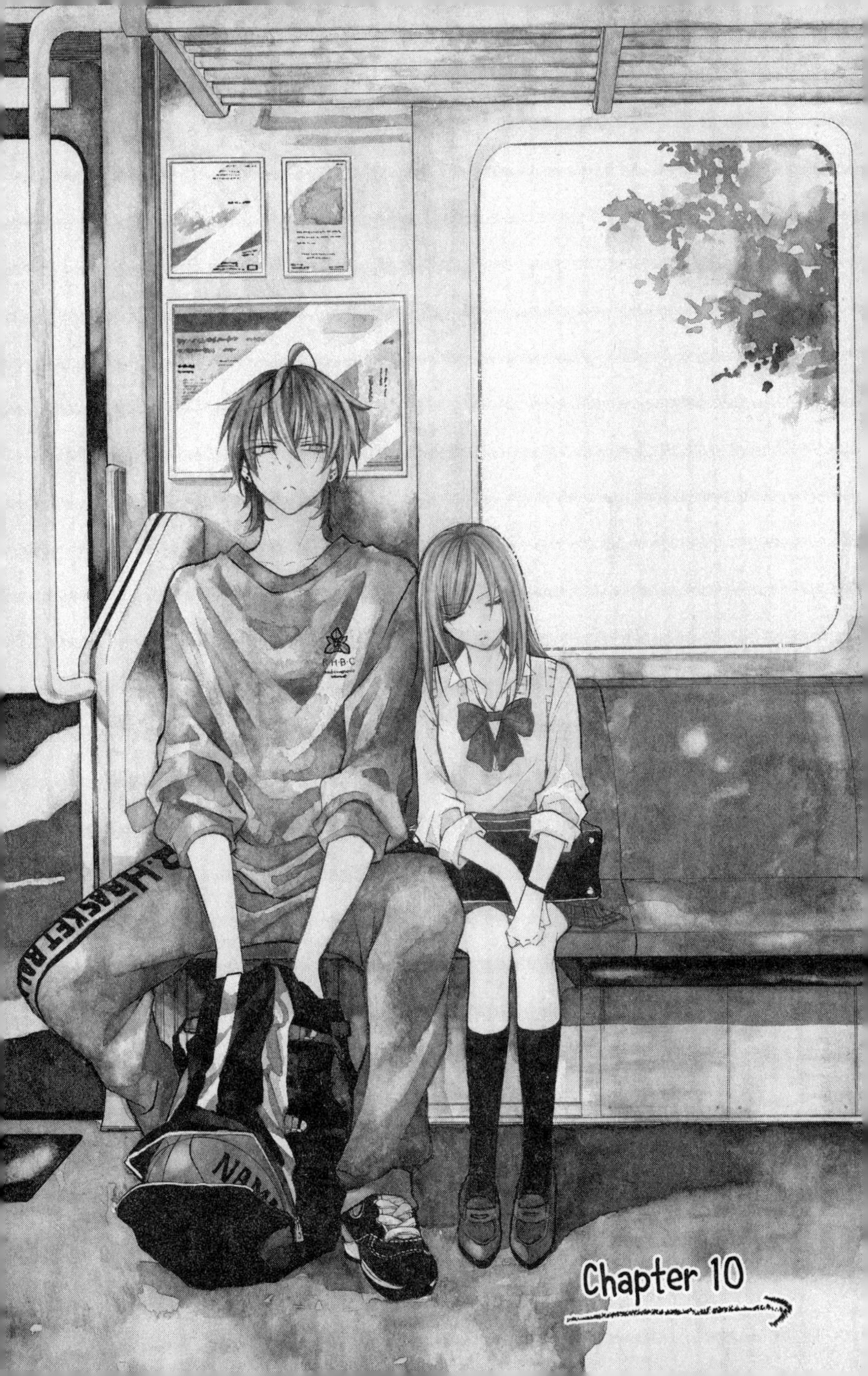
Chapter 10

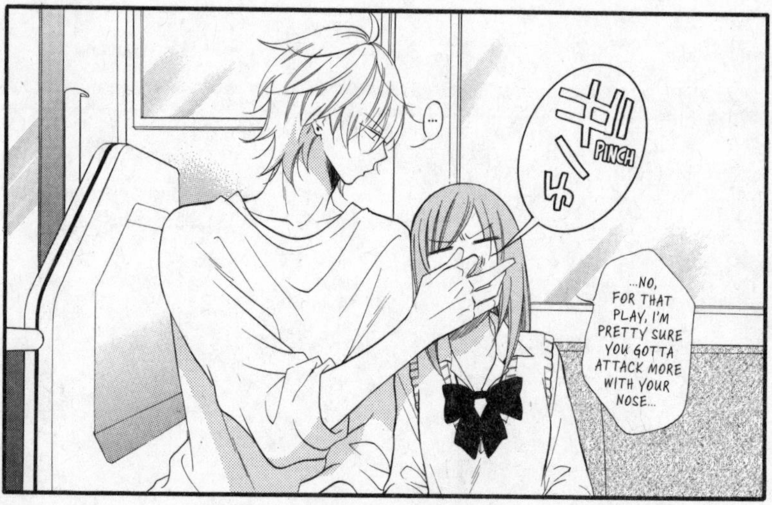

PINCH
...
...NO, FOR THAT PLAY, I'M PRETTY SURE YOU GOTTA ATTACK MORE WITH YOUR NOSE...

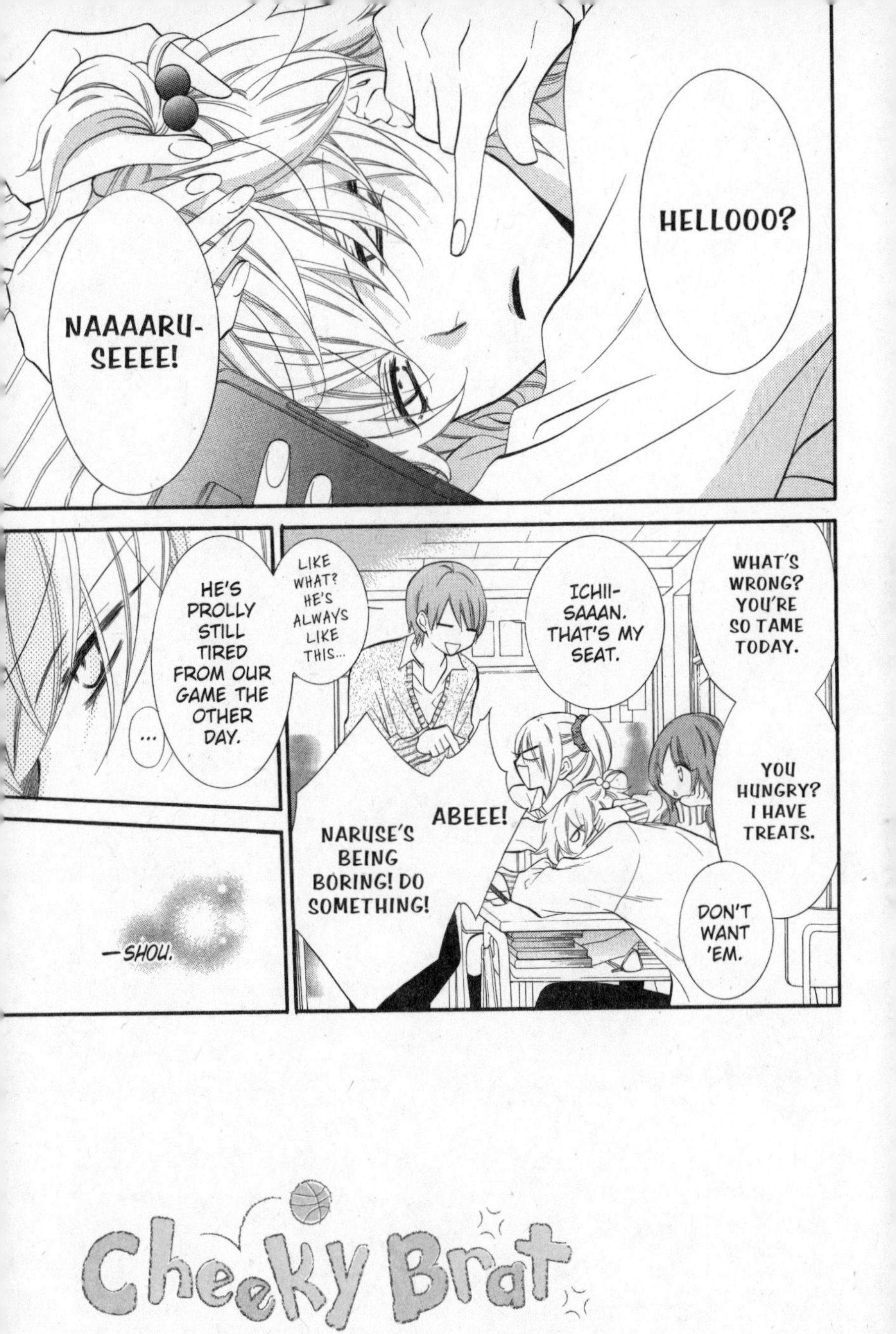
HELLOOO?
NAAAARU-SEEEE!
WHAT'S WRONG? YOU'RE SO TAME TODAY.
ICHII-SAAAN. THAT'S MY SEAT.
YOU HUNGRY? I HAVE TREATS.
LIKE WHAT? HE'S ALWAYS LIKE THIS...
DON'T WANT 'EM.
ABEEE!
NARUSE'S BEING BORING! DO SOMETHING!
HE'S PROLLY STILL TIRED FROM OUR GAME THE OTHER DAY.
...
—SHOU.
Cheeky Brat

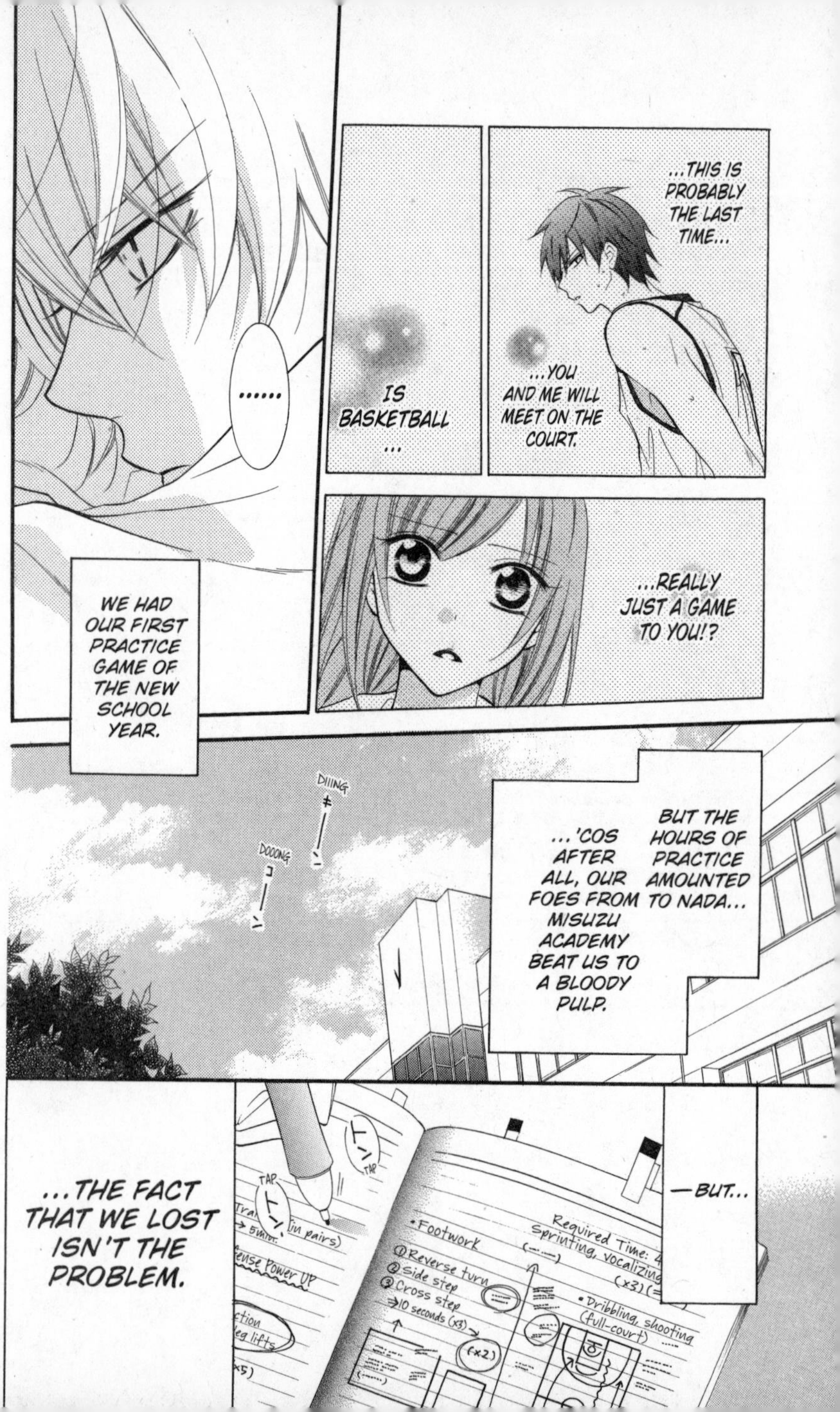
...THIS IS PROBABLY THE LAST TIME...
...YOU AND ME WILL MEET ON THE COURT.
IS BASKETBALL ...
...REALLY JUST A GAME TO YOU!?
......
WE HAD OUR FIRST PRACTICE GAME OF THE NEW SCHOOL YEAR.
DIIING
DOOONG
BUT THE HOURS OF PRACTICE AMOUNTED TO NADA...
...'COS AFTER ALL, OUR FOES FROM MISUZU ACADEMY BEAT US TO A BLOODY PULP.
—BUT...
TAP
TAP
•Footwork
Required Time:
Sprinting, vocalizing
(x3)
①Reverse turn
②Side step
③Cross step
→10 seconds (x3)
•Dribbling, shooting (full-court)
(x2)
(in pairs)
...THE FACT THAT WE LOST ISN'T THE PROBLEM.

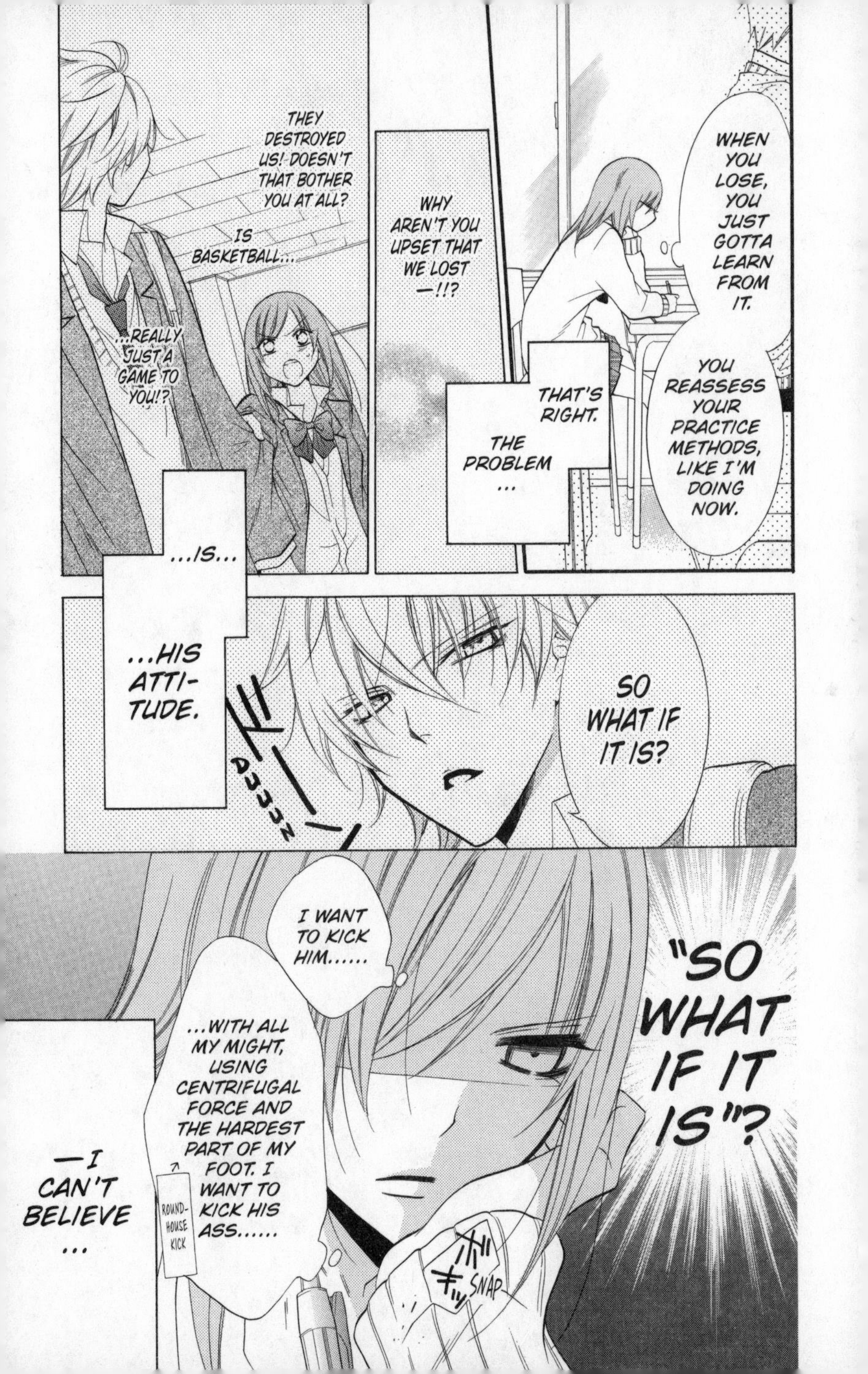
WHEN YOU LOSE, YOU JUST GOTTA LEARN FROM IT.
YOU REASSESS YOUR PRACTICE METHODS, LIKE I'M DOING NOW.
THAT'S RIGHT.
THE PROBLEM ...
WHY AREN'T YOU UPSET THAT WE LOST —!!?
THEY DESTROYED US! DOESN'T THAT BOTHER YOU AT ALL?
IS BASKETBALL...
...REALLY JUST A GAME TO YOU!?
...IS...
SO WHAT IF IT IS?
...HIS ATTI-TUDE.
"SO WHAT IF IT IS"?
I WANT TO KICK HIM......
...WITH ALL MY MIGHT, USING CENTRIFUGAL FORCE AND THE HARDEST PART OF MY FOOT. I WANT TO KICK HIS ASS......
ROUND-HOUSE KICK
SNAP
—I CAN'T BELIEVE ...

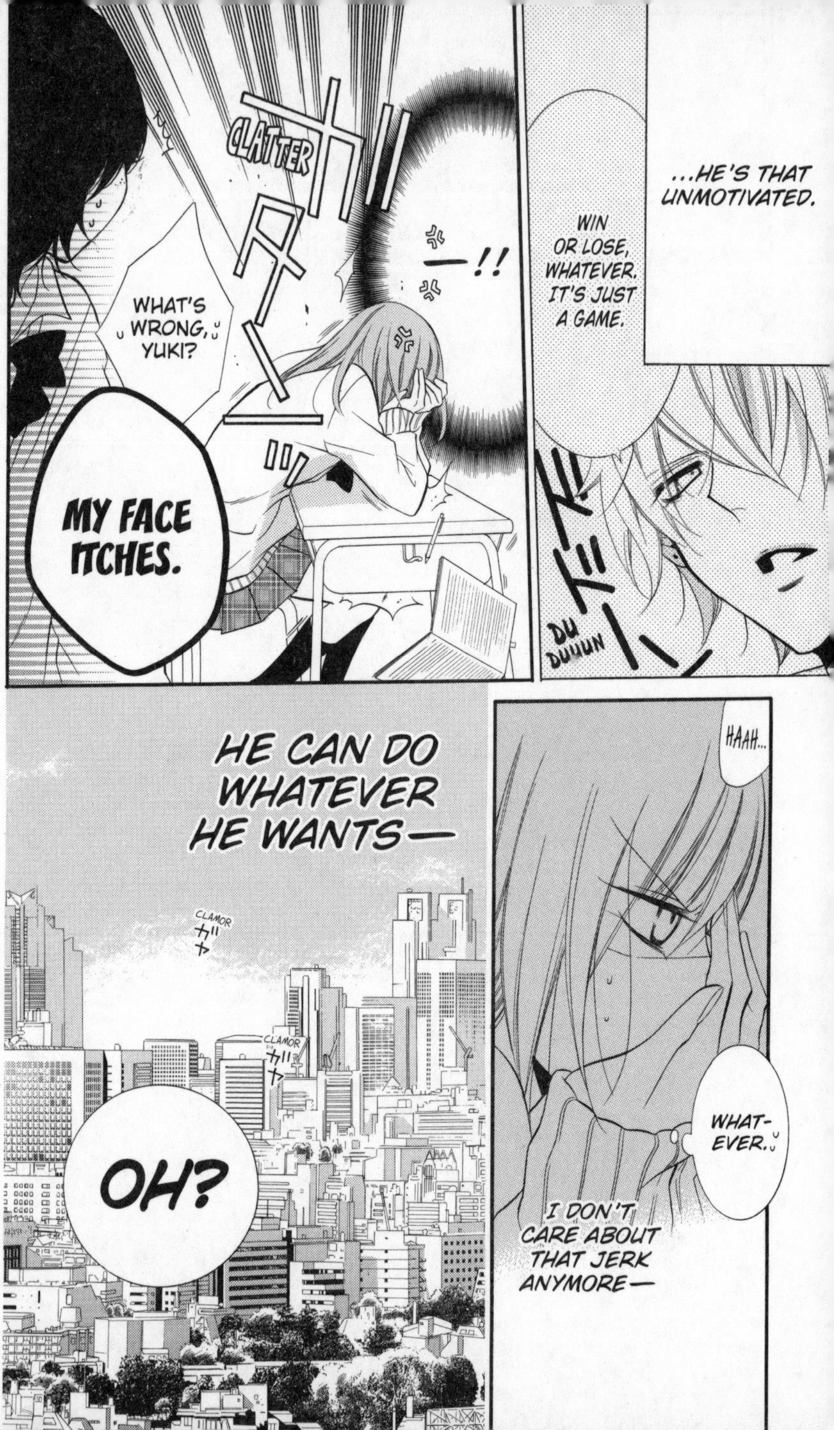
...HE'S THAT UNMOTIVATED.
WIN OR LOSE, WHATEVER. IT'S JUST A GAME.
DU DUUUN
CLATTER
—!!
WHAT'S WRONG, YUKI?
MY FACE ITCHES.
HAAH...
WHAT-EVER.
I DON'T CARE ABOUT THAT JERK ANYMORE—
HE CAN DO WHATEVER HE WANTS—
CLAMOR
CLAMOR
OH?

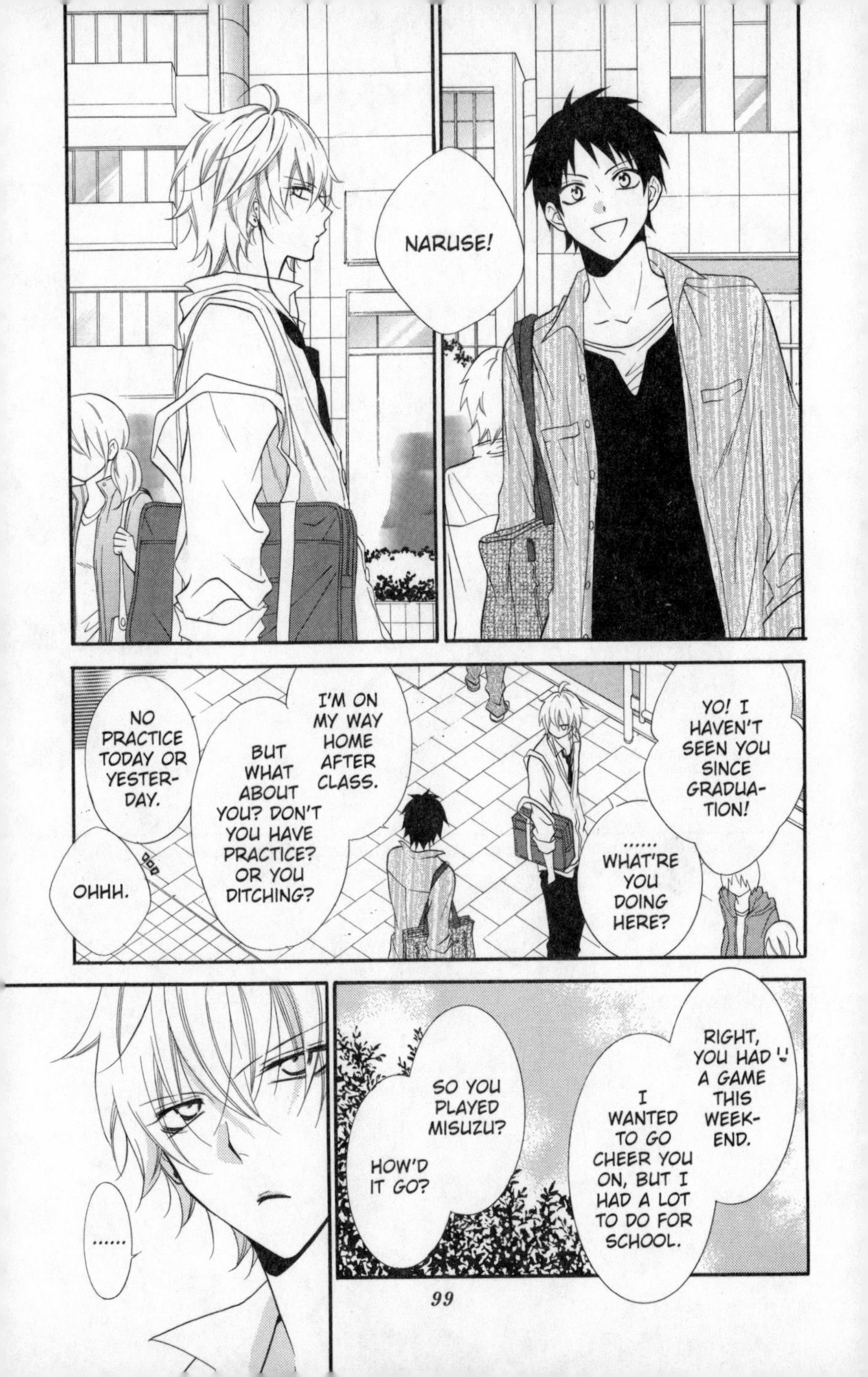
NARUSE!
YO! I HAVEN'T SEEN YOU SINCE GRADUA-TION!
...... WHAT'RE YOU DOING HERE?
I'M ON MY WAY HOME AFTER CLASS.
BUT WHAT ABOUT YOU? DON'T YOU HAVE PRACTICE? OR YOU DITCHING?
NO PRACTICE TODAY OR YESTER-DAY.
OHHH.
RIGHT, YOU HAD A GAME THIS WEEK-END.
I WANTED TO GO CHEER YOU ON, BUT I HAD A LOT TO DO FOR SCHOOL.
SO YOU PLAYED MISUZU?
HOW'D IT GO?
......

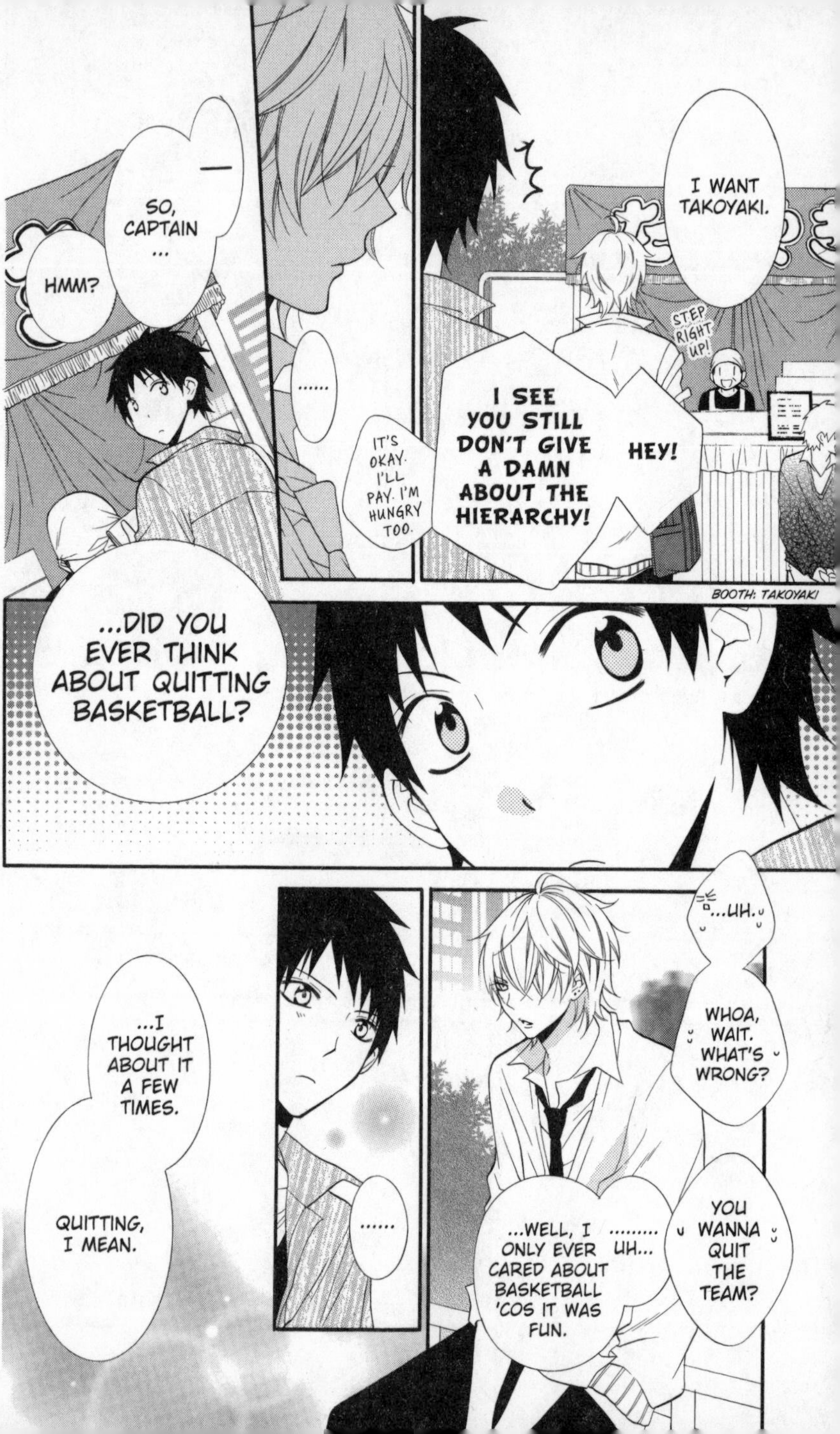
I WANT TAKOYAKI.
STEP RIGHT UP!
HEY!
I SEE YOU STILL DON'T GIVE A DAMN ABOUT THE HIERARCHY!
BOOTH: TAKOYAKI
......
IT'S OKAY. I'LL PAY. I'M HUNGRY TOO.
—
SO, CAPTAIN ...
HMM?
...DID YOU EVER THINK ABOUT QUITTING BASKETBALL?
...UH.
WHOA, WAIT. WHAT'S WRONG?
YOU WANNA QUIT THE TEAM?
.... UH...
...WELL, I ONLY EVER CARED ABOUT BASKETBALL 'COS IT WAS FUN.
......
...I THOUGHT ABOUT IT A FEW TIMES.
QUITTING, I MEAN.

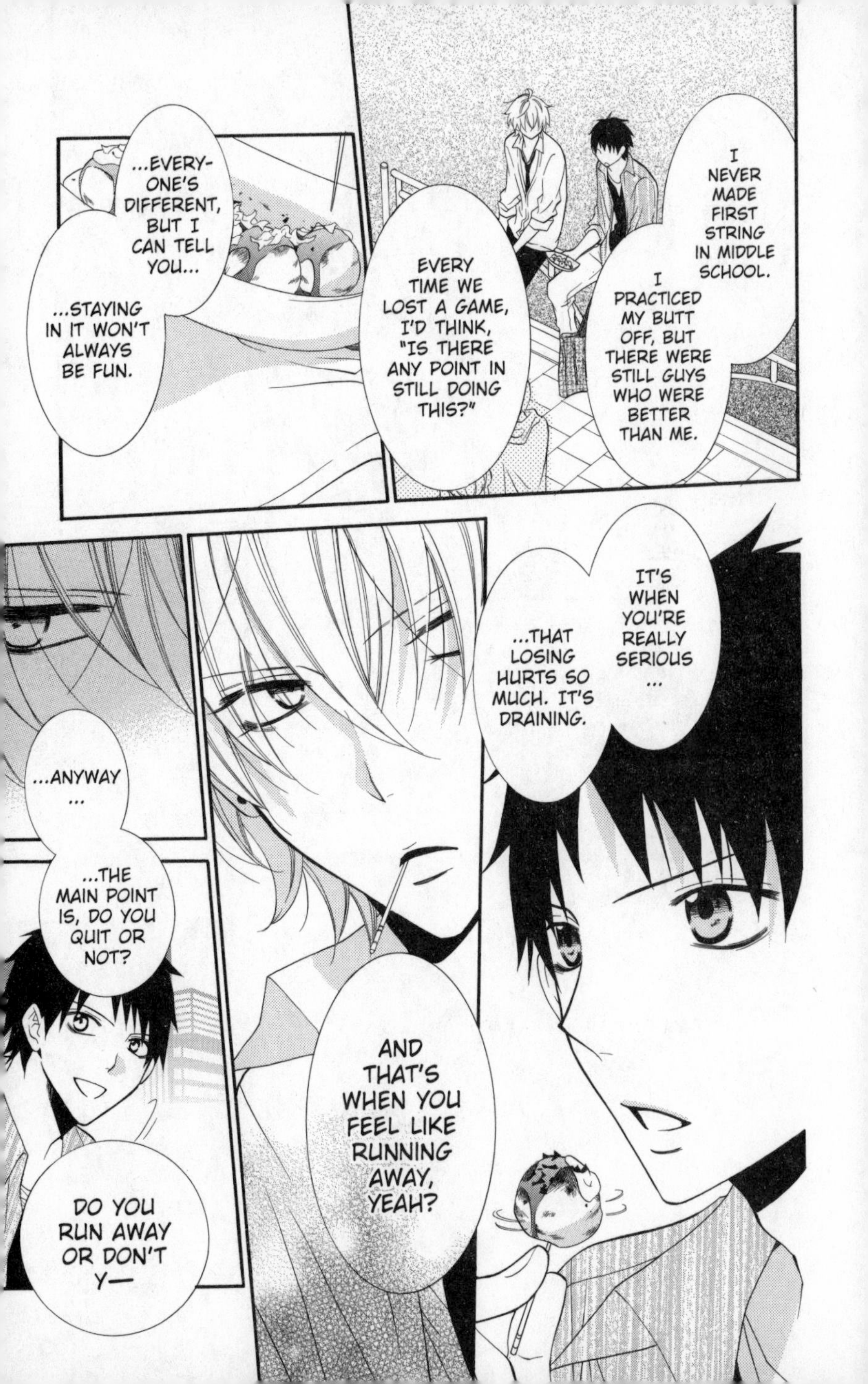
I NEVER MADE FIRST STRING IN MIDDLE SCHOOL.
I PRACTICED MY BUTT OFF, BUT THERE WERE STILL GUYS WHO WERE BETTER THAN ME.
EVERY TIME WE LOST A GAME, I'D THINK, "IS THERE ANY POINT IN STILL DOING THIS?"
...EVERY-ONE'S DIFFERENT, BUT I CAN TELL YOU...
...STAYING IN IT WON'T ALWAYS BE FUN.
IT'S WHEN YOU'RE REALLY SERIOUS...
...THAT LOSING HURTS SO MUCH. IT'S DRAINING.
AND THAT'S WHEN YOU FEEL LIKE RUNNING AWAY, YEAH?
...ANYWAY...
...THE MAIN POINT IS, DO YOU QUIT OR NOT?
DO YOU RUN AWAY OR DON'T Y—

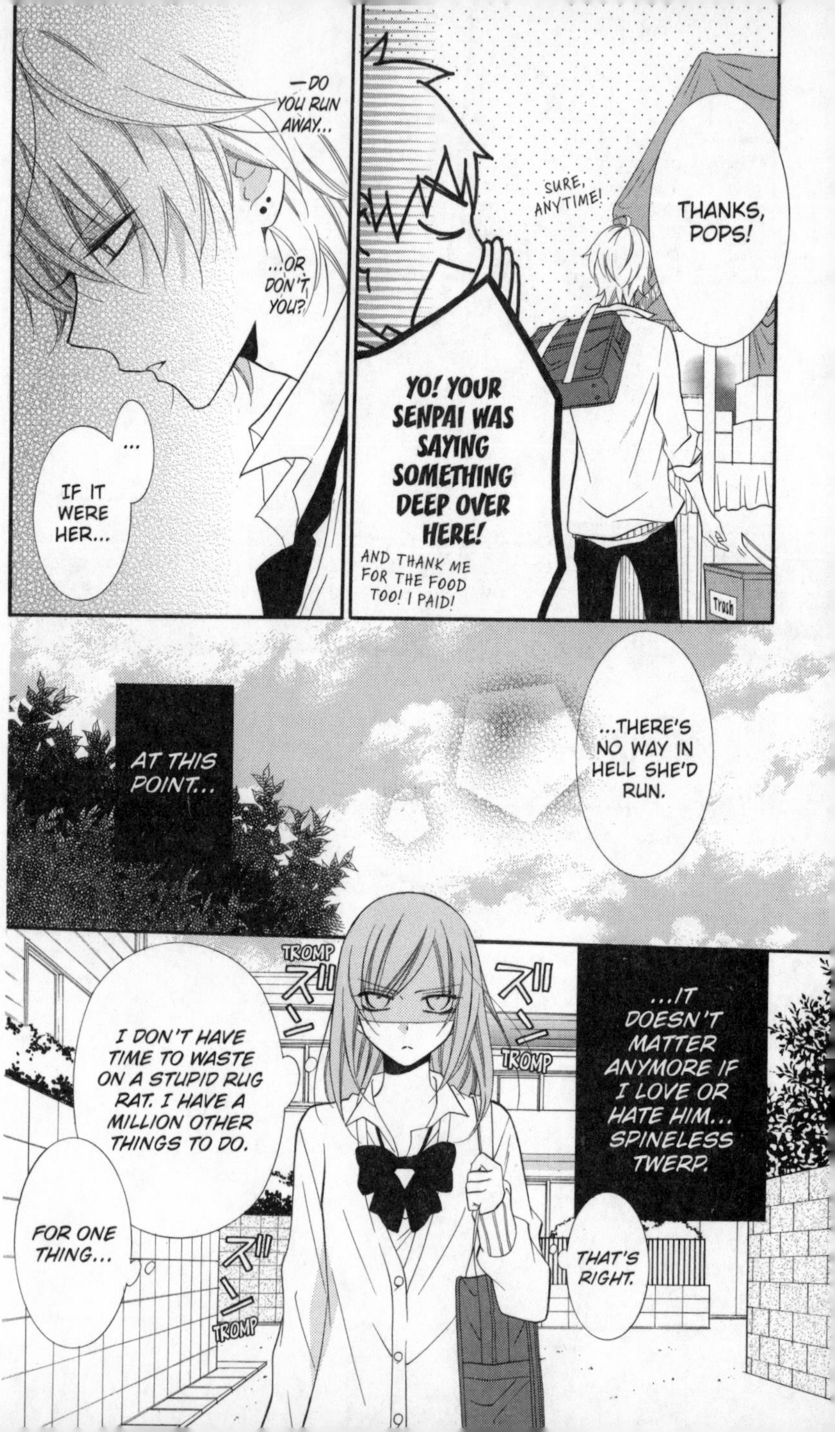
THANKS, POPS!
SURE, ANYTIME!
YO! YOUR SENPAI WAS SAYING SOMETHING DEEP OVER HERE!
AND THANK ME FOR THE FOOD TOO! I PAID!
Trash
—DO YOU RUN AWAY...
...OR DON'T YOU?
...
IF IT WERE HER...
...THERE'S NO WAY IN HELL SHE'D RUN.
AT THIS POINT...
...IT DOESN'T MATTER ANYMORE IF I LOVE OR HATE HIM... SPINELESS TWERP.
TROMP
TROMP
THAT'S RIGHT.
I DON'T HAVE TIME TO WASTE ON A STUPID RUG RAT. I HAVE A MILLION OTHER THINGS TO DO.
FOR ONE THING...
TROMP

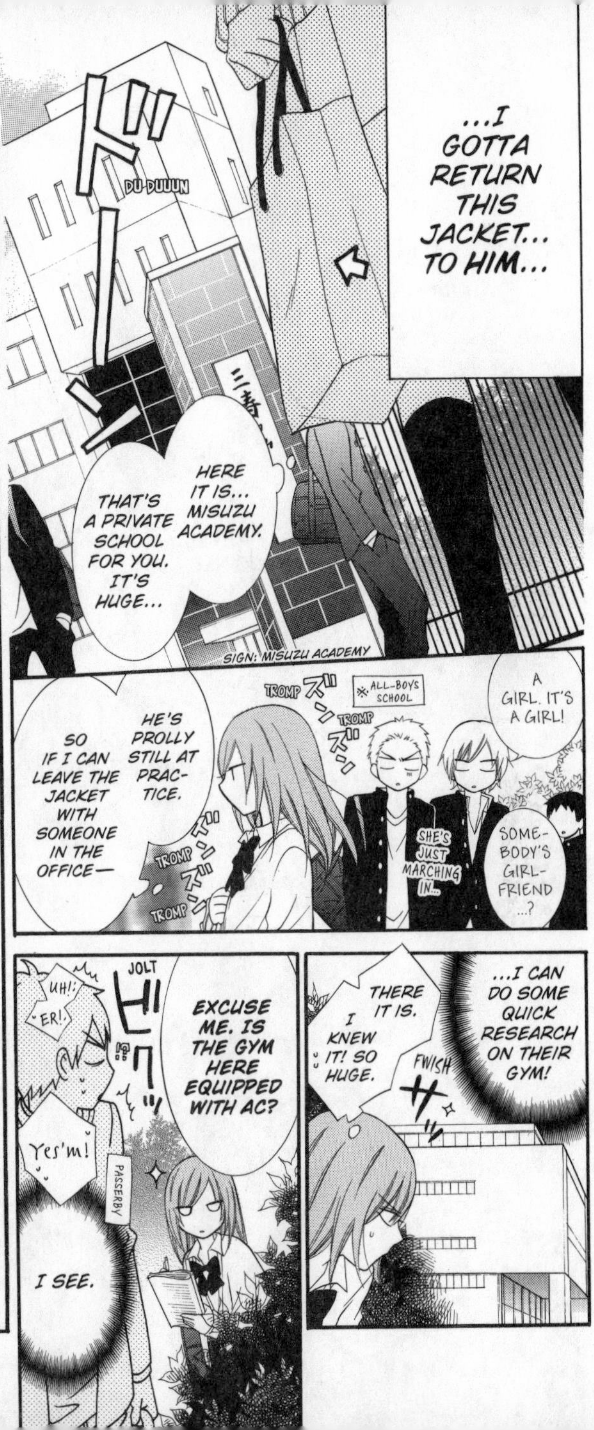
...I GOTTA RETURN THIS JACKET... TO HIM...
DU-DUUUN
HERE IT IS... MISUZU ACADEMY.
THAT'S A PRIVATE SCHOOL FOR YOU. IT'S HUGE...
SIGN: MISUZU ACADEMY
A GIRL. IT'S A GIRL!
SOMEBODY'S GIRLFRIEND ...?
※ALL-BOYS SCHOOL
TROMP
TROMP
SHE'S JUST MARCHING IN...
HE'S PROLLY STILL AT PRACTICE.
SO IF I CAN LEAVE THE JACKET WITH SOMEONE IN THE OFFICE—
TROMP
TROMP
...I CAN DO SOME QUICK RESEARCH ON THEIR GYM!
THERE IT IS.
I KNEW IT! SO HUGE.
FWISH
EXCUSE ME. IS THE GYM HERE EQUIPPED WITH AC?
JOLT
UH!
ER!
Yes'm!
PASSERBY
I SEE.

04

FIELD RESEARCH

I got to watch a basketball tournament that was held in Kanagawa Prefecture.

The game took place in a large gymnasium. I, myself, had never seen a real basketball game so close up before, so I was a bit overwhelmed.

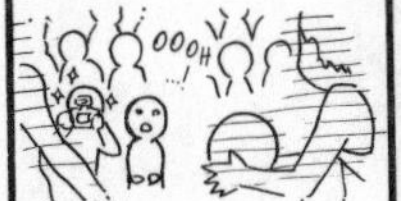
OOOH

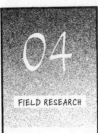

I mean, like, it was all I could do to keep track of the ball, so I only managed to get one picture on my camera. It wouldn't have made much difference if I'd left the camera at home. That's how riveted I was—my heart was pounding out of my chest from start to finish.
The players' passion for the game burned white-hot. So not surprisingly, some of them got injured...but they sat on the bench just long enough to get patched up and went right back out on the court. The fearlessness they exuded as I watched them go was just so... so...so...
It made me think I need to stop whining and claiming the callus on my pen finger will explode the second it gets hard to draw a manuscript....

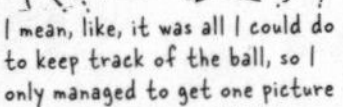
Uh-huh.
Jocks and I will never see eye to eye.

I also considered that maybe I should stop saying stuff like that just because I'm jealous of people who are good at sports. Everyone really was so awesome!! Thank you to everyone who helped me with this research. It was a terribly valuable experience, and I will make good use of it in my manga!!!

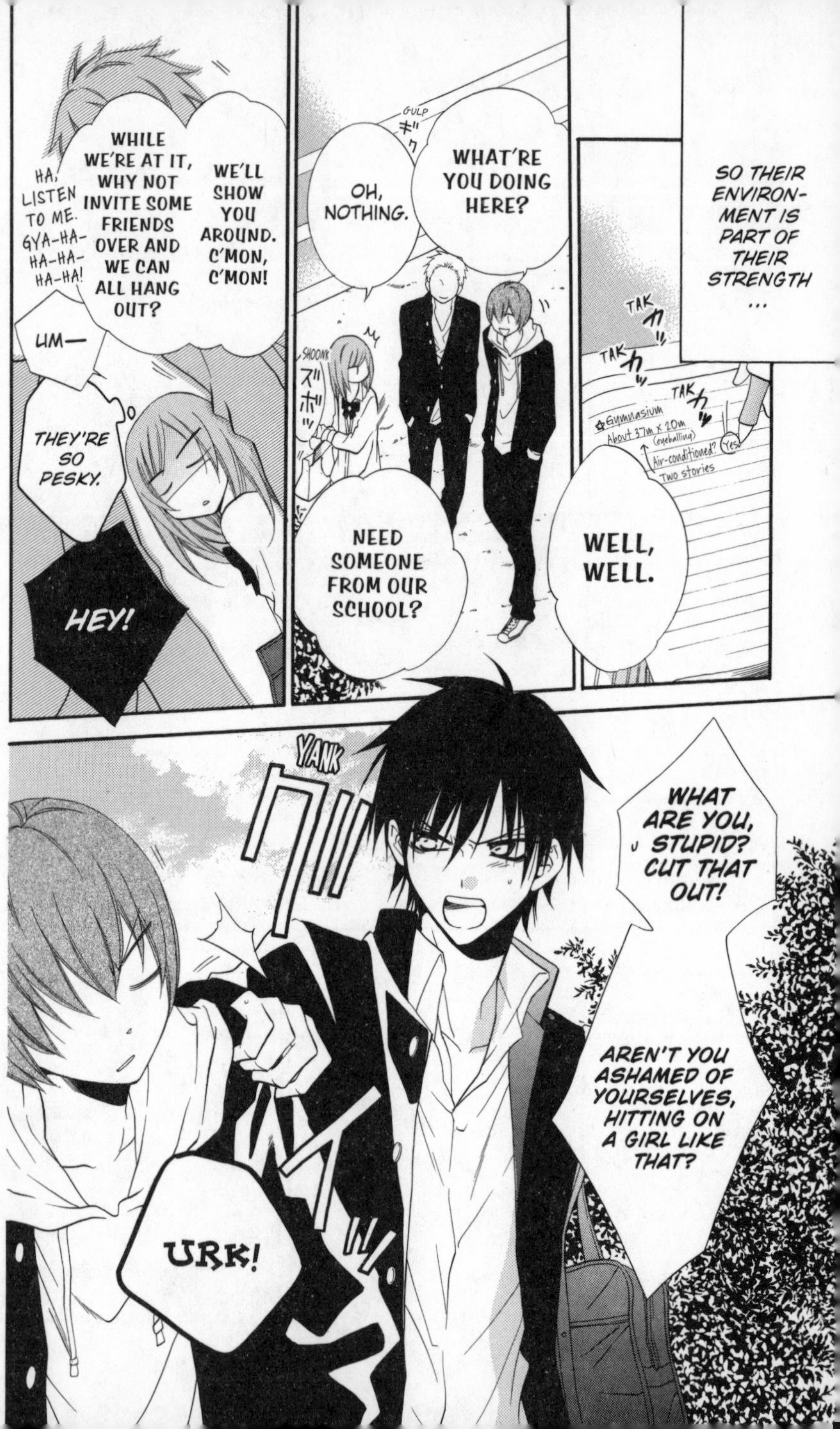
SO THEIR ENVIRONMENT IS PART OF THEIR STRENGTH...
TAK
TAK
TAK
Gymnasium
About 37m x 20m (eyeballing)
Air-conditioned? Yes
Two stories
WELL, WELL.
GULP
WHAT'RE YOU DOING HERE?
OH, NOTHING.
SHOONK
NEED SOMEONE FROM OUR SCHOOL?
WE'LL SHOW YOU AROUND. C'MON, C'MON!
WHILE WE'RE AT IT, WHY NOT INVITE SOME FRIENDS OVER AND WE CAN ALL HANG OUT?
HA, LISTEN TO ME. GYA-HA-HA-HA-HA-HA!
UM—
THEY'RE SO PESKY.
HEY!
WHAT ARE YOU, STUPID? CUT THAT OUT!
AREN'T YOU ASHAMED OF YOURSELVES, HITTING ON A GIRL LIKE THAT?
YANK
URK!

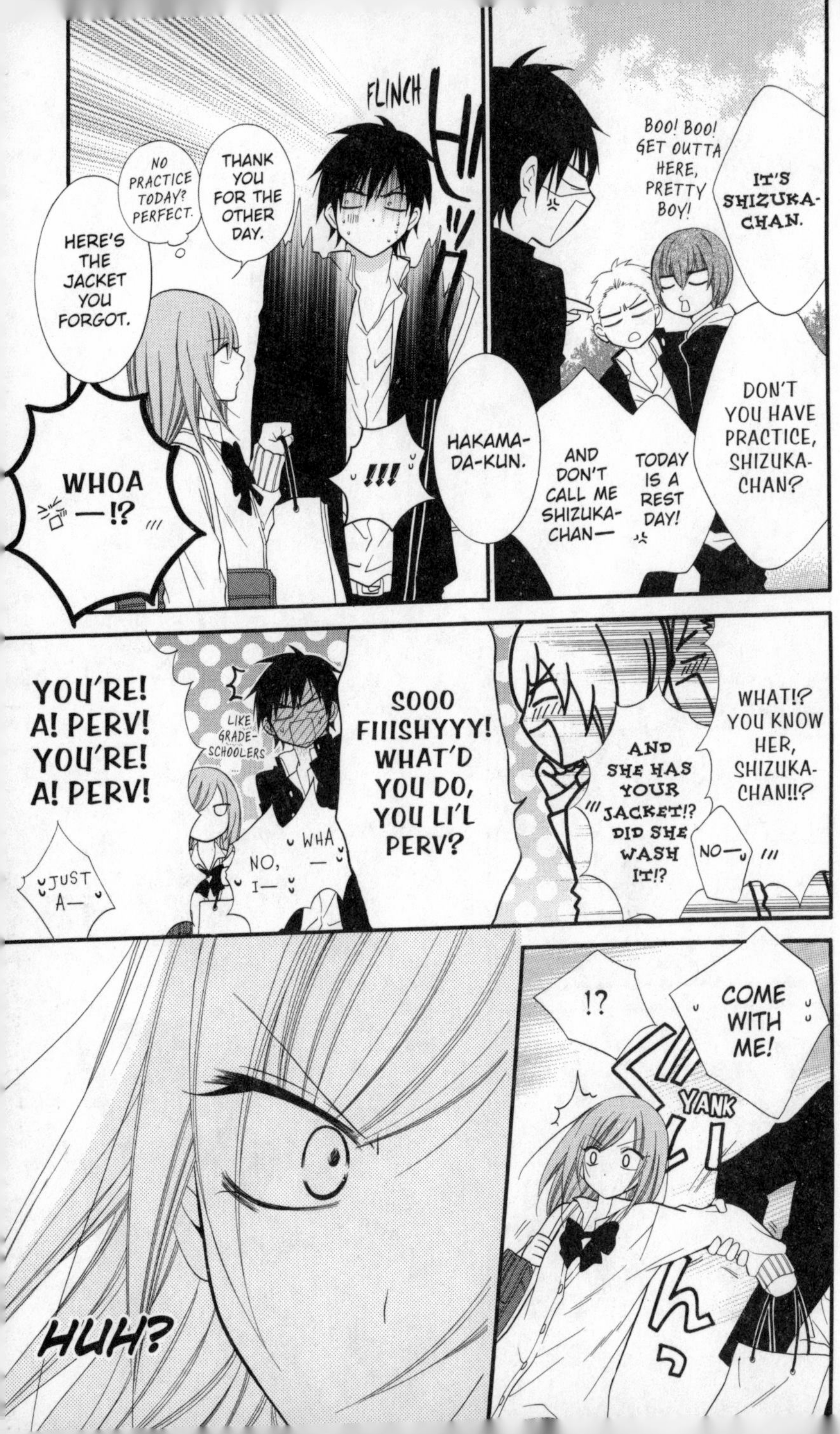
IT'S SHIZUKA-CHAN.
BOO! BOO! GET OUTTA HERE, PRETTY BOY!
DON'T YOU HAVE PRACTICE, SHIZUKA-CHAN?
TODAY IS A REST DAY!
AND DON'T CALL ME SHIZUKA-CHAN—
HAKAMA-DA-KUN.
FLINCH
THANK YOU FOR THE OTHER DAY.
NO PRACTICE TODAY? PERFECT.
HERE'S THE JACKET YOU FORGOT.
!!!
WHOA—!?
WHAT!? YOU KNOW HER, SHIZUKA-CHAN!!?
NO—
AND SHE HAS YOUR JACKET!? DID SHE WASH IT!?
SOOO FIIISHYYY! WHAT'D YOU DO, YOU LI'L PERV?
WHA—
NO, I—
LIKE GRADE-SCHOOLERS...
YOU'RE! A! PERV! YOU'RE! A! PERV!
JUST A—
COME WITH ME!
!?
YANK
HUH?

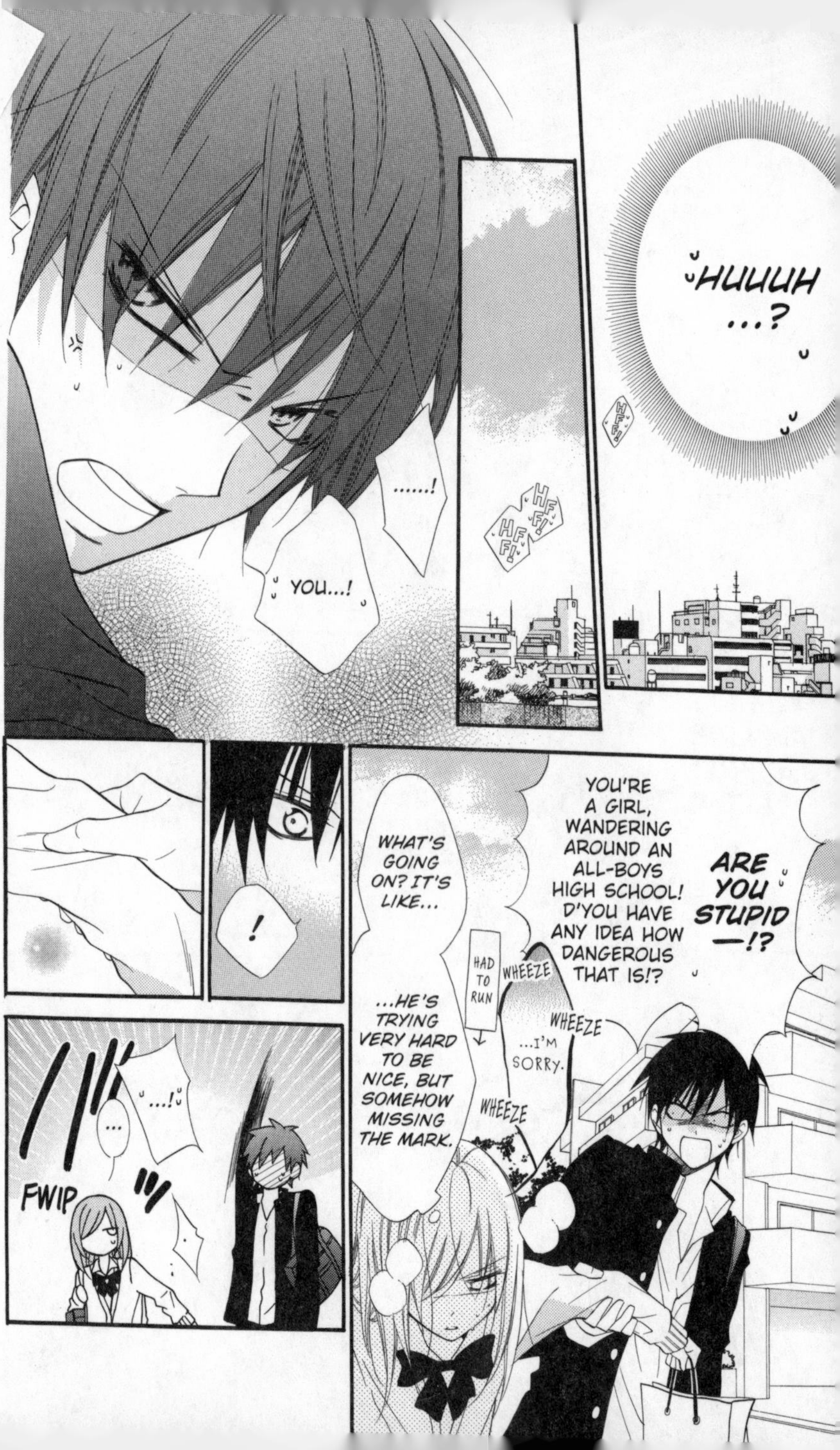
HUUUH ...?
HFF!
HFF!
HFF!
......!
YOU...!
ARE YOU STUPID—!?
YOU'RE A GIRL, WANDERING AROUND AN ALL-BOYS HIGH SCHOOL! D'YOU HAVE ANY IDEA HOW DANGEROUS THAT IS!?
HAD TO RUN
WHEEZE
WHEEZE
...I'M SORRY.
WHEEZE
WHAT'S GOING ON? IT'S LIKE...
...HE'S TRYING VERY HARD TO BE NICE, BUT SOMEHOW MISSING THE MARK.
!
...!
...
FWIP

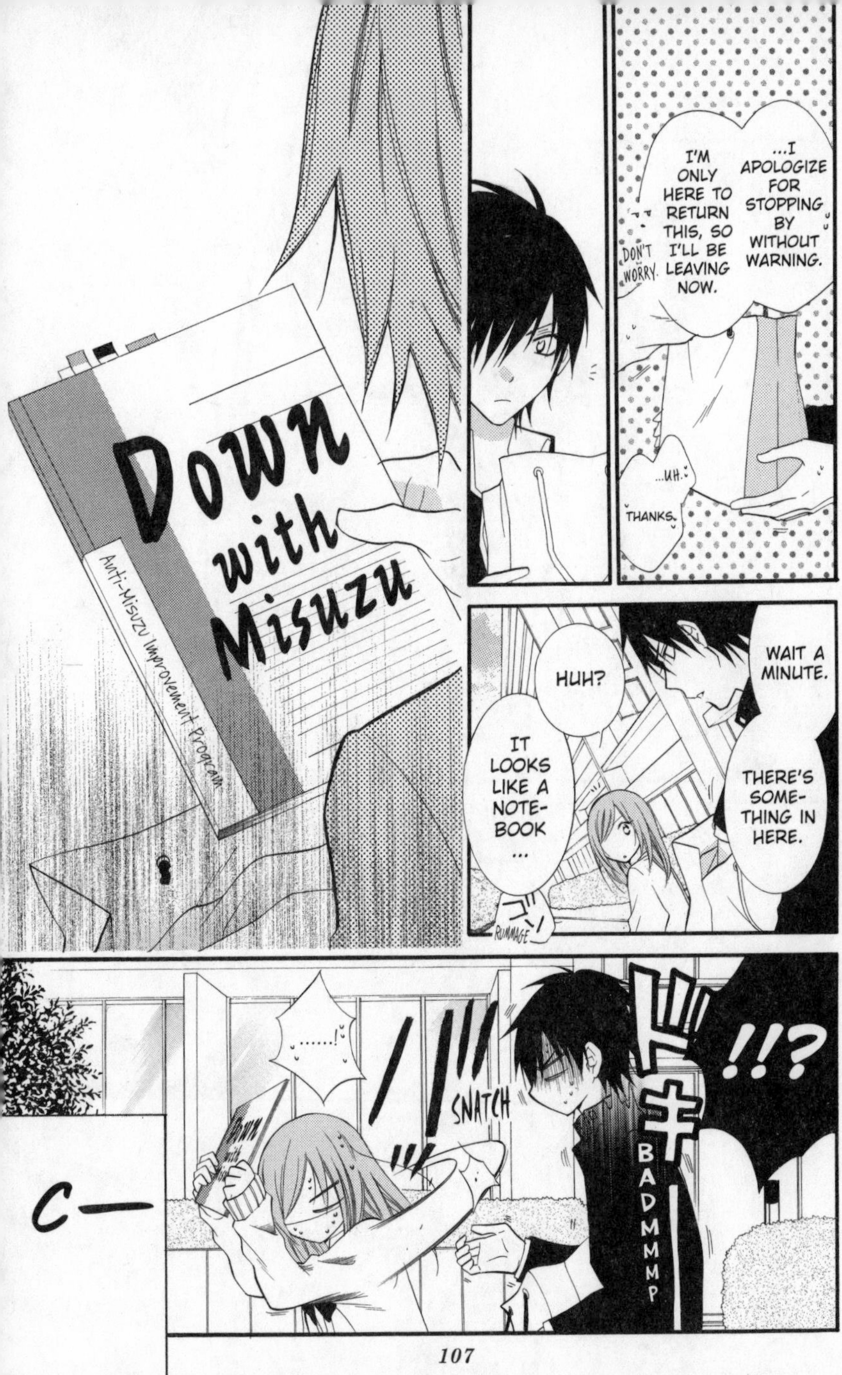
...I APOLOGIZE FOR STOPPING BY WITHOUT WARNING.
I'M ONLY HERE TO RETURN THIS, SO I'LL BE LEAVING NOW.
DON'T WORRY.
...UH.
THANKS.
WAIT A MINUTE.
THERE'S SOME-THING IN HERE.
HUH?
IT LOOKS LIKE A NOTE-BOOK...
RUMMAGE
Down with Misuzu
Anti-Misuzu Improvement Program
!!?
BADMMMP
SNATCH
......!
C—

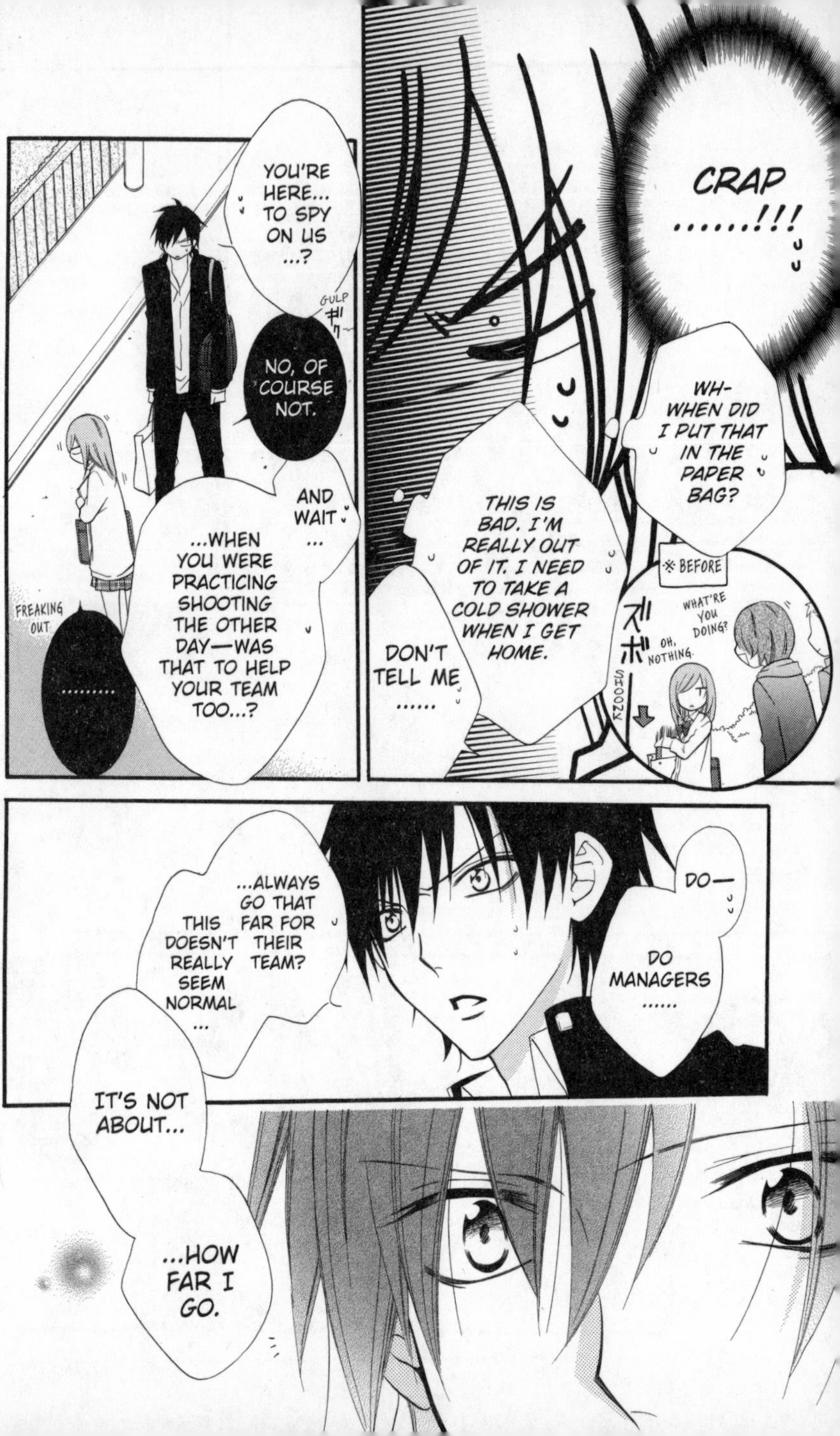
CRAP ......!!!
WH-WHEN DID I PUT THAT IN THE PAPER BAG?
※BEFORE
WHAT'RE YOU DOING?
OH, NOTHING.
SHOONK
THIS IS BAD. I'M REALLY OUT OF IT. I NEED TO TAKE A COLD SHOWER WHEN I GET HOME.
DON'T TELL ME ......
YOU'RE HERE... TO SPY ON US ...?
GULP
NO, OF COURSE NOT.
AND WAIT ...
...WHEN YOU WERE PRACTICING SHOOTING THE OTHER DAY—WAS THAT TO HELP YOUR TEAM TOO...?
FREAKING OUT
....
DO—
DO MANAGERS ......
...ALWAYS GO THAT FAR FOR THEIR TEAM?
THIS DOESN'T REALLY SEEM NORMAL ...
IT'S NOT ABOUT...
...HOW FAR I GO.

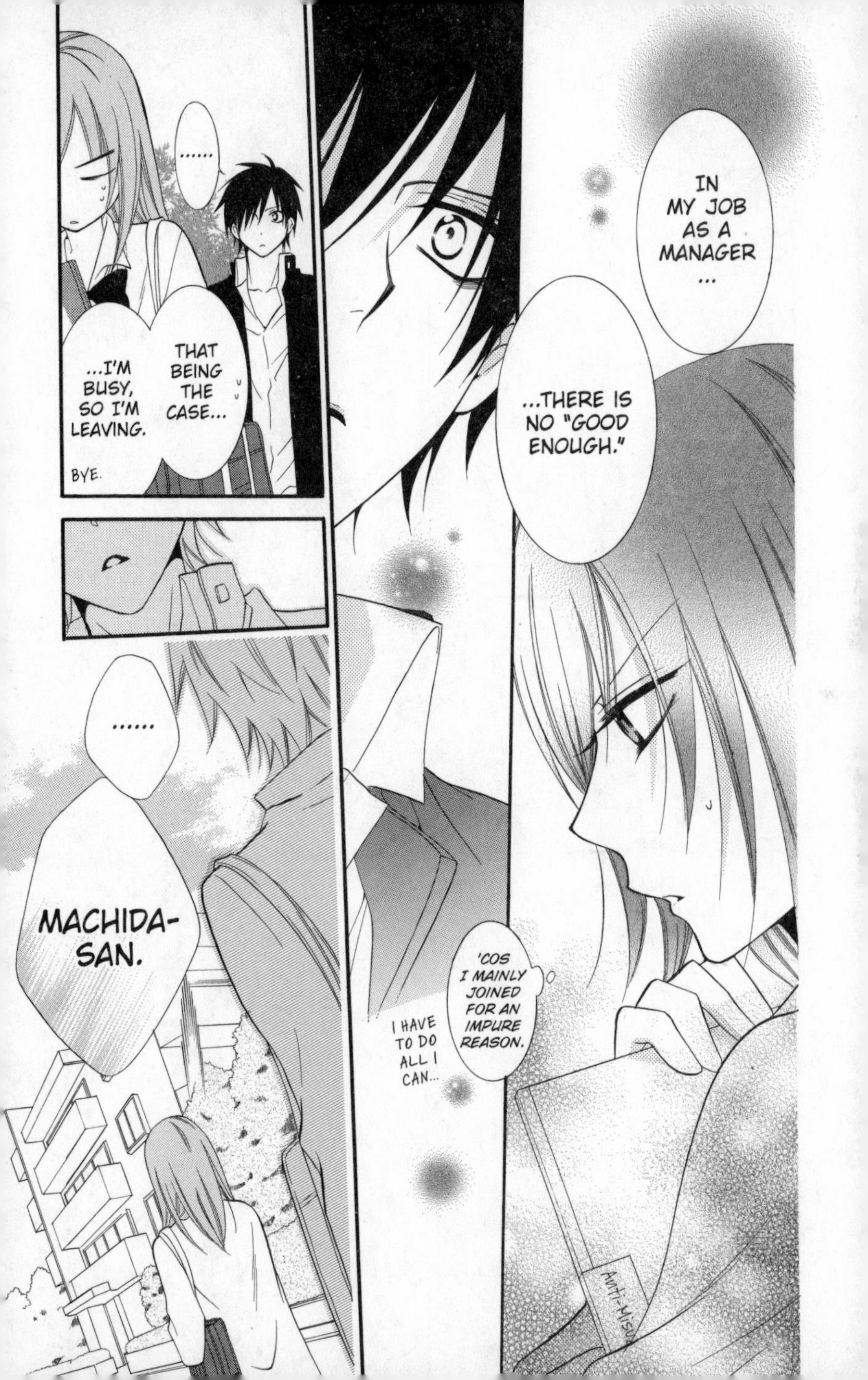
IN MY JOB AS A MANAGER...
...THERE IS NO "GOOD ENOUGH."
Anti-Misu
'COS I MAINLY JOINED FOR AN IMPURE REASON.
I HAVE TO DO ALL I CAN...
......
THAT BEING THE CASE...
...I'M BUSY, SO I'M LEAVING.
BYE.
......
MACHIDA-SAN.

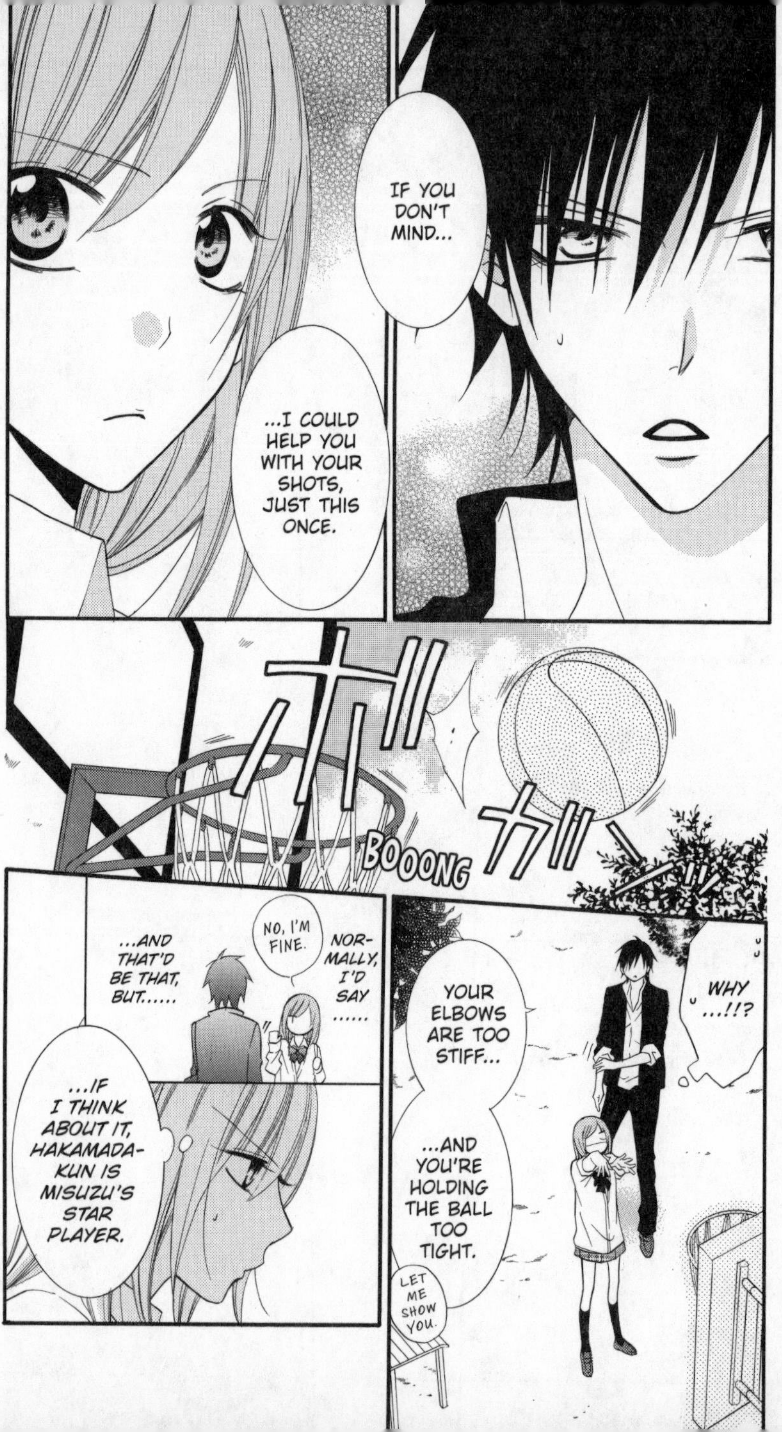
IF YOU DON'T MIND...
...I COULD HELP YOU WITH YOUR SHOTS, JUST THIS ONCE.
BOOONG
WHY ...!!?
YOUR ELBOWS ARE TOO STIFF...
...AND YOU'RE HOLDING THE BALL TOO TIGHT.
LET ME SHOW YOU.
NOR-MALLY, I'D SAY ......
NO, I'M FINE.
...AND THAT'D BE THAT, BUT......
...IF I THINK ABOUT IT, HAKAMADA-KUN IS MISUZU'S STAR PLAYER.

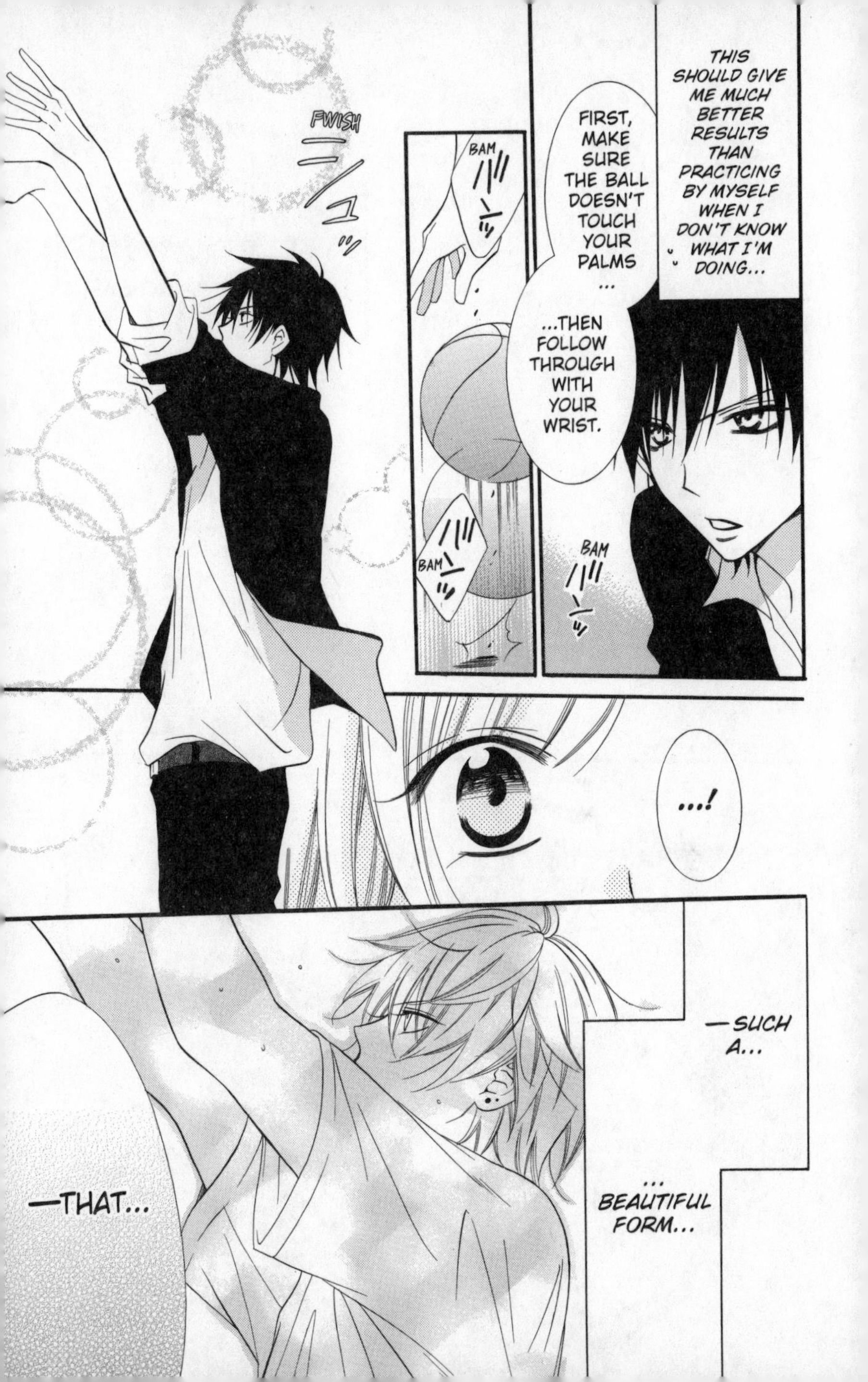
THIS SHOULD GIVE ME MUCH BETTER RESULTS THAN PRACTICING BY MYSELF WHEN I DON'T KNOW WHAT I'M DOING...
FIRST, MAKE SURE THE BALL DOESN'T TOUCH YOUR PALMS...
...THEN FOLLOW THROUGH WITH YOUR WRIST.
BAM
BAM
BAM
...!
FWISH
—SUCH A...
...BEAUTIFUL FORM...
—THAT...

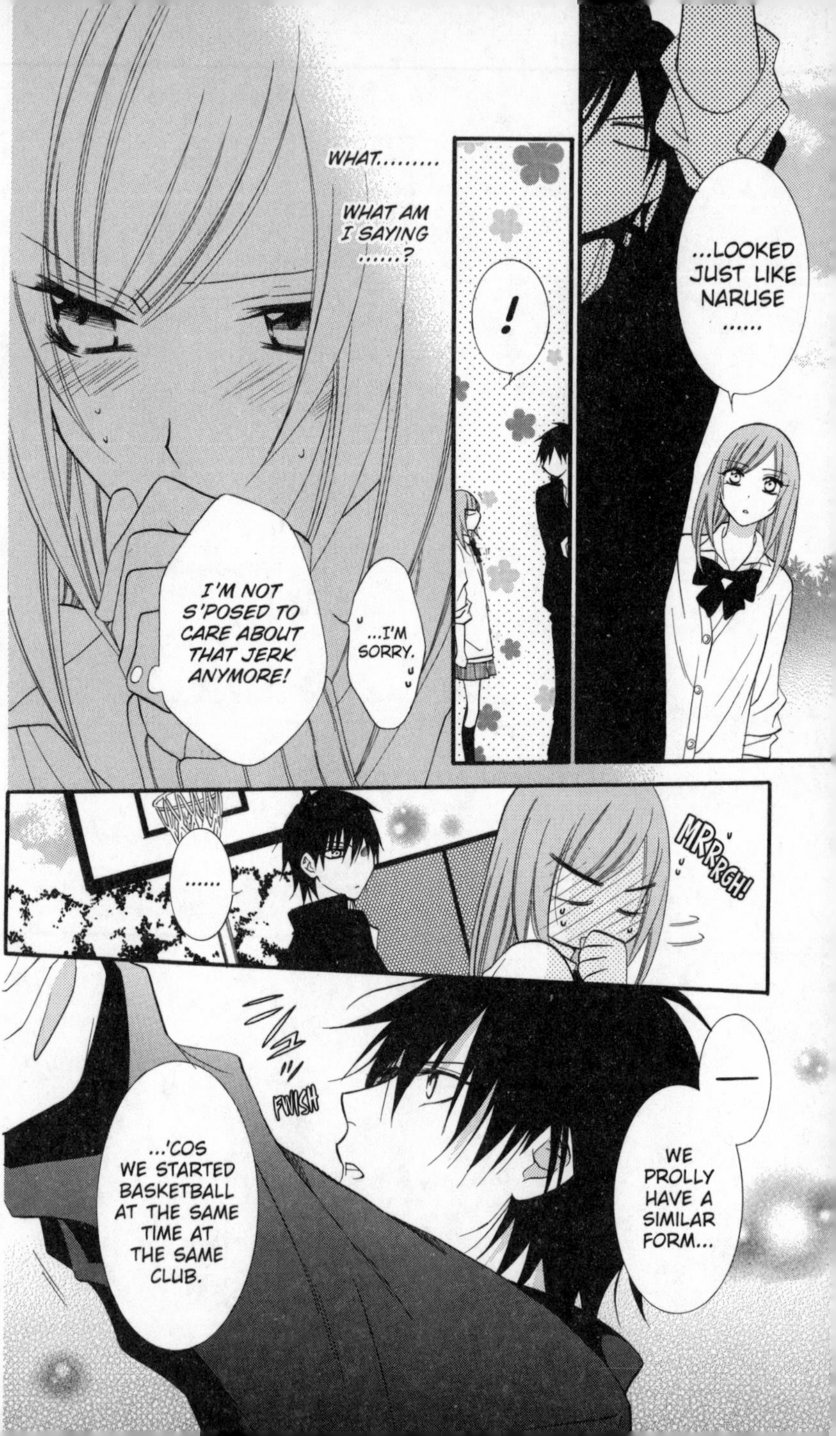
...LOOKED JUST LIKE NARUSE ......
!
WHAT........
WHAT AM I SAYING ......?
...I'M SORRY.
I'M NOT S'POSED TO CARE ABOUT THAT JERK ANYMORE!
MRRRGH!
......
—
WE PROLLY HAVE A SIMILAR FORM...
FWISH
...'COS WE STARTED BASKETBALL AT THE SAME TIME AT THE SAME CLUB.

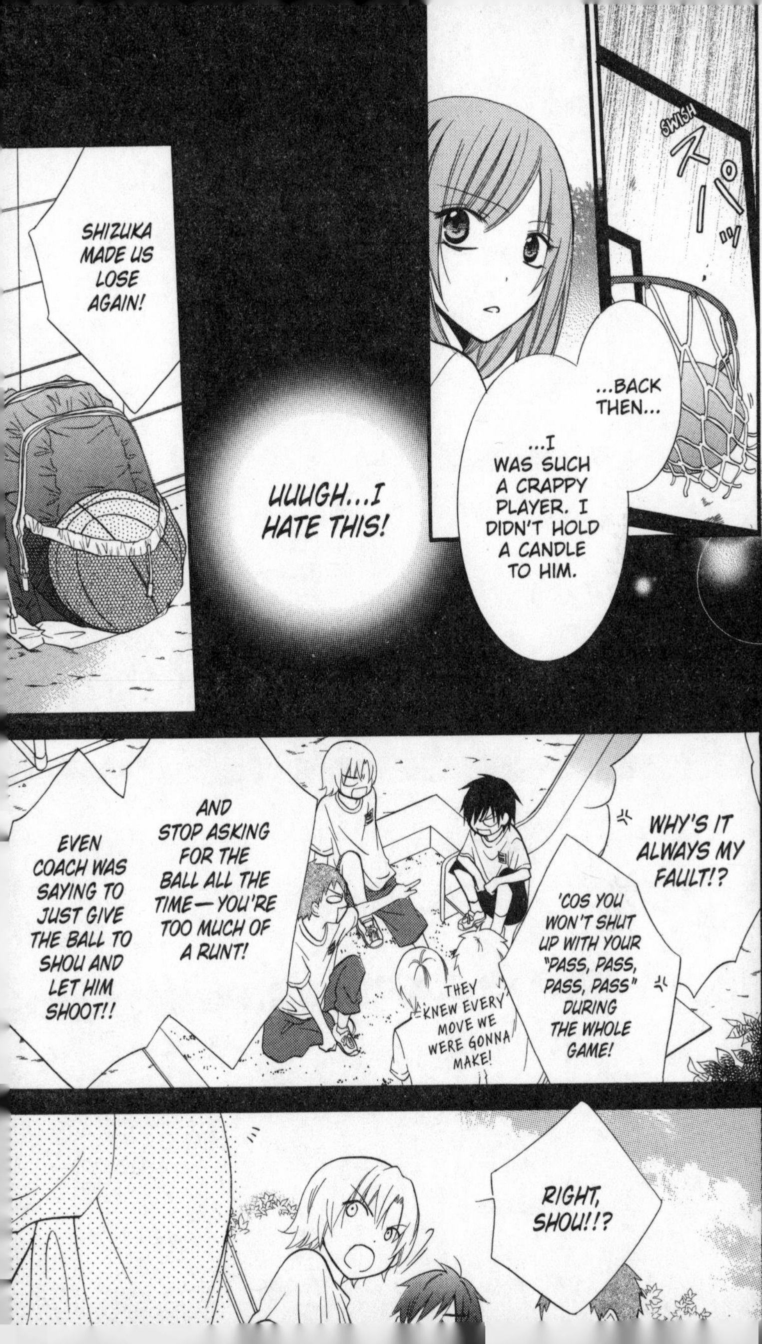
SWISH
...BACK THEN...
...I WAS SUCH A CRAPPY PLAYER. I DIDN'T HOLD A CANDLE TO HIM.
UUUGH...I HATE THIS!
SHIZUKA MADE US LOSE AGAIN!
WHY'S IT ALWAYS MY FAULT!?
'COS YOU WON'T SHUT UP WITH YOUR "PASS, PASS, PASS, PASS" DURING THE WHOLE GAME!
THEY KNEW EVERY MOVE WE WERE GONNA MAKE!
AND STOP ASKING FOR THE BALL ALL THE TIME—YOU'RE TOO MUCH OF A RUNT!
EVEN COACH WAS SAYING TO JUST GIVE THE BALL TO SHOU AND LET HIM SHOOT!!
RIGHT, SHOU!!?

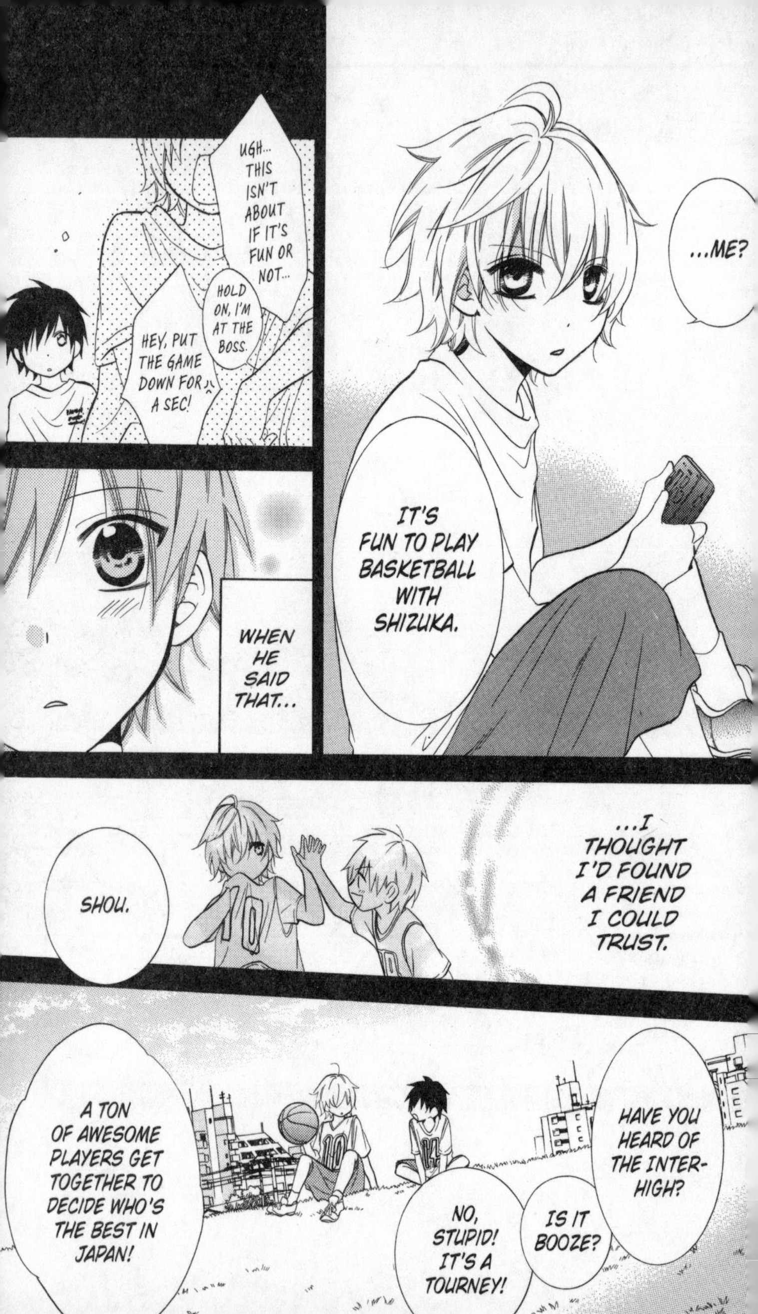
...ME?
IT'S FUN TO PLAY BASKETBALL WITH SHIZUKA.
UGH... THIS ISN'T ABOUT IF IT'S FUN OR NOT...
HOLD ON, I'M AT THE BOSS.
HEY, PUT THE GAME DOWN FOR A SEC!
WHEN HE SAID THAT...
...I THOUGHT I'D FOUND A FRIEND I COULD TRUST.
SHOU.
HAVE YOU HEARD OF THE INTER-HIGH?
IS IT BOOZE?
NO, STUPID! IT'S A TOURNEY!
A TON OF AWESOME PLAYERS GET TOGETHER TO DECIDE WHO'S THE BEST IN JAPAN!

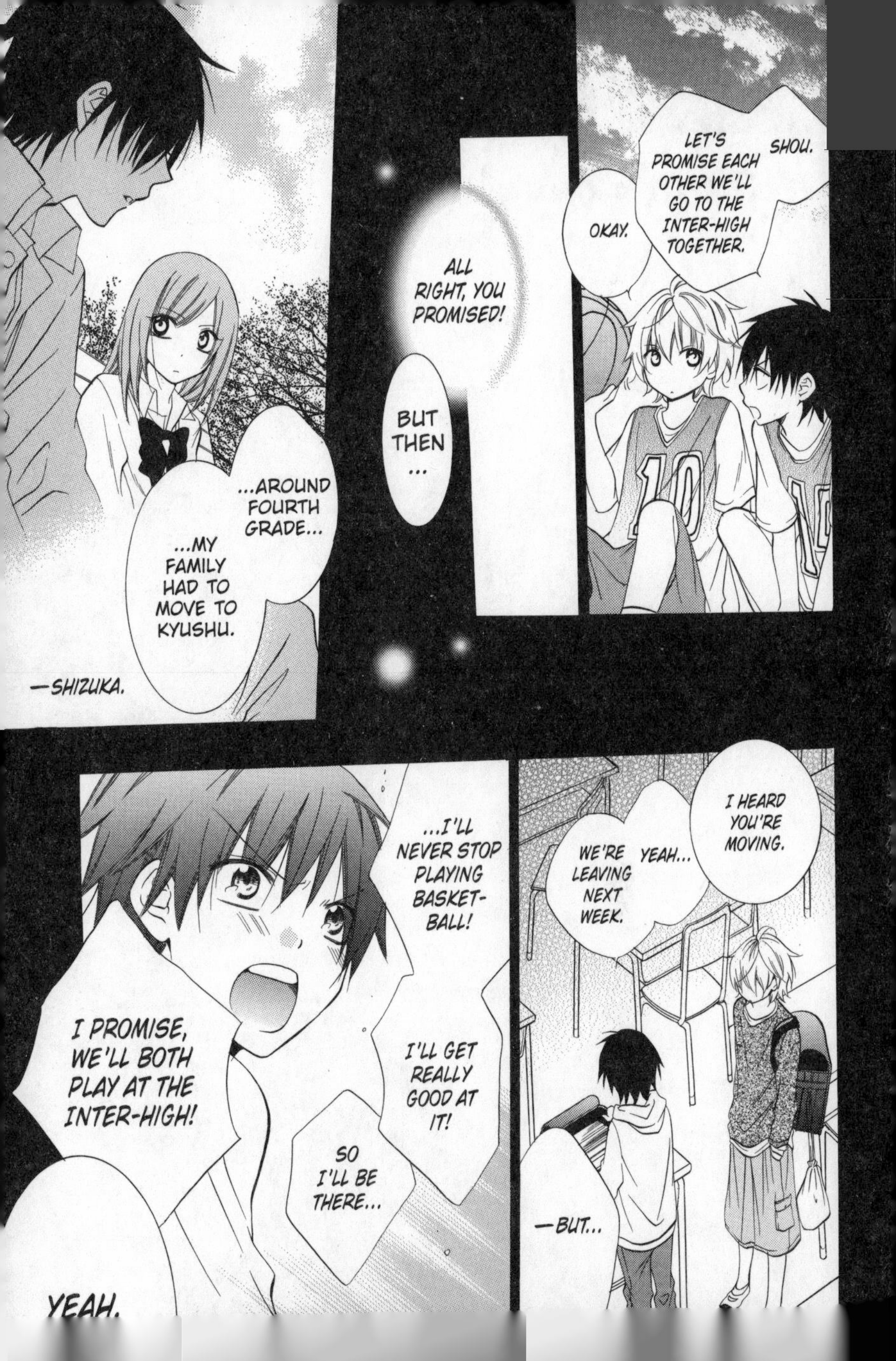
SHOU.
LET'S PROMISE EACH OTHER WE'LL GO TO THE INTER-HIGH TOGETHER.
OKAY.
ALL RIGHT, YOU PROMISED!
BUT THEN...
...AROUND FOURTH GRADE...
...MY FAMILY HAD TO MOVE TO KYUSHU.
—SHIZUKA.
I HEARD YOU'RE MOVING.
YEAH...
WE'RE LEAVING NEXT WEEK.
—BUT...
...I'LL NEVER STOP PLAYING BASKET-BALL!
I'LL GET REALLY GOOD AT IT!
SO I'LL BE THERE...
I PROMISE, WE'LL BOTH PLAY AT THE INTER-HIGH!
YEAH.

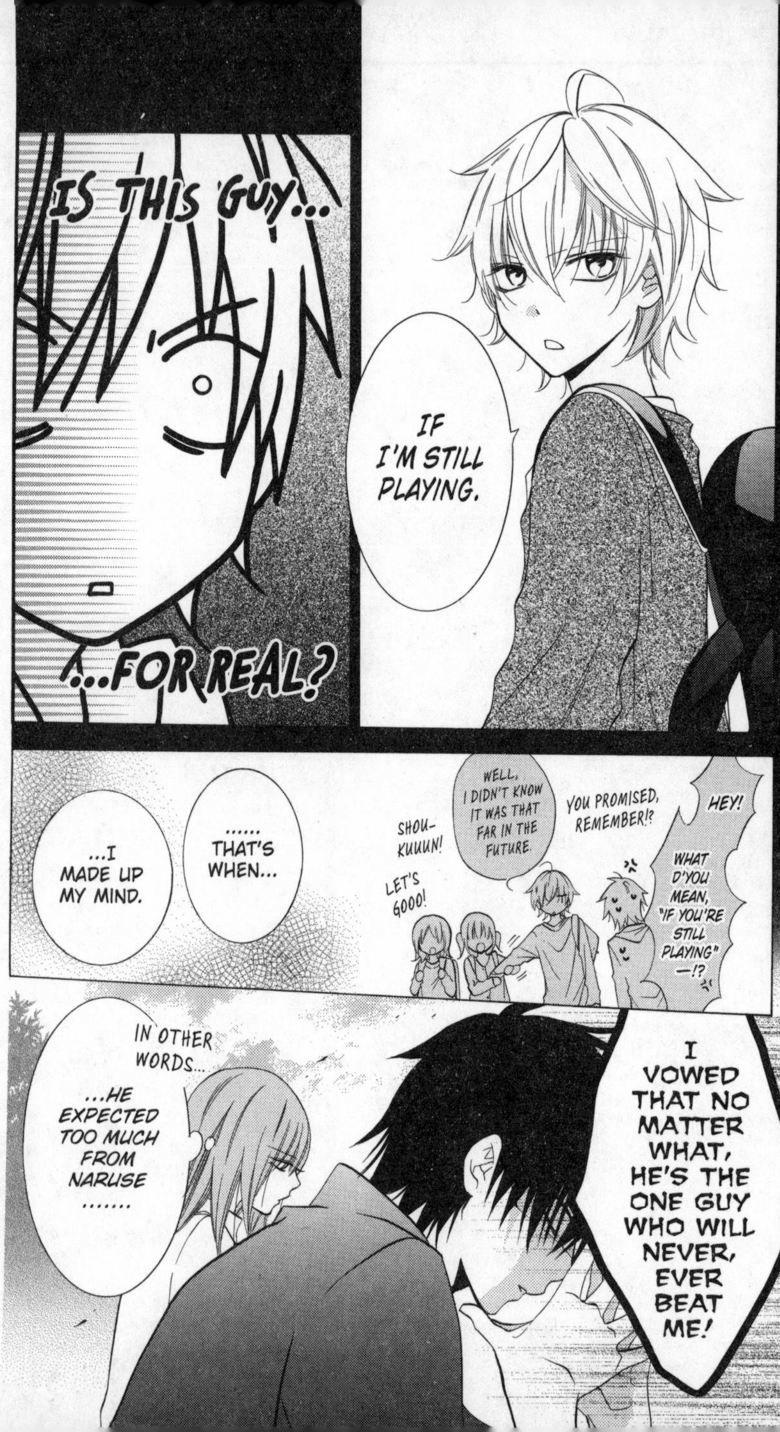
IF I'M STILL PLAYING.
IS THIS GUY...
...FOR REAL?
HEY!
WHAT D'YOU MEAN, "IF YOU'RE STILL PLAYING"—!?
YOU PROMISED, REMEMBER!?
WELL, I DIDN'T KNOW IT WAS THAT FAR IN THE FUTURE.
SHOU-KUUUN!
LET'S GOOO!
......THAT'S WHEN...
...I MADE UP MY MIND.
I VOWED THAT NO MATTER WHAT, HE'S THE ONE GUY WHO WILL NEVER, EVER BEAT ME!
IN OTHER WORDS...
...HE EXPECTED TOO MUCH FROM NARUSE ....

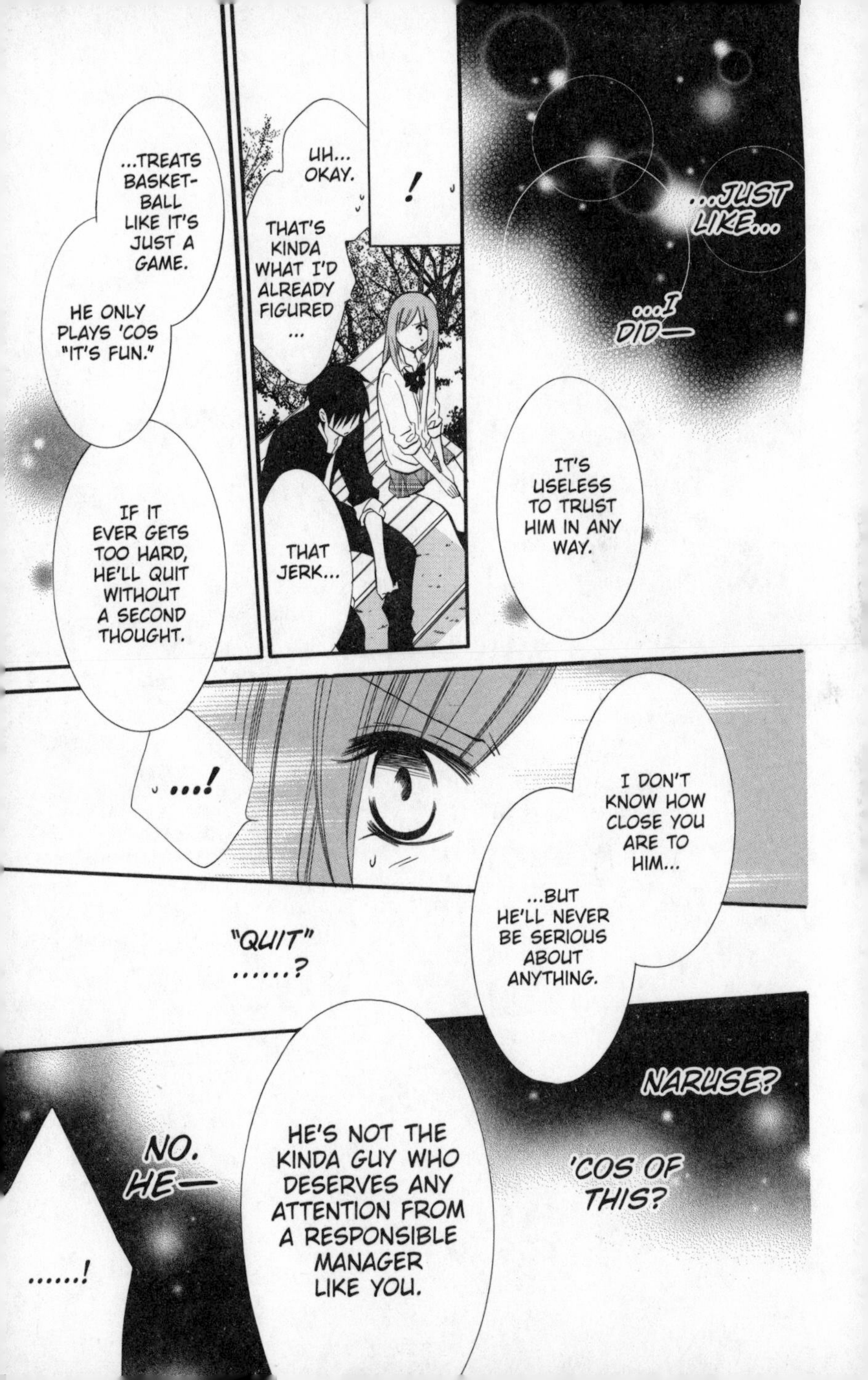
...JUST LIKE...
...I DID—
IT'S USELESS TO TRUST HIM IN ANY WAY.
UH... OKAY.
!
THAT'S KINDA WHAT I'D ALREADY FIGURED...
THAT JERK...
...TREATS BASKETBALL LIKE IT'S JUST A GAME.
HE ONLY PLAYS 'COS "IT'S FUN."
IF IT EVER GETS TOO HARD, HE'LL QUIT WITHOUT A SECOND THOUGHT.
I DON'T KNOW HOW CLOSE YOU ARE TO HIM...
...BUT HE'LL NEVER BE SERIOUS ABOUT ANYTHING.
...!
"QUIT" ......?
NARUSE?
'COS OF THIS?
HE'S NOT THE KINDA GUY WHO DESERVES ANY ATTENTION FROM A RESPONSIBLE MANAGER LIKE YOU.
NO. HE—
......!

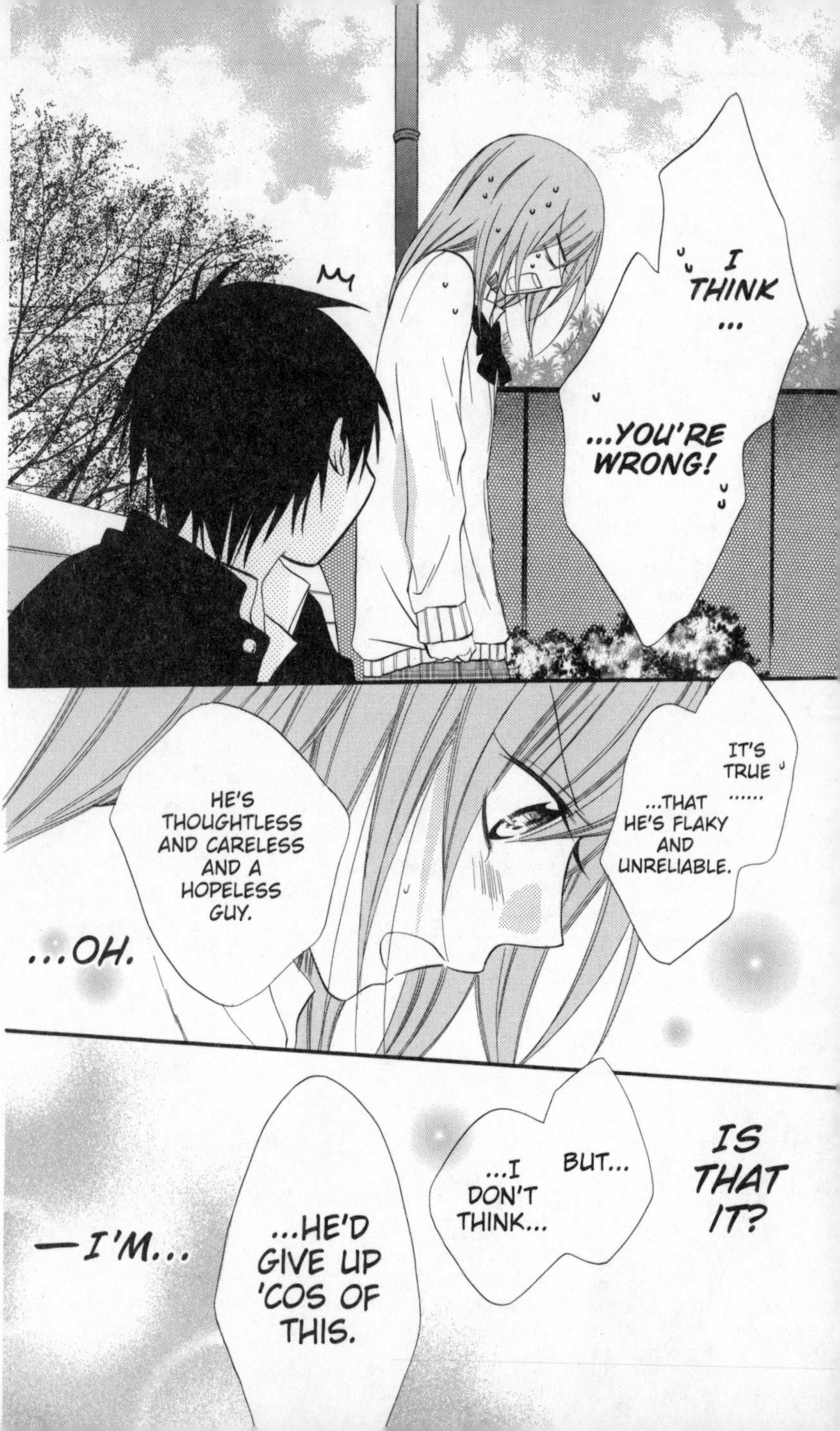
I THINK ...
...YOU'RE WRONG!
IT'S TRUE ......
...THAT HE'S FLAKY AND UNRELIABLE.
HE'S THOUGHTLESS AND CARELESS AND A HOPELESS GUY.
...OH.
IS THAT IT?
BUT...
...I DON'T THINK...
...HE'D GIVE UP 'COS OF THIS.
—I'M...

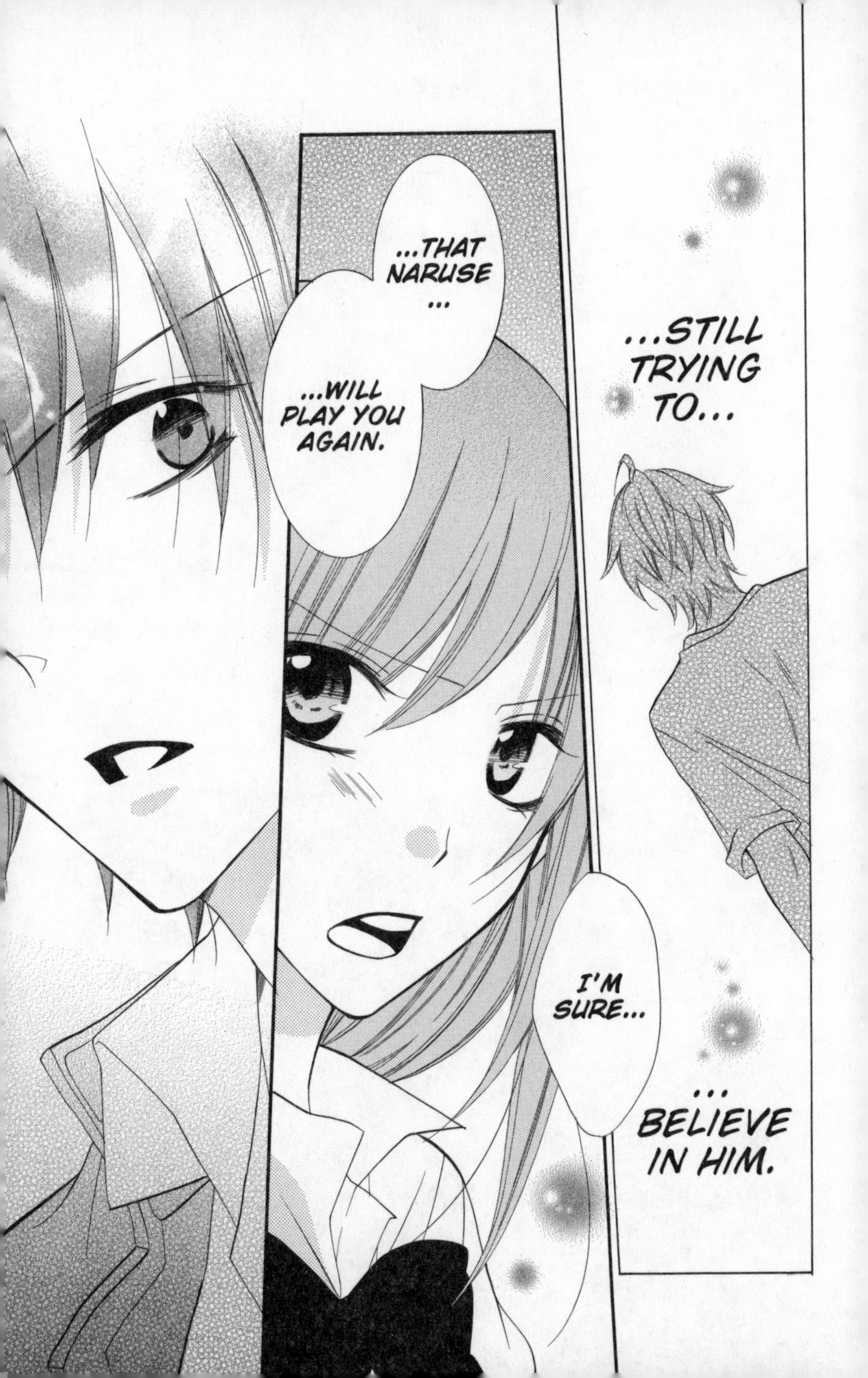
...STILL TRYING TO...
...BELIEVE IN HIM.
...THAT NARUSE...
...WILL PLAY YOU AGAIN.
I'M SURE...

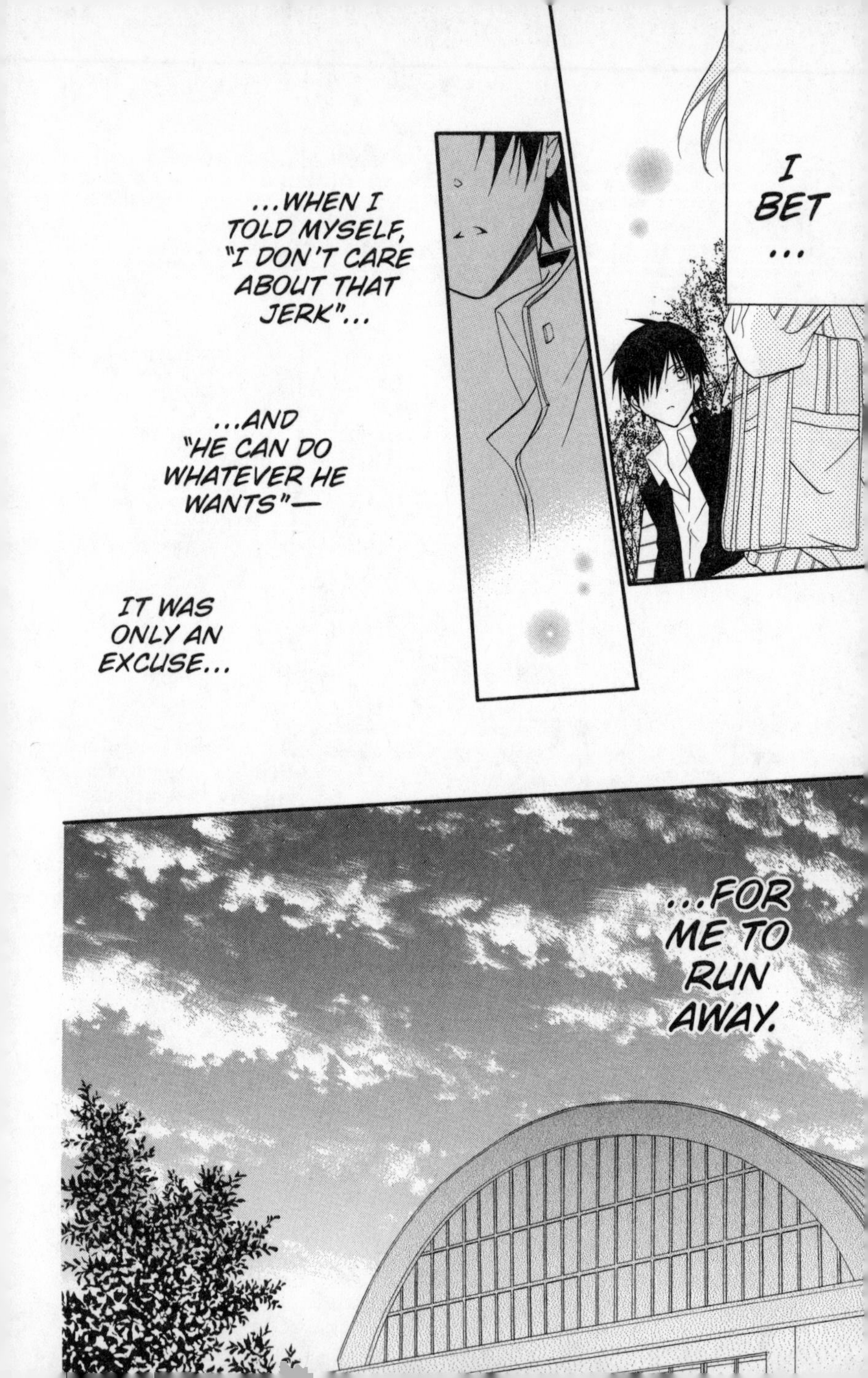
I BET ...
...WHEN I TOLD MYSELF, "I DON'T CARE ABOUT THAT JERK"...
...AND "HE CAN DO WHATEVER HE WANTS"—
IT WAS ONLY AN EXCUSE...
...FOR ME TO RUN AWAY.

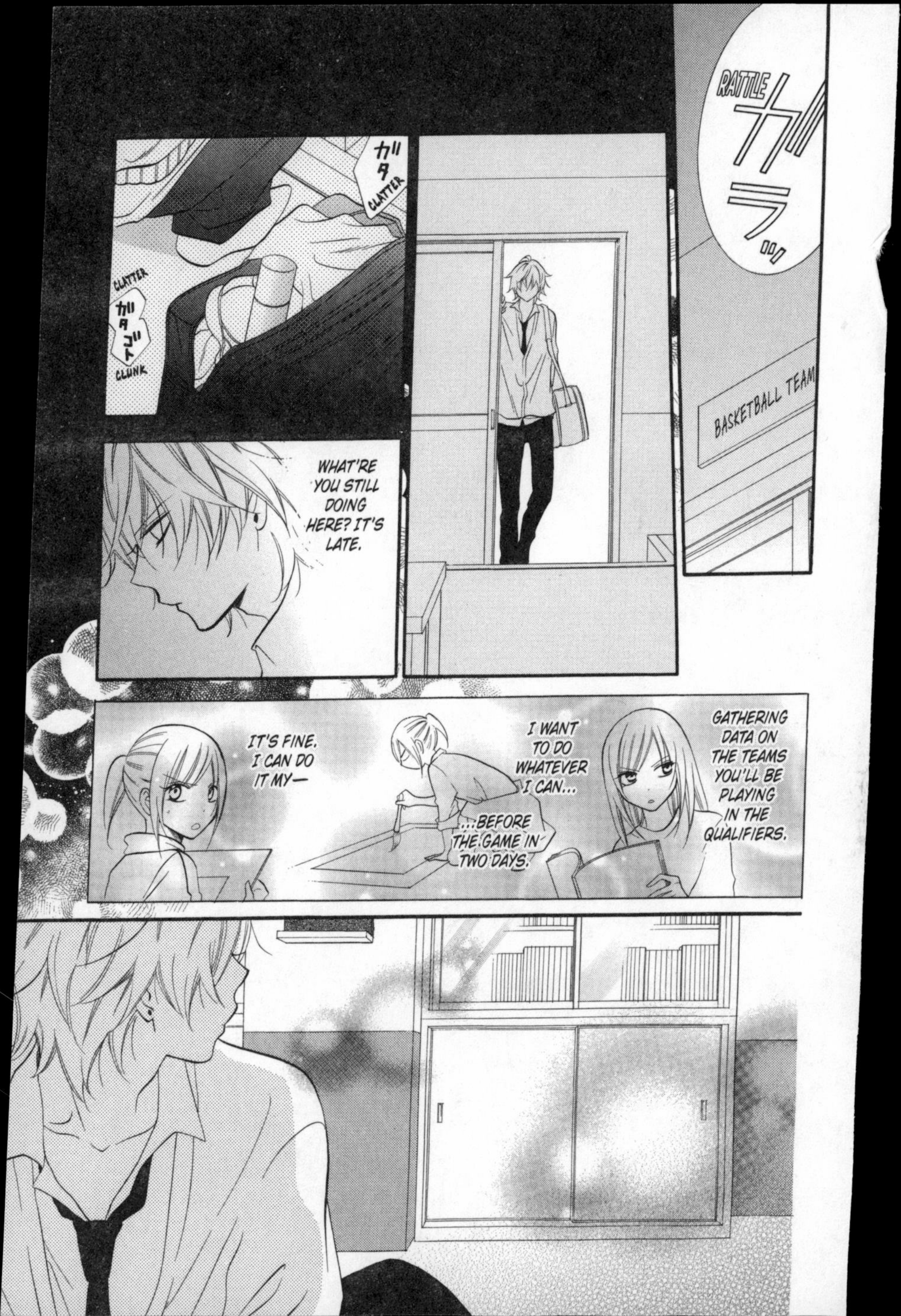
RATTLE
カラ…
BASKETBALL TEAM
ガタ
CLATTER
CLATTER
ガタゴト
CLUNK
WHAT'RE YOU STILL DOING HERE? IT'S LATE.
GATHERING DATA ON THE TEAMS YOU'LL BE PLAYING IN THE QUALIFIERS.
I WANT TO DO WHATEVER I CAN...
...BEFORE THE GAME IN TWO DAYS.
IT'S FINE. I CAN DO IT MY—

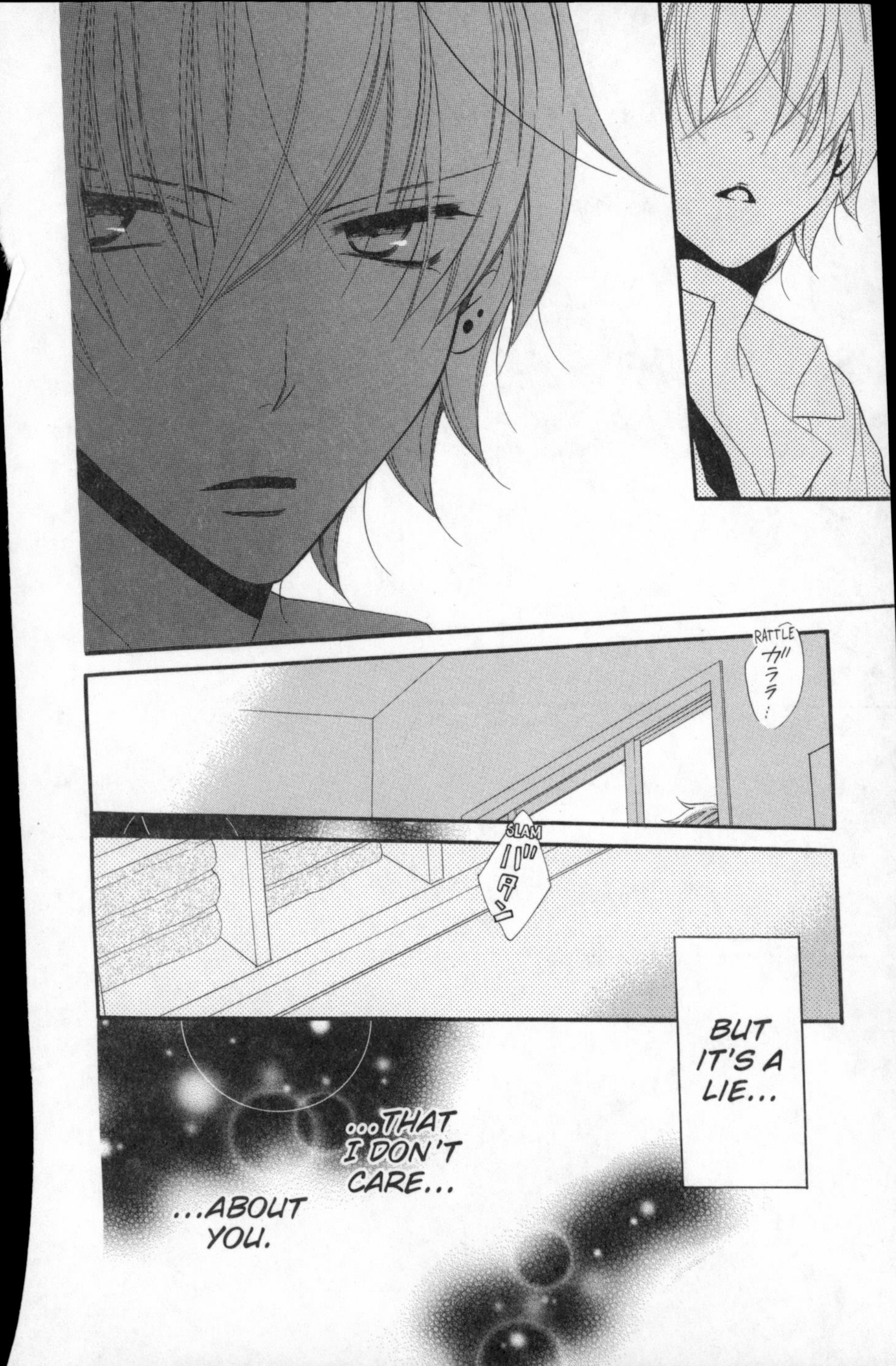
RATTLE
ガララ…
SLAM
バタン
BUT IT'S A LIE...
...THAT I DON'T CARE...
...ABOUT YOU.

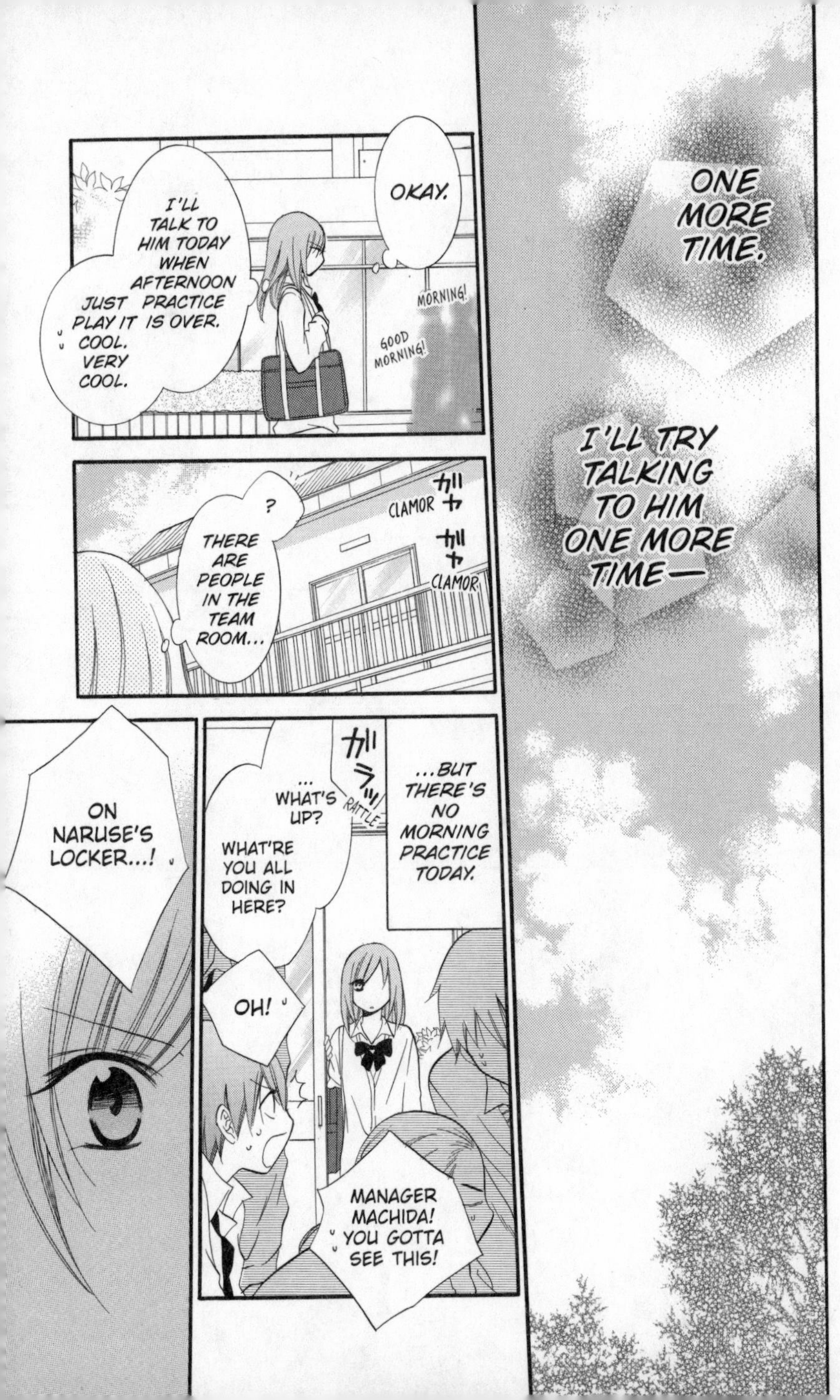
ONE MORE TIME.
I'LL TRY TALKING TO HIM ONE MORE TIME—
OKAY.
MORNING!
GOOD MORNING!
I'LL TALK TO HIM TODAY WHEN AFTERNOON PRACTICE IS OVER.
JUST PLAY IT COOL. VERY COOL.
ガヤ CLAMOR
ガヤ CLAMOR
?
THERE ARE PEOPLE IN THE TEAM ROOM...
...BUT THERE'S NO MORNING PRACTICE TODAY.
ガラッ RATTLE
...WHAT'S UP?
WHAT'RE YOU ALL DOING IN HERE?
OH!
MANAGER MACHIDA! YOU GOTTA SEE THIS!
ON NARUSE'S LOCKER...!

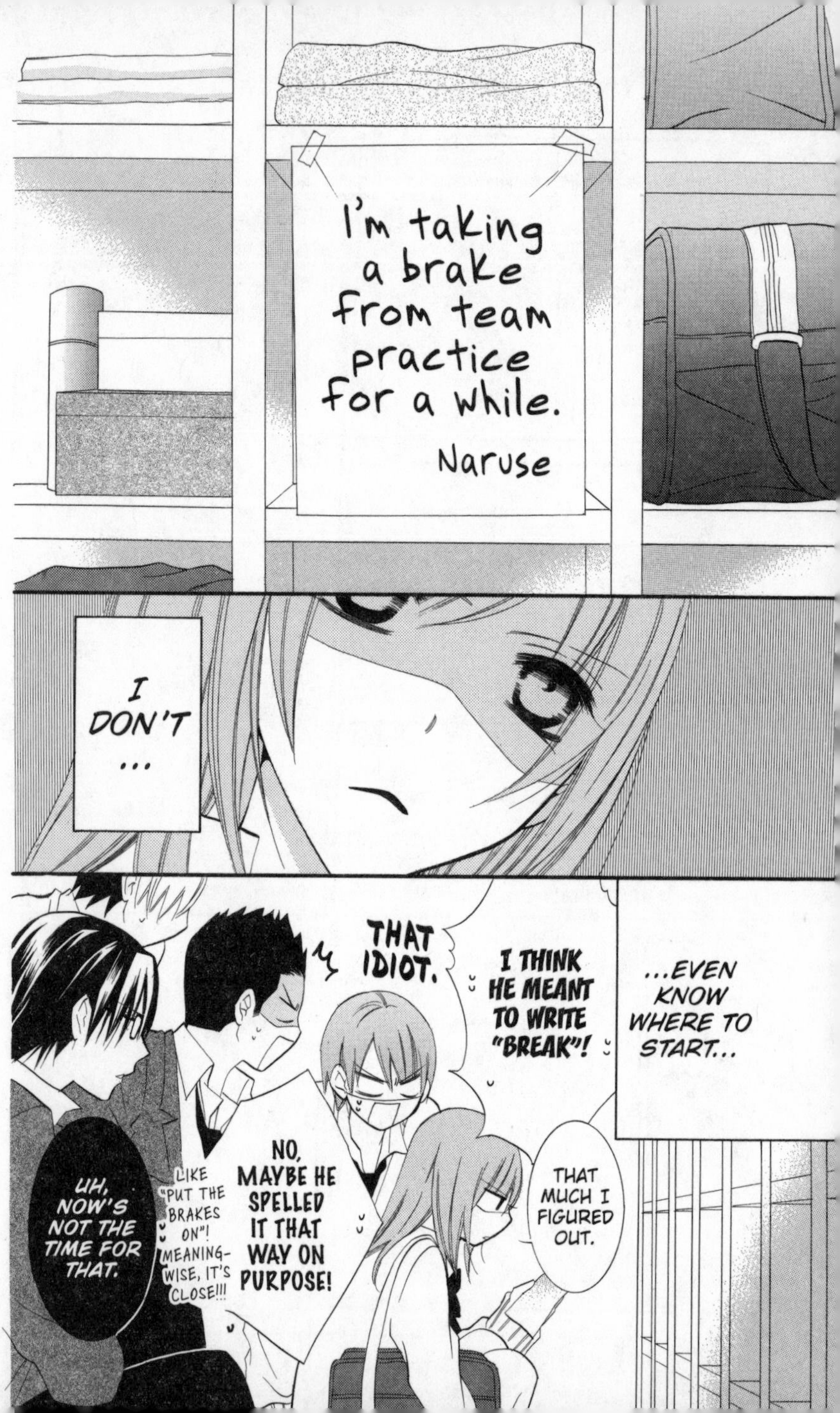
I'm taking a brake from team practice for a while.
Naruse
I DON'T ...
...EVEN KNOW WHERE TO START...
THAT IDIOT.
I THINK HE MEANT TO WRITE "BREAK"!
THAT MUCH I FIGURED OUT.
NO, MAYBE HE SPELLED IT THAT WAY ON PURPOSE!
LIKE "PUT THE BRAKES ON"! MEANING-WISE, IT'S CLOSE!!!
UH, NOW'S NOT THE TIME FOR THAT.

PURE-BOY HAKAMADA

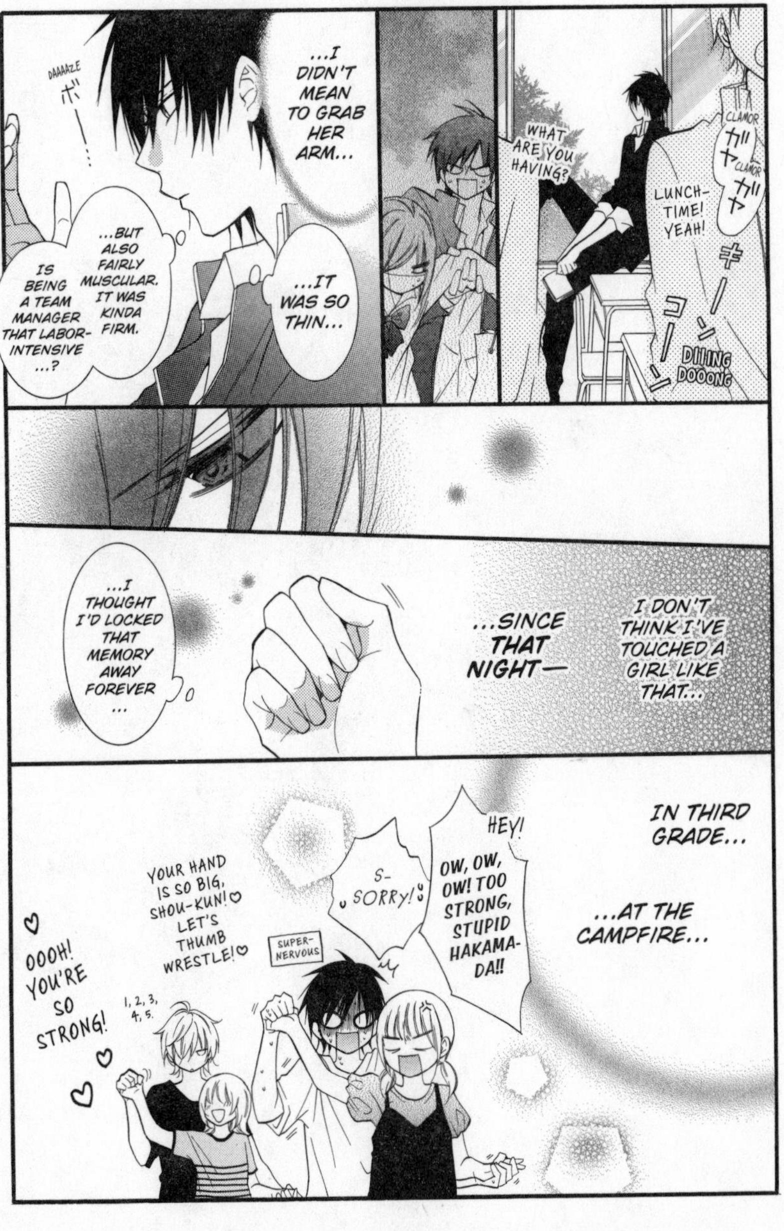

キーンコーン
DIIING DOOONG
LUNCH-TIME! YEAH!
ガヤガヤ
CLAMOR CLAMOR
WHAT ARE YOU HAVING?
...I DIDN'T MEAN TO GRAB HER ARM...
ボー……
DAAAAZE
...IT WAS SO THIN...
...BUT ALSO FAIRLY MUSCULAR. IT WAS KINDA FIRM.
IS BEING A TEAM MANAGER THAT LABOR-INTENSIVE ...?
I DON'T THINK I'VE TOUCHED A GIRL LIKE THAT...
...SINCE THAT NIGHT—
...I THOUGHT I'D LOCKED THAT MEMORY AWAY FOREVER ...
IN THIRD GRADE...
...AT THE CAMPFIRE...
HEY!
OW, OW, OW! TOO STRONG, STUPID HAKAMADA!!
S-SORRY!
SUPER-NERVOUS
YOUR HAND IS SO BIG, SHOU-KUN! ♡ LET'S THUMB WRESTLE! ♡
OOOH! YOU'RE SO STRONG!
1, 2, 3, 4, 5.

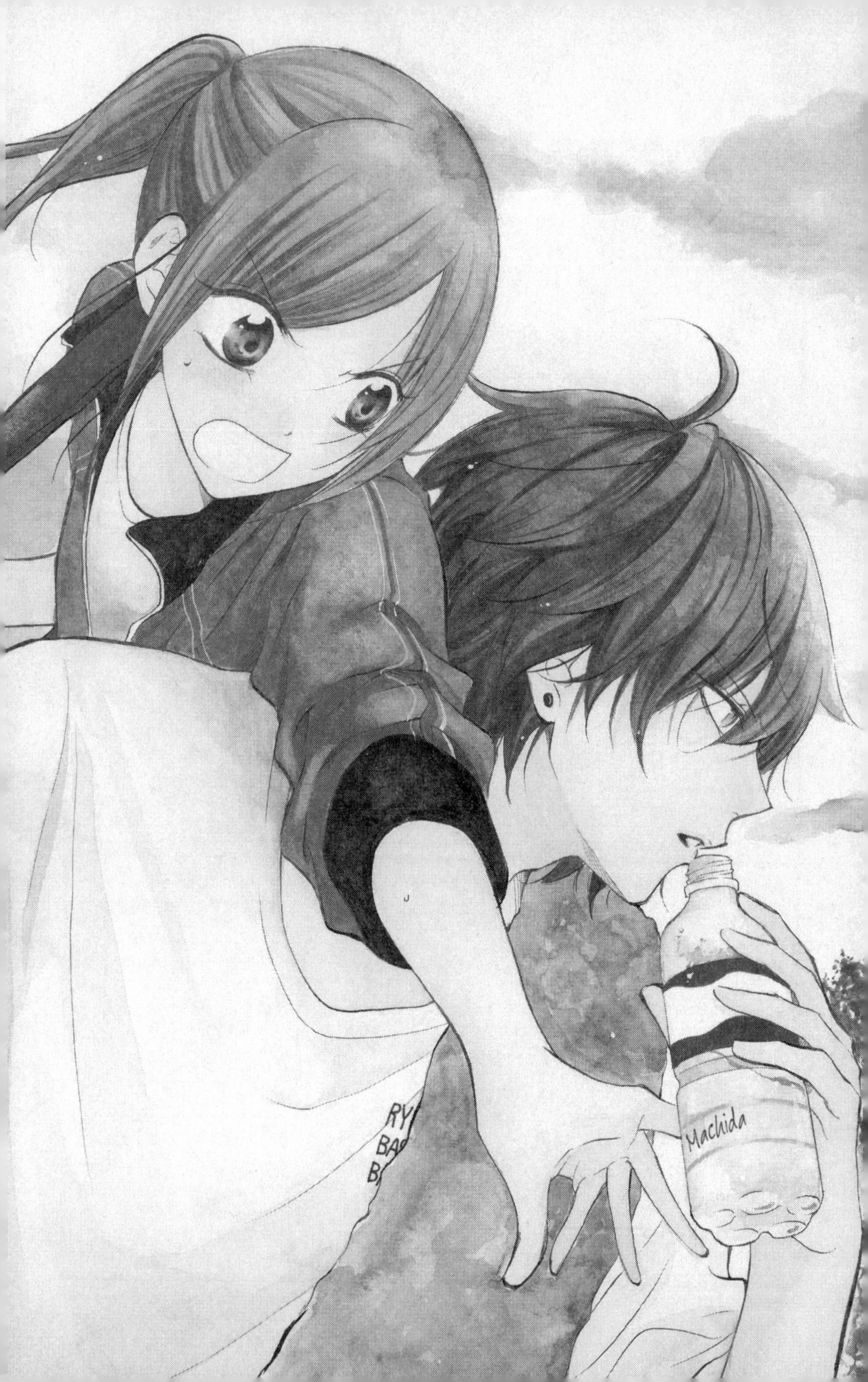
Machida

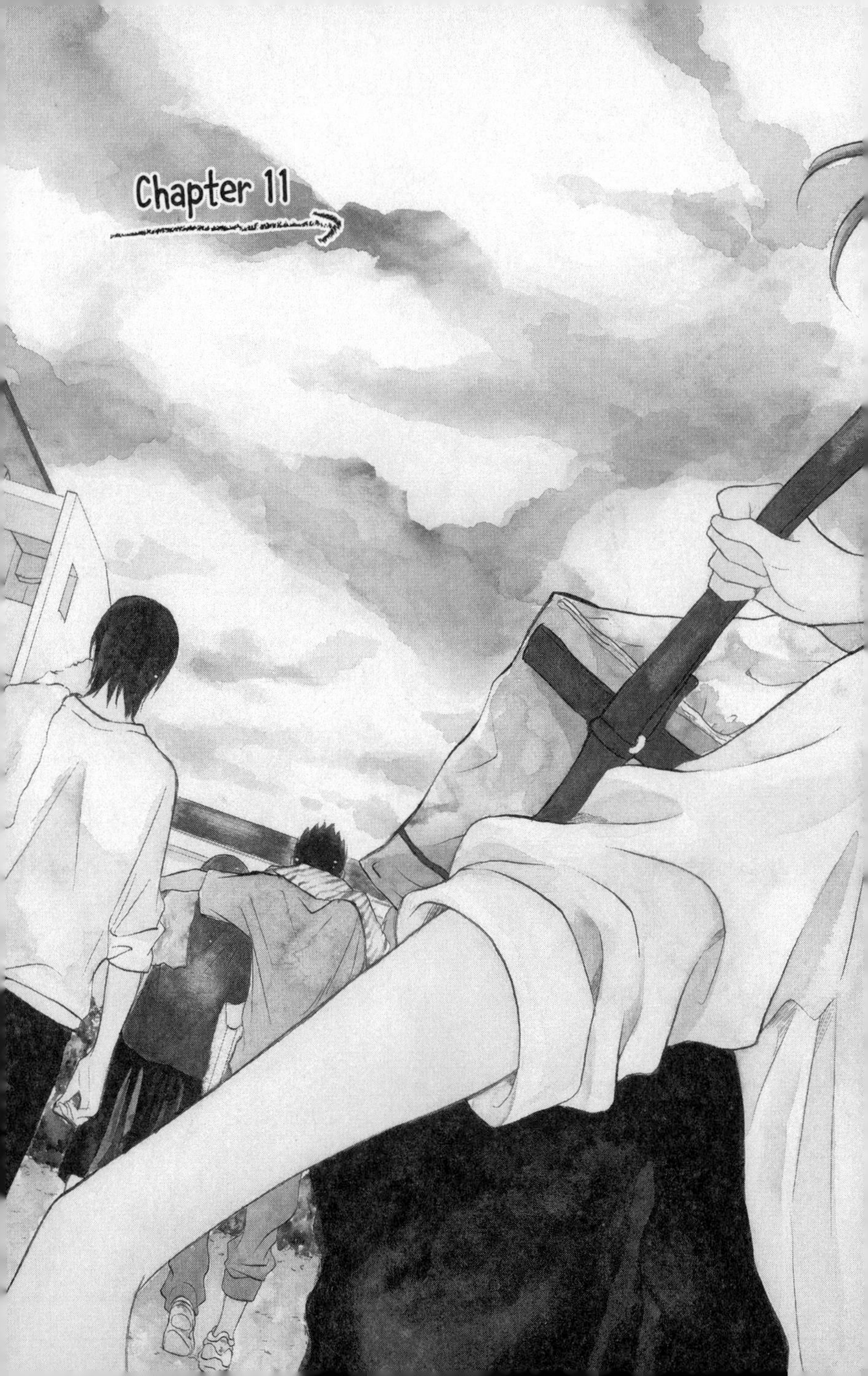
Chapter 11

CHEEKY BRAT

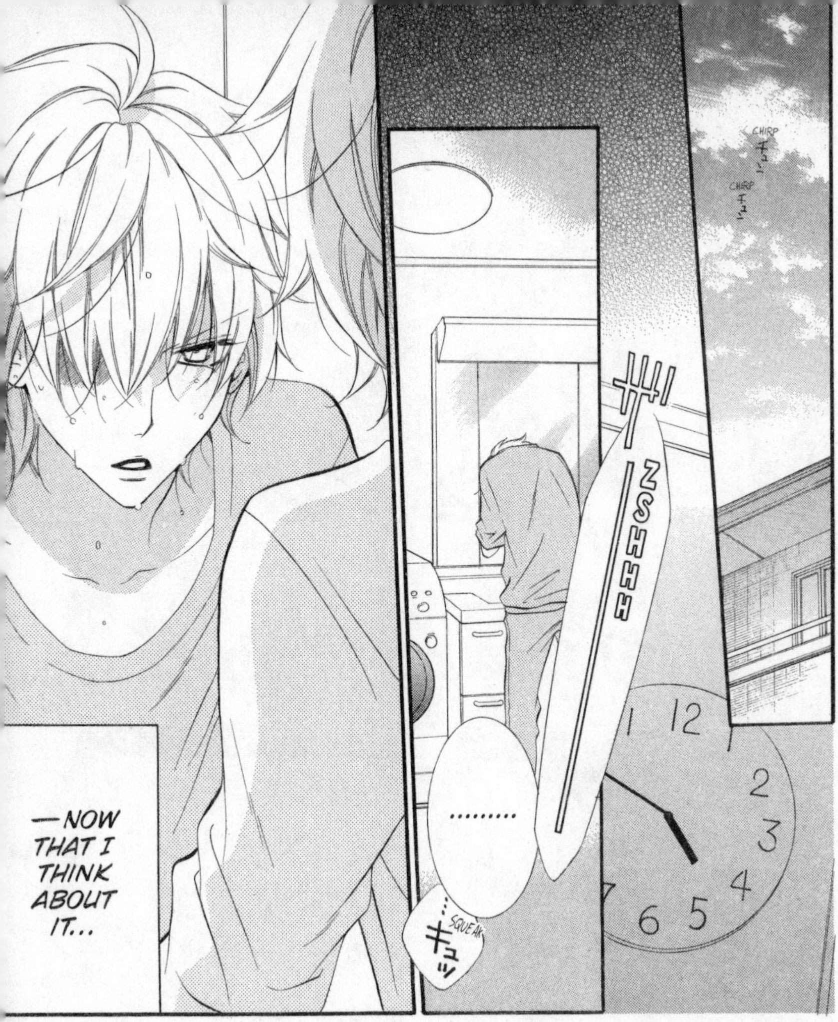
CHIRP
CHIRP
ZSHHHH
....
SQUEAK
—NOW THAT I THINK ABOUT IT...

Cheeky Brat

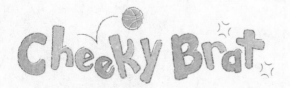

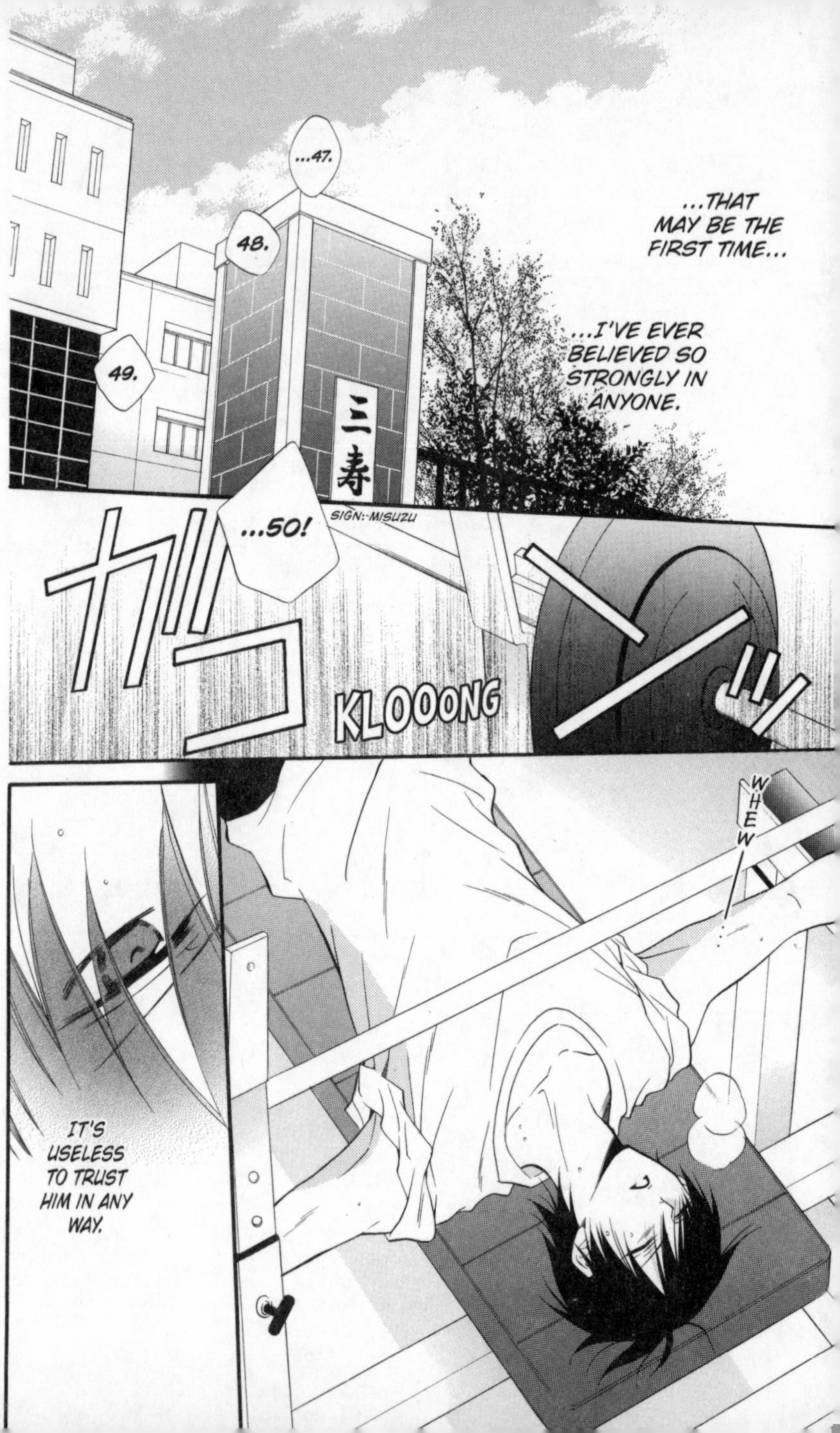
...THAT MAY BE THE FIRST TIME...
...47.
48.
49.
...I'VE EVER BELIEVED SO STRONGLY IN ANYONE.
三寿
SIGN: MISUZU
...50!
KLOOONG
WHEW
IT'S USELESS TO TRUST HIM IN ANY WAY.

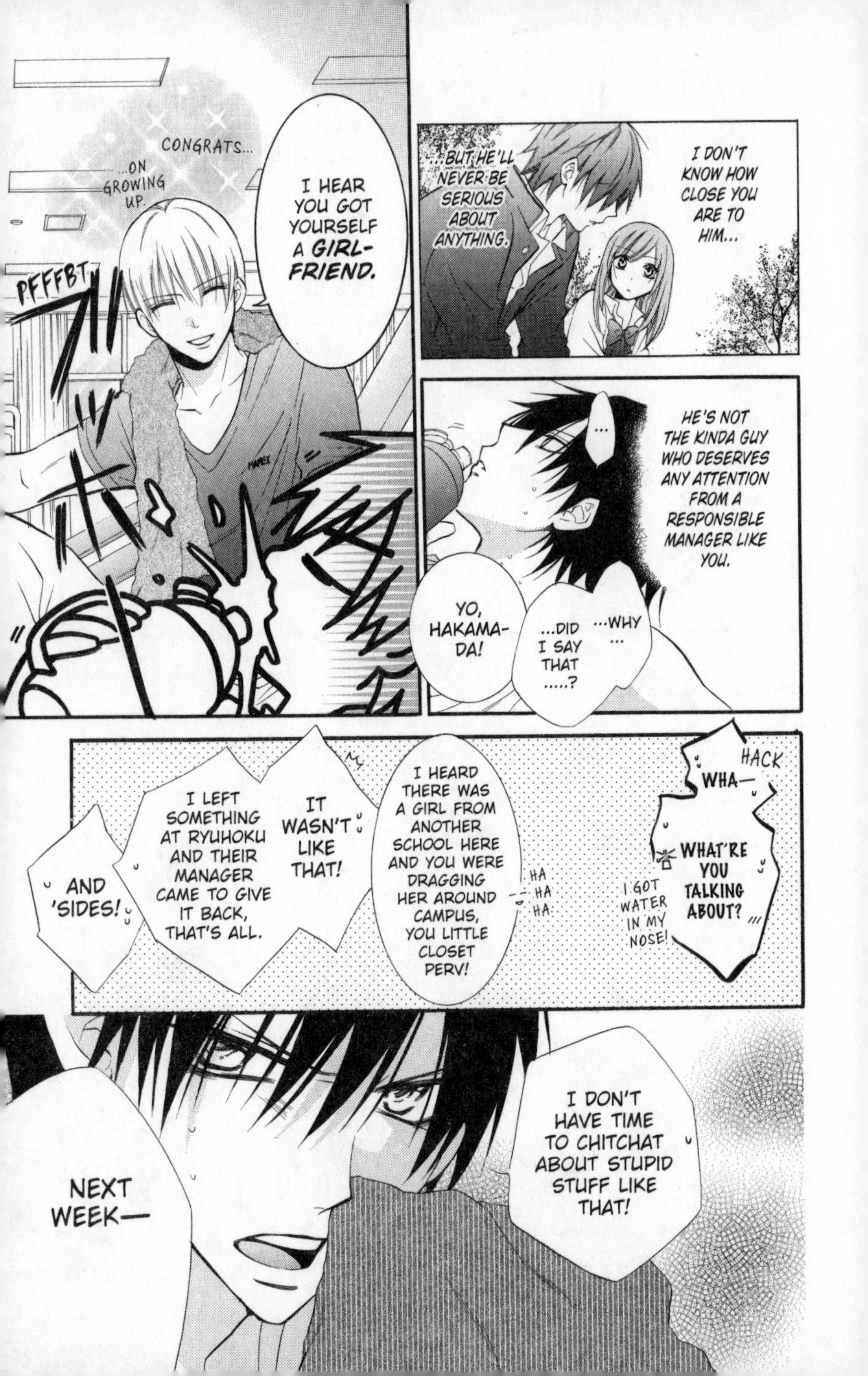
I DON'T KNOW HOW CLOSE YOU ARE TO HIM...
...BUT HE'LL NEVER BE SERIOUS ABOUT ANYTHING.
HE'S NOT THE KINDA GUY WHO DESERVES ANY ATTENTION FROM A RESPONSIBLE MANAGER LIKE YOU.
...
...WHY ...
...DID I SAY THAT .....?
YO, HAKAMA-DA!
I HEAR YOU GOT YOURSELF A GIRL-FRIEND.
CONGRATS...
...ON GROWING UP.
PFFFBT
HACK
WHA—
WHAT'RE YOU TALKING ABOUT?
I GOT WATER IN MY NOSE!
HA HA HA
I HEARD THERE WAS A GIRL FROM ANOTHER SCHOOL HERE AND YOU WERE DRAGGING HER AROUND CAMPUS, YOU LITTLE CLOSET PERV!
IT WASN'T LIKE THAT!
I LEFT SOMETHING AT RYUHOKU AND THEIR MANAGER CAME TO GIVE IT BACK, THAT'S ALL.
AND 'SIDES!
I DON'T HAVE TIME TO CHITCHAT ABOUT STUPID STUFF LIKE THAT!
NEXT WEEK—

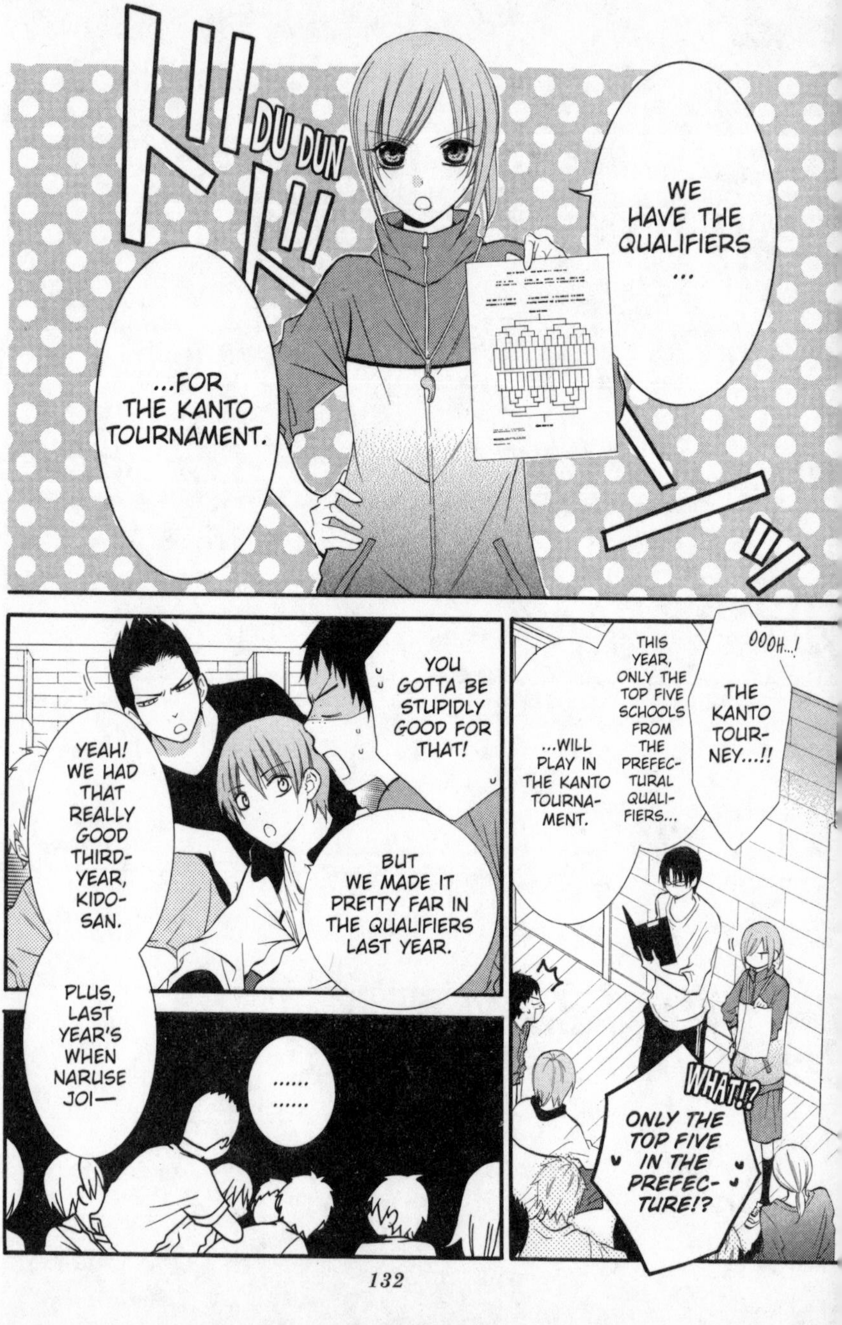
DU DUN
WE HAVE THE QUALIFIERS ...
...FOR THE KANTO TOURNAMENT.
OOOH...!
THE KANTO TOURNEY...!!
THIS YEAR, ONLY THE TOP FIVE SCHOOLS FROM THE PREFECTURAL QUALIFIERS...
...WILL PLAY IN THE KANTO TOURNAMENT.
WHAT!?
ONLY THE TOP FIVE IN THE PREFECTURE!?
YOU GOTTA BE STUPIDLY GOOD FOR THAT!
BUT WE MADE IT PRETTY FAR IN THE QUALIFIERS LAST YEAR.
YEAH! WE HAD THAT REALLY GOOD THIRD-YEAR, KIDO-SAN.
....
PLUS, LAST YEAR'S WHEN NARUSE JOI—

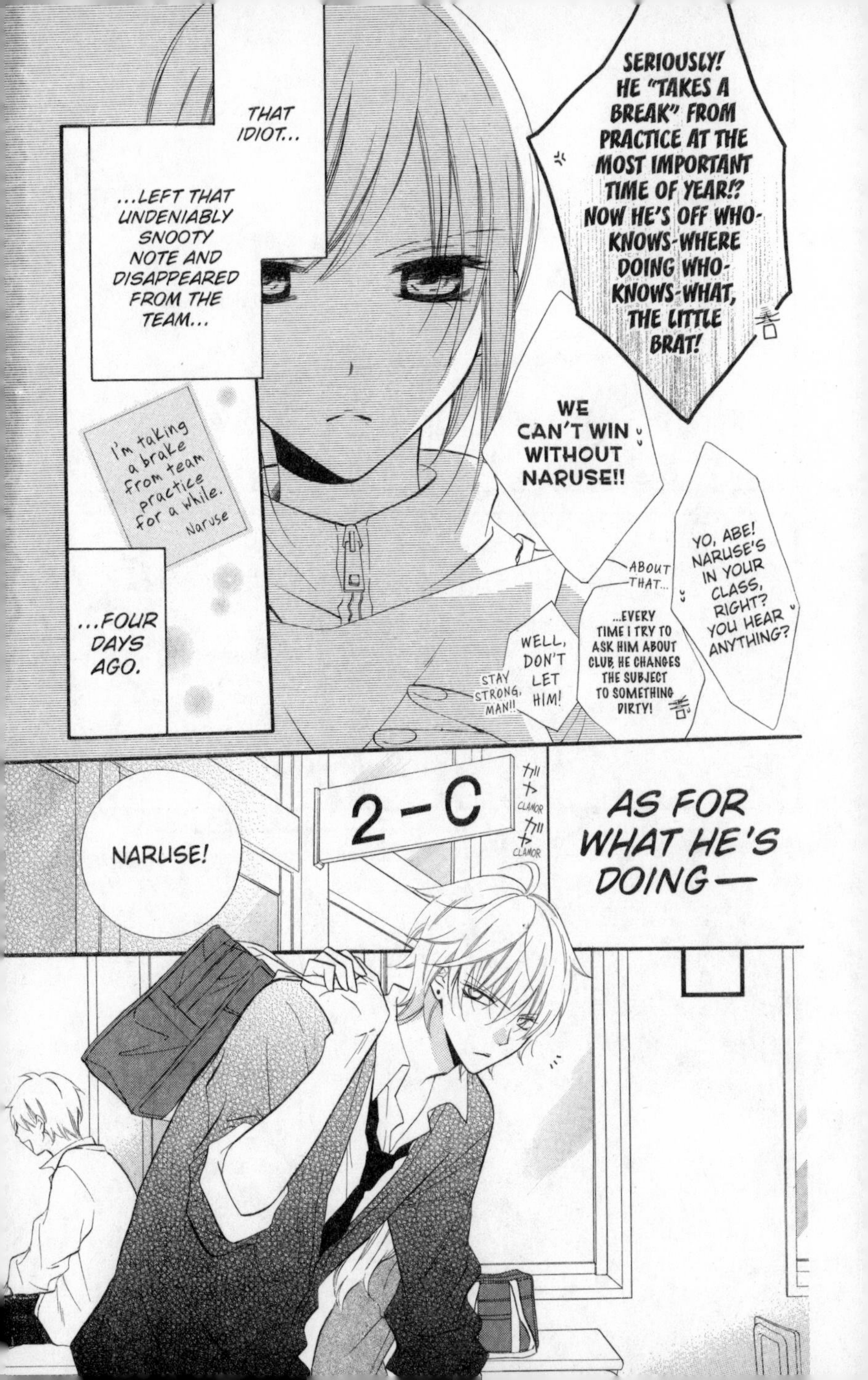
SERIOUSLY! HE "TAKES A BREAK" FROM PRACTICE AT THE MOST IMPORTANT TIME OF YEAR!? NOW HE'S OFF WHO-KNOWS-WHERE DOING WHO-KNOWS-WHAT, THE LITTLE BRAT!
WE CAN'T WIN WITHOUT NARUSE!!
YO, ABE! NARUSE'S IN YOUR CLASS, RIGHT? YOU HEAR ANYTHING?
ABOUT THAT...
...EVERY TIME I TRY TO ASK HIM ABOUT CLUB, HE CHANGES THE SUBJECT TO SOMETHING DIRTY!
WELL, DON'T LET HIM!
STAY STRONG, MAN!!
THAT IDIOT...
...LEFT THAT UNDENIABLY SNOOTY NOTE AND DISAPPEARED FROM THE TEAM...
I'm taking a brake from team practice for a while. Naruse
...FOUR DAYS AGO.
AS FOR WHAT HE'S DOING—
2-C
CLAMOR
CLAMOR
NARUSE!

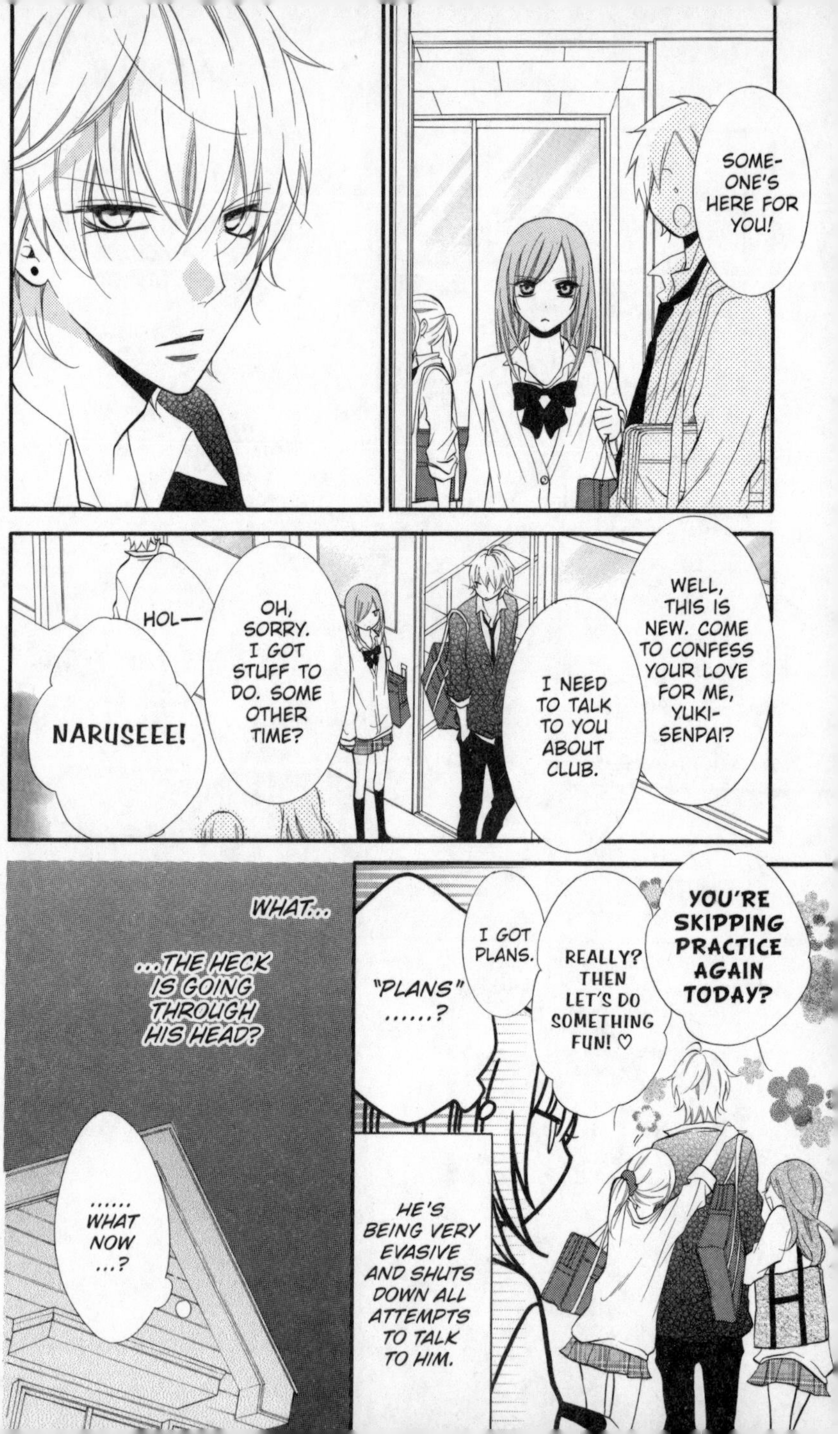
SOME-ONE'S HERE FOR YOU!
WELL, THIS IS NEW. COME TO CONFESS YOUR LOVE FOR ME, YUKI-SENPAI?
I NEED TO TALK TO YOU ABOUT CLUB.
OH, SORRY. I GOT STUFF TO DO. SOME OTHER TIME?
HOL—
NARUSEEE!
YOU'RE SKIPPING PRACTICE AGAIN TODAY?
REALLY? THEN LET'S DO SOMETHING FUN! ♡
I GOT PLANS.
"PLANS" ......?
HE'S BEING VERY EVASIVE AND SHUTS DOWN ALL ATTEMPTS TO TALK TO HIM.
WHAT...
...THE HECK IS GOING THROUGH HIS HEAD?
......WHAT NOW...?

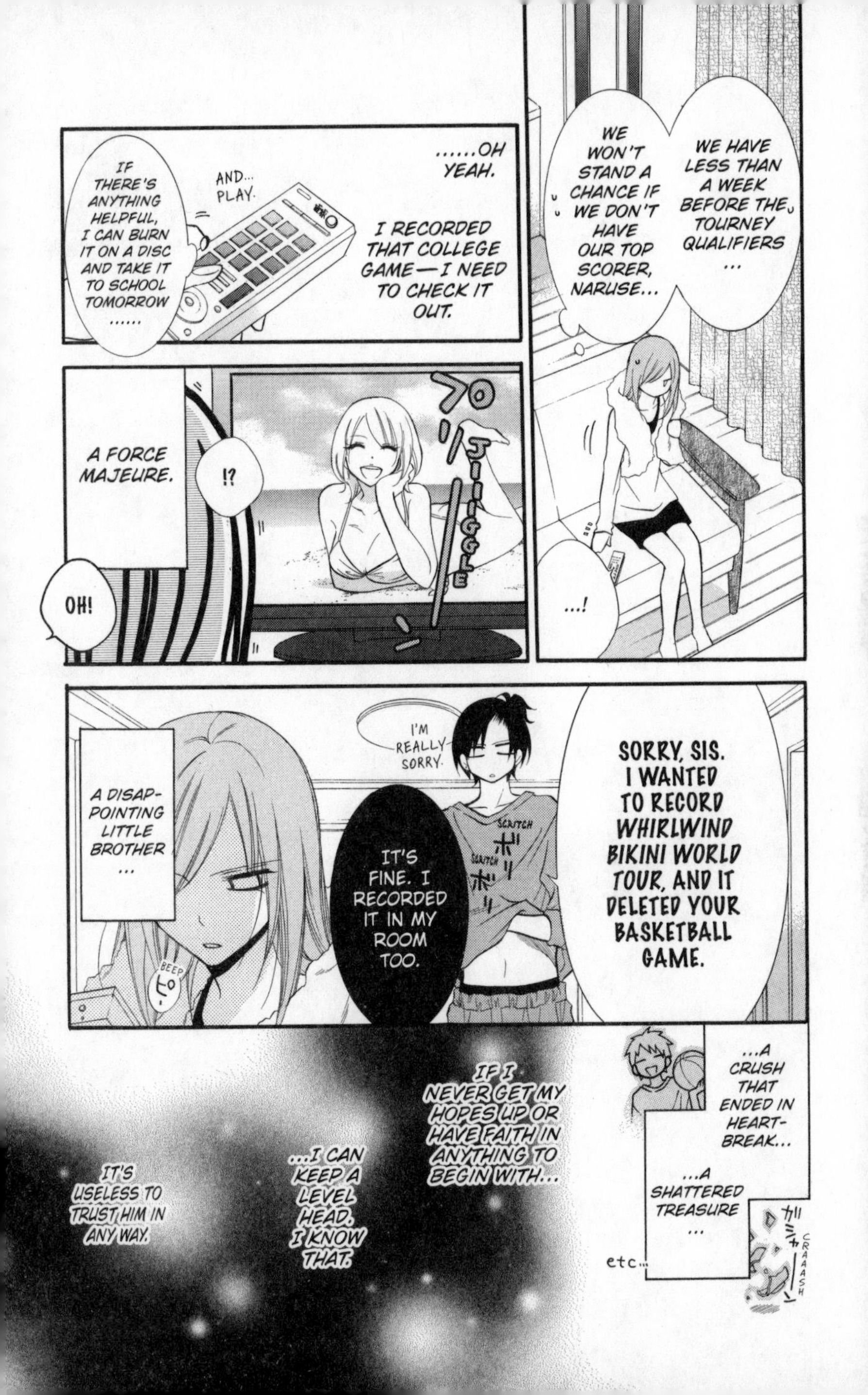
WE HAVE LESS THAN A WEEK BEFORE THE TOURNEY QUALIFIERS ...
WE WON'T STAND A CHANCE IF WE DON'T HAVE OUR TOP SCORER, NARUSE...
...!
......OH YEAH.
I RECORDED THAT COLLEGE GAME—I NEED TO CHECK IT OUT.
AND... PLAY.
IF THERE'S ANYTHING HELPFUL, I CAN BURN IT ON A DISC AND TAKE IT TO SCHOOL TOMORROW ......
JIIIGGLE
!?
A FORCE MAJEURE.
OH!
SORRY, SIS. I WANTED TO RECORD WHIRLWIND BIKINI WORLD TOUR, AND IT DELETED YOUR BASKETBALL GAME.
I'M REALLY SORRY.
SCRITCH
SCRITCH
IT'S FINE. I RECORDED IT IN MY ROOM TOO.
BEEP
A DISAP-POINTING LITTLE BROTHER ...
...A CRUSH THAT ENDED IN HEART-BREAK...
...A SHATTERED TREASURE ...
CRAAASH
etc...
IF I NEVER GET MY HOPES UP OR HAVE FAITH IN ANYTHING TO BEGIN WITH...
...I CAN KEEP A LEVEL HEAD. I KNOW THAT.
IT'S USELESS TO TRUST HIM IN ANY WAY.

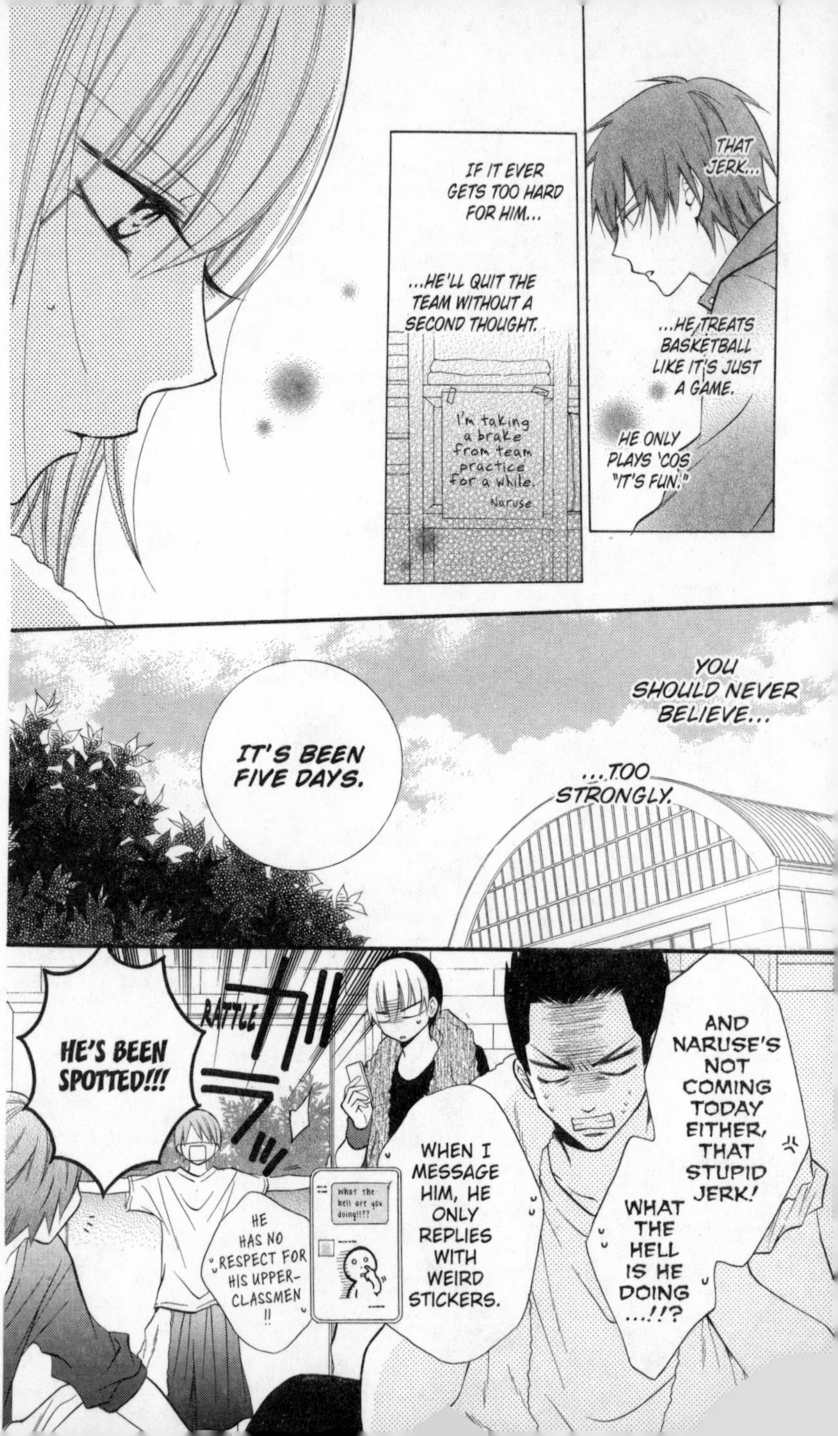
THAT JERK...
...HE TREATS BASKETBALL LIKE IT'S JUST A GAME.
HE ONLY PLAYS 'COS "IT'S FUN."
IF IT EVER GETS TOO HARD FOR HIM...
...HE'LL QUIT THE TEAM WITHOUT A SECOND THOUGHT.
I'm taking a brake from team practice for a while. Naruse
YOU SHOULD NEVER BELIEVE...
...TOO STRONGLY.
IT'S BEEN FIVE DAYS.
AND NARUSE'S NOT COMING TODAY EITHER, THAT STUPID JERK!
WHAT THE HELL IS HE DOING ...!!?
WHEN I MESSAGE HIM, HE ONLY REPLIES WITH WEIRD STICKERS.
What the hell are you doing!!??
HE HAS NO RESPECT FOR HIS UPPER-CLASSMEN!!
RATTLE
HE'S BEEN SPOTTED!!!

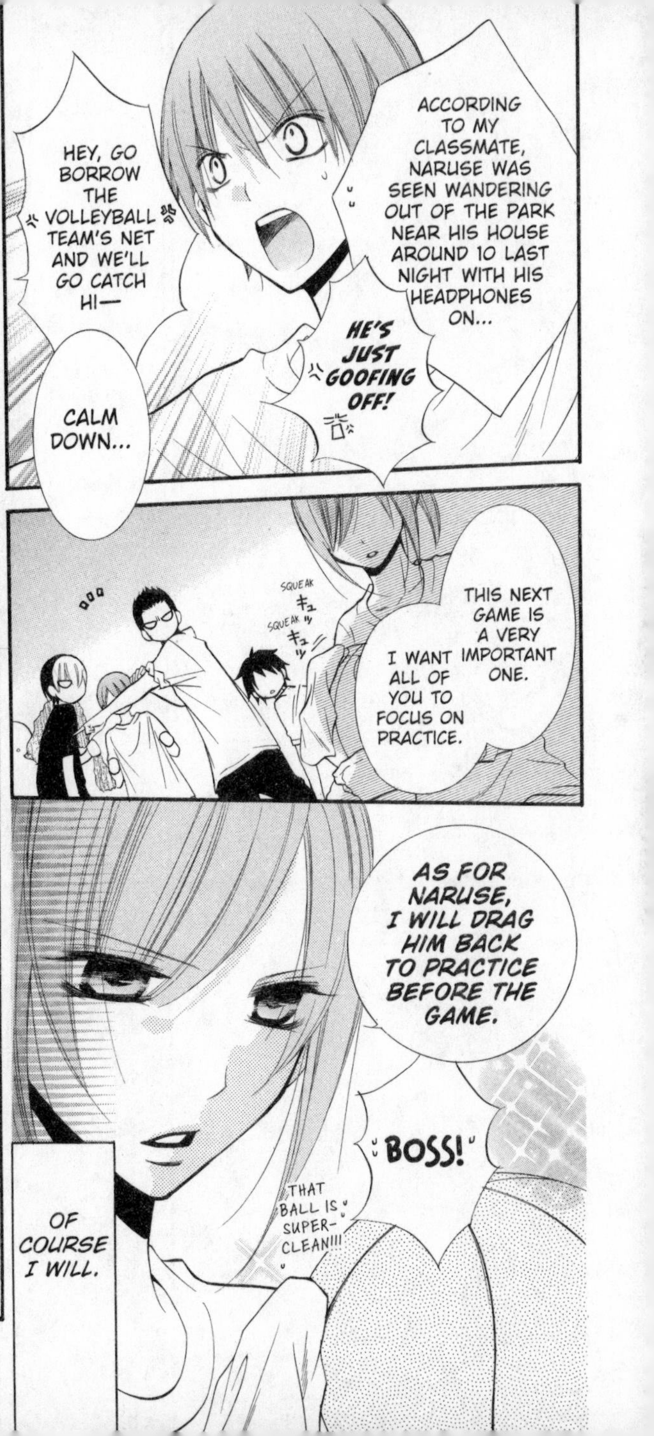
ACCORDING TO MY CLASSMATE, NARUSE WAS SEEN WANDERING OUT OF THE PARK NEAR HIS HOUSE AROUND 10 LAST NIGHT WITH HIS HEADPHONES ON...
HE'S JUST GOOFING OFF!
HEY, GO BORROW THE VOLLEYBALL TEAM'S NET AND WE'LL GO CATCH HI—
CALM DOWN...
THIS NEXT GAME IS A VERY IMPORTANT ONE.
I WANT ALL OF YOU TO FOCUS ON PRACTICE.
SQUEAK
SQUEAK
AS FOR NARUSE, I WILL DRAG HIM BACK TO PRACTICE BEFORE THE GAME.
BOSS!
THAT BALL IS SUPER-CLEAN!!!
OF COURSE I WILL.

05

PROFILES: YUKI AND NARUSE

At the autograph signing and in letters and such, people keep saying to me, "Give us character profiles!" So I will now present the profiles of the two main characters. I doubt you'll think they give anything that's too in-depth away.

Yuki Machida
(currently 17)
Born: September 12
Virgo, blood type A
The eldest of six.
Surprisingly sweet-toothed, unexpectedly fond of soft, fluffy things.
Favorite color:
None in particular (she claims, but it's pink)
Dislikes:
Nothing in particular (she claims, but she doesn't like scary stories or bitter coffee)
Favorite type:
A responsible, faithful gentleman with a handsome smile

Shou Naruse
(currently 16)
Born: July 25
Leo, blood type B
The youngest. (Has a sister.)
A dog person who loves cats.
Plays video games in his spare time, but gives up on RPGs before beating them.
Favorite color: black
Dislikes: mushrooms, natto, tomatoes, bluefish, carrots, kanji, cold places, etc.
Favorite type:
A prim and proper type with straight long hair. More of a breast guy than a butt guy.

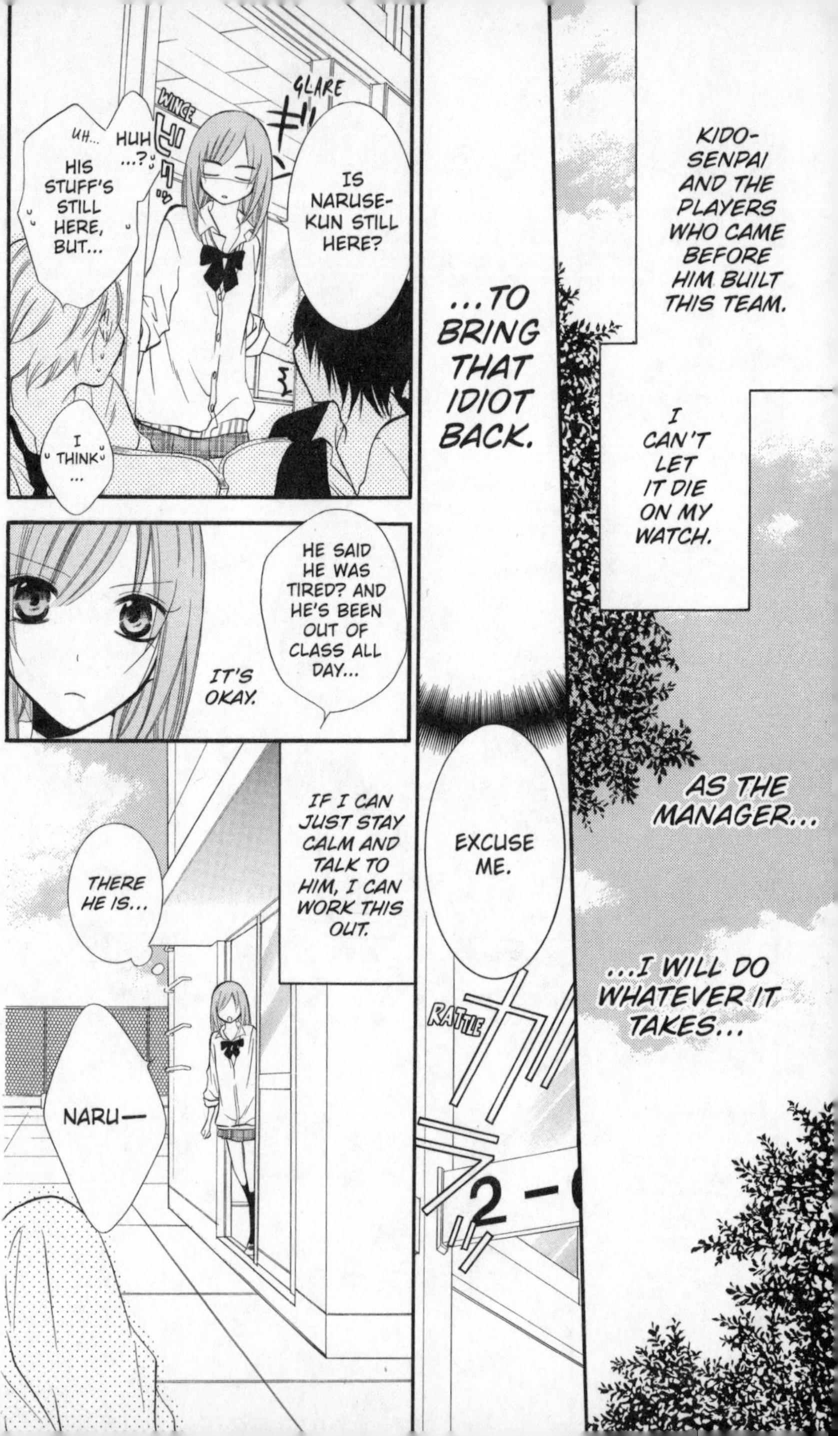
KIDO-SENPAI AND THE PLAYERS WHO CAME BEFORE HIM BUILT THIS TEAM.
I CAN'T LET IT DIE ON MY WATCH.
AS THE MANAGER...
...I WILL DO WHATEVER IT TAKES...
...TO BRING THAT IDIOT BACK.
EXCUSE ME.
RATTLE
IS NARUSE-KUN STILL HERE?
GLARE
WINCE
HUH ...?
UH... HIS STUFF'S STILL HERE, BUT...
I THINK ...
HE SAID HE WAS TIRED? AND HE'S BEEN OUT OF CLASS ALL DAY...
IT'S OKAY.
IF I CAN JUST STAY CALM AND TALK TO HIM, I CAN WORK THIS OUT.
THERE HE IS...
NARU—

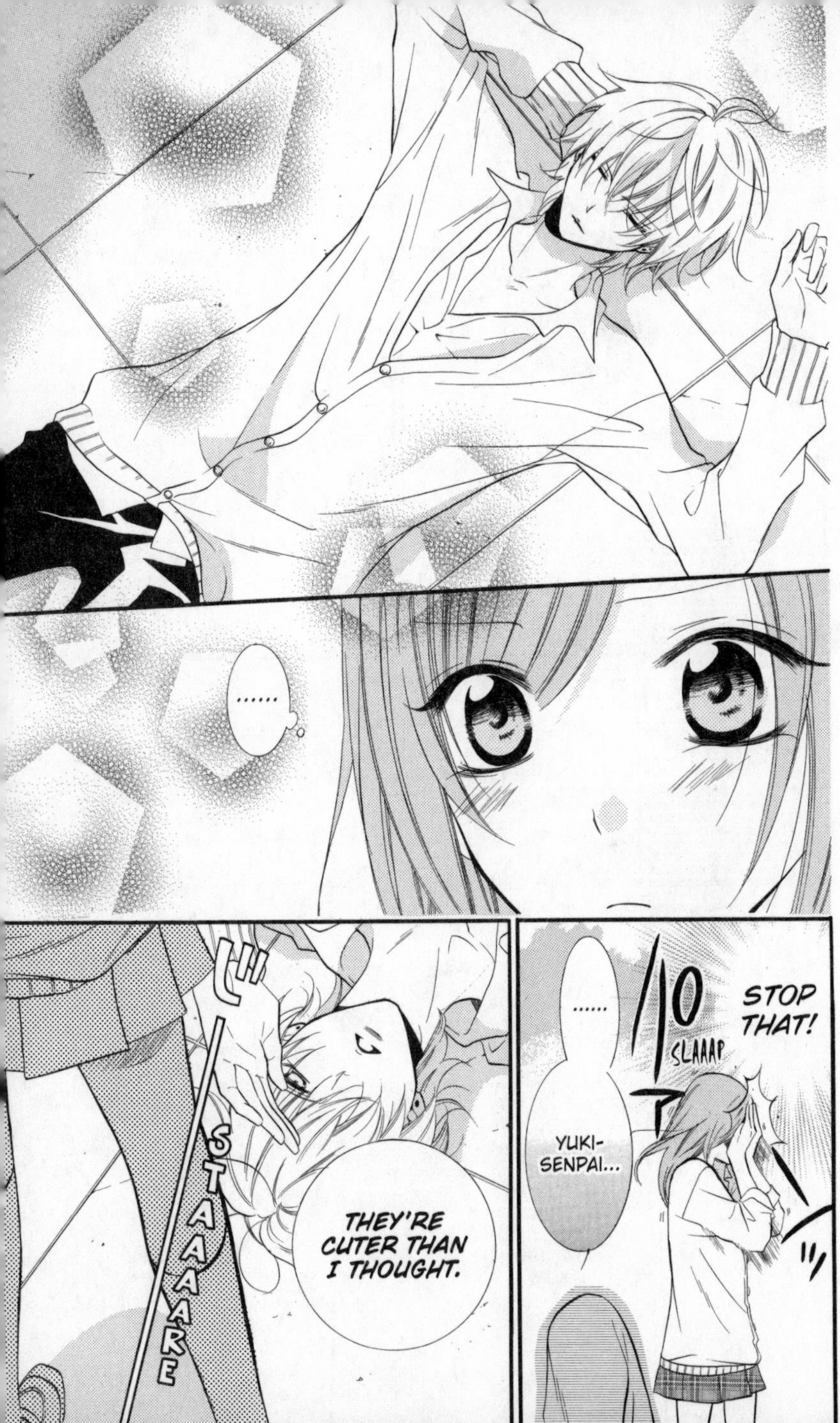
......
STOP THAT!
SLAAAP
......
YUKI-SENPAI...
THEY'RE CUTER THAN I THOUGHT.
STAAAAARE

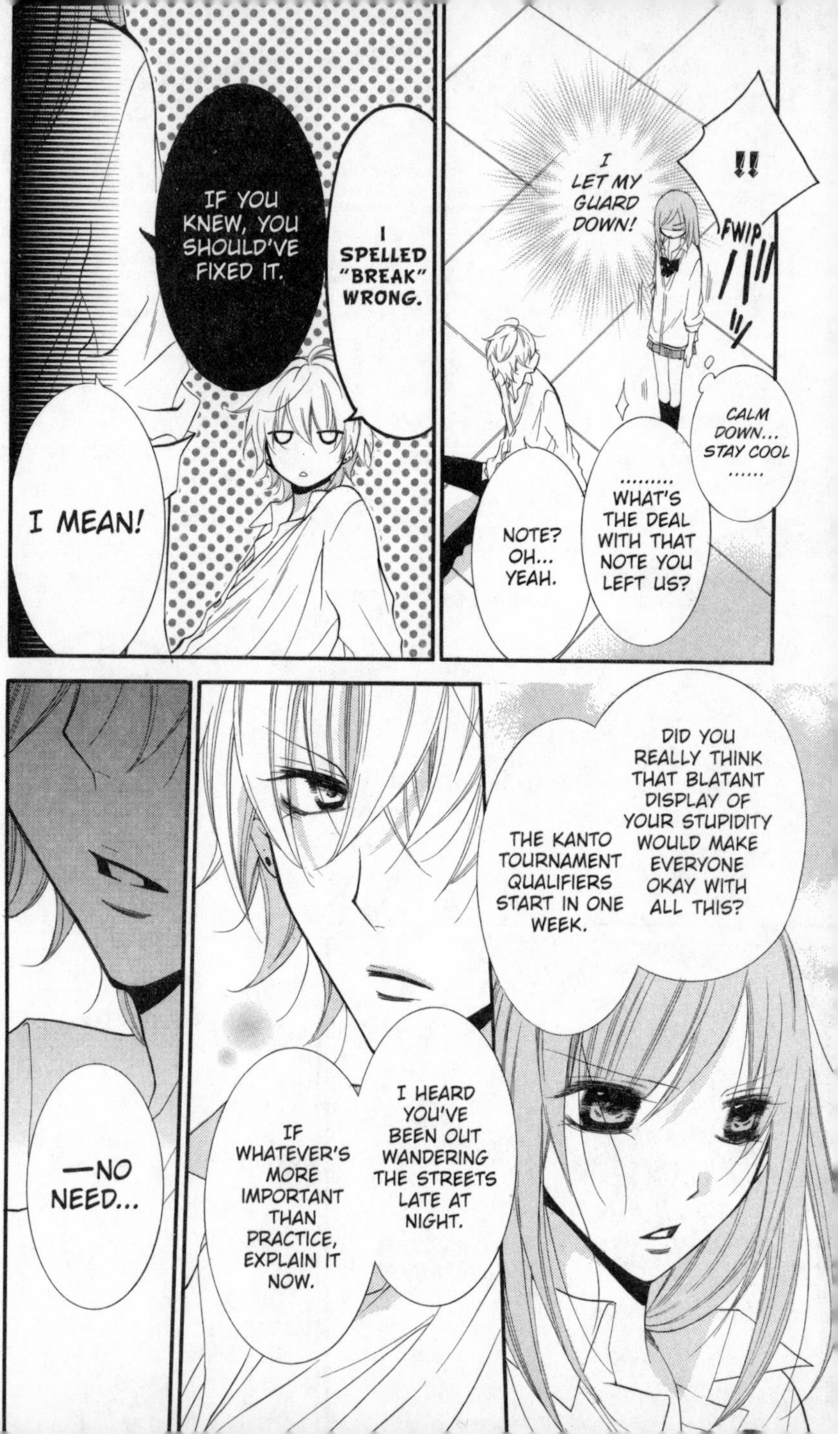
!!
FWIP
I LET MY GUARD DOWN!
CALM DOWN... STAY COOL ......
.... WHAT'S THE DEAL WITH THAT NOTE YOU LEFT US?
NOTE? OH... YEAH.
I SPELLED "BREAK" WRONG.
IF YOU KNEW, YOU SHOULD'VE FIXED IT.
I MEAN!
DID YOU REALLY THINK THAT BLATANT DISPLAY OF YOUR STUPIDITY WOULD MAKE EVERYONE OKAY WITH ALL THIS?
THE KANTO TOURNAMENT QUALIFIERS START IN ONE WEEK.
I HEARD YOU'VE BEEN OUT WANDERING THE STREETS LATE AT NIGHT.
IF WHATEVER'S MORE IMPORTANT THAN PRACTICE, EXPLAIN IT NOW.
—NO NEED...

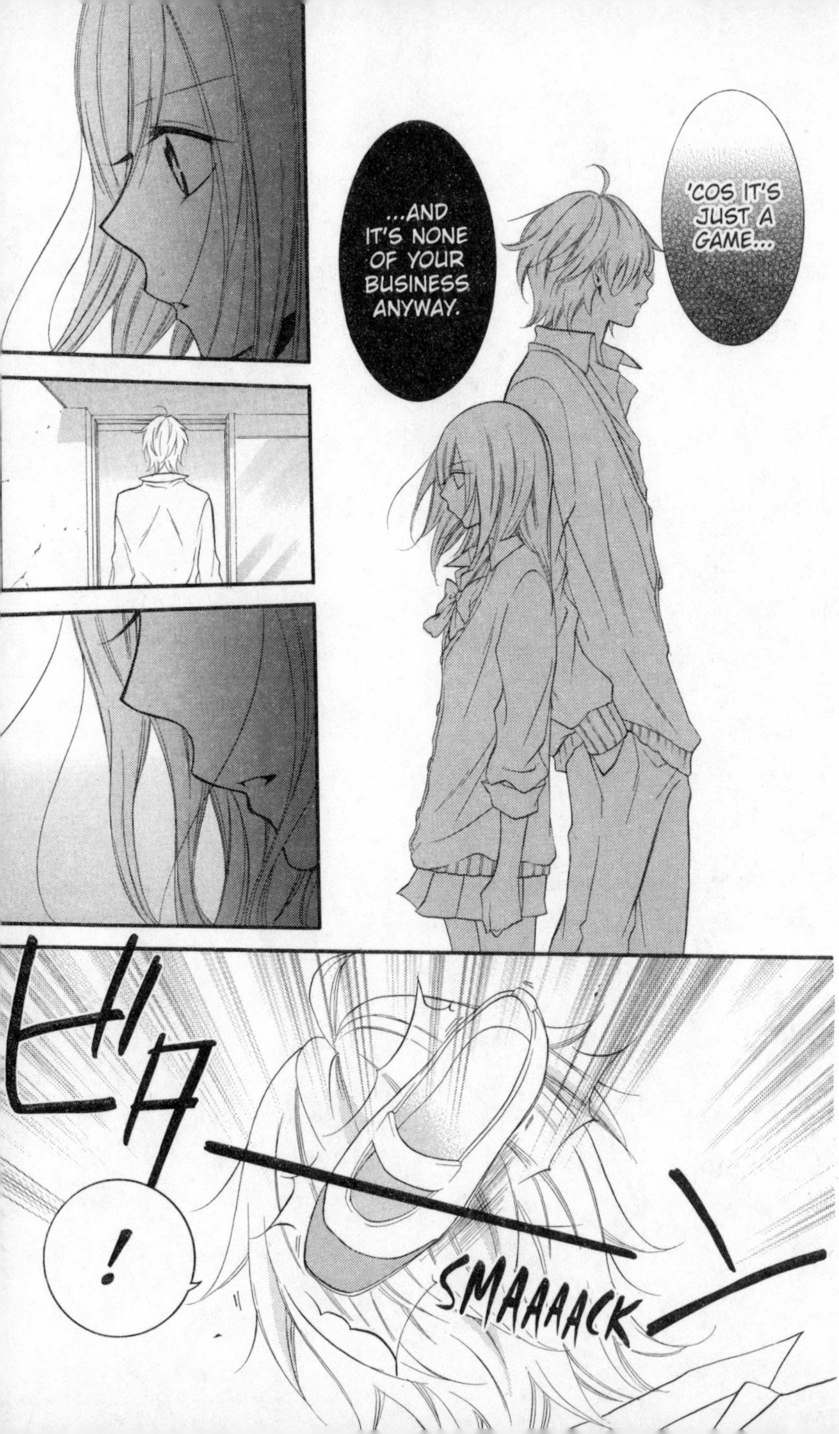
'COS IT'S JUST A GAME...
...AND IT'S NONE OF YOUR BUSINESS ANYWAY.
!
SMAAAACK

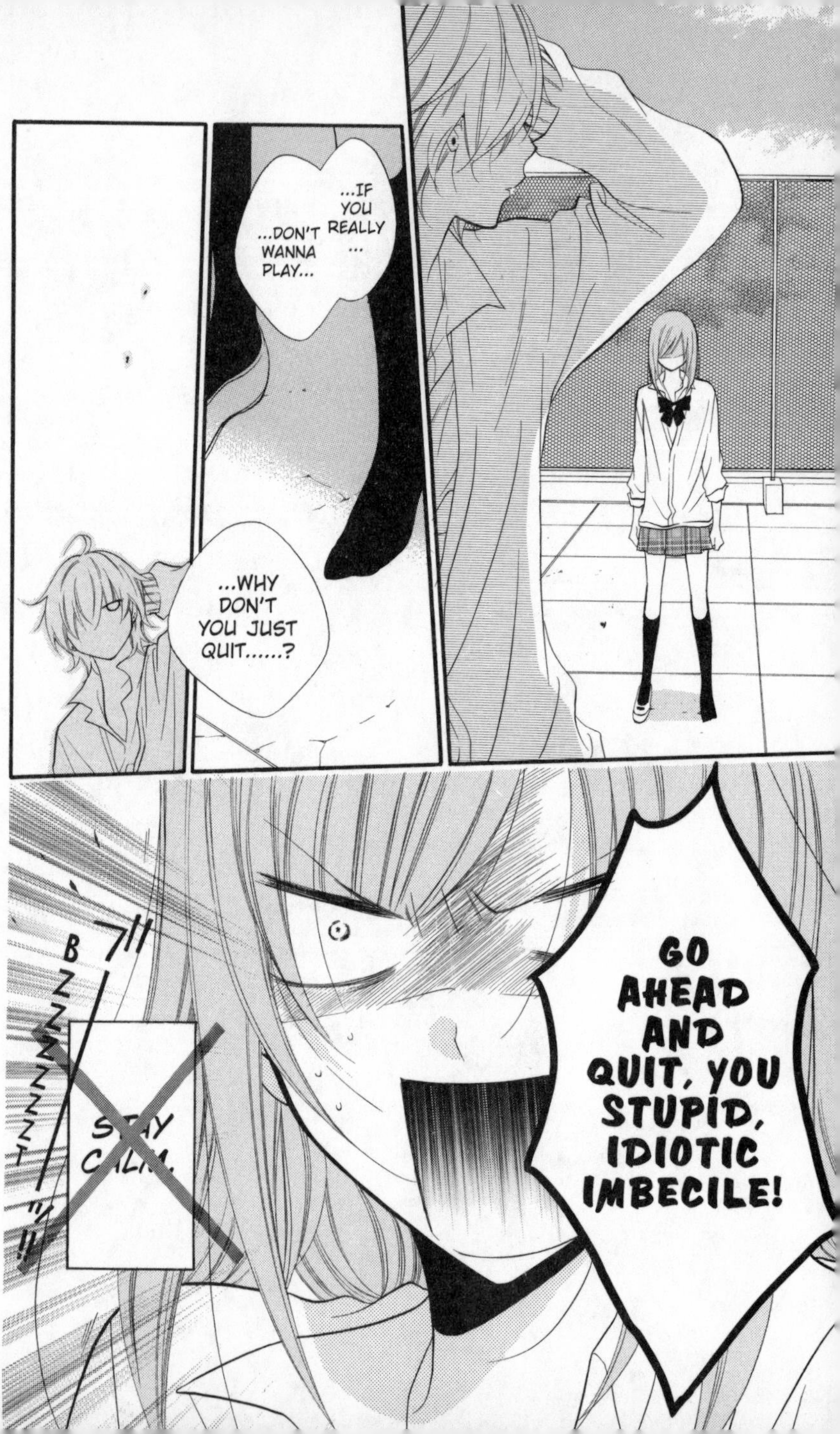
...IF YOU REALLY ... ...DON'T WANNA PLAY...
...WHY DON'T YOU JUST QUIT......?
GO AHEAD AND QUIT, YOU STUPID, IDIOTIC IMBECILE!
STAY CALM.

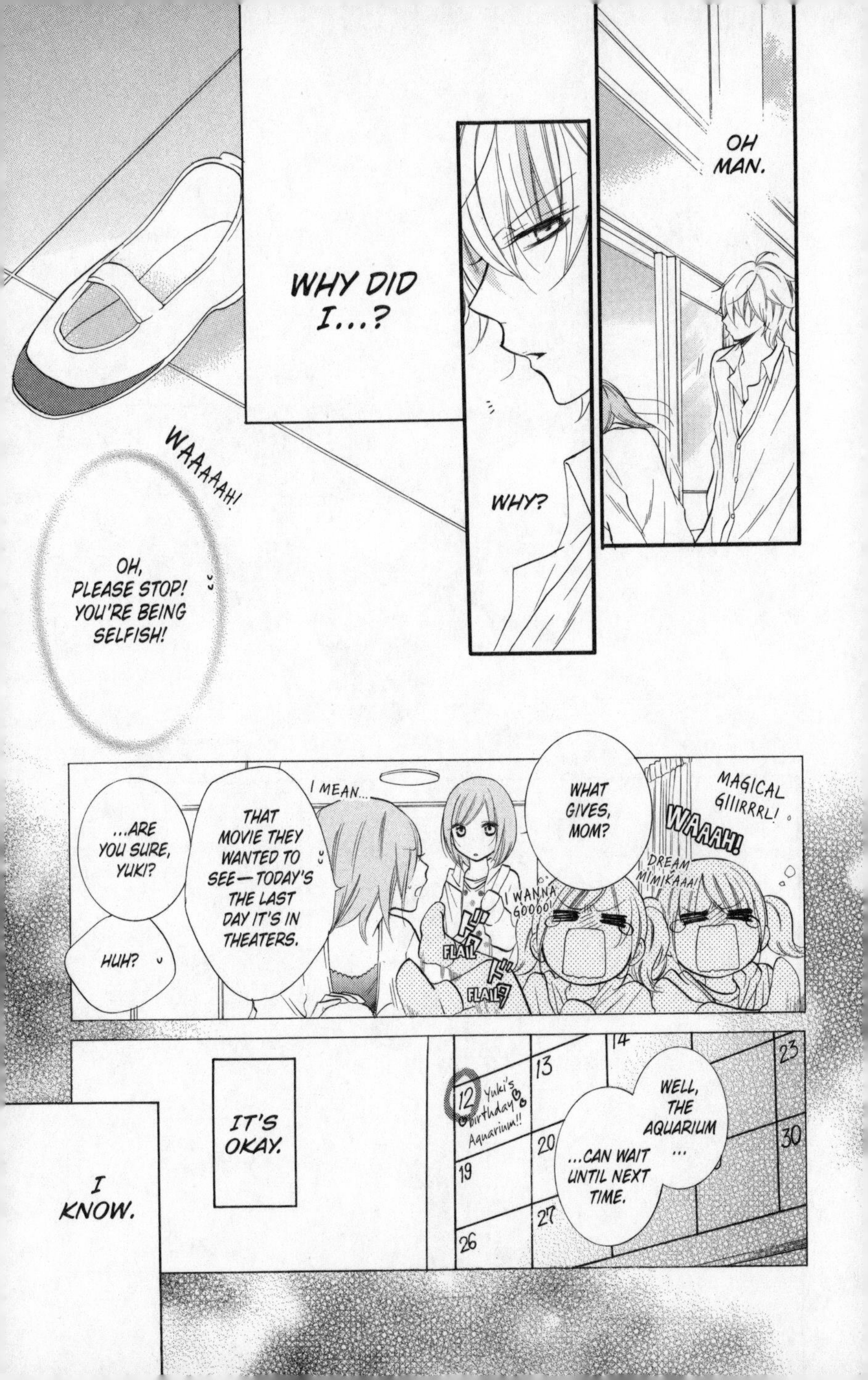

OH MAN.
WHY DID I...?
WHY?
WAAAAAH!
OH, PLEASE STOP! YOU'RE BEING SELFISH!
MAGICAL GIIIRRRL!
WAAAH!
DREAM MIMIKAAA!
WHAT GIVES, MOM?
I WANNA GOOOO!
FLAIL
FLAIL
I MEAN...
THAT MOVIE THEY WANTED TO SEE—TODAY'S THE LAST DAY IT'S IN THEATERS.
...ARE YOU SURE, YUKI?
HUH?
14
13
23
12 Yuki's birthday Aquarium!!
30
20
19
27
26
WELL, THE AQUARIUM ...
...CAN WAIT UNTIL NEXT TIME.
IT'S OKAY.
I KNOW.

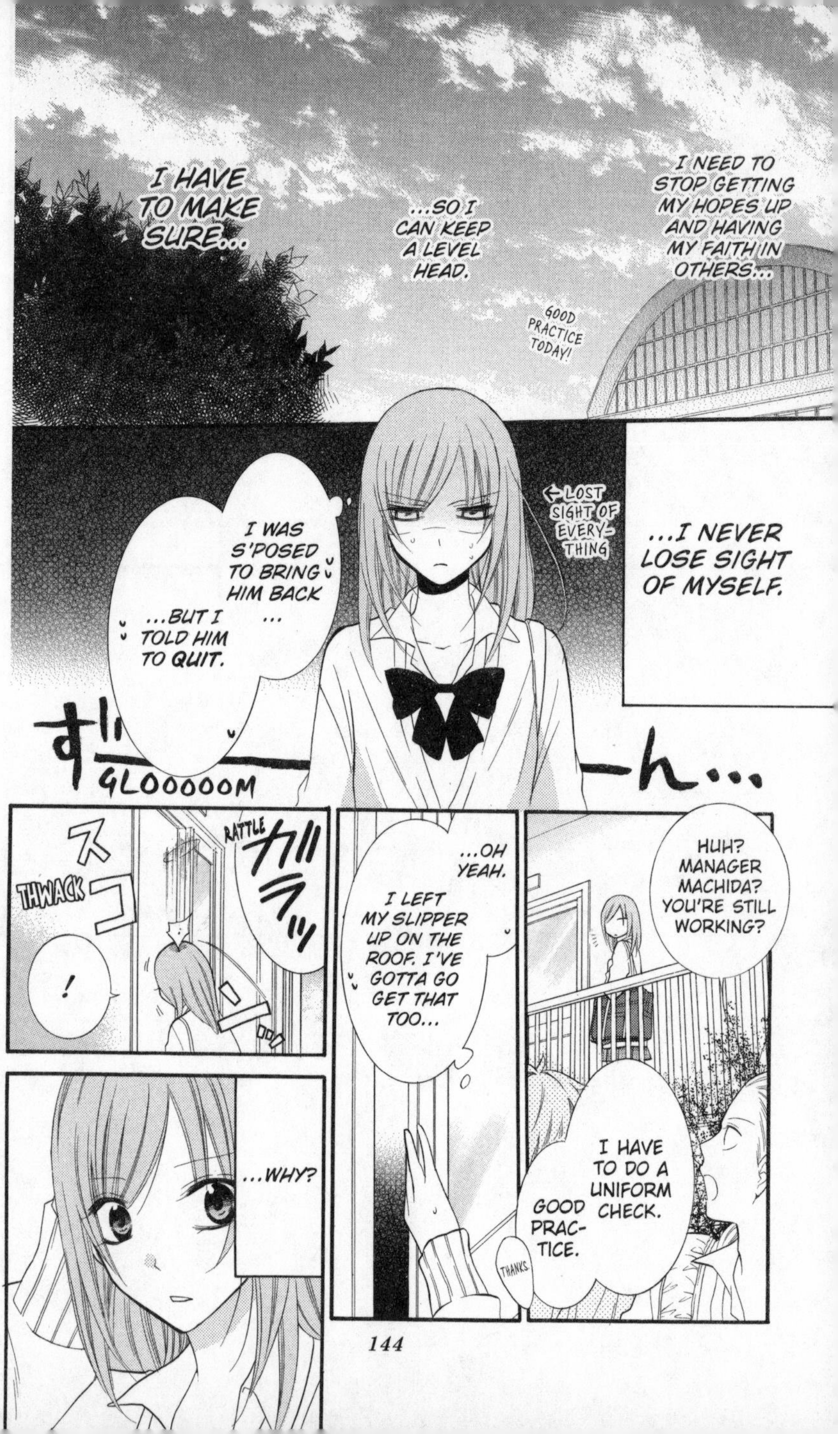
I NEED TO STOP GETTING MY HOPES UP AND HAVING MY FAITH IN OTHERS...
...SO I CAN KEEP A LEVEL HEAD.
I HAVE TO MAKE SURE...
GOOD PRACTICE TODAY!
...I NEVER LOSE SIGHT OF MYSELF.
← LOST SIGHT OF EVERY-THING
I WAS S'POSED TO BRING HIM BACK...
...BUT I TOLD HIM TO QUIT.
GLOOOOOM
HUH? MANAGER MACHIDA? YOU'RE STILL WORKING?
I HAVE TO DO A UNIFORM CHECK.
GOOD PRAC-TICE.
THANKS.
...OH YEAH.
I LEFT MY SLIPPER UP ON THE ROOF. I'VE GOTTA GO GET THAT TOO...
RATTLE
THWACK
!
...WHY?

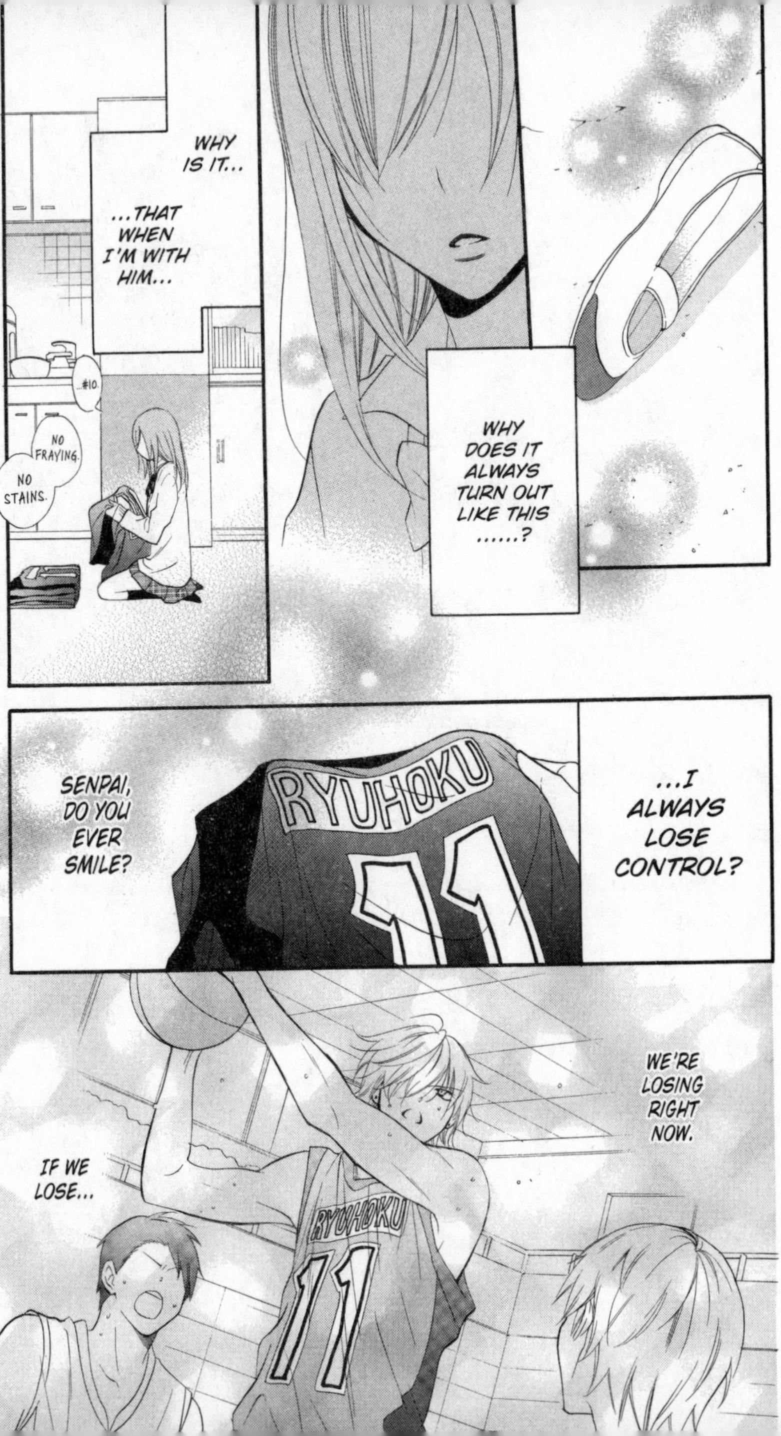
WHY DOES IT ALWAYS TURN OUT LIKE THIS ......?
WHY IS IT...
...THAT WHEN I'M WITH HIM...
...#10.
NO FRAYING.
NO STAINS.
...I ALWAYS LOSE CONTROL?
RYUHOKU 11
SENPAI, DO YOU EVER SMILE?
WE'RE LOSING RIGHT NOW.
RYUHOKU 11
IF WE LOSE...

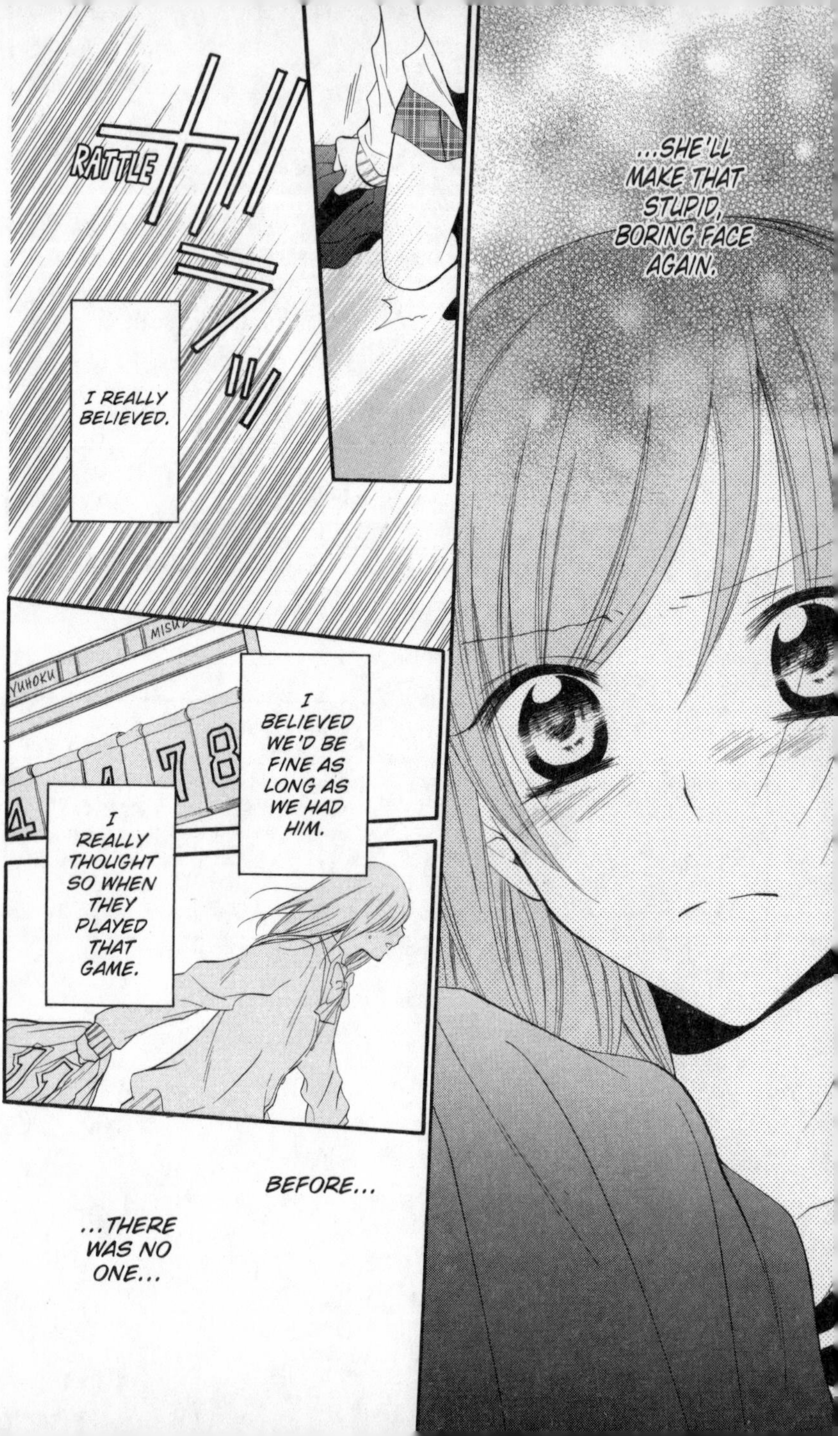
...SHE'LL MAKE THAT STUPID, BORING FACE AGAIN.
RATTLE
I REALLY BELIEVED.
YUHOKU
I BELIEVED WE'D BE FINE AS LONG AS WE HAD HIM.
I REALLY THOUGHT SO WHEN THEY PLAYED THAT GAME.
BEFORE...
...THERE WAS NO ONE...

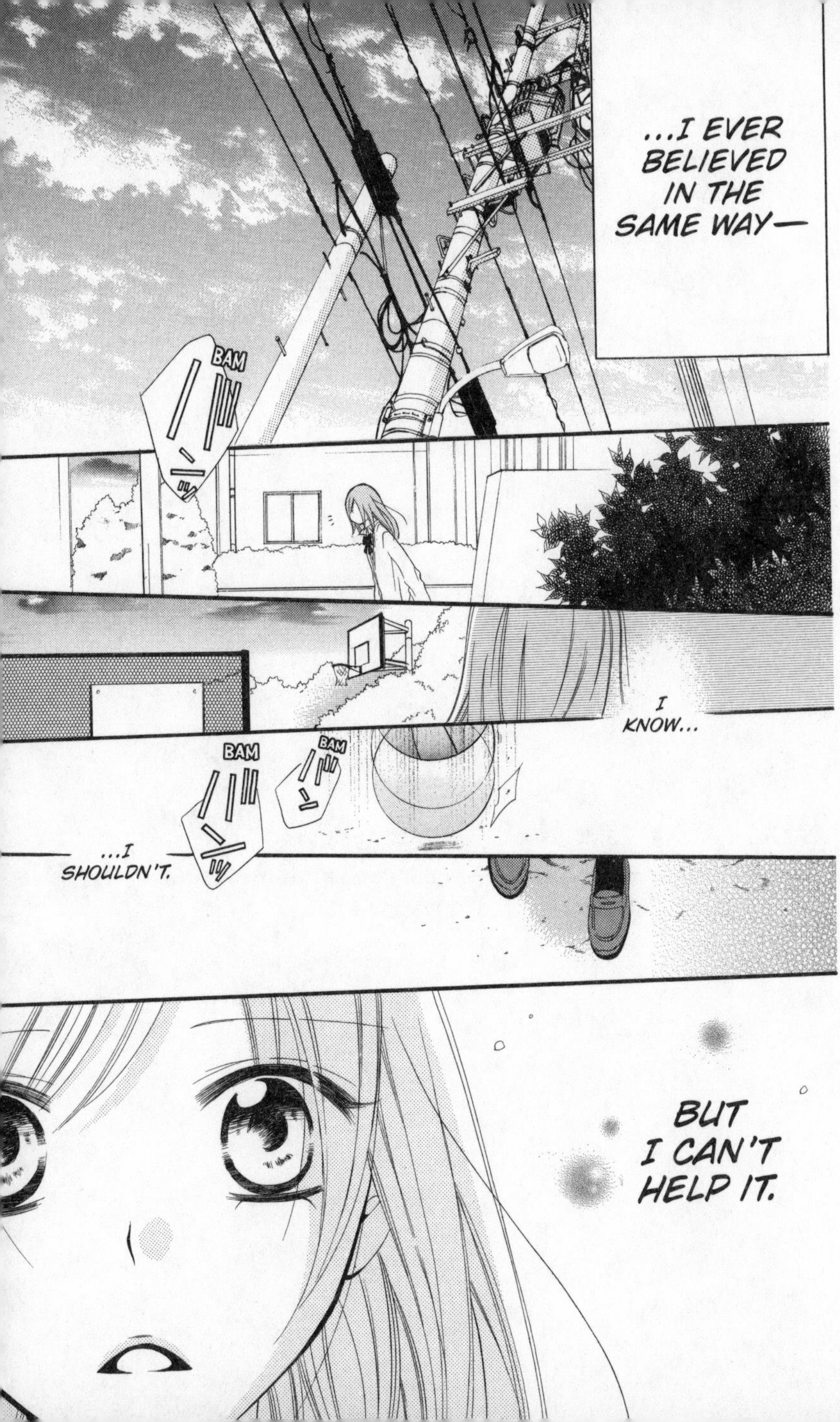
...I EVER BELIEVED IN THE SAME WAY—
BAM
I KNOW...
BAM
BAM
...I SHOULDN'T.
BUT I CAN'T HELP IT.

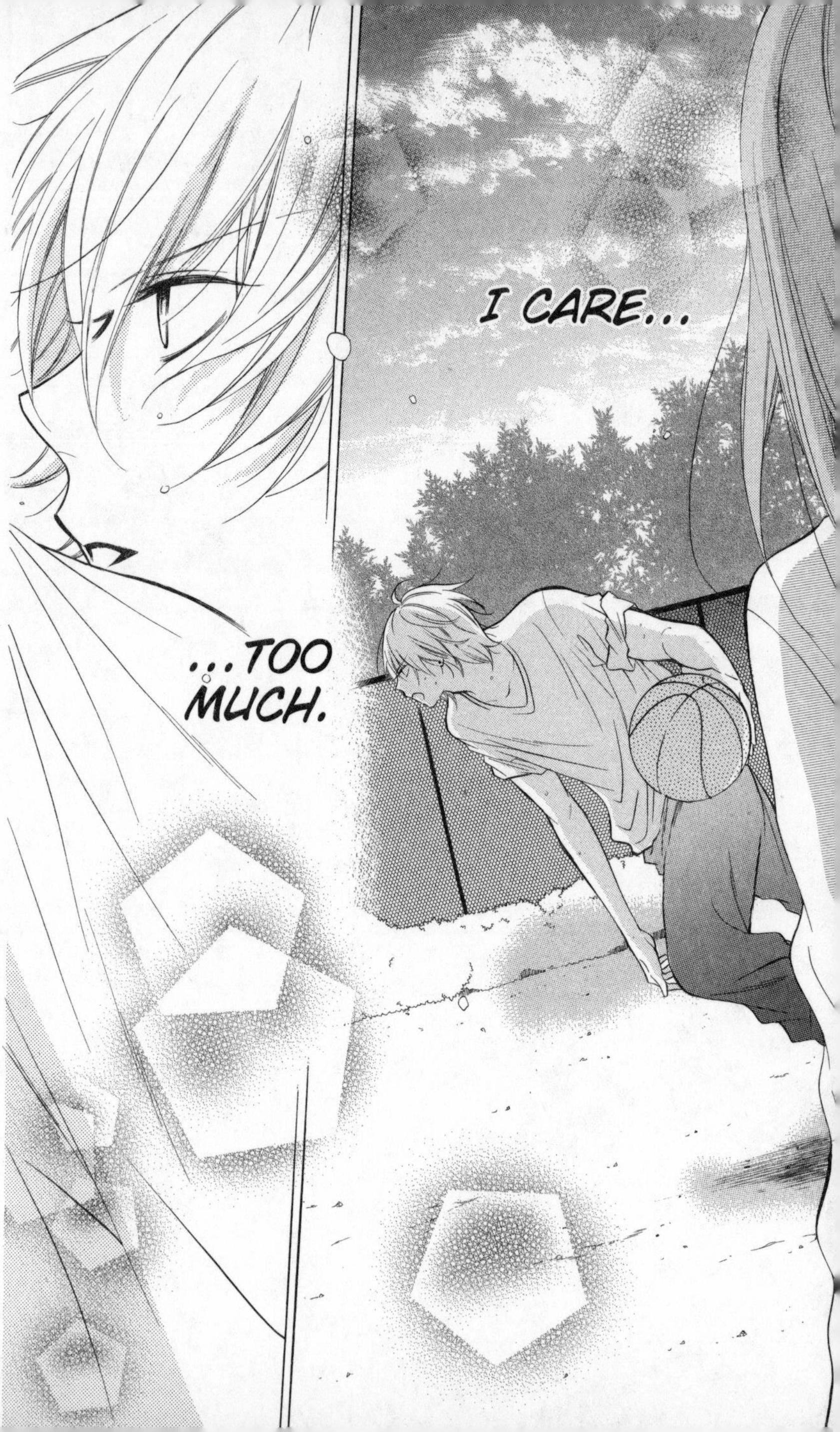
I CARE...
...TOO MUCH.

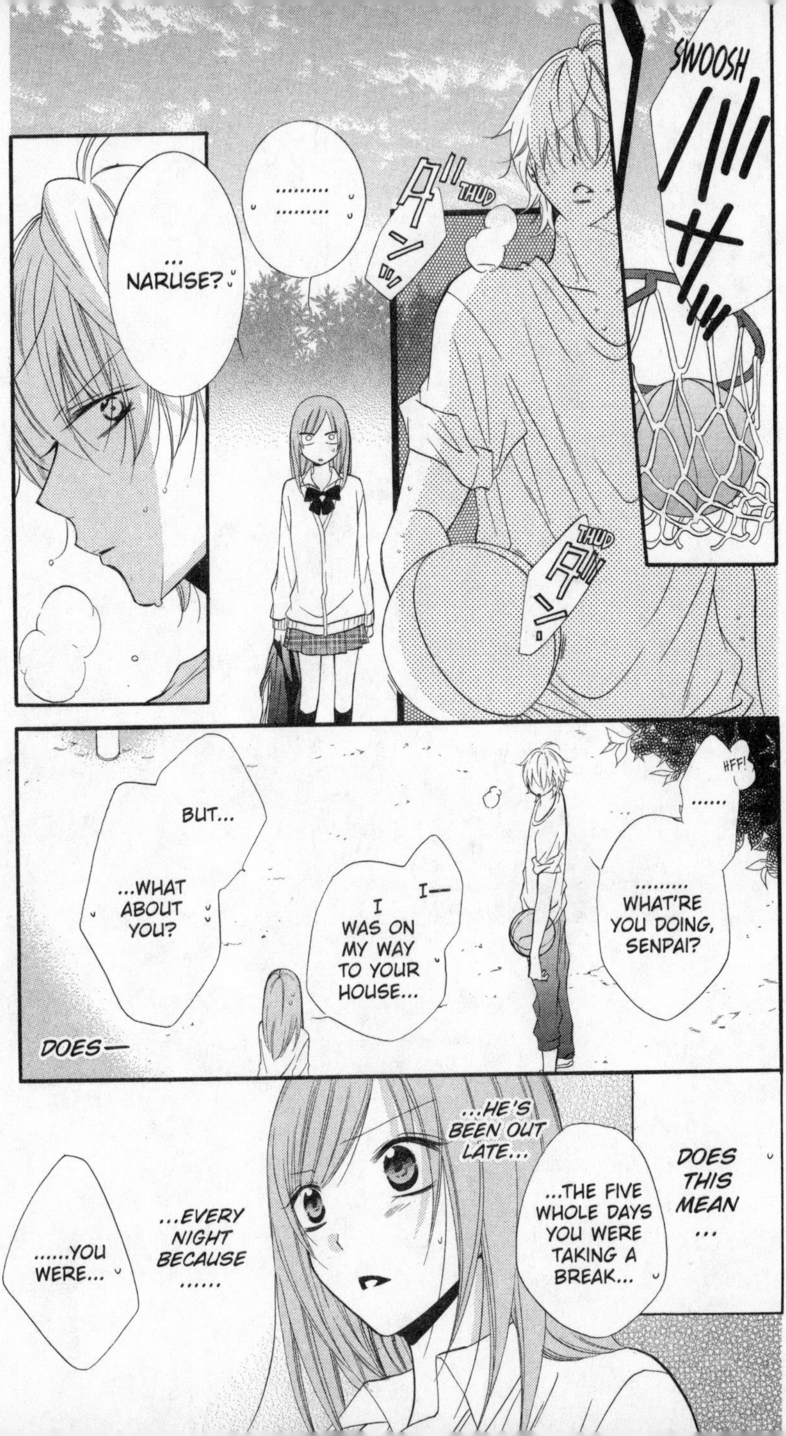
SWOOSH
THUD
....
....
THUD
... NARUSE?
HFF!
......
.... WHAT'RE YOU DOING, SENPAI?
I— I WAS ON MY WAY TO YOUR HOUSE...
BUT...
...WHAT ABOUT YOU?
DOES—
DOES THIS MEAN ...
...THE FIVE WHOLE DAYS YOU WERE TAKING A BREAK...
...HE'S BEEN OUT LATE...
...EVERY NIGHT BECAUSE ......
......YOU WERE...

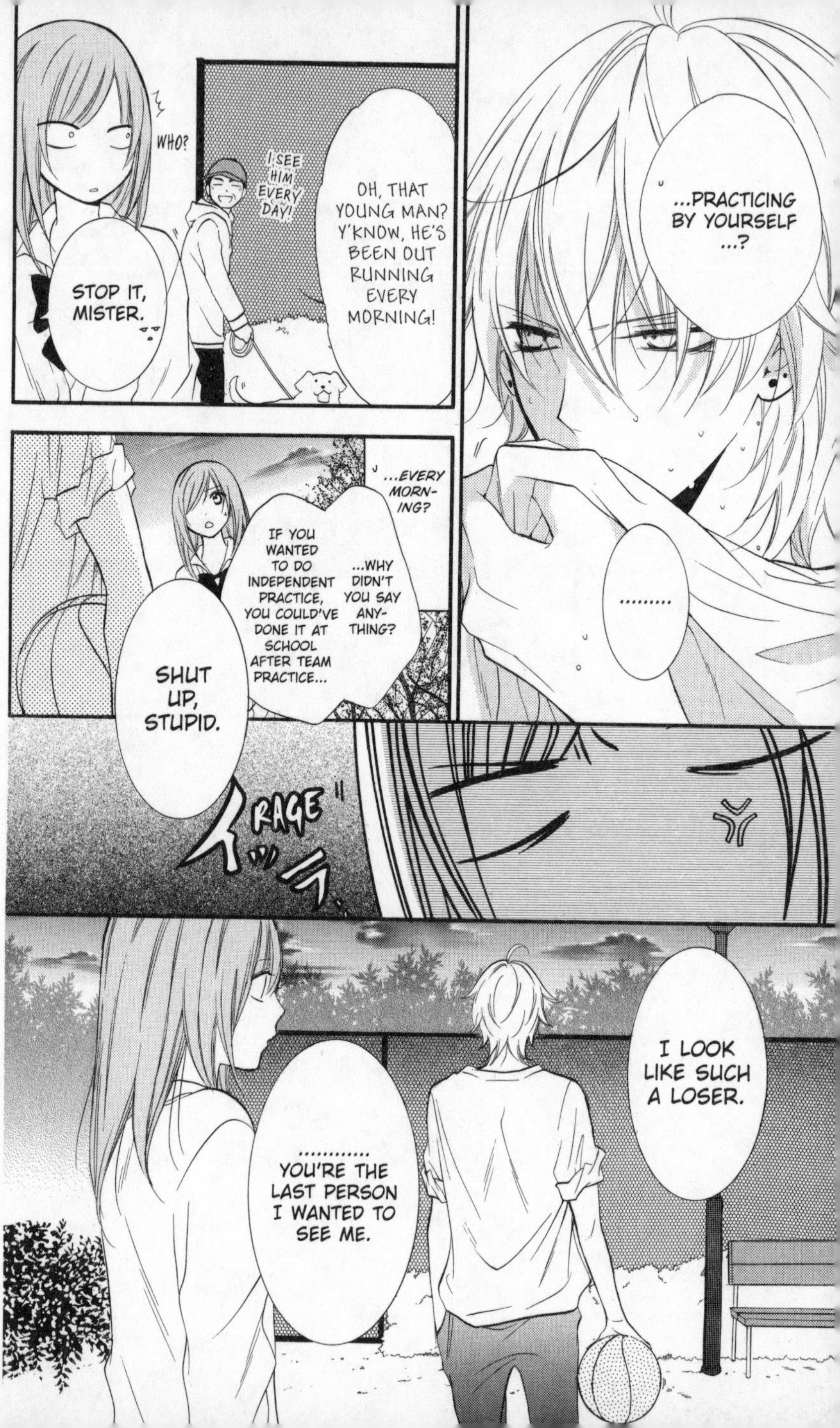
...PRACTICING BY YOURSELF ...?
....
OH, THAT YOUNG MAN? Y'KNOW, HE'S BEEN OUT RUNNING EVERY MORNING!
I SEE HIM EVERY DAY!
WHO?
STOP IT, MISTER.
...EVERY MORNING?
...WHY DIDN'T YOU SAY ANY-THING?
IF YOU WANTED TO DO INDEPENDENT PRACTICE, YOU COULD'VE DONE IT AT SCHOOL AFTER TEAM PRACTICE...
SHUT UP, STUPID.
RAGE
I LOOK LIKE SUCH A LOSER.
.... YOU'RE THE LAST PERSON I WANTED TO SEE ME.

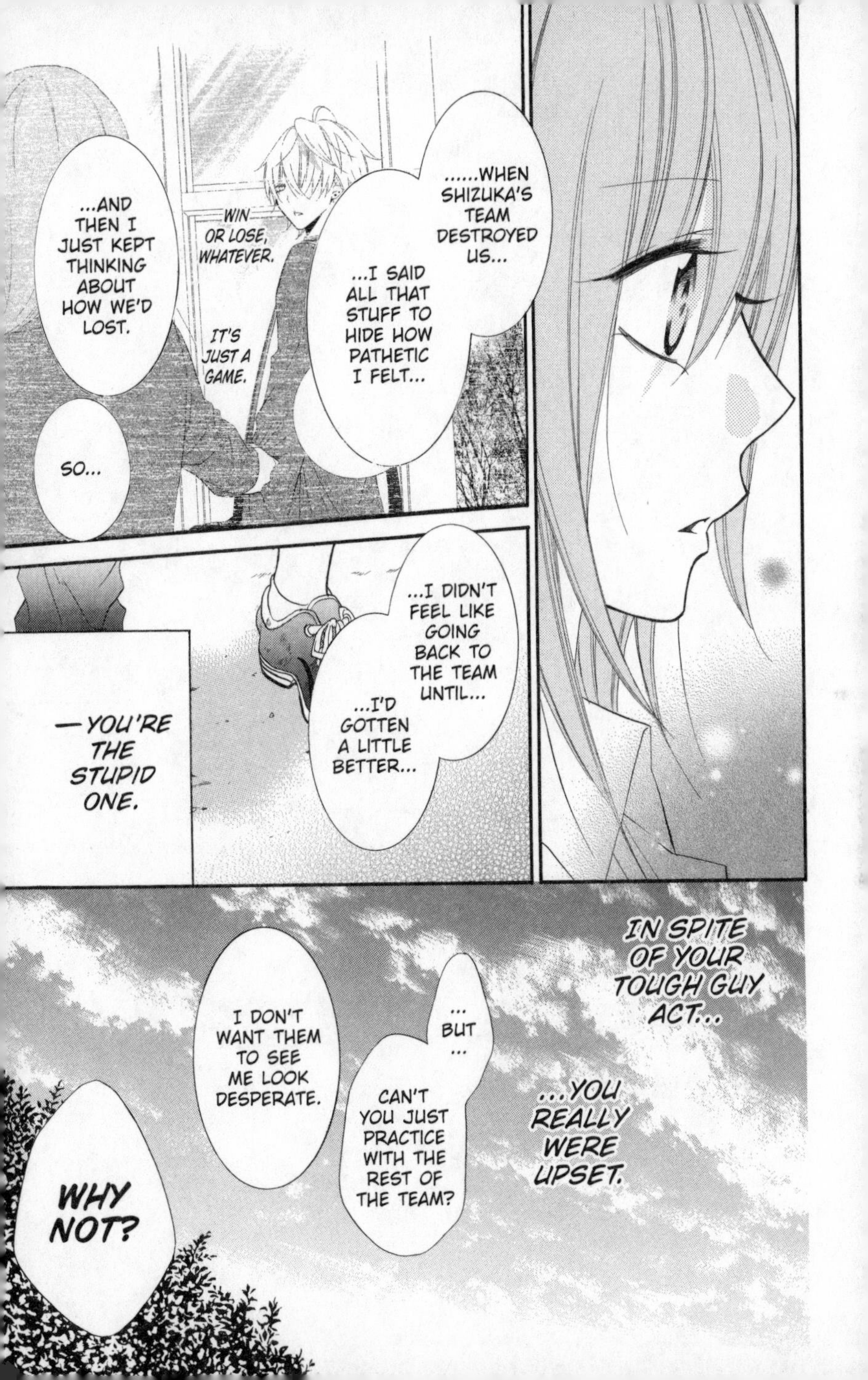
......WHEN SHIZUKA'S TEAM DESTROYED US...
...I SAID ALL THAT STUFF TO HIDE HOW PATHETIC I FELT...
WIN OR LOSE, WHATEVER.
IT'S JUST A GAME.
...AND THEN I JUST KEPT THINKING ABOUT HOW WE'D LOST.
SO...
...I DIDN'T FEEL LIKE GOING BACK TO THE TEAM UNTIL...
...I'D GOTTEN A LITTLE BETTER...
—YOU'RE THE STUPID ONE.
IN SPITE OF YOUR TOUGH GUY ACT...
...YOU REALLY WERE UPSET.
...BUT...
CAN'T YOU JUST PRACTICE WITH THE REST OF THE TEAM?
I DON'T WANT THEM TO SEE ME LOOK DESPERATE.
WHY NOT?

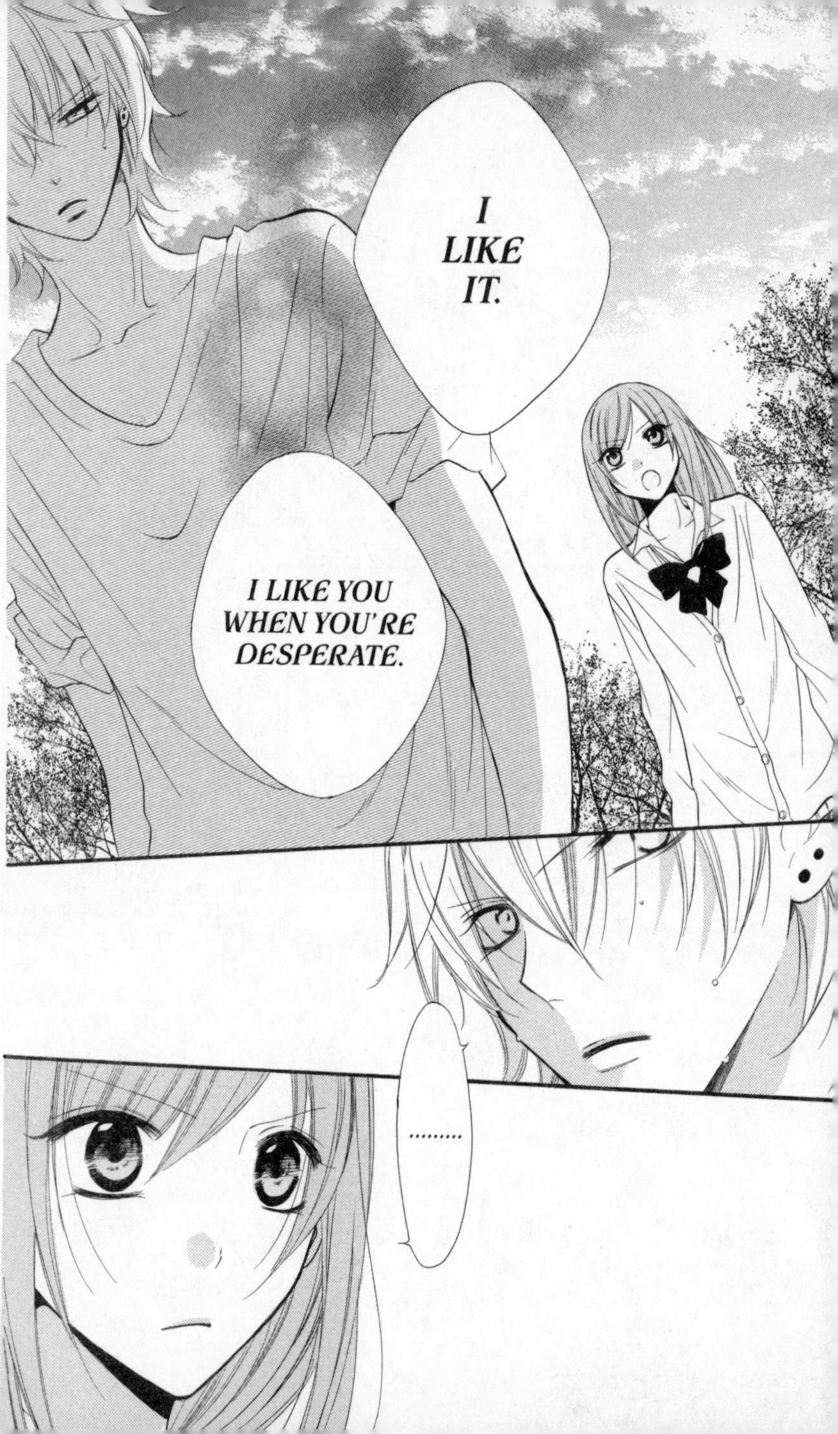
I LIKE IT.
I LIKE YOU WHEN YOU'RE DESPERATE.
....

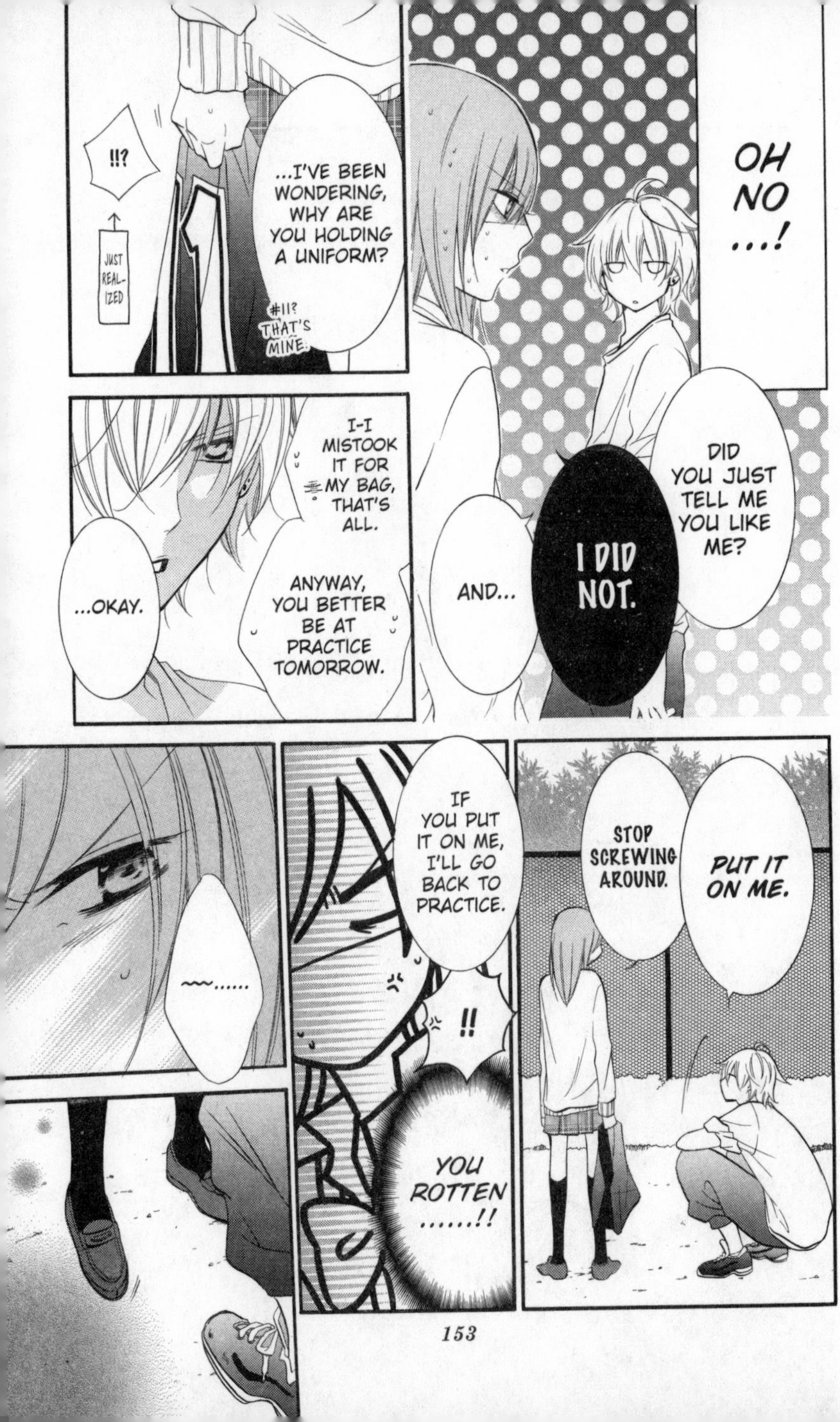
OH NO ...!
...I'VE BEEN WONDERING, WHY ARE YOU HOLDING A UNIFORM?
#11? THAT'S MINE.
!!?
JUST REAL-IZED
DID YOU JUST TELL ME YOU LIKE ME?
I DID NOT.
AND...
I-I MISTOOK IT FOR MY BAG, THAT'S ALL.
ANYWAY, YOU BETTER BE AT PRACTICE TOMORROW.
...OKAY.
PUT IT ON ME.
STOP SCREWING AROUND.
IF YOU PUT IT ON ME, I'LL GO BACK TO PRACTICE.
!!
YOU ROTTEN ......!!
~~......

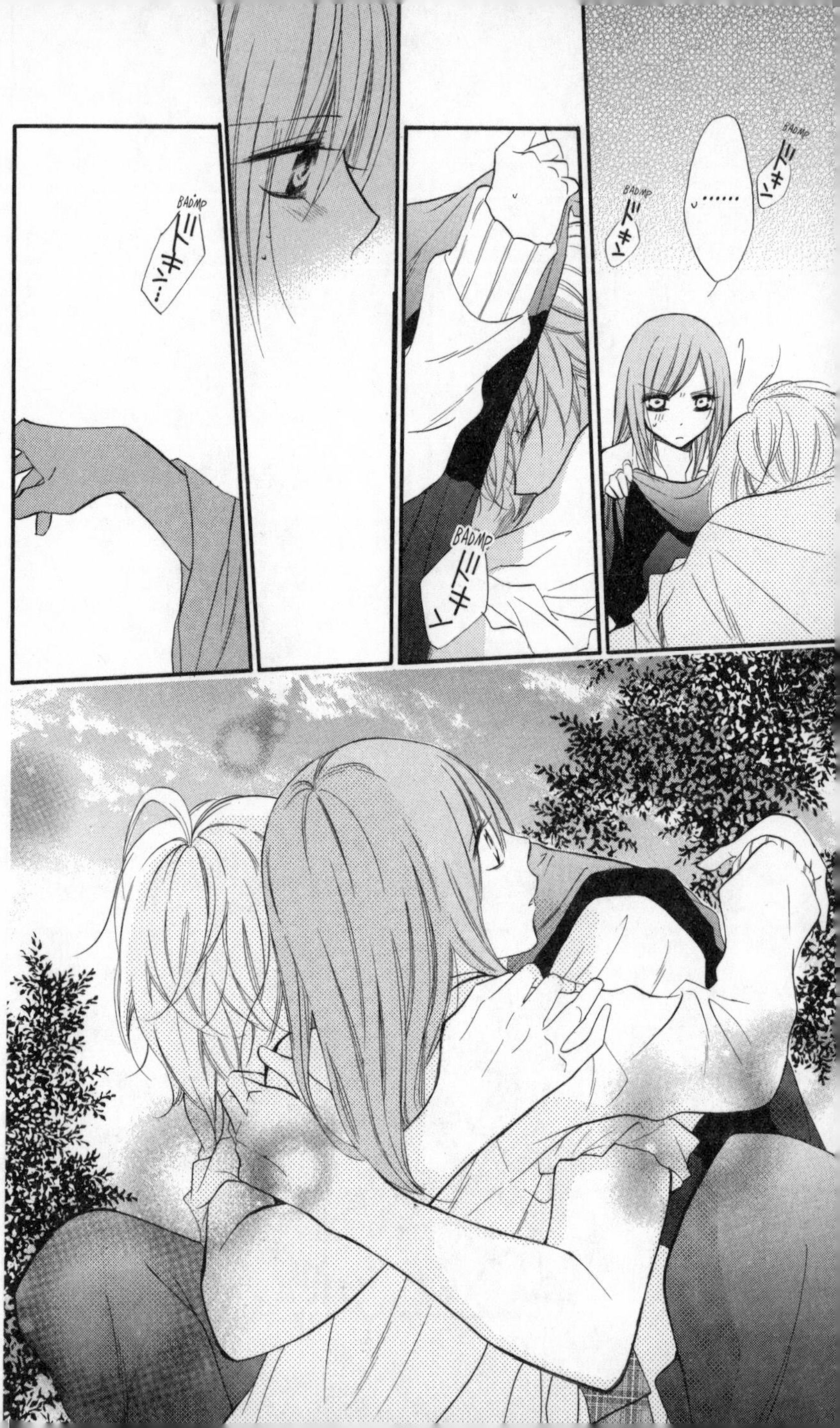
BADMP
……
BADMP
BADMP
BADMP

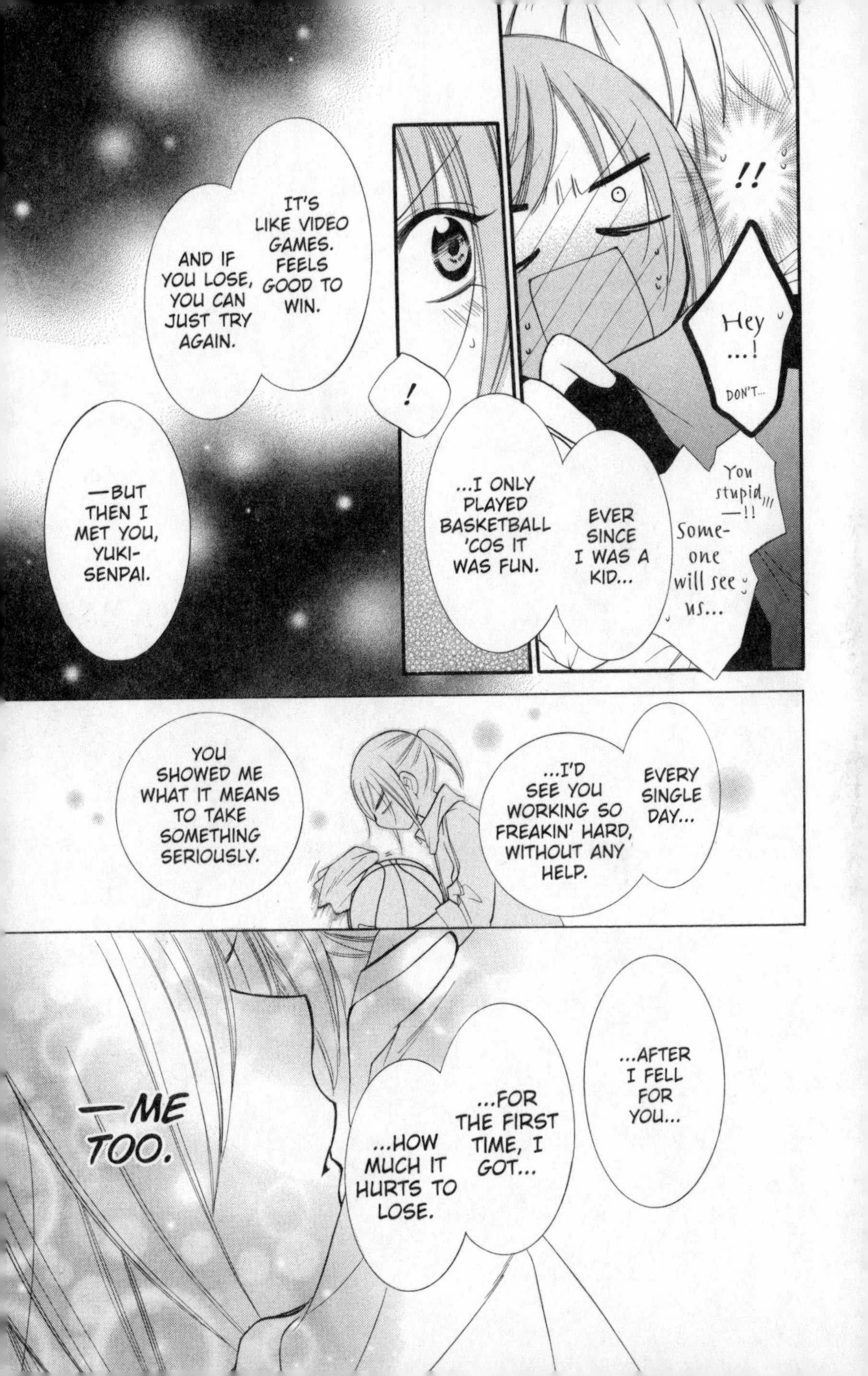
!!
Hey...!
DON'T...
You stupid—!!
Someone will see us...
!
EVER SINCE I WAS A KID...
...I ONLY PLAYED BASKETBALL 'COS IT WAS FUN.
IT'S LIKE VIDEO GAMES. FEELS GOOD TO WIN.
AND IF YOU LOSE, YOU CAN JUST TRY AGAIN.
—BUT THEN I MET YOU, YUKI-SENPAI.
EVERY SINGLE DAY...
...I'D SEE YOU WORKING SO FREAKIN' HARD, WITHOUT ANY HELP.
YOU SHOWED ME WHAT IT MEANS TO TAKE SOMETHING SERIOUSLY.
...AFTER I FELL FOR YOU...
...FOR THE FIRST TIME, I GOT...
...HOW MUCH IT HURTS TO LOSE.
—ME TOO.

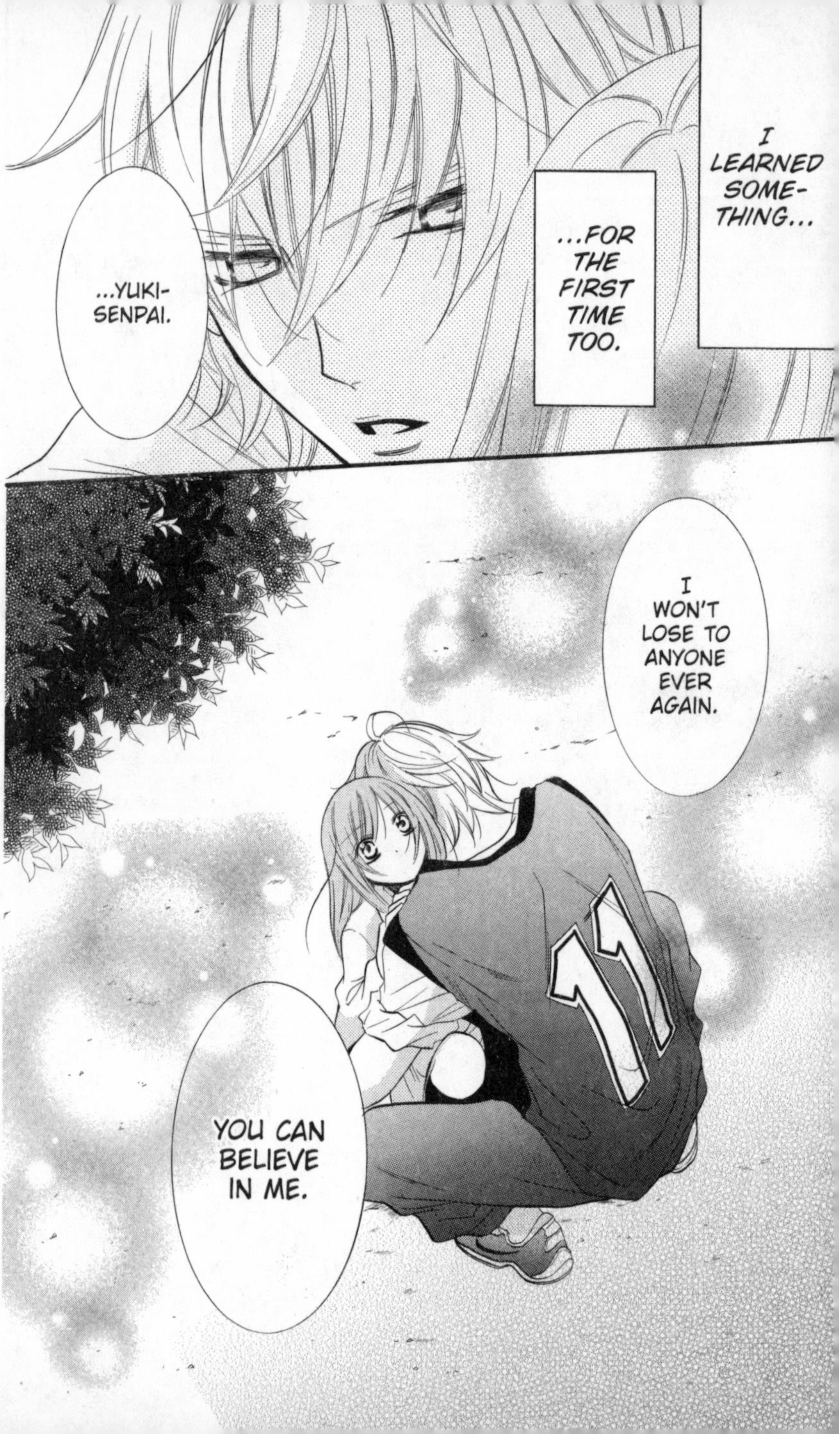
I LEARNED SOMETHING...
...FOR THE FIRST TIME TOO.
...YUKI-SENPAI.
I WON'T LOSE TO ANYONE EVER AGAIN.
YOU CAN BELIEVE IN ME.

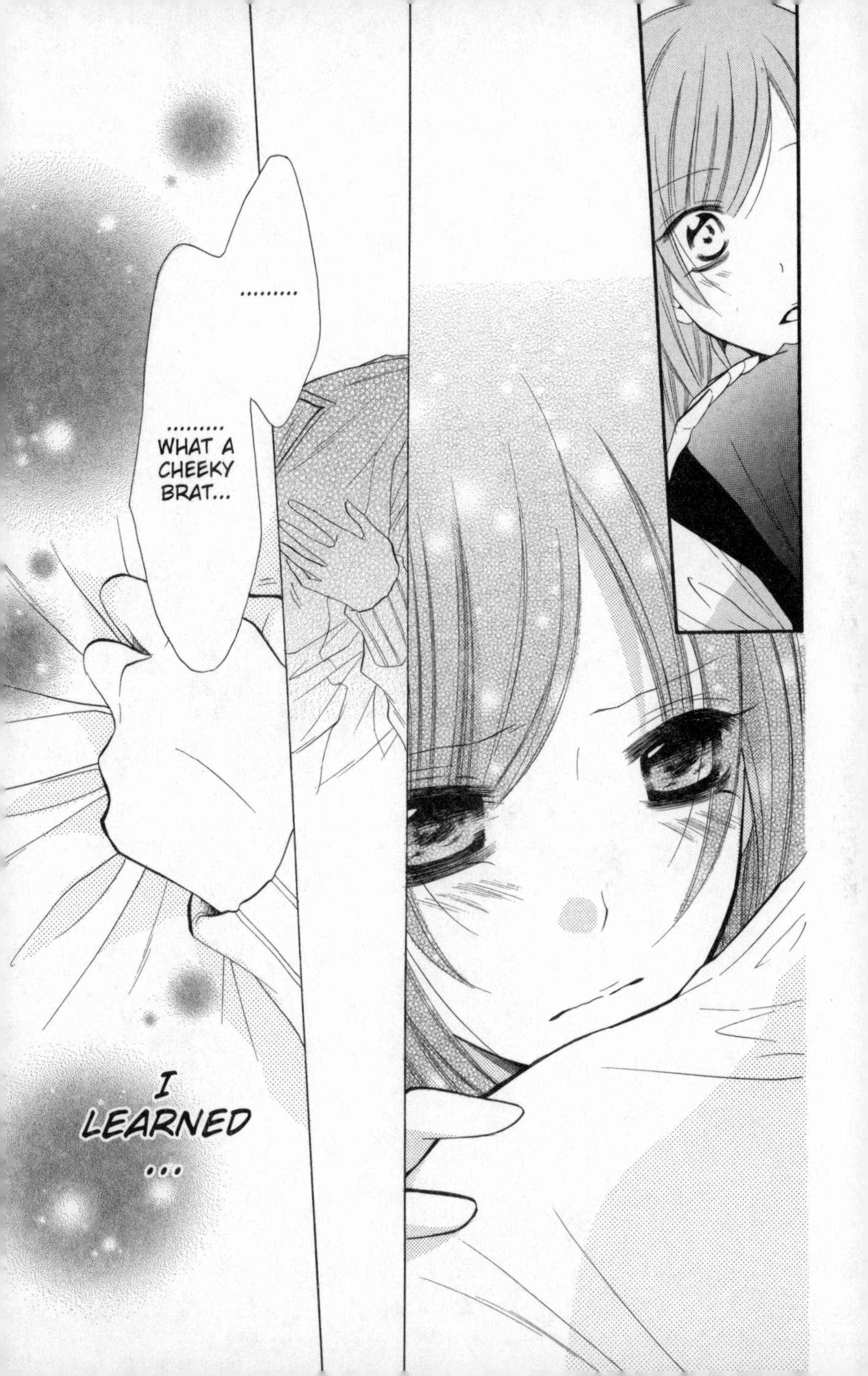
....
.... WHAT A CHEEKY BRAT...
I LEARNED ...

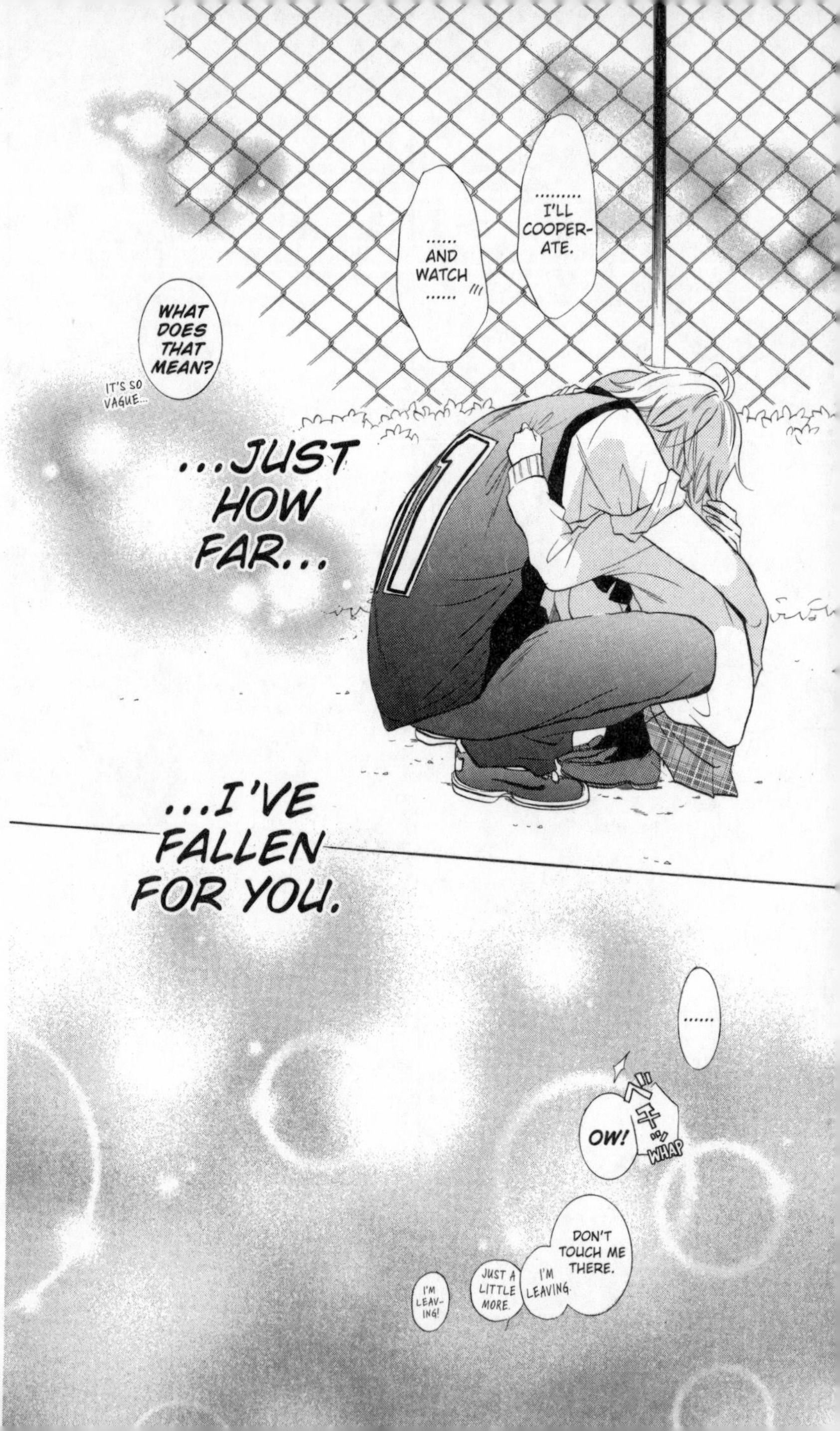

....
I'LL COOPERATE.
......
AND WATCH
......
WHAT DOES THAT MEAN?
IT'S SO VAGUE...
...JUST HOW FAR...
...I'VE FALLEN FOR YOU.
......
WHAP
OW!
DON'T TOUCH ME THERE.
I'M LEAVING.
JUST A LITTLE MORE.
I'M LEAVING!

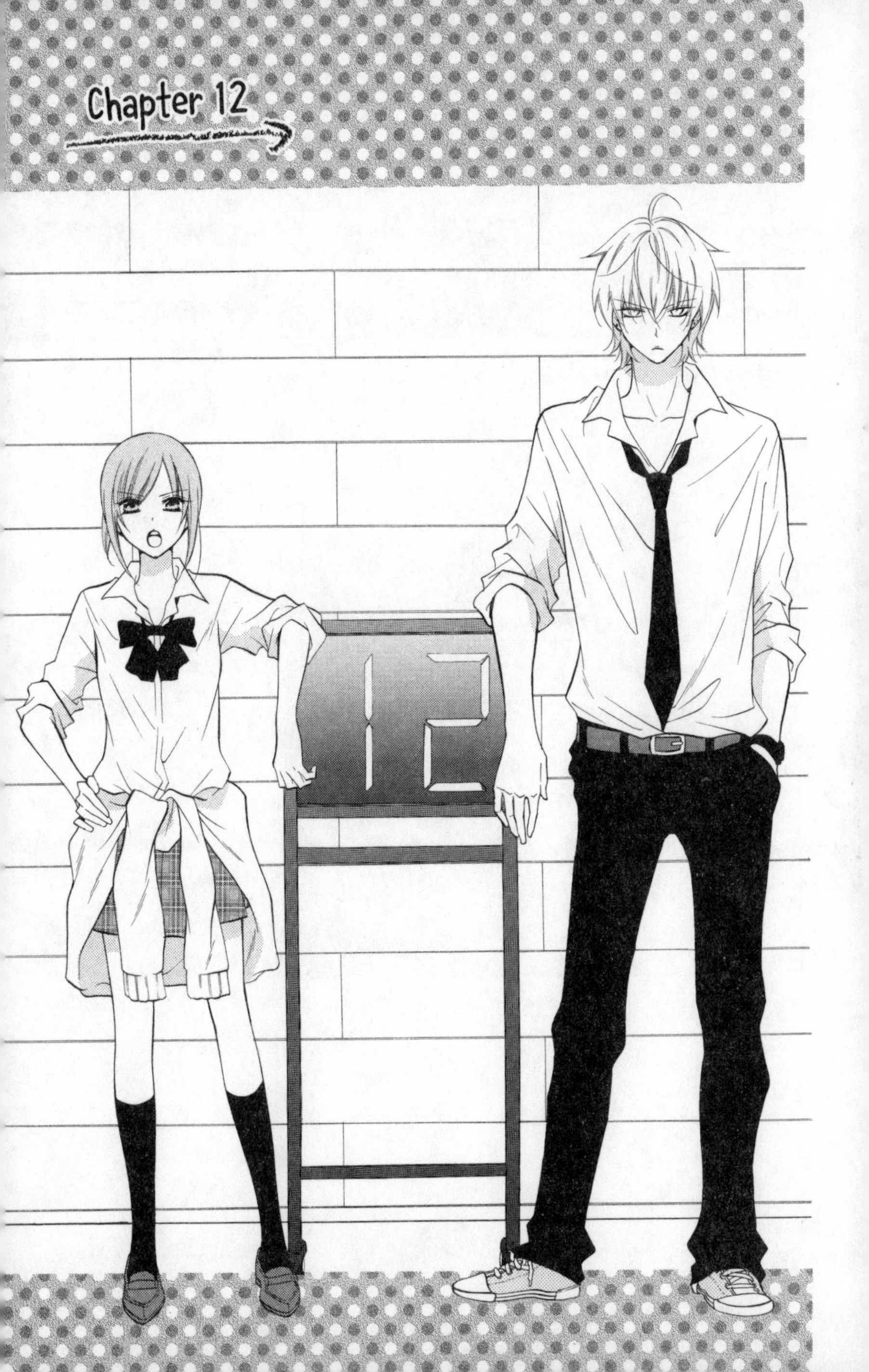
Chapter 12
12

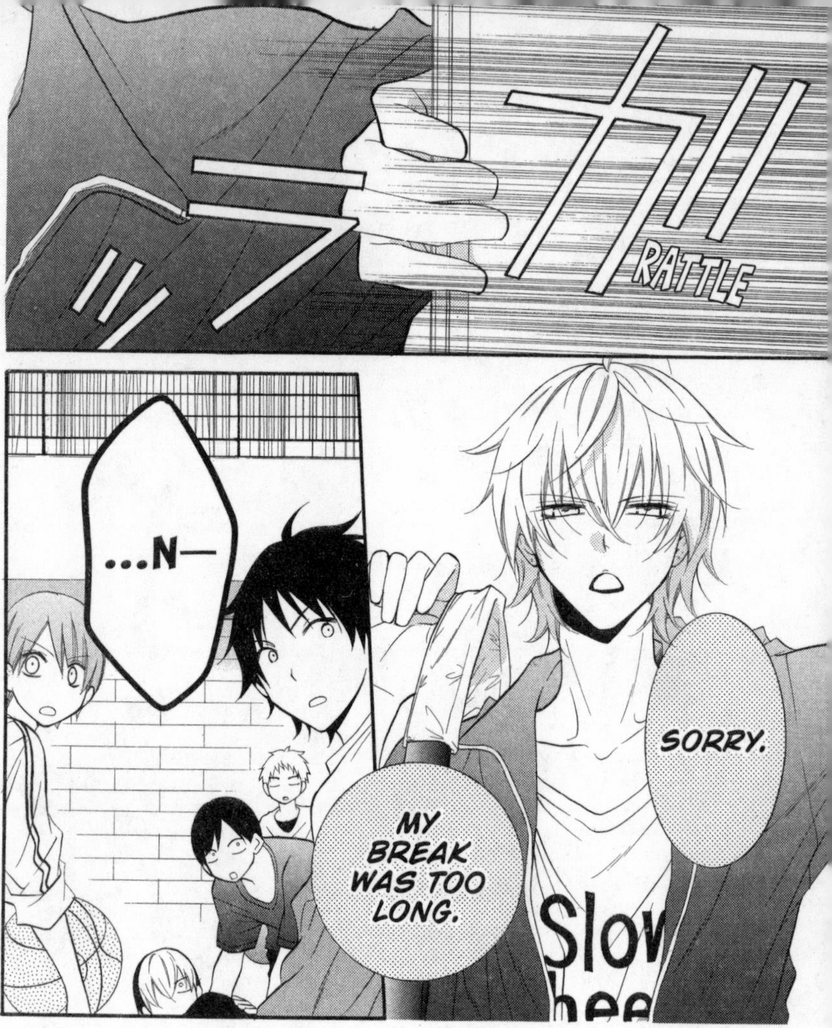
RATTLE
SORRY.
MY BREAK WAS TOO LONG.
...N—

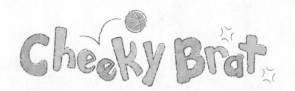

Cheeky Brat

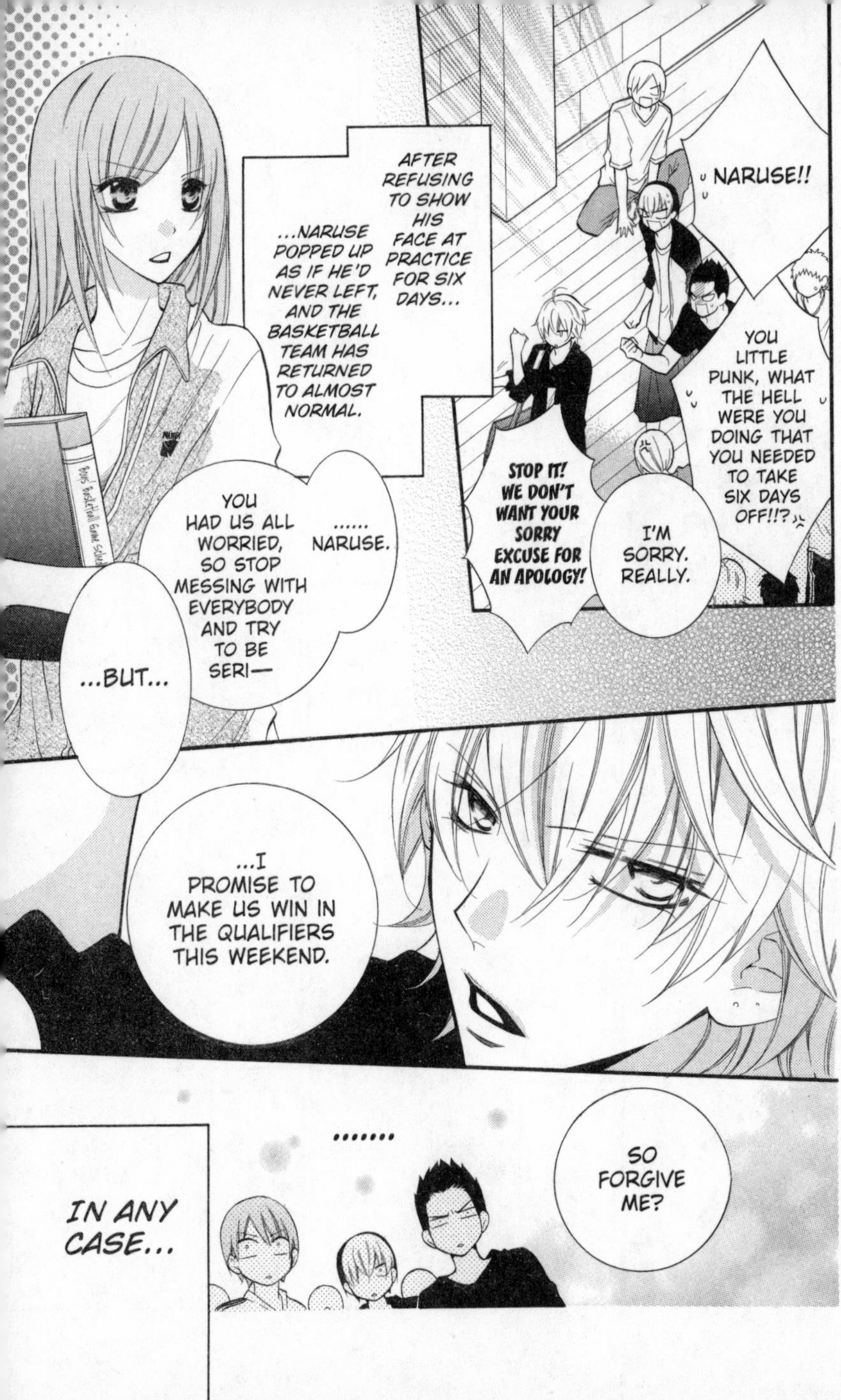
NARUSE!!
YOU LITTLE PUNK, WHAT THE HELL WERE YOU DOING THAT YOU NEEDED TO TAKE SIX DAYS OFF!!?
I'M SORRY. REALLY.
STOP IT! WE DON'T WANT YOUR SORRY EXCUSE FOR AN APOLOGY!
AFTER REFUSING TO SHOW HIS FACE AT PRACTICE FOR SIX DAYS...
...NARUSE POPPED UP AS IF HE'D NEVER LEFT, AND THE BASKETBALL TEAM HAS RETURNED TO ALMOST NORMAL.
......NARUSE.
YOU HAD US ALL WORRIED, SO STOP MESSING WITH EVERYBODY AND TRY TO BE SERI—
...BUT...
...I PROMISE TO MAKE US WIN IN THE QUALIFIERS THIS WEEKEND.
SO FORGIVE ME?
....
IN ANY CASE...

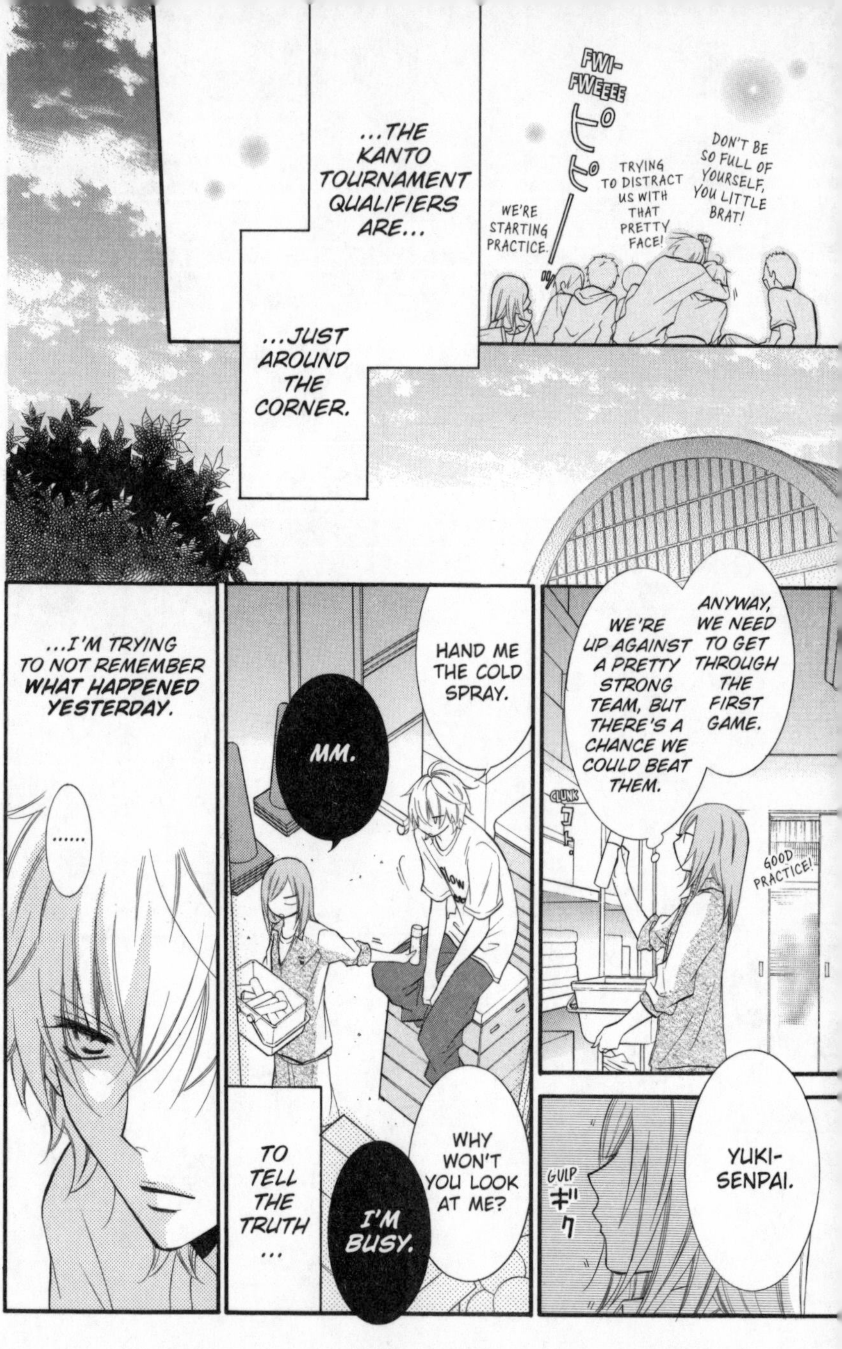
FWI-FWEEEE
ピピー
DON'T BE SO FULL OF YOURSELF, YOU LITTLE BRAT!
TRYING TO DISTRACT US WITH THAT PRETTY FACE!
WE'RE STARTING PRACTICE.
...THE KANTO TOURNAMENT QUALIFIERS ARE...
...JUST AROUND THE CORNER.
ANYWAY, WE NEED TO GET THROUGH THE FIRST GAME.
WE'RE UP AGAINST A PRETTY STRONG TEAM, BUT THERE'S A CHANCE WE COULD BEAT THEM.
CLUNK
コト
GOOD PRACTICE!
HAND ME THE COLD SPRAY.
MM.
YUKI-SENPAI.
GULP
ギク
WHY WON'T YOU LOOK AT ME?
I'M BUSY.
TO TELL THE TRUTH...
...I'M TRYING TO NOT REMEMBER WHAT HAPPENED YESTERDAY.
......

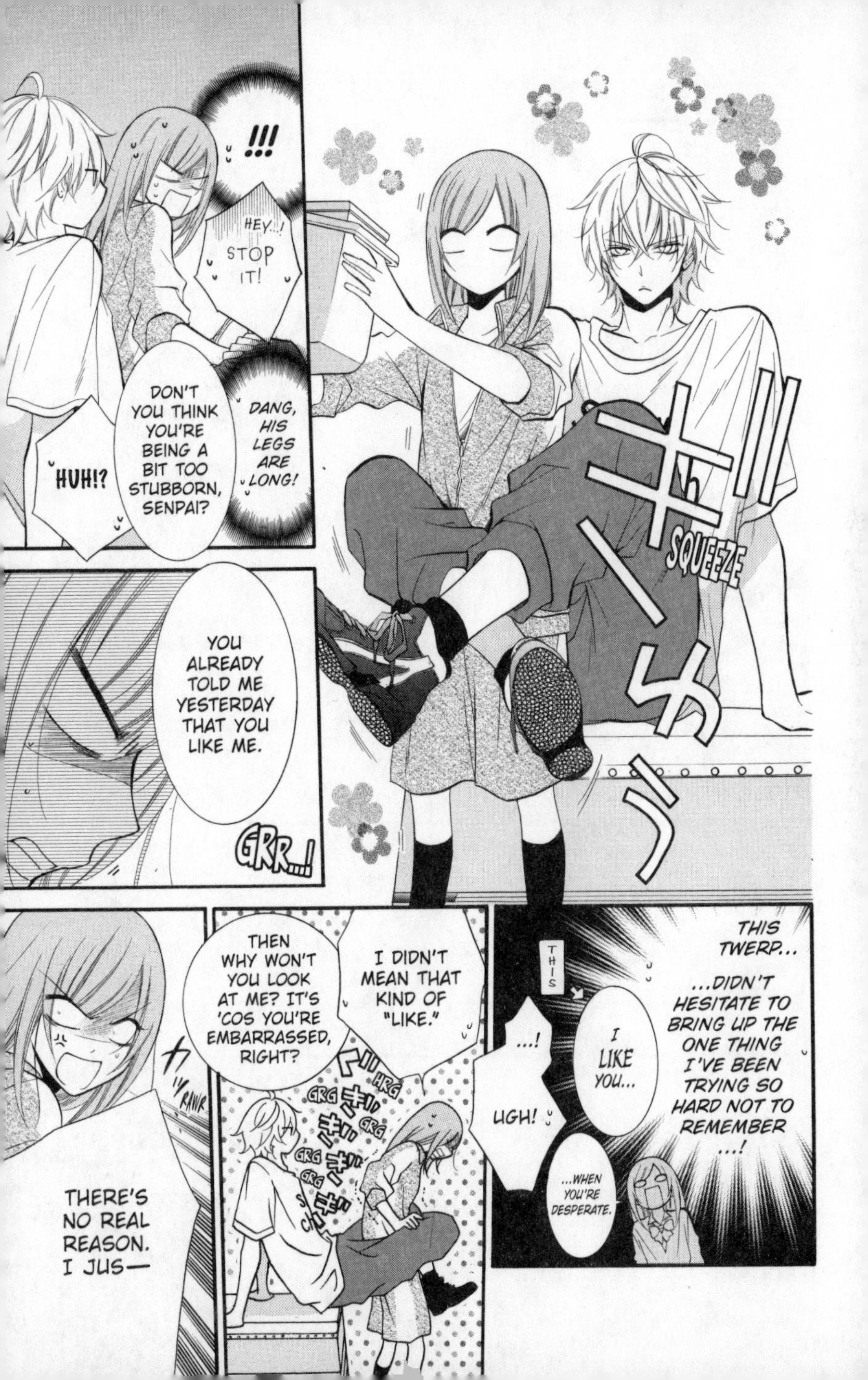
SQUEEZE
!!!
HEY...! STOP IT!
DANG, HIS LEGS ARE LONG!
DON'T YOU THINK YOU'RE BEING A BIT TOO STUBBORN, SENPAI?
HUH!?
YOU ALREADY TOLD ME YESTERDAY THAT YOU LIKE ME.
GRR...!
THIS TWERP...
...DIDN'T HESITATE TO BRING UP THE ONE THING I'VE BEEN TRYING SO HARD NOT TO REMEMBER...!
THIS
I LIKE YOU...
...!
UGH!
...WHEN YOU'RE DESPERATE.
I DIDN'T MEAN THAT KIND OF "LIKE."
THEN WHY WON'T YOU LOOK AT ME? IT'S 'COS YOU'RE EMBARRASSED, RIGHT?
HRG
GRG
GRG
GRG
GRG
RAWR
THERE'S NO REAL REASON. I JUS—

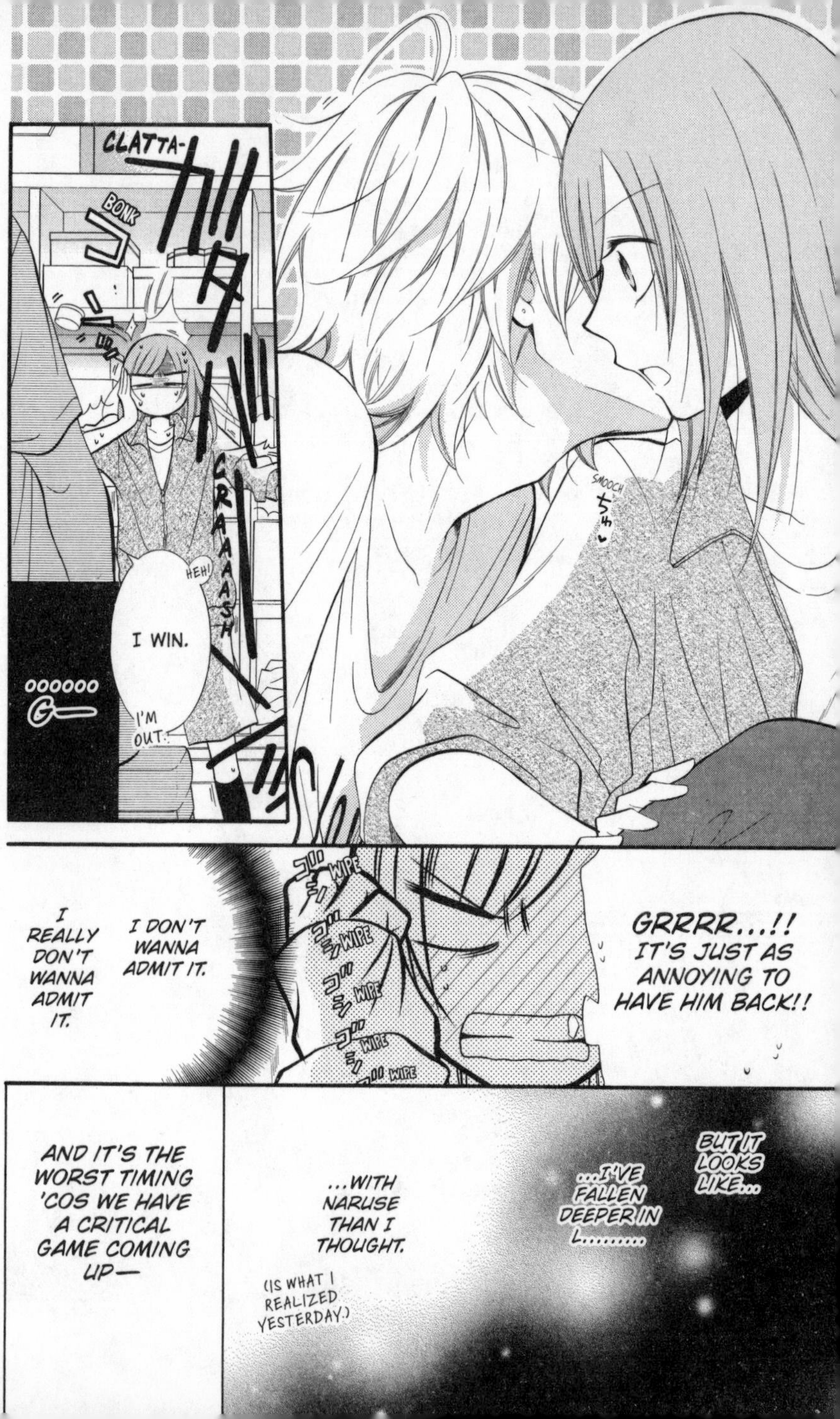

SMOOCH
CLATTA-
BONK
CRAAAASH
HEH!
I WIN.
I'M OUT.
OOOOOO G—
GRRRR...!! IT'S JUST AS ANNOYING TO HAVE HIM BACK!!
WIPE
WIPE
WIPE
WIPE
WIPE
I DON'T WANNA ADMIT IT.
I REALLY DON'T WANNA ADMIT IT.
BUT IT LOOKS LIKE...
...I'VE FALLEN DEEPER IN L..........
...WITH NARUSE THAN I THOUGHT.
(IS WHAT I REALIZED YESTERDAY.)
AND IT'S THE WORST TIMING 'COS WE HAVE A CRITICAL GAME COMING UP—

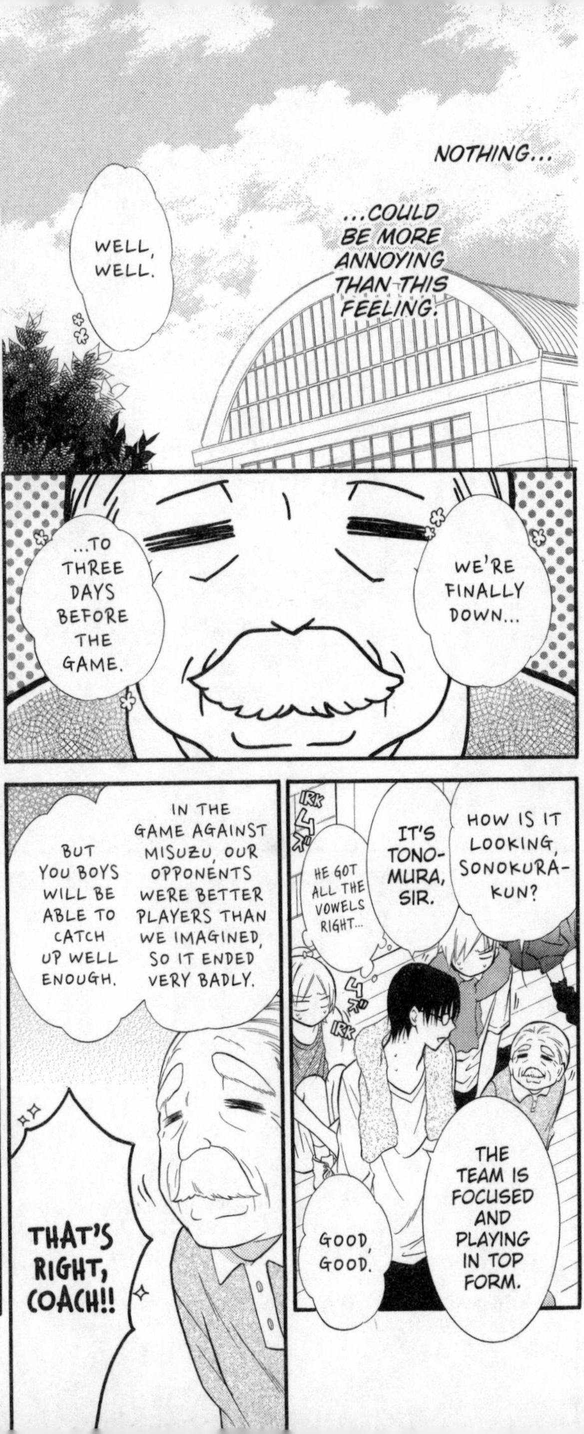
NOTHING...
...COULD BE MORE ANNOYING THAN THIS FEELING.
WELL, WELL.
WE'RE FINALLY DOWN...
...TO THREE DAYS BEFORE THE GAME.
HOW IS IT LOOKING, SONOKURA-KUN?
IT'S TONOMURA, SIR.
IRK
HE GOT ALL THE VOWELS RIGHT...
IRK
THE TEAM IS FOCUSED AND PLAYING IN TOP FORM.
GOOD, GOOD.
IN THE GAME AGAINST MISUZU, OUR OPPONENTS WERE BETTER PLAYERS THAN WE IMAGINED, SO IT ENDED VERY BADLY.
BUT YOU BOYS WILL BE ABLE TO CATCH UP WELL ENOUGH.
THAT'S RIGHT, COACH!!

06

Every time I write these, I want to thank all of you who actually read the messy handwriting in this tiny space. Thank you very much.

How did you like *Cheeky Brat 2*?

It has the "Naruse grows just a little" plotline, so I can't help feeling that it has a heavier emphasis on basketball.

So if you're thinking, "Can't you give us more makeout scenes!?", I apologize. There aren't as many kisses and whatnot as volume 1. I'm very sorry.

I think that in volume 3, Naruse will let some of his pent-up emotions explode in a big way, so I hope you'll look forward to that!!!!!

Also, sometimes the chapters have colored pages and stuff, so I hope you'll look at the *Hana to Yume* magazine too. You can see them there. Oh, and someone asked me this once—I use watercolors.

Please, please, please let me know what you think. Please, please, please, please send requests for what you want me to make Naruse do.

Mitsubachi Miyuki
Yen Press
150 West 30th Street,
19th Floor
New York, NY 10001

Send them here!!!
I hope we can meet again in the next volume!!!!!

Miyuki

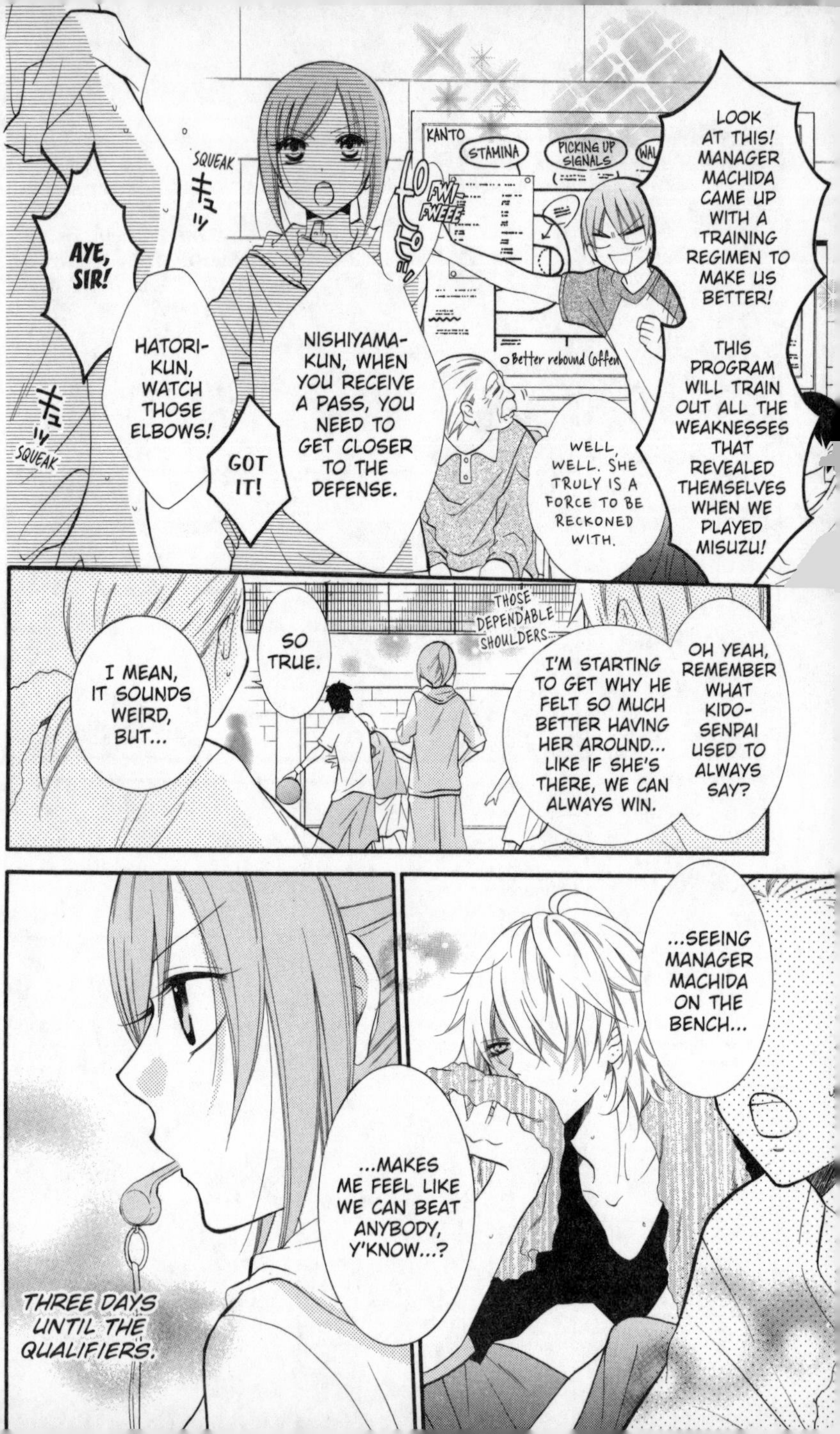
LOOK AT THIS! MANAGER MACHIDA CAME UP WITH A TRAINING REGIMEN TO MAKE US BETTER!
THIS PROGRAM WILL TRAIN OUT ALL THE WEAKNESSES THAT REVEALED THEMSELVES WHEN WE PLAYED MISUZU!
WELL, WELL. SHE TRULY IS A FORCE TO BE RECKONED WITH.
KANTO
STAMINA
PICKING UP SIGNALS
FWI-FWEEE
NISHIYAMA-KUN, WHEN YOU RECEIVE A PASS, YOU NEED TO GET CLOSER TO THE DEFENSE.
GOT IT!
HATORI-KUN, WATCH THOSE ELBOWS!
SQUEAK
AYE, SIR!
SQUEAK
OH YEAH, REMEMBER WHAT KIDO-SENPAI USED TO ALWAYS SAY?
I'M STARTING TO GET WHY HE FELT SO MUCH BETTER HAVING HER AROUND... LIKE IF SHE'S THERE, WE CAN ALWAYS WIN.
THOSE DEPENDABLE SHOULDERS...
SO TRUE.
I MEAN, IT SOUNDS WEIRD, BUT...
...SEEING MANAGER MACHIDA ON THE BENCH...
...MAKES ME FEEL LIKE WE CAN BEAT ANYBODY, Y'KNOW...?
THREE DAYS UNTIL THE QUALIFIERS.

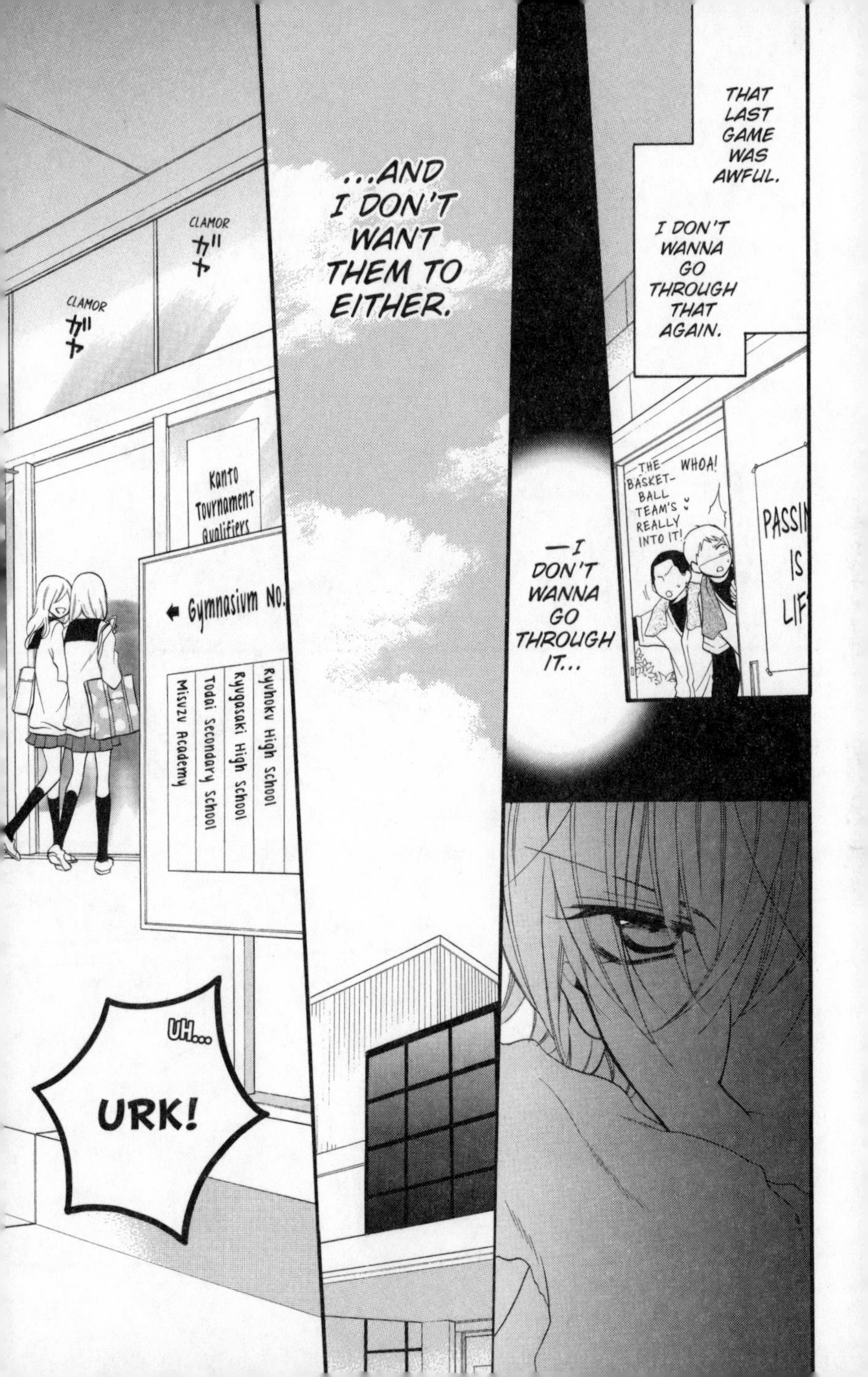
THAT LAST GAME WAS AWFUL.
I DON'T WANNA GO THROUGH THAT AGAIN.
WHOA!
THE BASKET-BALL TEAM'S REALLY INTO IT!
PASSIN
IS
LIF
—I DON'T WANNA GO THROUGH IT...
...AND I DON'T WANT THEM TO EITHER.
CLAMOR
ガヤ
CLAMOR
ガヤ
Kanto Tournament Qualifiers
Gymnasium No.
Ryuhoku High School
Ryugasaki High School
Todai Secondary School
Misuzu Academy
UH...
URK!

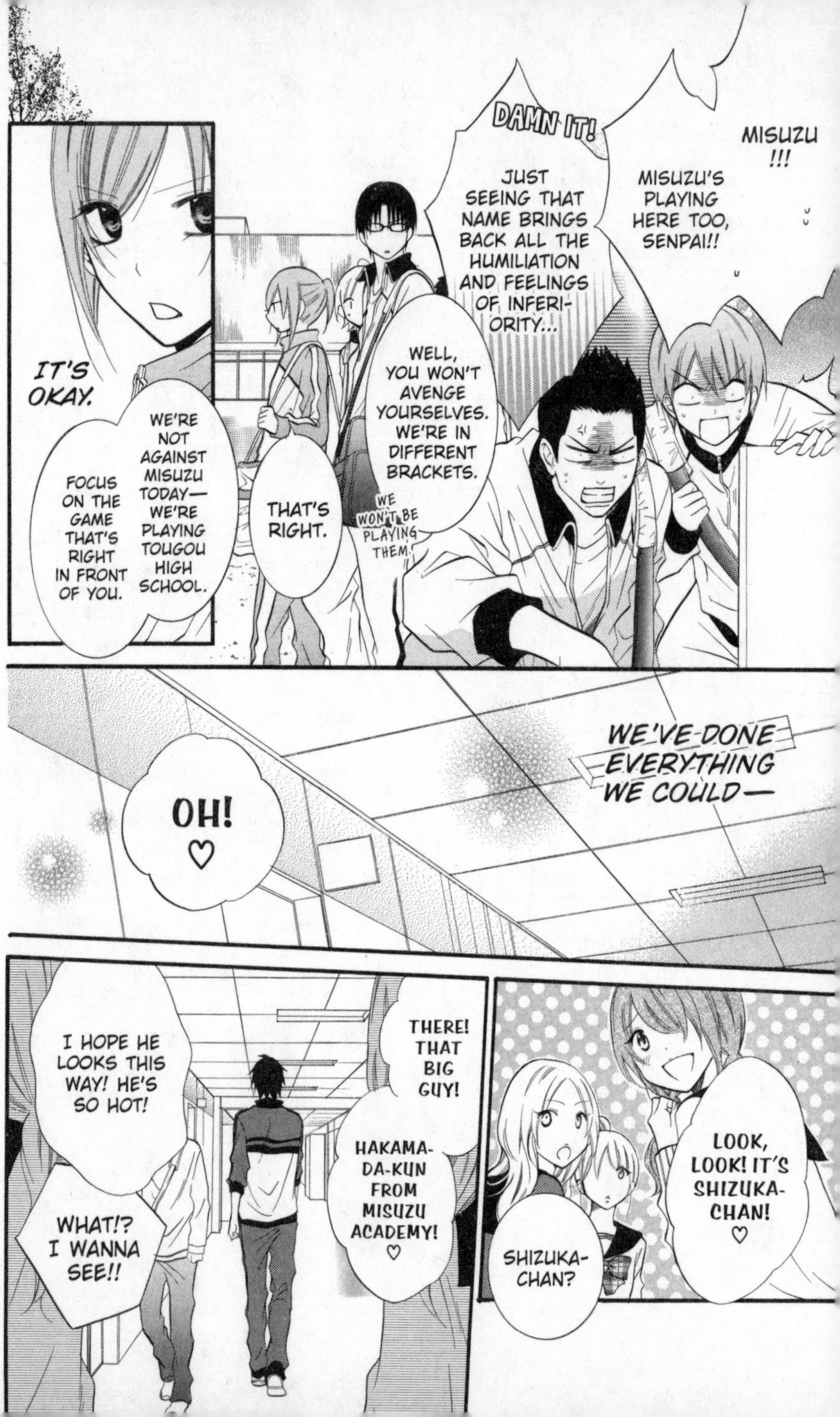
MISUZU !!!
MISUZU'S PLAYING HERE TOO, SENPAI!!
DAMN IT!
JUST SEEING THAT NAME BRINGS BACK ALL THE HUMILIATION AND FEELINGS OF INFERIORITY...
WELL, YOU WON'T AVENGE YOURSELVES. WE'RE IN DIFFERENT BRACKETS.
WE WON'T BE PLAYING THEM.
THAT'S RIGHT.
IT'S OKAY.
WE'RE NOT AGAINST MISUZU TODAY—WE'RE PLAYING TOUGOU HIGH SCHOOL.
FOCUS ON THE GAME THAT'S RIGHT IN FRONT OF YOU.
WE'VE DONE EVERYTHING WE COULD—
OH! ♡
LOOK, LOOK! IT'S SHIZUKA-CHAN! ♡
SHIZUKA-CHAN?
THERE! THAT BIG GUY!
HAKAMA-DA-KUN FROM MISUZU ACADEMY! ♡
I HOPE HE LOOKS THIS WAY! HE'S SO HOT!
WHAT!? I WANNA SEE!!

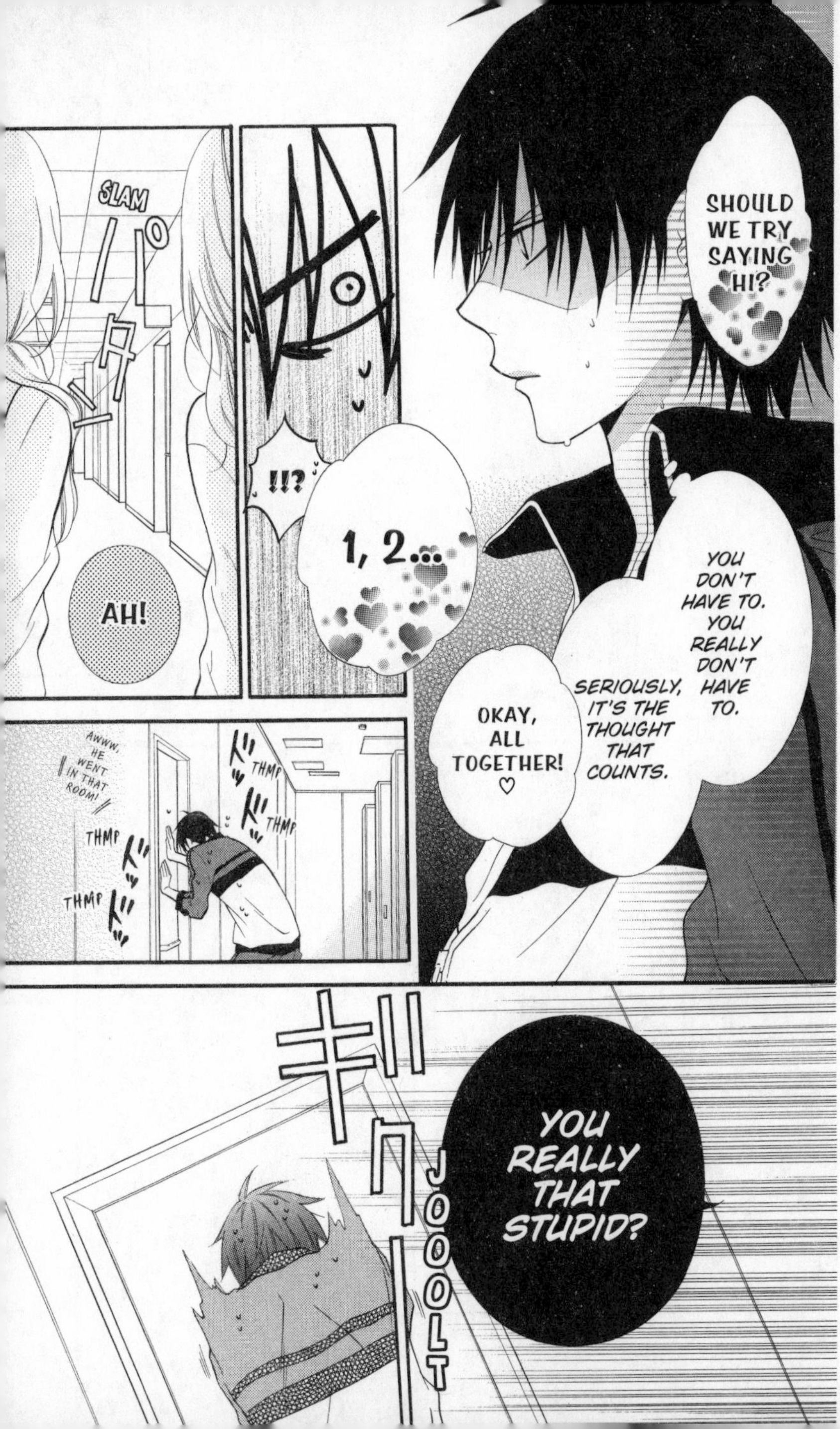

SHOULD WE TRY SAYING HI?
YOU DON'T HAVE TO. YOU REALLY DON'T HAVE TO.
SERIOUSLY, IT'S THE THOUGHT THAT COUNTS.
OKAY, ALL TOGETHER! ♡
1, 2...
!!?
SLAM
AH!
AWWW, HE WENT IN THAT ROOM!
THMP
THMP
THMP
THMP
JOOOLT
YOU REALLY THAT STUPID?

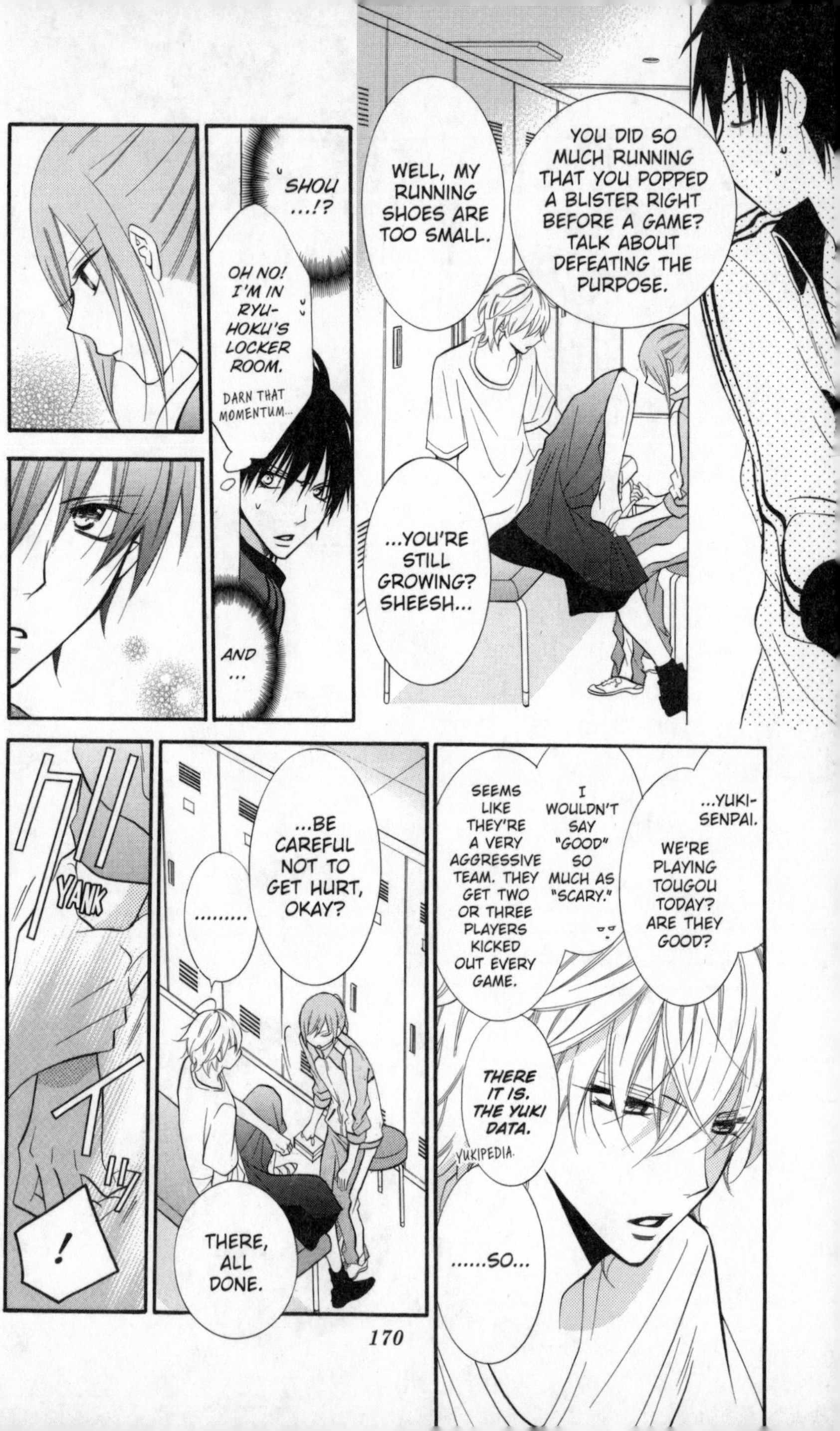
YOU DID SO MUCH RUNNING THAT YOU POPPED A BLISTER RIGHT BEFORE A GAME? TALK ABOUT DEFEATING THE PURPOSE.
WELL, MY RUNNING SHOES ARE TOO SMALL.
...YOU'RE STILL GROWING? SHEESH...
SHOU ...!?
OH NO! I'M IN RYU-HOKU'S LOCKER ROOM.
DARN THAT MOMENTUM...
AND ...
...YUKI-SENPAI.
WE'RE PLAYING TOUGOU TODAY? ARE THEY GOOD?
I WOULDN'T SAY "GOOD" SO MUCH AS "SCARY."
SEEMS LIKE THEY'RE A VERY AGGRESSIVE TEAM. THEY GET TWO OR THREE PLAYERS KICKED OUT EVERY GAME.
THERE IT IS. THE YUKI DATA.
YUKIPEDIA.
......SO...
...BE CAREFUL NOT TO GET HURT, OKAY?
....
THERE, ALL DONE.
YANK
!

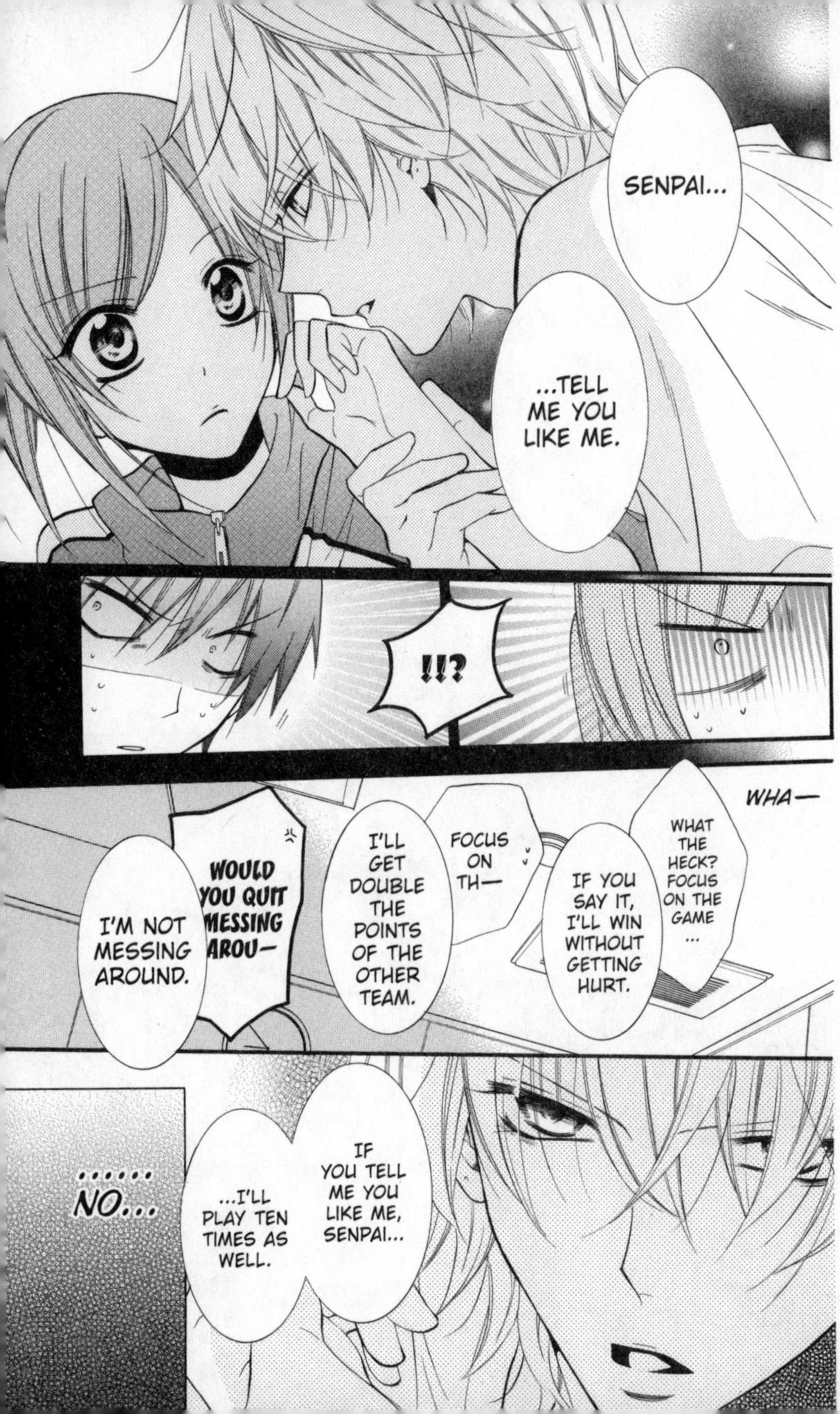
SENPAI...
...TELL ME YOU LIKE ME.
!!?
WHA—
WHAT THE HECK? FOCUS ON THE GAME ...
IF YOU SAY IT, I'LL WIN WITHOUT GETTING HURT.
FOCUS ON TH—
I'LL GET DOUBLE THE POINTS OF THE OTHER TEAM.
WOULD YOU QUIT MESSING AROU—
I'M NOT MESSING AROUND.
IF YOU TELL ME YOU LIKE ME, SENPAI...
...I'LL PLAY TEN TIMES AS WELL.
...... NO...

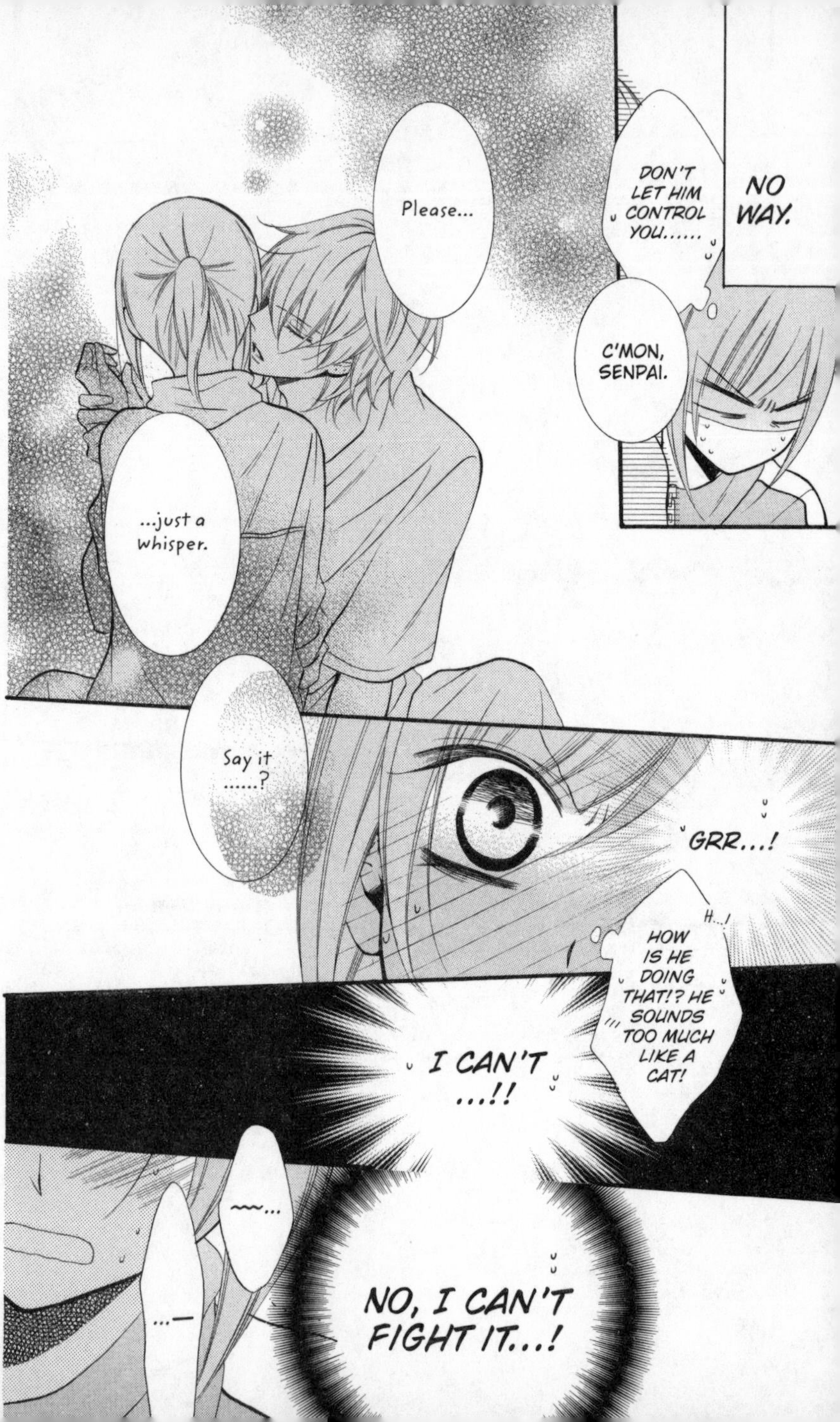

NO WAY.
DON'T LET HIM CONTROL YOU......
C'MON, SENPAI.
Please...
...just a whisper.
Say it ......?
GRR...!
H...! HOW IS HE DOING THAT!? HE SOUNDS TOO MUCH LIKE A CAT!
I CAN'T ...!!
NO, I CAN'T FIGHT IT...!
~~...
...—

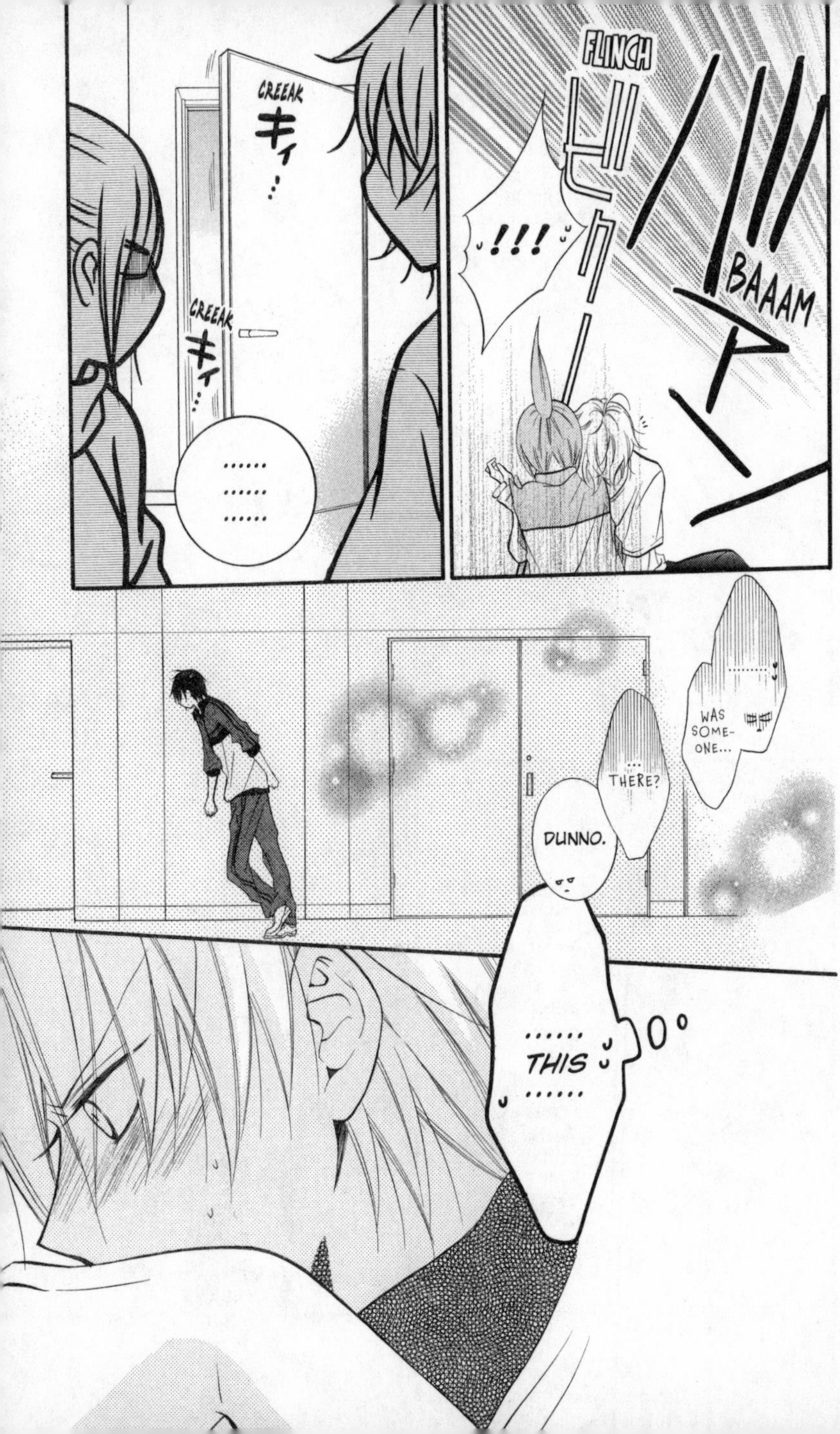
FLINCH
BAAAM
!!!
CREEAK
キィ…
CREEAK
キィ…
......
......
......
....
WAS SOME-ONE...
... THERE?
DUNNO.
......
THIS
......

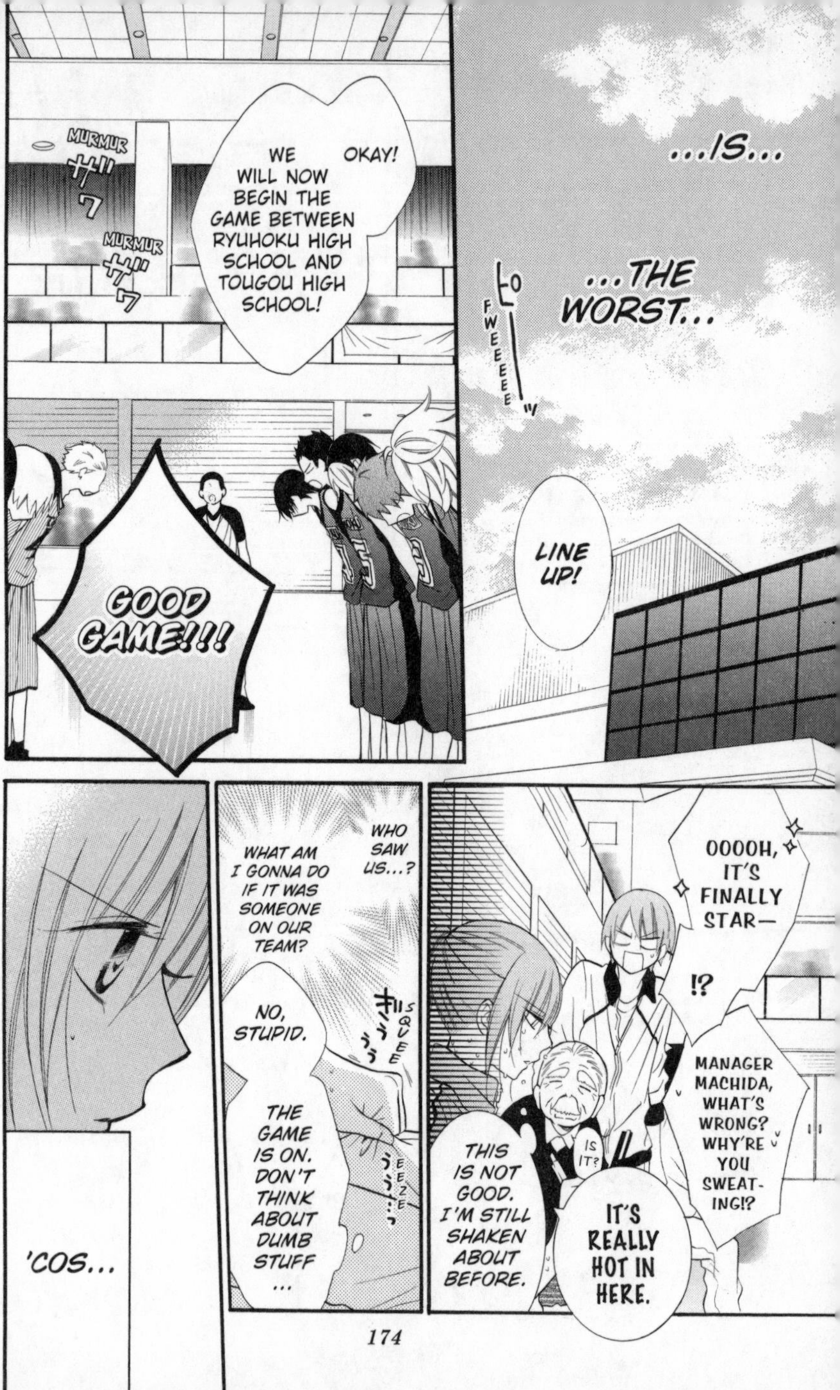
...IS...
...THE WORST...
FWEEEEEE
LINE UP!
MURMUR
MURMUR
OKAY! WE WILL NOW BEGIN THE GAME BETWEEN RYUHOKU HIGH SCHOOL AND TOUGOU HIGH SCHOOL!
GOOD GAME!!!
OOOOH, IT'S FINALLY STAR—
!?
MANAGER MACHIDA, WHAT'S WRONG? WHY'RE YOU SWEATING!?
IS IT?
IT'S REALLY HOT IN HERE.
THIS IS NOT GOOD. I'M STILL SHAKEN ABOUT BEFORE.
WHO SAW US...?
WHAT AM I GONNA DO IF IT WAS SOMEONE ON OUR TEAM?
SQUEEEEZE
NO, STUPID.
THE GAME IS ON. DON'T THINK ABOUT DUMB STUFF...
'COS...

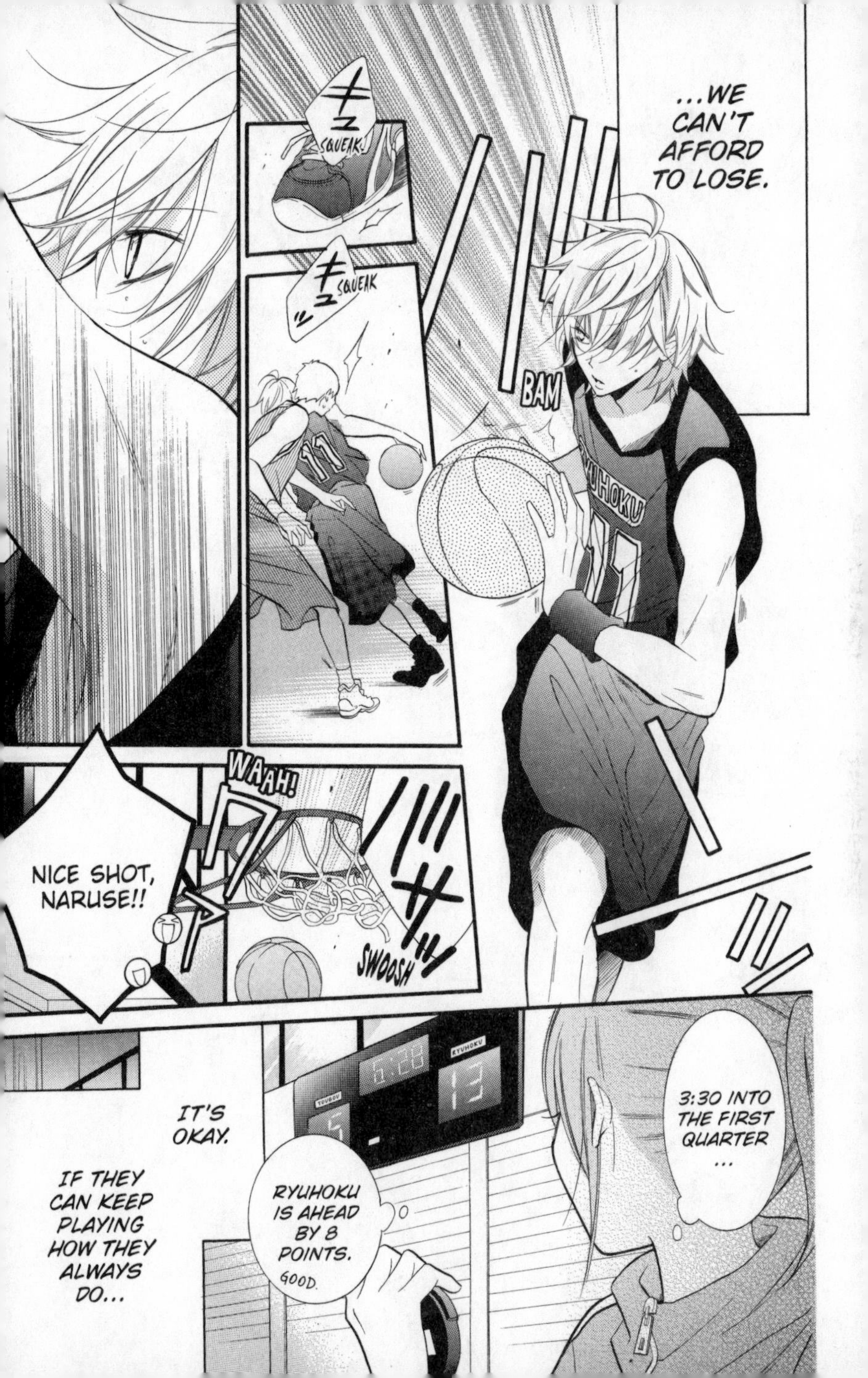
...WE CAN'T AFFORD TO LOSE.
BAM
SQUEAK!
SQUEAK
WAAH!
SWOOSH
NICE SHOT, NARUSE!!
3:30 INTO THE FIRST QUARTER...
RYUHOKU IS AHEAD BY 8 POINTS.
GOOD.
IT'S OKAY.
IF THEY CAN KEEP PLAYING HOW THEY ALWAYS DO...

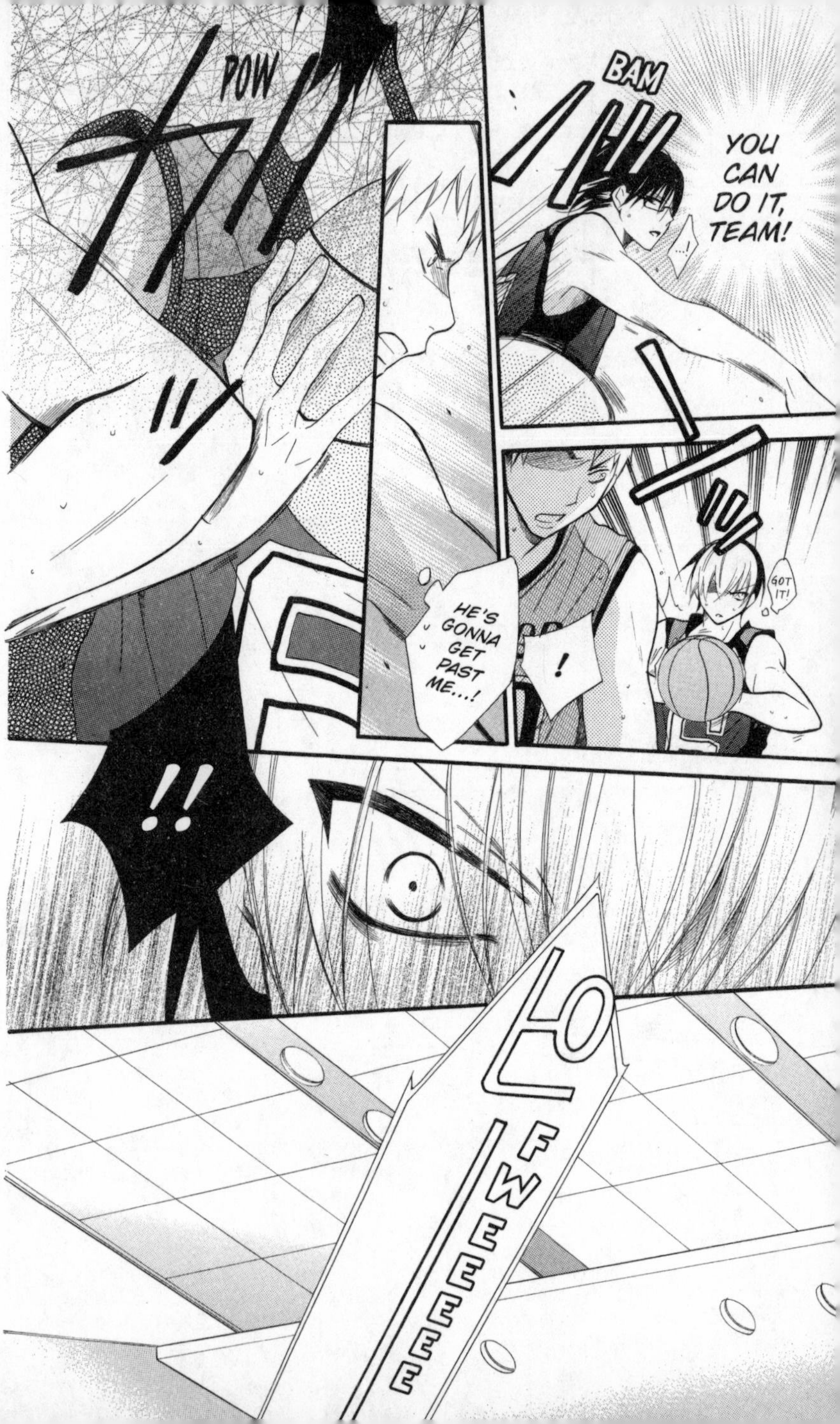
BAM
YOU CAN DO IT, TEAM!
...!
GOT IT!
!
HE'S GONNA GET PAST ME...!
POW
!!
FWEEEEE

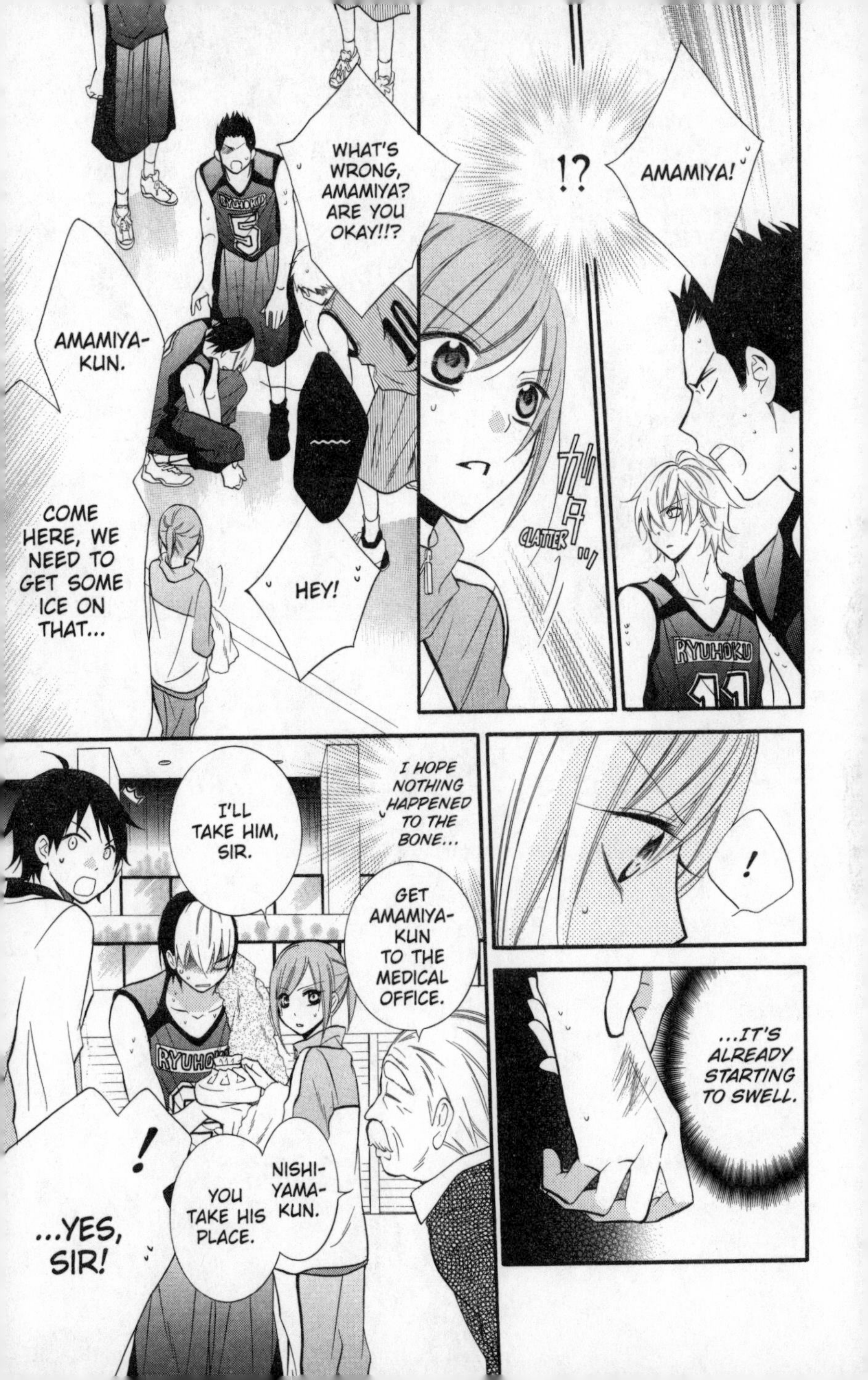
AMAMIYA!
!?
CLATTER
WHAT'S WRONG, AMAMIYA? ARE YOU OKAY!!?
HEY!
AMAMIYA-KUN.
COME HERE, WE NEED TO GET SOME ICE ON THAT...
!
...IT'S ALREADY STARTING TO SWELL.
I HOPE NOTHING HAPPENED TO THE BONE...
GET AMAMIYA-KUN TO THE MEDICAL OFFICE.
I'LL TAKE HIM, SIR.
NISHI-YAMA-KUN.
YOU TAKE HIS PLACE.
!
...YES, SIR!

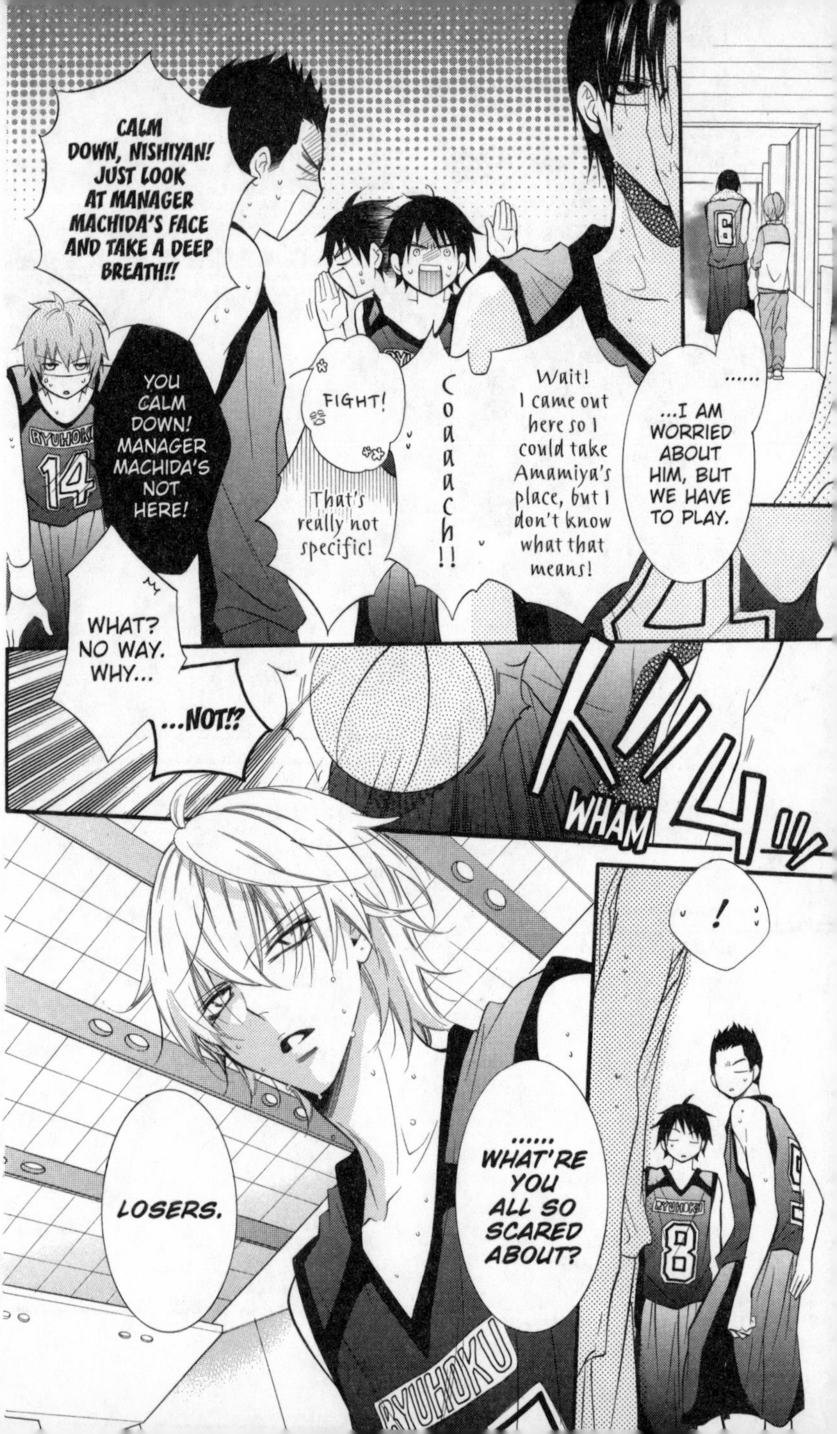
......
...I AM WORRIED ABOUT HIM, BUT WE HAVE TO PLAY.
Wait! I came out here so I could take Amamiya's place, but I don't know what that means!
Coaaach!!
FIGHT!
That's really not specific!
CALM DOWN, NISHIYAN! JUST LOOK AT MANAGER MACHIDA'S FACE AND TAKE A DEEP BREATH!!
YOU CALM DOWN! MANAGER MACHIDA'S NOT HERE!
WHAT? NO WAY. WHY...
...NOT!?
WHAM
!
...... WHAT'RE YOU ALL SO SCARED ABOUT?
LOSERS.

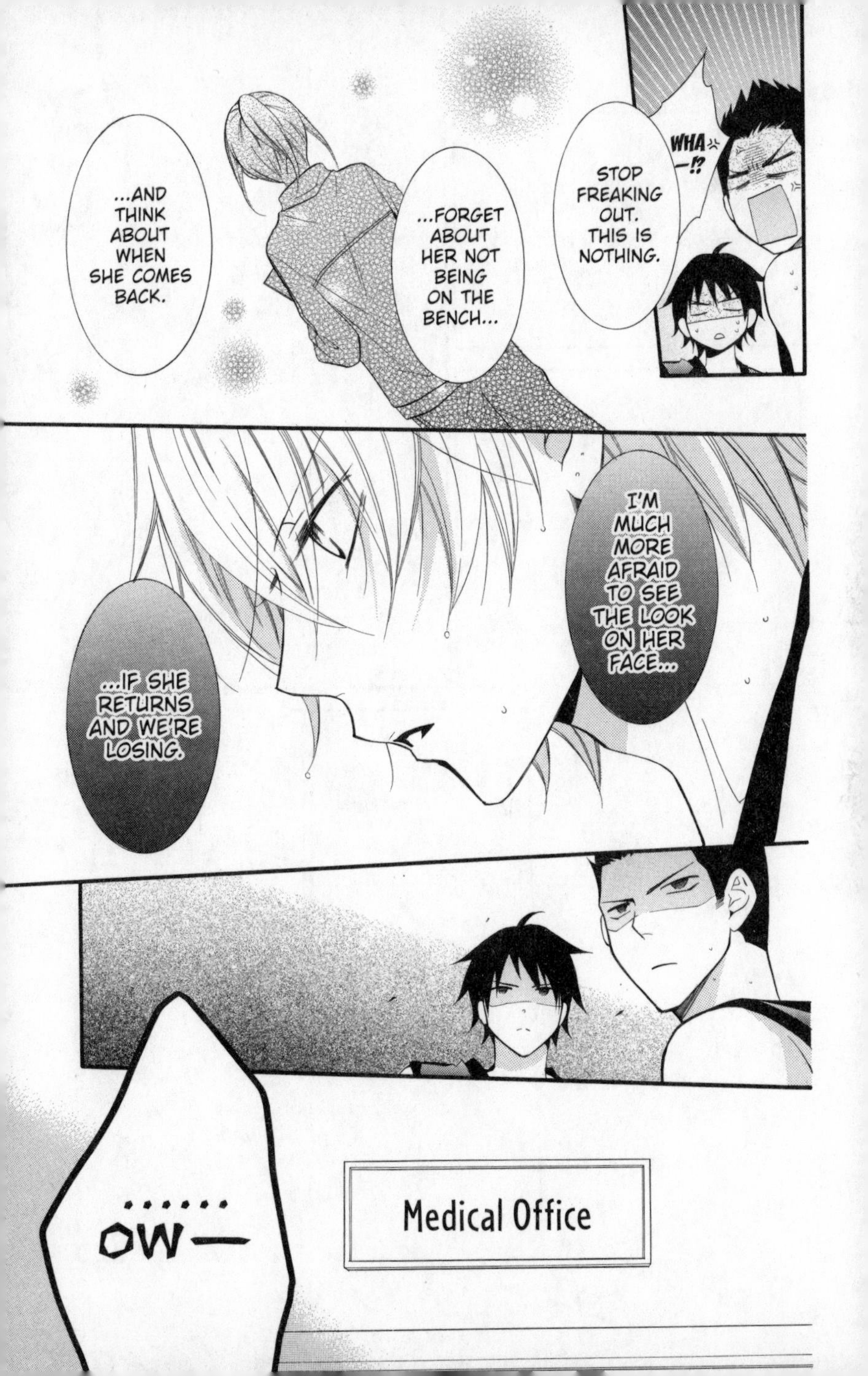
WHA—!?
STOP FREAKING OUT. THIS IS NOTHING.
...FORGET ABOUT HER NOT BEING ON THE BENCH...
...AND THINK ABOUT WHEN SHE COMES BACK.
I'M MUCH MORE AFRAID TO SEE THE LOOK ON HER FACE...
...IF SHE RETURNS AND WE'RE LOSING.
Medical Office
......
OW—

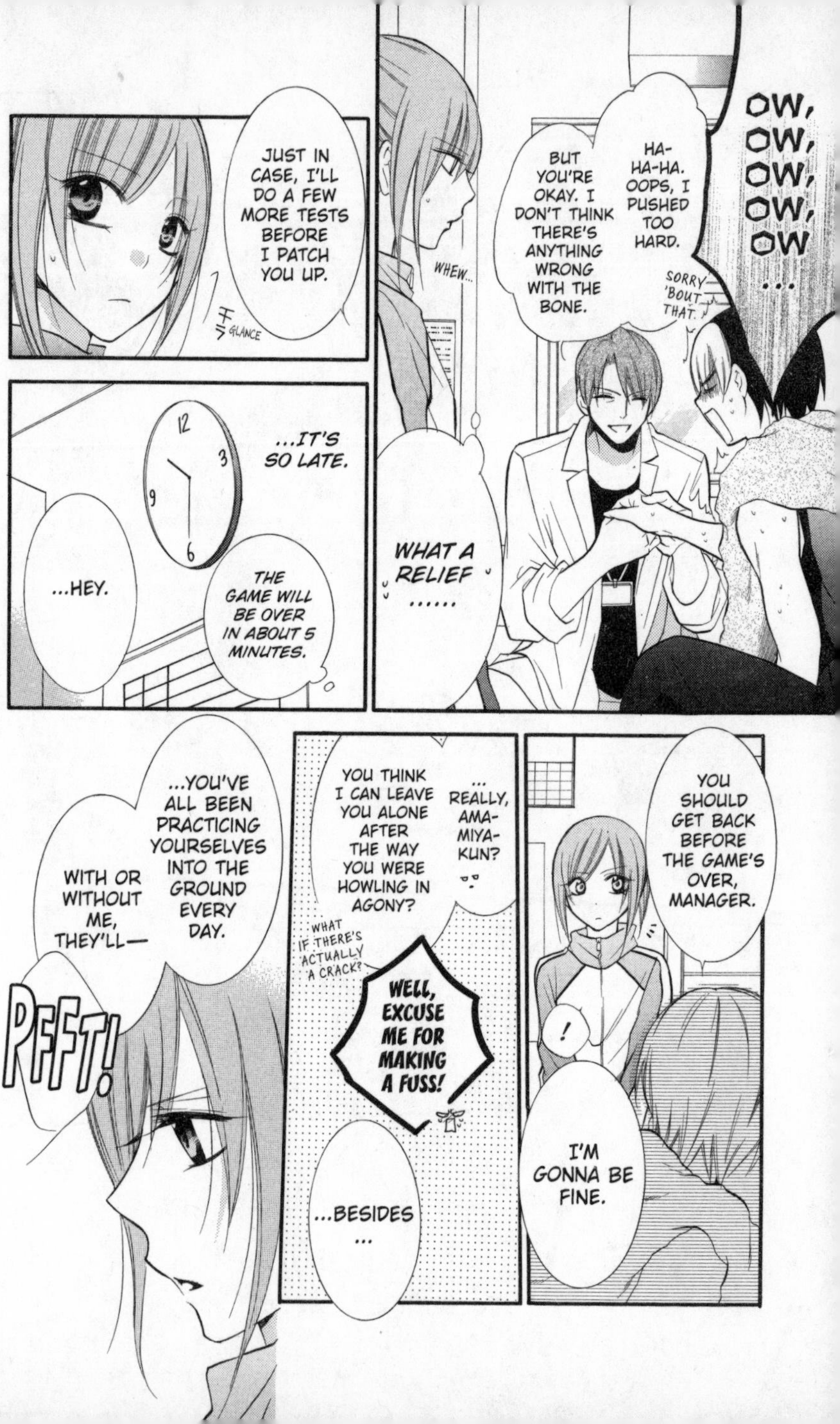
OW, OW, OW, OW, OW...
HA-HA-HA. OOPS, I PUSHED TOO HARD.
SORRY 'BOUT THAT.
BUT YOU'RE OKAY. I DON'T THINK THERE'S ANYTHING WRONG WITH THE BONE.
WHEW...
WHAT A RELIEF......
JUST IN CASE, I'LL DO A FEW MORE TESTS BEFORE I PATCH YOU UP.
GLANCE
...IT'S SO LATE.
THE GAME WILL BE OVER IN ABOUT 5 MINUTES.
...HEY.
YOU SHOULD GET BACK BEFORE THE GAME'S OVER, MANAGER.
!
I'M GONNA BE FINE.
...REALLY, AMAMIYA-KUN?
YOU THINK I CAN LEAVE YOU ALONE AFTER THE WAY YOU WERE HOWLING IN AGONY?
WHAT IF THERE'S ACTUALLY A CRACK?
WELL, EXCUSE ME FOR MAKING A FUSS!
...BESIDES...
...YOU'VE ALL BEEN PRACTICING YOURSELVES INTO THE GROUND EVERY DAY.
WITH OR WITHOUT ME, THEY'LL—
PFFT!

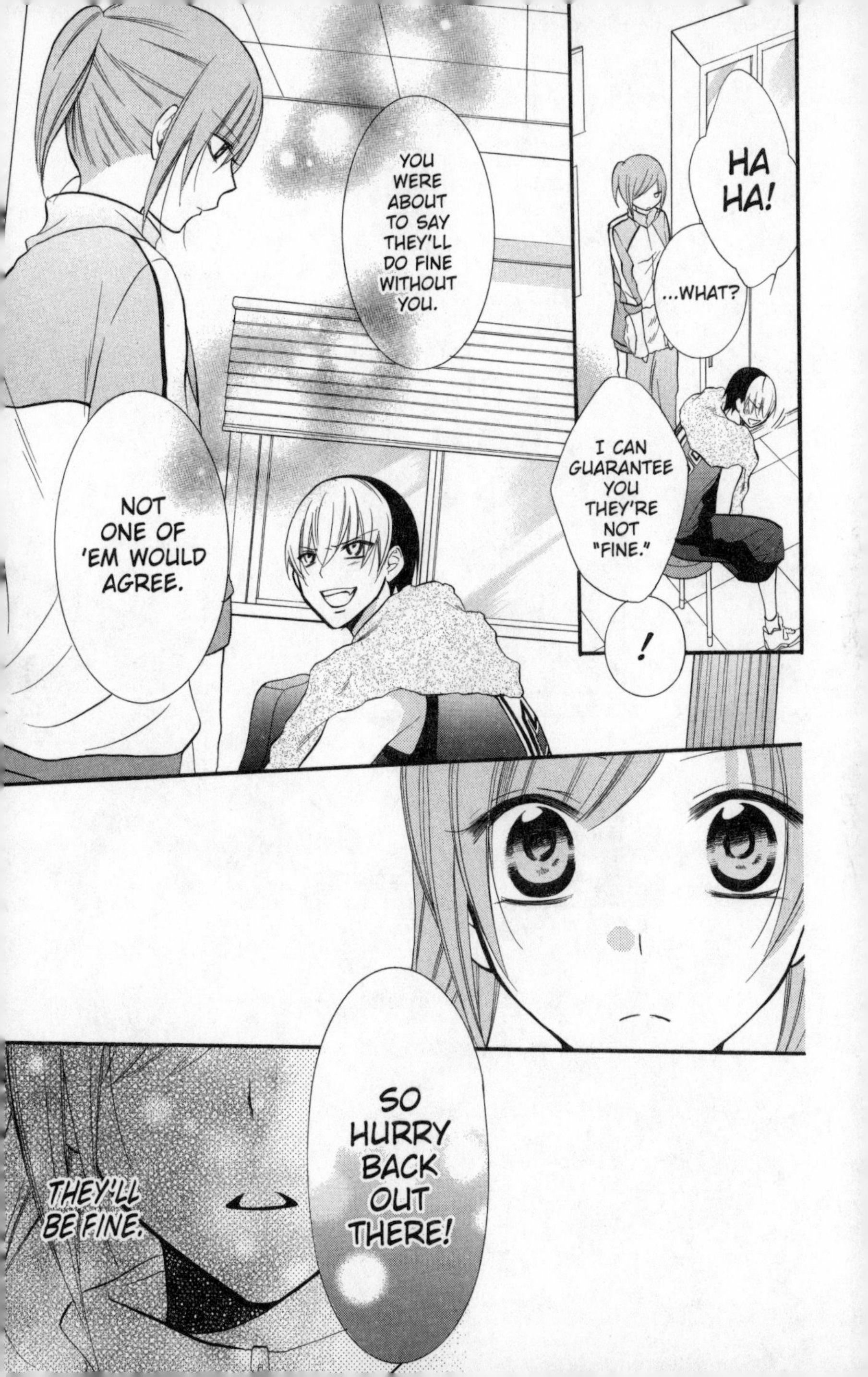
HA HA!
...WHAT?
I CAN GUARANTEE YOU THEY'RE NOT "FINE."
!
YOU WERE ABOUT TO SAY THEY'LL DO FINE WITHOUT YOU.
NOT ONE OF 'EM WOULD AGREE.
SO HURRY BACK OUT THERE!
THEY'LL BE FINE.

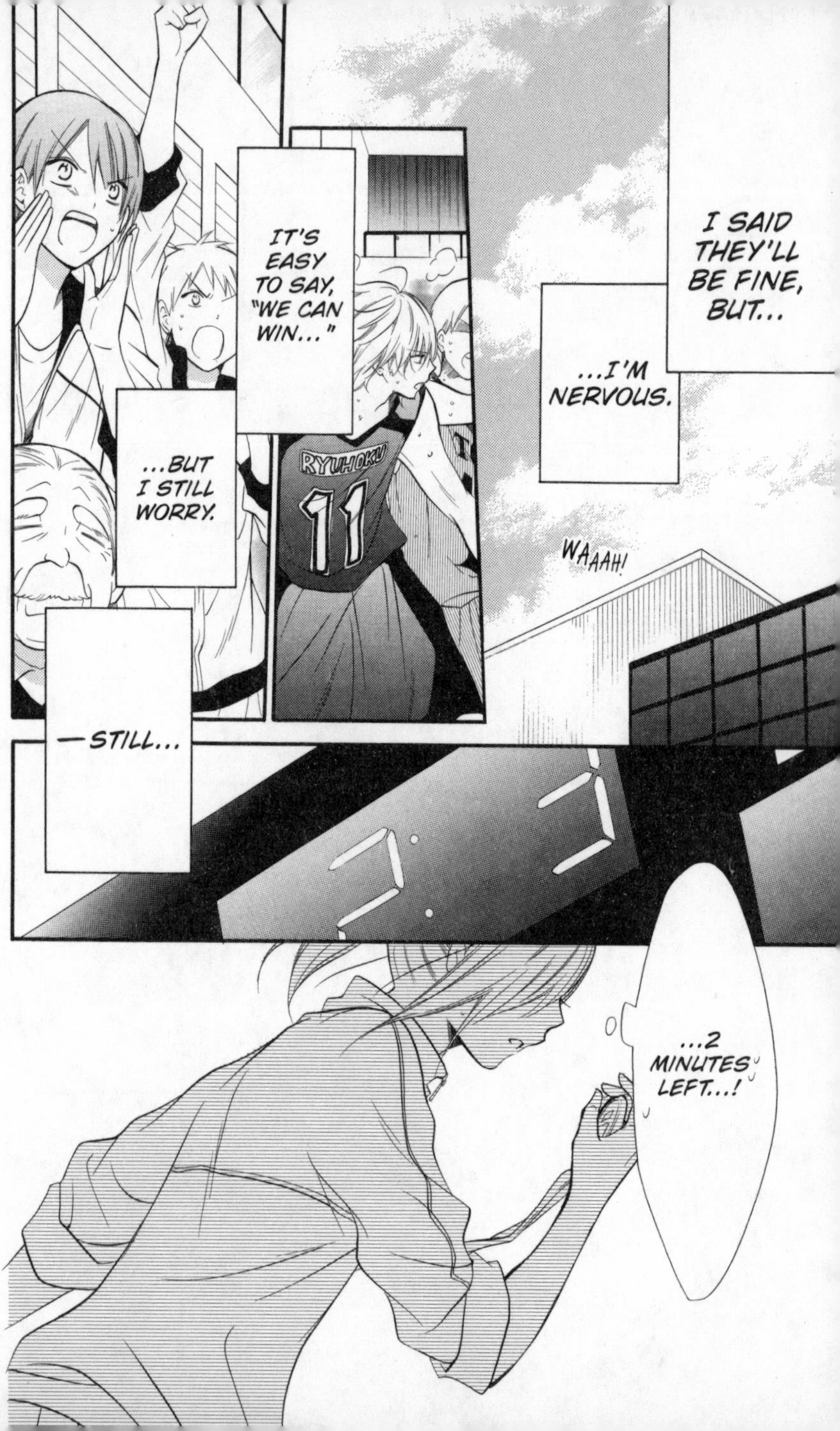
I SAID THEY'LL BE FINE, BUT...
...I'M NERVOUS.
WAAAH!
IT'S EASY TO SAY, "WE CAN WIN..."
...BUT I STILL WORRY.
RYUHOKU 11
—STILL...
...2 MINUTES LEFT...!

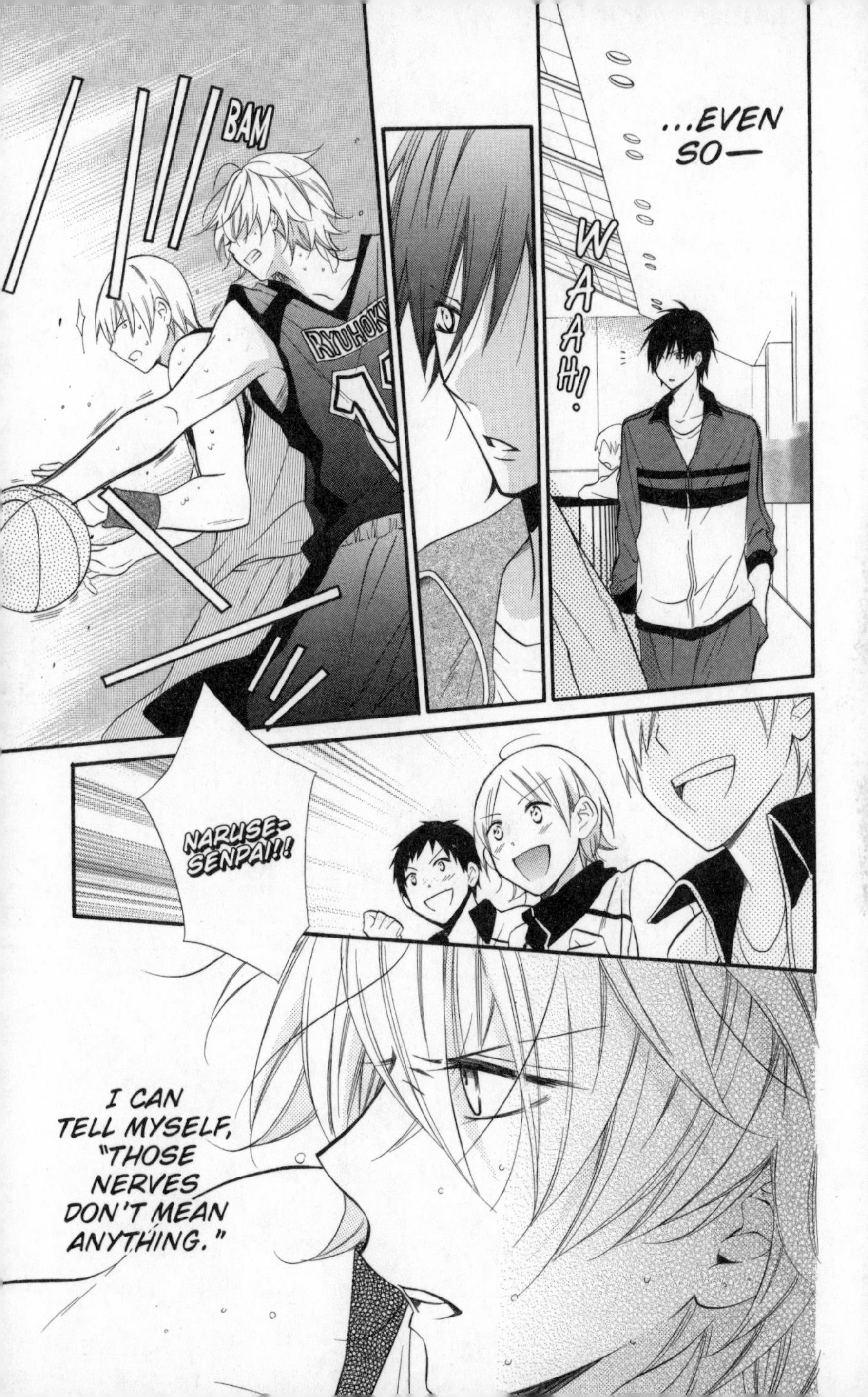
...EVEN SO—
WAAAH!
BAM
RYUHOKU
NARUSE-SENPAI!!
I CAN TELL MYSELF, "THOSE NERVES DON'T MEAN ANYTHING."

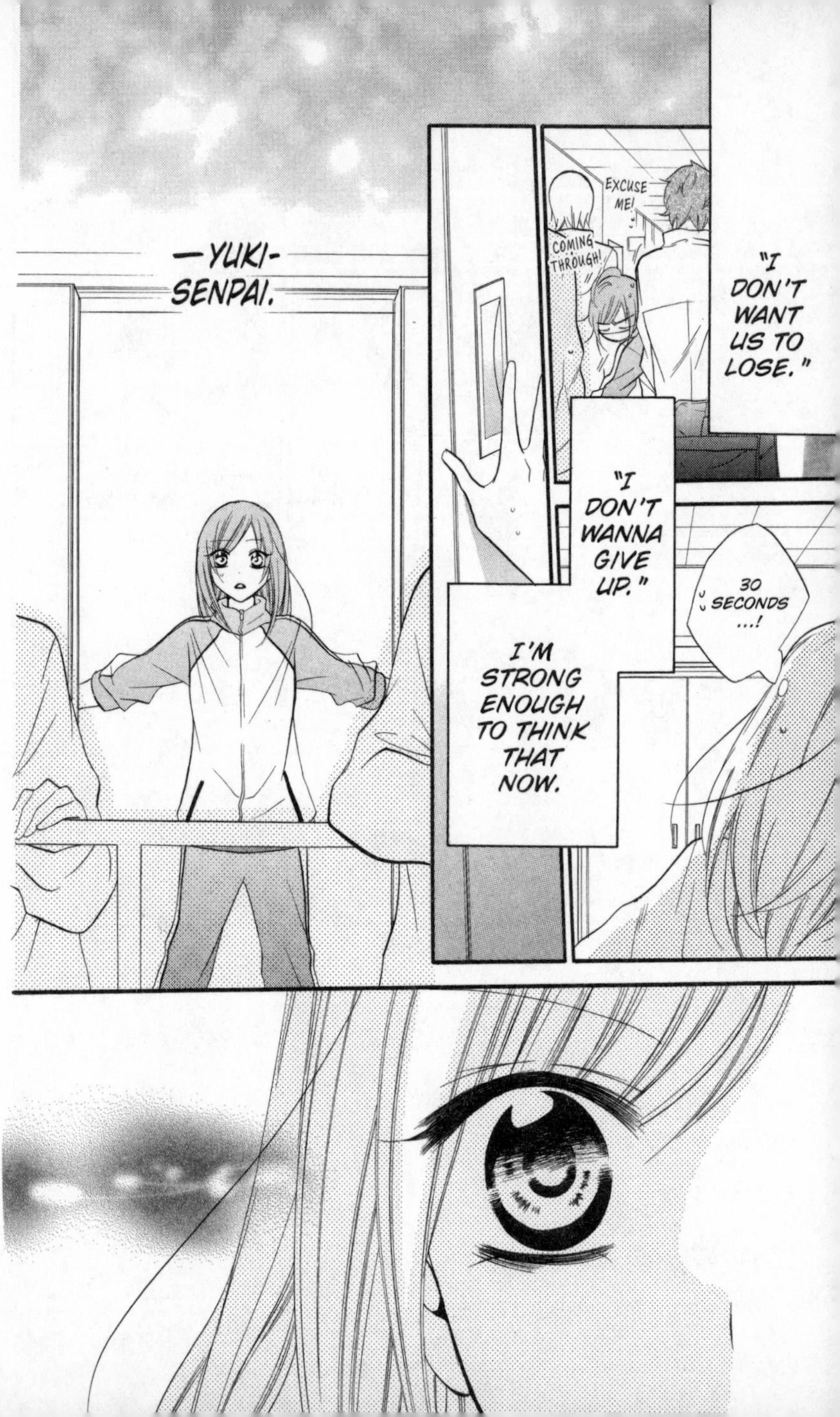
"I DON'T WANT US TO LOSE."
EXCUSE ME!
COMING THROUGH!
"I DON'T WANNA GIVE UP."
30 SECONDS ...!
I'M STRONG ENOUGH TO THINK THAT NOW.
—YUKI-SENPAI.

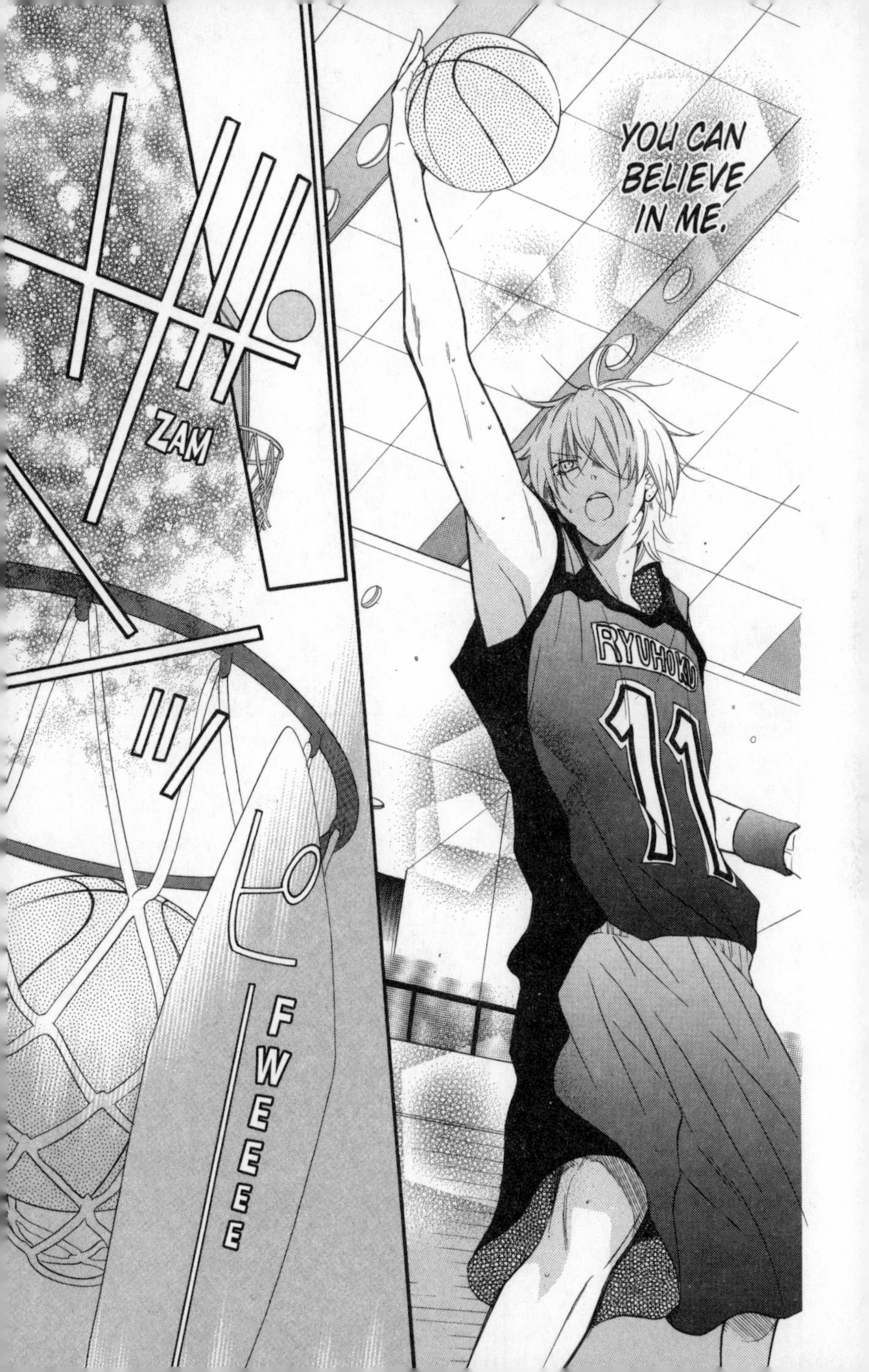
YOU CAN BELIEVE IN ME.
RYUHOKU
11
ZAM
FWEEEEE

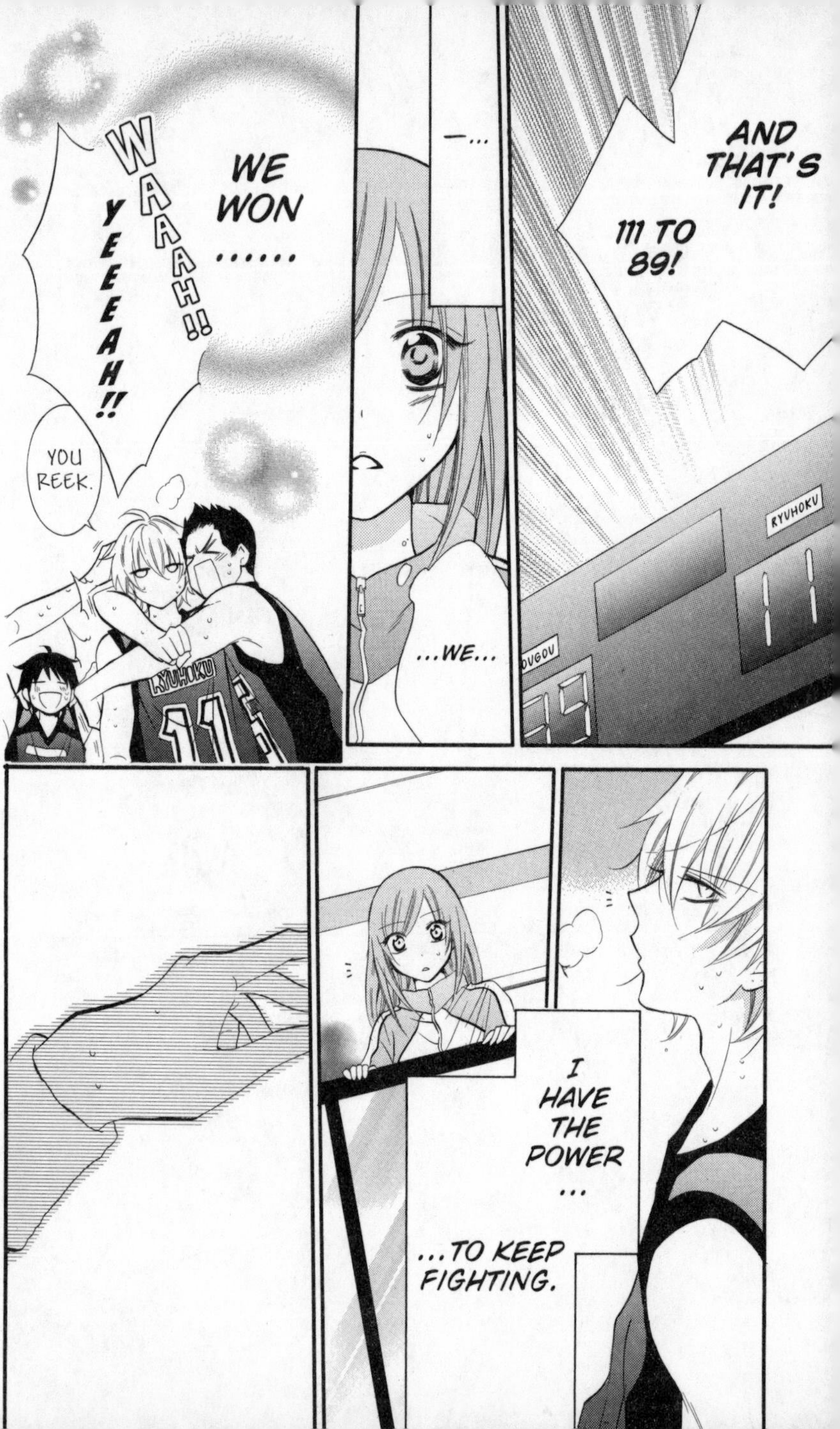
AND THAT'S IT!
111 TO 89!
RYUHOKU
—...
...WE...
WE WON ......
WAAAAH!!
YEEEEAH!!
YOU REEK.
RYUHOKU
I HAVE THE POWER ...
...TO KEEP FIGHTING.

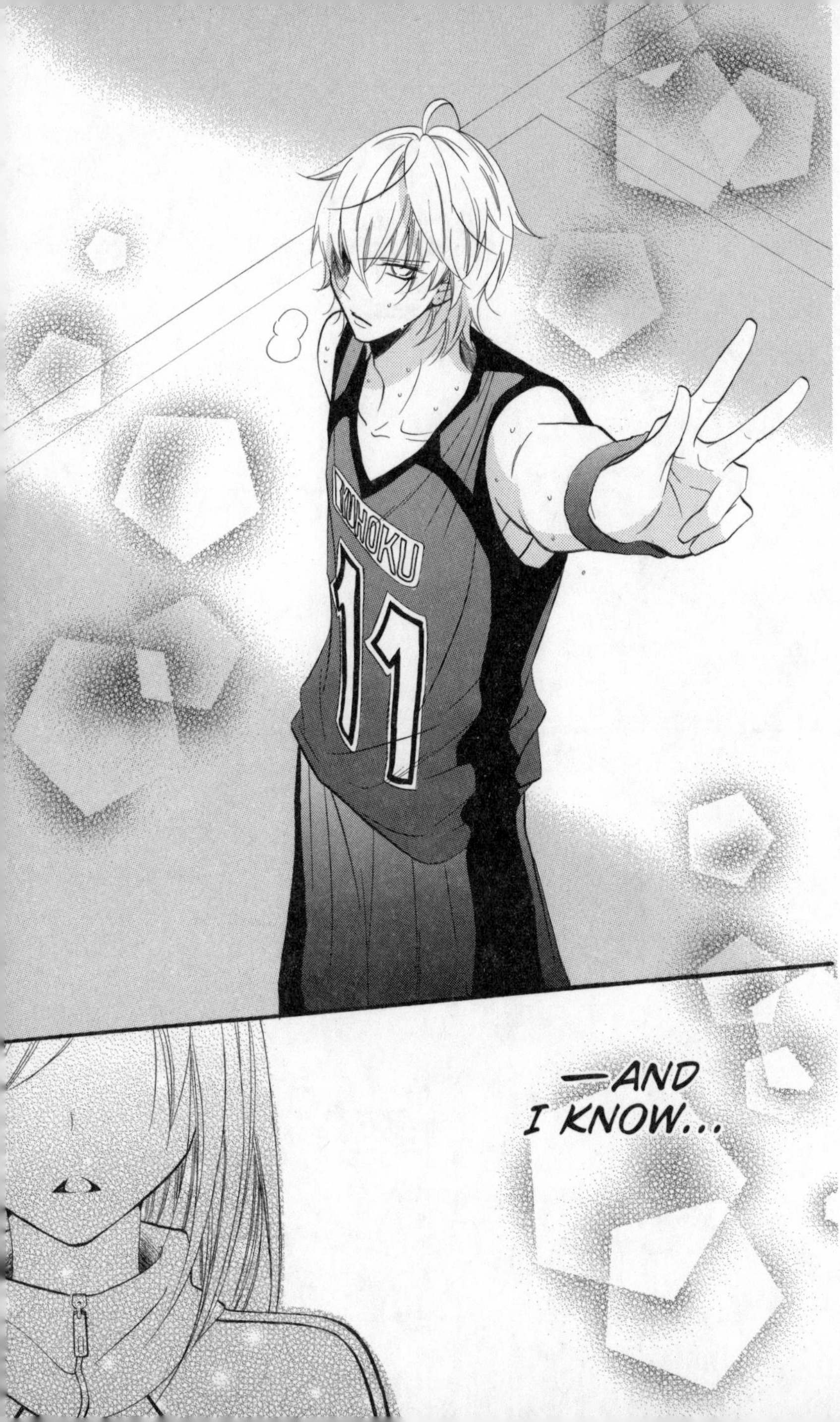
—AND I KNOW...

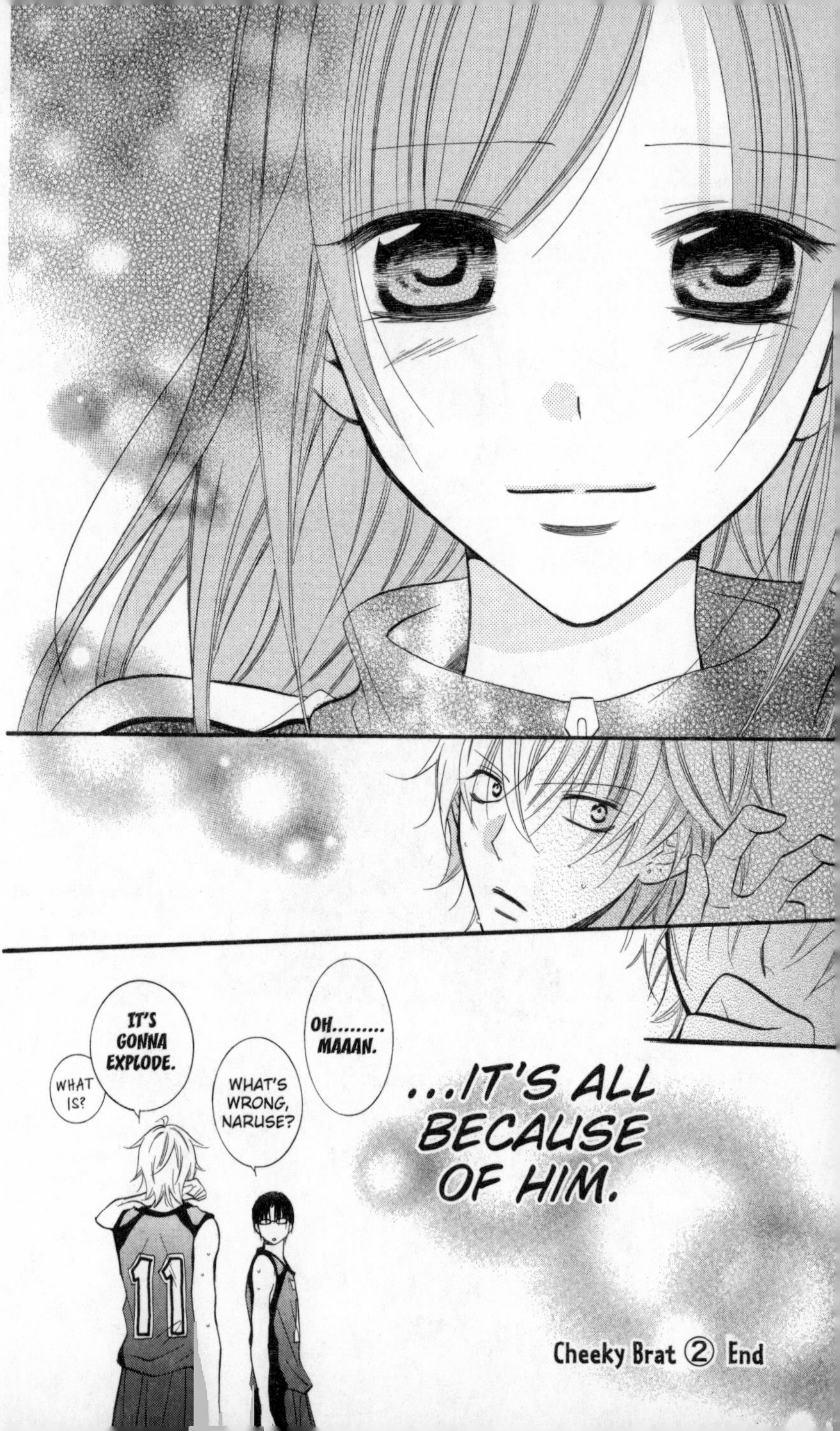
...IT'S ALL BECAUSE OF HIM.
OH......... MAAAN.
WHAT'S WRONG, NARUSE?
IT'S GONNA EXPLODE.
WHAT IS?
Cheeky Brat ② End

INTROSPECTION

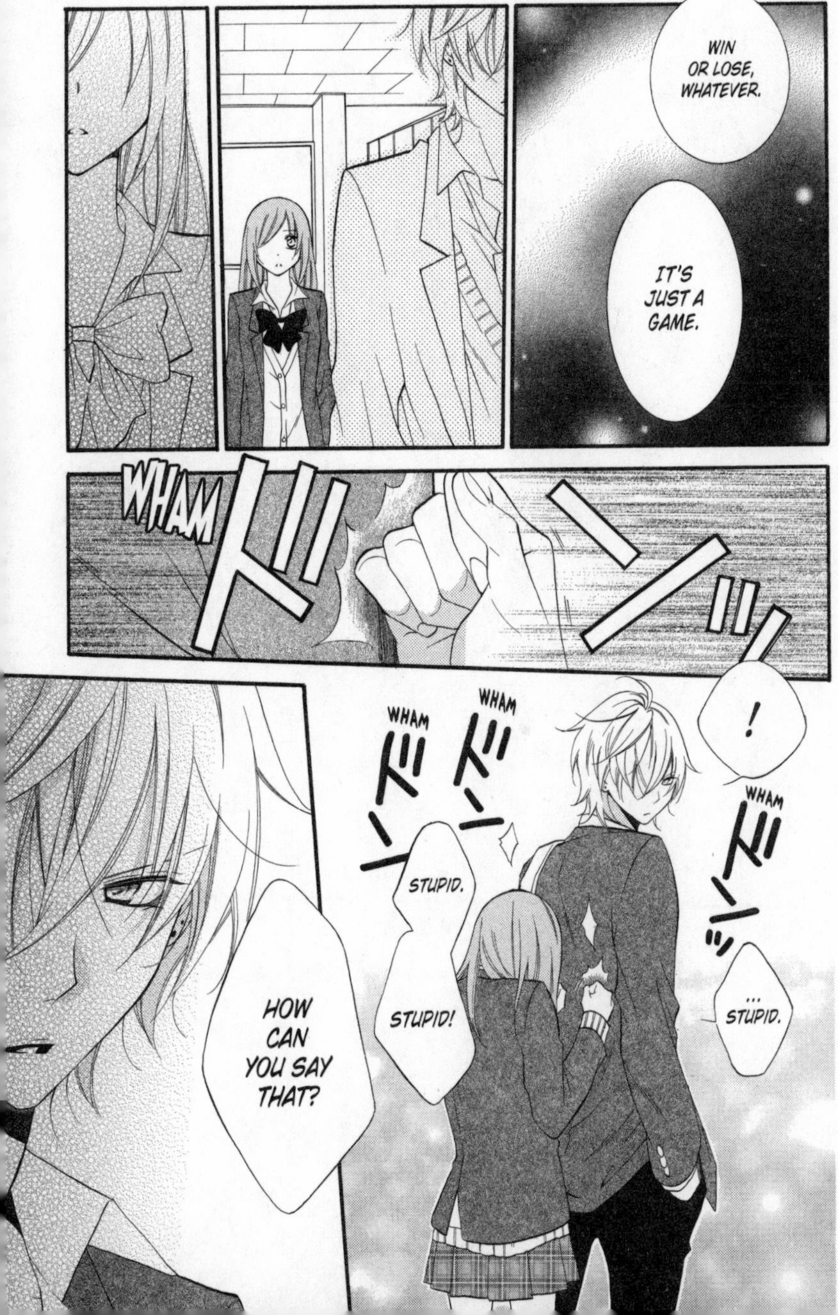

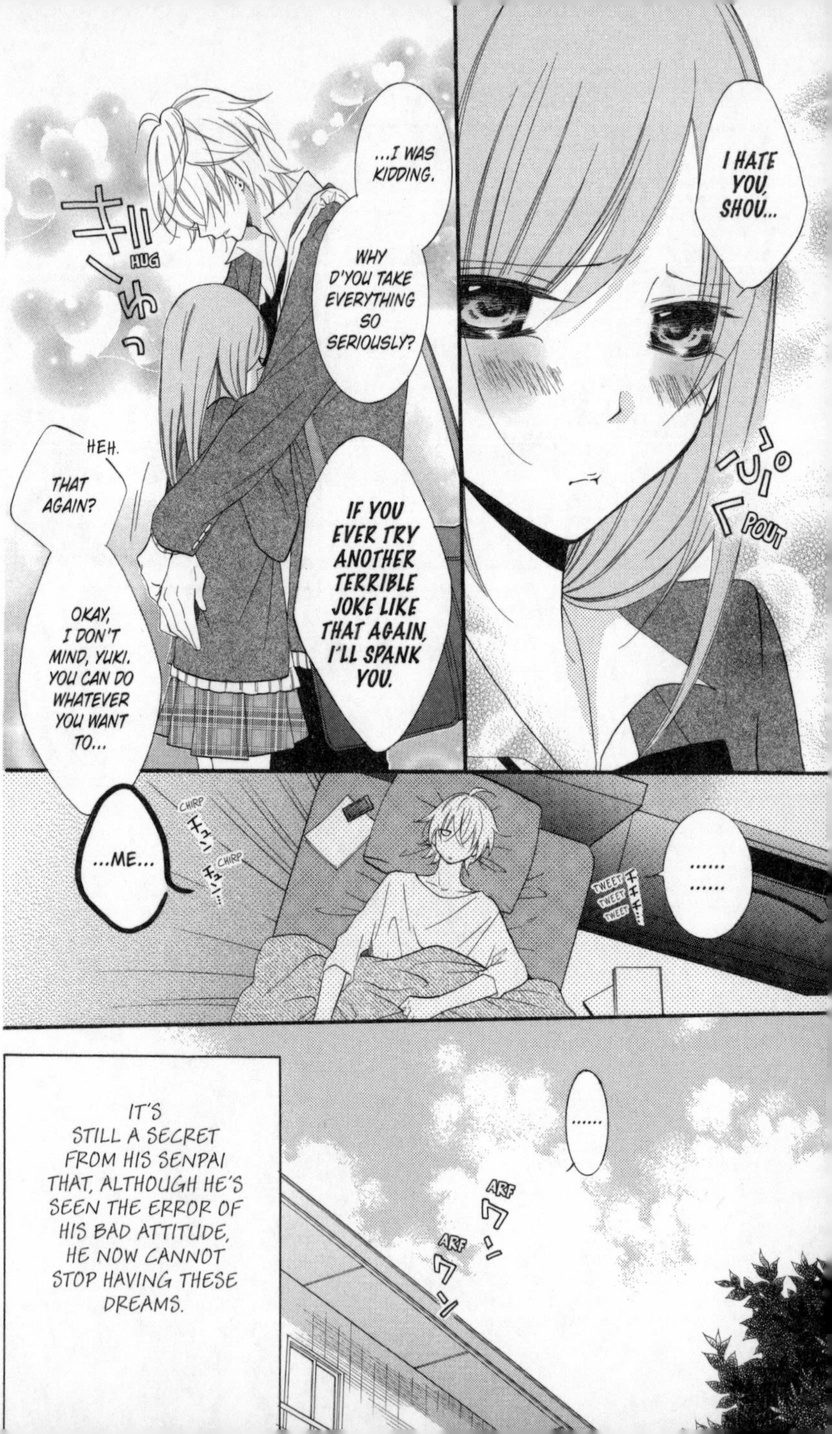
I HATE YOU, SHOU...
POUT
...I WAS KIDDING.
WHY D'YOU TAKE EVERYTHING SO SERIOUSLY?
IF YOU EVER TRY ANOTHER TERRIBLE JOKE LIKE THAT AGAIN, I'LL SPANK YOU.
HUG
HEH.
THAT AGAIN?
OKAY, I DON'T MIND, YUKI. YOU CAN DO WHATEVER YOU WANT TO...
......
......
TWEET TWEET TWEET
CHIRP
CHIRP
...ME...
......
ARF
ARF
IT'S STILL A SECRET FROM HIS SENPAI THAT, ALTHOUGH HE'S SEEN THE ERROR OF HIS BAD ATTITUDE, HE NOW CANNOT STOP HAVING THESE DREAMS.

Translation Notes

PAGE 8

White Day is a similar holiday to Valentine's Day in Japan. It is the day when anyone, usually guys, who was lucky enough to receive chocolate or other gifts on Valentine's Day will return the kindness with a gift of their own. Traditionally, the gift is something marshmallow-related (hence the name White Day), but these days, the gifts are not restricted to those kinds of things. It falls on March 14, while spring break comes at the end of March. Because the practice session was happening during spring break, it seems that White Day was at least a week before.

PAGE 34

Onee-chan is a friendly way of addressing an older (but not old) woman, and means "older sister." It's also used to address one's actual older sister. Use of *onee-chan* is sometimes retained instead of getting translated as "Big Sis," depending on what matches the tone of the speaker and the situation better.

PAGE 34

The **Battle of Sekigahara** was the decisive battle marking the end of the unification period following the Muromachi period and the Era of the Warring States (1336–1590 CE). Unification began when the last Ashikaga shogun (the military family in charge at the time) was driven out of power by Oda Nobunaga in 1568. Toyotomi Hideyoshi and Tokugawa Ieyasu finshed subduing the rest of the feudal lords over the next 32 years, ending after the Battle of Sekigahara in 1600. And so began the Tokugawa period, when the Tokugawa family was in power from 1603-1867. Like most battles, it was a period of chaos and confusion, and thus is used as a comparison for Yuki's home life.

PAGE 124

Break vs. brake: Naruse's note includes only one of the Chinese characters, known as *kanji*, that most Japanese high schoolers would usually be able to read and write. On top of that, the only *kanji* included was written incorrectly. The word for "rest" or "take a break" is usually written as 休, but Naruse wrote 体. The added stroke changes the meaning "body." The second kanji is typically read as *karada* or *tai* and so, as his teammate helpfully (?) suggested, it's possibly a fancy way of writing *taimu*, because the English word "time," would not normally be written in *kanji*. His suggestion is actually, "Maybe he meant to say, 'I'm taking a time out,' while using fancy *kanji*." As Naruse himself points out later, however, it was actually a simple spelling mistake, hence the use of the homonym "brake" in the translation.

Cheeky Brat 2

Mitsubachi Miyuki

Translation: Alethea Nibley and Athena Nibley
Lettering: Lys Blakeslee

This book is a work of fiction. Names, characters, places, and incidents are the product of the author's imagination or are used fictitiously. Any resemblance to actual events, locales, or persons, living or dead, is coincidental.

Namaiki Zakari by Mitsubachi Miyuki
© Mitsubachi Miyuki 2014
All rights reserved.
First published in Japan in 2014 by HAKUSENSHA, Inc., Tokyo.
English language translation rights in U.S.A., Canada and U.K. arranged with HAKUSENSHA, Inc., Tokyo through Tuttle-Mori Agency, Inc., Tokyo.

English translation © 2022 by Yen Press, LLC

Yen Press
150 West 30th Street, 19th Floor
New York, NY 10001

Visit us at yenpress.com
facebook.com/yenpress
twitter.com/yenpress
yenpress.tumblr.com
instagram.com/yenpress

First Yen Press Edition: February 2022

Yen Press is an imprint of Yen Press, LLC.
The Yen Press name and logo are trademarks of Yen Press, LLC.

The publisher is not responsible for websites (or their content) that are not owned by the publisher.

Library of Congress Control Number: 2021946316

ISBNs: 978-1-9753-3437-6 (paperback)
978-1-9753-3438-3 (ebook)

10 9 8 7 6 5 4 3 2 1

WOR

Printed in the United States of America

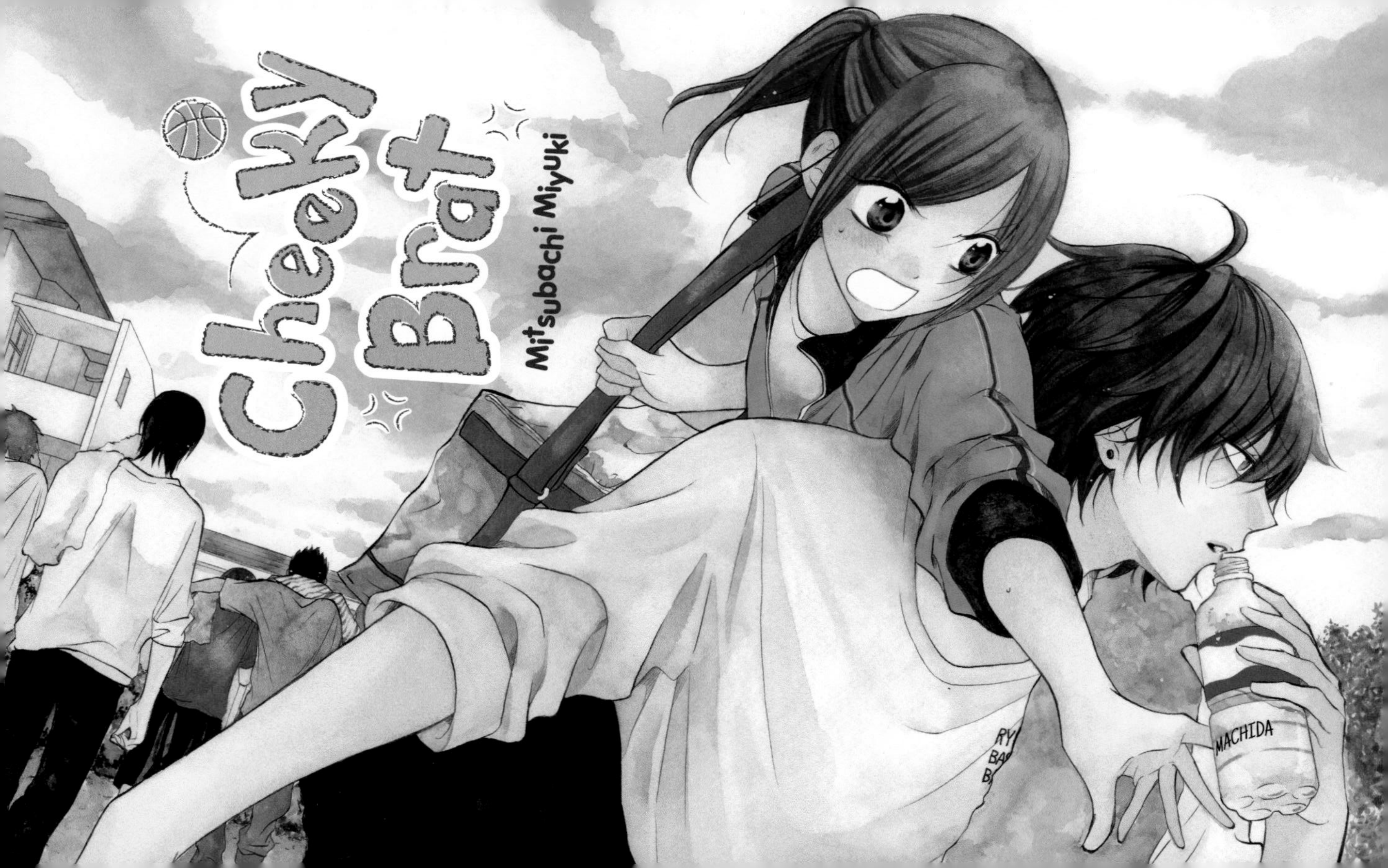
Cheeky Brat
Mitsubachi Miyuki
MACHIDA

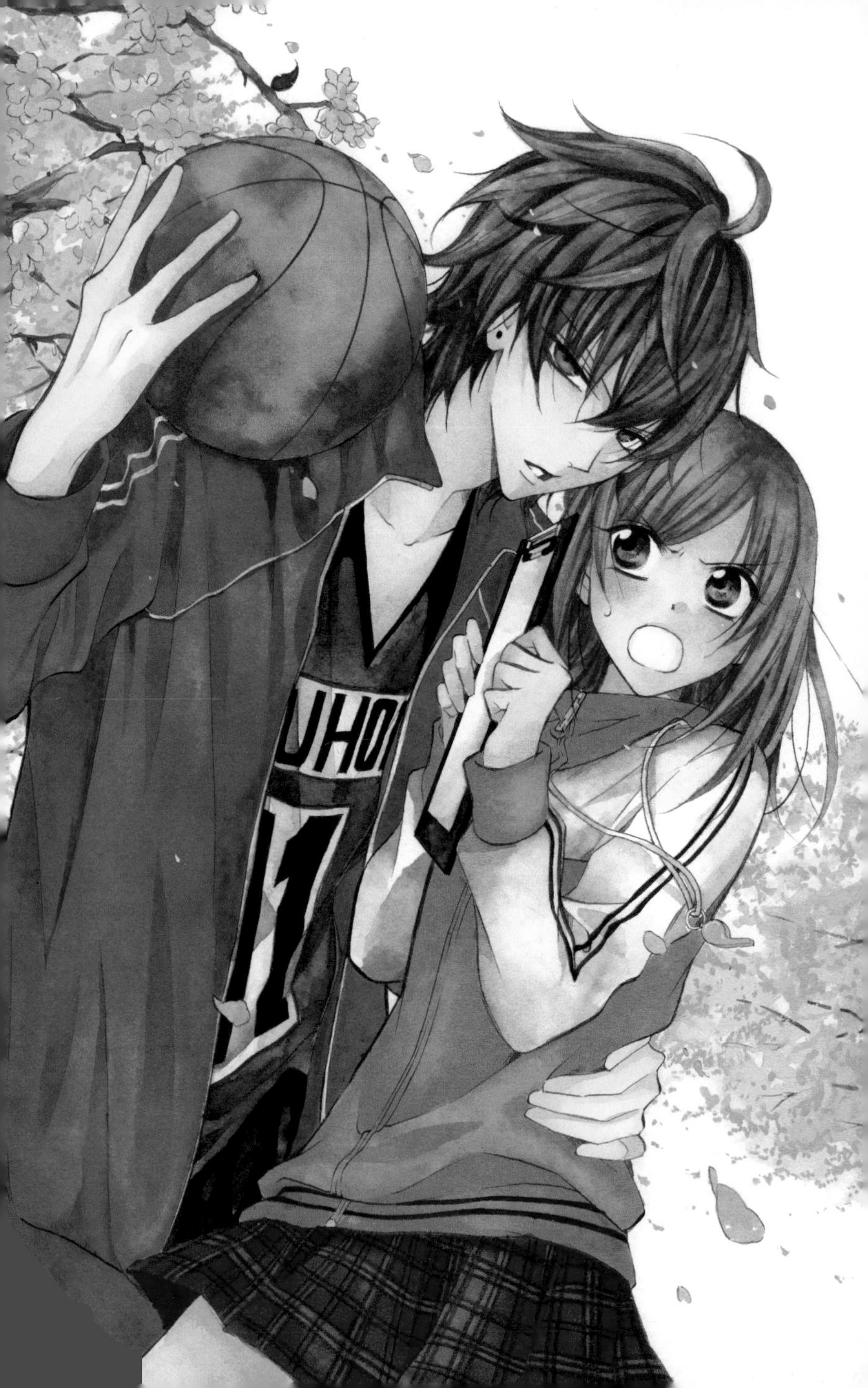